From Miracle
to Maturity

The Growth of the Korean Economy

This volume is part of the multivolume study
Rising to the Challenges of Democratization and Globalization in Korea,
1987–2007

Harvard East Asian Monographs 350

From Miracle
to Maturity

The Growth of the Korean Economy

Barry Eichengreen,
Dwight H. Perkins,
and
Kwanho Shin

Published by the Harvard University Asia Center
and distributed by Harvard University Press
Cambridge (Massachusetts) and London, 2012

Printed in the United States of America

The Harvard University Asia Center publishes a monograph series and, in coordination with the Fairbank Center for Chinese Studies, the Korea Institute, the Reischauer Institute of Japanese Studies, and other faculties and institutes, administers research projects designed to further scholarly understanding of China, Japan, Vietnam, Korea, and other Asian countries. The Center also sponsors projects addressing multidisciplinary and regional issues in Asia.

Library of Congress Cataloging-in-Publication Data

Eichengreen, Barry.
   From miracle to maturity : the growth of the Korean economy / Barry Eichengreen, Dwight H. Perkins, and Kwanho Shin.
      p. cm. — (Harvard East Asian monographs ; 350)
   Includes bibliographical references and index.
   ISBN 978-0-674-06675-5 (hbk. : alk. paper)   1. Economic development—Korea (South)   2. Korea (South)—Economic policy—1988–   3. Korea (South)—Economic conditions—1988–   I. Perkins, Dwight H. (Dwight Heald), 1934–   II. Sin, Kwan-ho, 1963–   III. Title.
   HC467.96.E43 2012

   330.95195—dc23   2012019146

   Index by Enid Zafran

⊗ Printed on acid-free paper

Last figure below indicates year of this printing

22   21   20   19   18   17   16   15   14   13

Acknowledgments

A book like this one is necessarily many years coming to fruition, and many debts are incurred along the way. Our first debt is to Yung Chul Park, who got us involved in the project. Throughout, we have had the support and encouragement of the Korea Development Institute—its successive presidents, Jung Taik Hyun and Oh-Seok Hyun, as well as its staff of professional economists, notably the estimable Wonhyuk Lim. We thank Jaehan Cho for his excellent and devoted research assistance. Valuable research assistance was also provided by Jisoo Kim and Won Ju. We had the benefit of comments on the book by Joshua Aizenman, Robert Dekle, Dominique Dwor-Frecaut, and Jung-ho Yoo at conferences in Cambridge, Palo Alto, and Seoul. Extensive comments and suggestions for improving the final manuscript were provided by Marcus Noland and Peter Petri. We are also grateful to Gretchen O'Connor for careful editing and for the help of William Hammell and others at the Harvard University Asia Center for shepherding the book into print.

Contents

Tables and Figures

Tables

Figures

From Miracle
to Maturity

The Growth of the Korean Economy

CHAPTER I

Introduction

Economic growth is a central preoccupation in Korea. It is central to the country's self-image, the government's legitimacy, and the nation's security. This fact flows from Korea's history, the country having been among the poorest in the world as recently as half a century ago. It flows from Korea's geographic position between two economic powers, Japan and China. It flows from the difficult security situation posed by North Korea and the economic challenges of Korean reunification.

From the 1960s through the mid-1990s, economic growth in South Korea averaged 9 percent. Growth at this pace is not without parallel. Japan grew as quickly in the 1950s and 1960s. Taiwan grew as rapidly in the 1960s and 1970s. China has grown at comparable rates since the 1980s. But there are few other countries that have grown as quickly or where the starting point was so unpromising. The resulting transformation has been profound. There are good reasons, in other words, why Korea's experience is seen as an economic miracle.

Be this as it may, in recent years a sense of disquiet has developed around the economy's performance. Since the turn of the century, growth has slowed. From 2001 to 2007 gross domestic product (GDP) growth averaged only 4.7 percent, a noticeable decline from earlier years. Lee Myung-Bak campaigned for the presidency in 2007 on a pledge to boost the growth rate to 7 percent, more in line with historical norms. While his presidential campaign was successful, his pledge was not: growth slumped further, to 2.3 percent, in 2008, and fell to 0.3 percent in 2009, before recovering by 6.2 percent in 2010.[1] Pessimistic analysts blamed the decline in investment following the financial crisis of 1997–1998.

They pointed to competition from a rapidly growing China abundantly endowed with cheap labor, and to the difficulties that Korea faced in moving up market, given the similarity of its resources and product mix to those of richer and more technologically advanced Japan. They complained that manufacturing was being hollowed out by Korean companies' foreign investments in China, while Korea itself was finding it increasingly difficult to compete with other potential hosts for foreign direct investment (FDI). They worried that Korea's economic growth was especially susceptible to being disrupted by financial problems, given how the country was disproportionately affected by financial volatility both in 1997–1998 and 2008–2009.[2]

These dual perspectives, derived from the record of the past and trepidation about the future, frame our analysis of Korean economic growth. We argue that the prevailing sense of angst is excessive, although there are economic problems requiring urgent attention. In Chapter 2, we chart the course of growth in South Korea. The data confirm that growth has slowed in recent years relative to the high-growth period that commenced in the first half of the 1960s.

But we argue that there is nothing aberrant about this development. The rapid growth characteristic of a once-poor economy that has successfully broken free of its low-level equilibrium trap does not last forever. Success in catching up means higher labor costs and therefore less ability to compete on price. It means less scope for growing simply by importing technology; it becomes necessary to invest in more costly and difficult indigenous technological development instead. With economic maturity and convergence, growth inevitably slows down.

Typically that slowdown occurs when per capita income reaches a level of about $14,000 (in 2000 U.S. purchasing-power-parity dollars). We show in Chapter 2 that this was precisely the case in Korea. Similarly, there is no advanced economy in which growth has exceeded 4 percent per annum for any extended period. This provides a metric for what Korea can expect, now that it is a member of the Organization for Economic Cooperation and Development (OECD) and on the verge of joining the ranks of the advanced economies.

If there is something distinctive about South Korea's experience, it is that its slowdown was successfully resisted for a period of years. In the first half of the 1990s investment rates were boosted to artificially high levels, with much of the additional investment financed by borrowing abroad. This kept growth going at rates resembling those of the 1960s, 1970s, and 1980s but at the cost of increasingly high corporate gearing of the Korean banking system toward short-term external debt. With the outbreak of the Asian financial crisis in the second half of 1997, this house of cards came tumbling down. The secular slowdown became apparent.

Nor is there anything anomalous about the relative decline of manufacturing in Korea. Falling shares of manufacturing output and employment are predictable corollaries of economic maturity. As economies grow rich, an increasing fraction of resources is allocated to the service sector. In Chapter 3, where we turn to growth at the sectoral level, we show that this is precisely the pattern in Korea. The share of manufacturing in GDP and employment peaked in 1988 and 1989, respectively. The employment share then fell sharply, although the output share remained relatively stable.[3] In most countries, the share of employment in manufacturing begins to decline before it reaches 30 percent of the total. Korea is right in line with this experience.

There are some distinctive aspects of the Korean experience that give pause, however. First, deindustrialization has been unusually rapid. The share of employment in manufacturing declined by 0.91 percent per annum for ten years following its peak in 1989—faster than in any other economy with the exception of Taiwan. The level of GDP at the point when deindustrialization in this sense set in was also unusually low. It is tempting to argue, both on a priori grounds and by comparison with Taiwan, that the decline in the share of employment was unusually rapid because the growth of that share had been unusually rapid, and that the transition from manufacturing to services occurred relatively early in per capita income terms because Korea was a latecomer to economic growth. But the pace at which manufacturing employment has contracted remains unsettling.

It is more unsettling insofar as the service sector, which generally is expected to take up the output- and employment-growth slack, displays chronic low productivity. This is the case in wholesale and retail trade, health care, and education, among other activities, as we show in Chapter 4. To be sure, Korea has a technologically progressive service subsector centered on information and communications, but that progressive segment accounts for only a fraction of service sector employment. Moreover, there is little evidence of strong productivity spillovers from these high-tech activities to the remainder of the service sector.

Economic growth and export growth are virtually synonymous in Korea. The country's dearth of energy and raw materials means that, in order to import these essential inputs, it must export manufactured goods and services. The economic miracle that commenced in the 1960s was closely connected—some would say ignited—by the shift to export-led growth. The competitiveness of exports is therefore a key indicator of Korean economic performance.

In Chapter 5 we analyze Korean exports in detail. While there has been some deceleration in the rate of growth of exports, this too is in line with the unexceptional deceleration in overall economic growth. We situate the break at the point when the rate of growth of exports decelerated from an exceptional 20 percent to a more customary 10 percent, not in the 1990s, when China emerged as a serious competitor, but in the 1980s. The exceptional surge in exports associated with the artificially high investment and rapid growth of the first half of the 1990s tended to disguise this change, but the evidence is now clear. Today the rate of growth of exports is precisely in line with what one would expect of a country at Korea's level of economic development and with its other observable characteristics. Similarly, the technological sophistication of Korea's merchandise exports is almost exactly what one would expect from its per capita income and the behavior of other countries.

If there is a problem, it lies in the fact that increases in merchandise exports, which have traditionally been the engine of employment growth, are creating less employment than before. Increases in merchandise exports do less to boost output and employment because a growing share of the value of those sales is accounted for by imported inputs—by parts and components from countries like China. This too is a predictable consequence of economic maturation. As incomes rise and Korean labor becomes more expensive, it is normal for routine, labor-intensive inputs into the products of the country's export industries to be sourced abroad.

But if the pattern is normal, it is no less disquieting for that fact. It is especially disquieting insofar as Korea underperforms as an exporter of services. This of course is simply another manifestation of the problem of lagging service sector productivity, analyzed in Chapter 4. Where exports of services represent more than 10 percent of GDP in the typical

OECD country, in Korea they were only 7 percent of GDP in 2010. This is troubling for an economy that, going forward, will be forced to rely increasingly on exports of services.

Foreign direct investment is another lens through which the competitiveness of the Korean economy can be observed, as we show in Chapter 6. Historically, the Korean authorities discouraged foreign investment in Korean business, or inward FDI, preferring imported equipment and licensing as vehicles for technology transfer. To avoid compromising corporate control, potential joint-venture partners, notably the *chaebol* (the large family-run conglomerates that dominated Korean industry), preferred to finance their expansion by issuing debt rather than by selling equity stakes to foreigners. Partly as a result of these legacies, Korea continues to attract less FDI than one would expect on the basis of its economic characteristics. There is also evidence that China's emergence as a magnet for FDI has made it more difficult for Korea to attract investors. In addition, foreign investors point to the continuing importance of family connections in Korea, lack of transparency and predictability in the business environment, and strained labor relations as deterrents to FDI. This suggests that there are things that Korea can do to become a more attractive destination for foreign investment.

In contrast to the unusually low level of inward FDI in Korea, there is nothing unusual about the level of outward FDI by Korean companies. This is in contrast to popular complaints that Korea's outward FDI is excessive and is "hollowing out" the economy. Once upon a time, in the 1980s and 1990s, FDI outflows were larger than predicted for a country with Korea's characteristics. But this is no longer the case. Since 2001, Korea's FDI outflow has, in fact, been just what would be expected. Insofar as domestic investment has fallen, it is not the result of unusually high levels of outward FDI.

A final aspect of Korean growth performance that is widely viewed as troubling is the economy's susceptibility to crises. The country's recent history has been punctuated by economic crises: in the early 1970s, in the early 1980s, in 1997–1998, and, most recently, in 2008–2009. On each occasion, growth fell sharply. Some of these crises, notably that in 1997–1998, resulted in major output losses. In Chapter 7 we therefore analyze the connections between crises and economic growth. In fact, four crises in four decades is not exceptional—more than a few other middle-income countries have had similar experiences. That said, Korea is somewhat more crisis prone than average: some 60 percent of comparator countries have had fewer crises since the mid-1960s. We show that Korea's susceptibility to crises is a corollary of a development strategy favoring debt over equity finance, short-term debt in particular. The high levels of leverage and potential debt rollover problems resulting from this strategy have heightened crisis risk.

We also show that the 2008–2009 crisis differed from its predecessors. While short-term debt again played a role (there was a maturity mismatch between the banks' short-term dollar liabilities and long-term dollar assets), other long-standing sources of financial fragility, such as high leverage ratios, had been significantly reduced. In 2008–2009 Korea suffered financially not for the reasons that it and other emerging markets had historically experienced financial crises (problems with domestic policies and institutions). Ironically, it suffered because its economy and financial system had matured, and the 2008–2009 financial crisis was a crisis of the mature economies.

Thus, many aspects of the recent economic performance of South Korea, from the deceleration in growth to the changing sectoral composition of activity, the behavior of exports, the growth of outward FDI, and the changing nature of financial crises, are corollaries of economic maturation. These changes are natural consequences of the success of Korean economic performance in the past. This is not to deny the existence of problems. We devote considerable attention to those problems in Chapters 2 through 7, and to their potential solutions in Chapter 8. But to accurately identify the problems, and especially to prescribe solutions, it is first necessary to identify what is normal about Korea's growth experience. And this in turn requires putting that experience in context.

CHAPTER 2

The Aggregate Sources of Growth

Two methodologies are commonly used to examine why countries experience varying rates of economic growth. The first, growth accounting, approaches the question from the supply side, seeking to explain performance in terms of the supply of capital and labor inputs and increases in productivity. Variants of this methodology have been widely used to analyze why Korea's economy grew so rapidly from the 1960s through the 1980s.

Although we take growth accounting as the point of departure for our analysis (if nothing else, this facilitates comparisons with previous work), our approach differs from other studies in the periods we cover and their definition, and in the questions we pose. We cover both the high-growth period and the subsequent slowdown. We estimate the sources of growth not only for the entire economy but also for the economy excluding agriculture.[1] And we focus on the question of why growth slowed in the 1990s.

A second widely used methodology, cross-country growth regression, is best thought of as summarizing, in reduced form, the relative importance of different supply- and demand-side factors in economic growth. In reviewing this work, we focus on whether the implications of the international comparisons highlighted by this approach are consistent with our growth accounting results and whether they provide additional insights.

Aggregate Growth Accounting Methodology

Assume a standard production function of the form in equation (1).

$$Y_t = A_t F(K_t, h_t L_t) \tag{1}$$

where Y_t is the aggregate output, A_t is the level of total factor productivity (TFP), K_t is the capital stock, h_t is the average human capital, and L_t is the quantity of labor at time t. Further assuming a translog structure and constant-returns-to-scale technology, we can convert equation (1) to

$$\ln\left(\frac{Y_t}{Y_{t-1}}\right) = V_K(t,t-1)\ln\left(\frac{K_t}{K_{t-1}}\right) + V_L(t,t-1)\ln\left(\frac{h_t}{h_{t-1}}\right)$$
$$+ V_L(t,t-1)\ln\left(\frac{L_t}{L_{t-1}}\right) + \ln\left(\frac{A_t}{A_{t-1}}\right) \tag{2}$$

where $V_K(t,t-1)$ and $V_L(t,t-1)$ are the average of capital and income shares in t and t - 1. Equation (2) shows that the growth of output can be decomposed into the contributions of physical capital accumulation, human capital accumulation, labor input growth, and technological improvement.[2]

Equation (2) can be further rearranged to express the growth of per capita output as:

$$\ln\left(\frac{Y_t/P_t}{Y_{t-1}/P_t}\right) = V_K(t,t-1)\ln\left(\frac{K_t/L_t}{K_{t-1}/L_t}\right) + V_L(t,t-1)\ln\left(\frac{h_t}{h_{t-1}}\right)$$
$$+ V_L(t,t-1)\ln\left(\frac{L_t/P_t}{L_{t-1}/P_t}\right) + \ln\left(\frac{A_t}{A_{t-1}}\right) \tag{3}$$

where P_t is population at time t. Equation (3) says that the growth of per capita output can be decomposed into the contributions of capital deepening, human capital accumulation, the increase in labor input per person, and TFP growth.

Controversies over this framework have a long history, extending back to the "Cambridge-versus-Cambridge" debate of the 1960s. When applied to developing countries, the methodology suffers from additional problems associated with assumptions that are strained in that context, such as that factors of production are paid their marginal product. Ultimately, however, the proof of the pudding is in the eating: the value of the approach depends on whether it can shed light on growth experience, and specifically on whether it has value as a rough-and-ready device for separating out growth due to increasing factor inputs from growth due to increases in productivity.

It is in this spirit that we explore what this approach tells us about Korea. But in doing so we relate our measurements to the timing of fundamental changes in policy.[3] We also pursue some extensions that allow us to decompose efficiency into components associated with movements in the global technological frontier and changes in the extent of country-specific catch-up, in the manner of Kumar and Russell (2002).[4]

Data

We obtain value added in constant year-2000 prices from the national accounts data of Bank of Korea. Labor input is man-hours, calculated by multiplying the number of employees and average weekly hours. Industry-level data on the number of employees and weekly hours are taken from the *Annual Report on the Economic Active Population Survey* and the *Yearbook of Labor Statistics*, respectively.[5] Number of workers includes permanent and temporary employees, self-employed workers, and family workers.

Because the national accounts report the income share of labor based on compensation provided to employees on payroll, we need to estimate wage compensation for self-employed and family workers to construct the income share of the total labor force. We assume that wage compensation of self-employed and family workers is two-thirds that of employees on payroll in wholesale and retail trade, restaurants and hotels, and community, social, and personal services.[6] For manufacturing and other service sectors, the wage compensation of self-employed and family workers is assumed to be four-fifths that of employees on payroll in the same industries.

To measure human capital, we use the Jorgenson and Fraumeni (1989, 1992a, 1992b) lifetime-labor-income method. Instead of using years of education, this approach measures the human capital embodied in individuals based on total income received over their lifetime.[7] We divide workers into nine sectors, the two sexes, two employment types (employees and the self-employed), and five educational levels (primary, junior secondary, higher secondary, college, and university). All differences in wage rates among different education levels are assumed to be due to different levels of human capital accumulation.[8] Wage data are collected from the *Report on Wage Survey by Occupational Category*.

Physical capital stock is net fixed capital stock by industry, as constructed by Pyo, Chung, and Cho (2007). They follow the approach of the EU KLEMS project, estimating national wealth by asset and industry using a modified perpetual inventory method and a polynomial-benchmark-year estimation method, using four benchmark-year estimates. The capital stock is then obtained by summing five types of capital goods: residential structures, nonresidential structures, other construction, machinery, and transportation equipment.

Basic Growth Accounting Results

Tables 2.1 and 2.2 show the results of these calculations (see also Table 2.A1 in the appendix to this chapter). Table 2.1 is a more detailed calculation excluding agriculture and mining. Table 2.2 adds those sectors but omits some variables for lack of data. The results, like those of other studies, suggest that the growth of capital accounts for the largest share of output growth in the 1970s. TFP growth in this period was very slow. In the 1980s, TFP growth accelerated before decelerating again in the run-up to the 1997–1998 financial crisis. Following the crisis, the contribution of capital fell while that of TFP rose. It is tempting to interpret this in terms of the decrease in investment and increase in efficiency associated with post-crisis reforms. The contribution of labor and human capital also declined relative to earlier years; in this case the interpretation is less clear.[9]

Capital is of course the standard explanation for economic growth used by everyone from Ricardo to Marx. To be sure, Adam Smith did not agree with this view, and Robert Solow influentially demonstrated that growth in the United States was largely driven by total factor productivity. Much recent work on growth accounting, however, has concluded that capital is as important as TFP in developing economies.[10] It is difficult in practice to distinguish the effects of capital deepening from

Table 2.1. Growth Accounting Decomposition of Aggregate Gross Domestic Product, Excluding Agriculture and Mining (1971–2005)

Year	Aggregate GDP growth rate	Contribution to aggregate GDP					Labor income share
		Capital	Human capital	Employment	Labor hours	TFP	
1971–1979	8.47%	3.54%	0.42%	4.88%	−0.55%	0.17%	0.66
(1971–1982)	(7.44%)	(3.71%)	(0.29%)	(4.02%)	(0.00%)	(−0.58%)	(0.66)
1982–1989	9.48%	3.98%	0.44%	3.85%	−0.84%	2.05%	0.69
1989–1997	7.32%	3.22%	0.41%	2.76%	−0.47%	1.40%	0.74
(1989–1998)	(5.86%)	(3.02%)	(0.54%)	(1.82%)	(−0.58%)	(1.06%)	(0.74)
1998–2005	5.75%	1.61%	0.37%	1.91%	−0.20%	2.06%	0.74
(1999–2005)	(5.29%)	(1.60%)	(0.42%)	(1.91%)	(−0.68%)	(2.04%)	(0.74)
Total period	7.10%	3.15%	0.40%	2.97%	−0.37%	0.94%	0.70

Note: TFP = total factor productivity. The sample period, 1971–2005, is divided into four subsample periods, excluding the crisis years. The results for subsample periods that include the crisis years are also reported, in parentheses. Value added at 2000 year constant prices is obtained from National Accounts, Bank of Korea. Employment is the number of employees, and labor hours are average weekly hours. Data on the number of employees and the weekly hours are taken from Korea's *Annual Report on the Economic Active Population Survey* and the *Yearbook of Labor Statistics* (Geneva: International Labour Organization), respectively. The construction of human capital follows the lifetime-labor-income method of Jorgenson and Fraumeni (1989, 1992a, 1992b). Physical capital stock is net fixed capital stock constructed by Pyo, Chung, and Cho (2007). To construct the income share of the total labor force (i.e., labor income share), we add compensation for self-employed and family workers to that for employees on payroll.

Table 2.2. Growth Accounting Decomposition of Aggregate GDP, Including Agriculture and Mining (1964–1979)

Year	Aggregate GDP growth rate	Contribution to aggregate GDP				Labor income share
		Capital	Human capital	Employment	TFP	
1964–1966	9.20%	3.87%	0.59%	1.89%	2.84%	0.59
1967–1971	9.54%	7.35%	0.27%	2.10%	−0.18%	0.59
1972–1979	7.93%	3.81%	0.38%	2.41%	1.34%	0.63
Total period	8.67%	4.93%	0.38%	2.22%	1.15%	0.61

Note: TFP = total factor productivity.

those of productivity because they are so intertwined. Investment is not exogenous, even if it is treated as such in standard growth accounting; it reflects the decisions of individuals undertaking that investment because they anticipate high rates of return. And the higher the rate of return, the more likely they are to invest.

In the typical high-income country, the rate of return is driven by improvements in technological and organizational knowledge that produce supernormal returns for first movers. The high growth rates resulting from such innovations lead to high rates of return and hence to high rates of investment. In developing countries like Korea in the 1960s and 1970s, the precipitating factors are often reforms and policy changes undertaken by the government to change an unfriendly business environment. But in both contexts, changes in technology and in the way the economy is organized are what lead to higher productivity.[11] The higher growth that results then raises the return to capital and the rate of investment.

When considering the relative importance of innovation and accumulation in Korea, it is important to recall that there is little that is unusual about the country's investment and savings rates. In Table 2.3 we regress savings and investment rates on growth rates, per capita incomes, and dependency ratios, including quadratic terms to allow for nonlinearities, and on country and period dummies. As in other developing countries, saving is driven by the growth of income and changes in the dependency ratio. Investment is driven by increases in GDP, as in the accelerator model. The Korea dummy, whether specified for the entire period or for each individual decade, is not statistically significant. This suggests that saving and investment rates in Korea are well explained by standard fundamentals like growth rates and demography.[12]

Data for the 1960s are not as reliable as for later years, but the story they tell is clear. Soon after the military coup in 1961, Korea undertook radical reforms to open the economy. Growth accelerated beginning in 1963, averaging 9 percent through the end of the decade. But gross domestic capital formation as a share of GDP remained well below 20 percent through 1965 and below 22 percent in 1966 and 1967, before rising to 26 and 29 percent in 1968 and 1969. Evidently something other than just capital formation explains the transition to rapid growth.[13]

This same conclusion flows from the fact that GDP grew at an average rate of 9.7 percent in the period from 1964 to 1969, with capital ac-

Table 2.3. Saving and Investment Regressions, Time Fixed Effects

	Saving			Investment		
GDP growth	0.880*** [0.105]	0.884*** [0.105]	0.885*** [0.106]	0.672*** [0.077]	0.666*** [0.078]	0.668*** [0.078]
Lagged GDP growth	0.826*** [0.102]	0.830*** [0.102]	0.828*** [0.103]	0.509*** [0.068]	0.505*** [0.069]	0.502*** [0.069]
Income	0.008 [0.050]	0.008 [0.050]	0.009 [0.050]	0.110*** [0.034]	0.110*** [0.034]	0.111*** [0.034]
Income squared	0.002 [0.003]	0.002 [0.003]	0.002 [0.003]	−0.006*** [0.002]	−0.006*** [0.002]	−0.006*** [0.002]
Life expectancy	0.045 [0.028]	0.045 [0.028]	0.046 [0.028]	0.031 [0.022]	0.031 [0.022]	0.031 [0.022]
Old Age dependency	−0.657*** [0.086]	−0.663*** [0.087]	−0.657*** [0.087]	−0.230*** [0.059]	−0.223*** [0.059]	−0.219*** [0.059]
Youth dependency	−0.114*** [0.025]	−0.116*** [0.025]	−0.115*** [0.026]	−0.026 [0.019]	−0.024 [0.020]	−0.024 [0.020]
Korea dummy		−0.01 [0.024]			0.016 [0.021]	
Korea 1960s			−0.019 [0.067]			−0.011 [0.058]
Korea 1970s			−0.05 [0.048]			−0.001 [0.041]
Korea 1980s			−0.001 [0.048]			0.007 [0.041]
Korea 1990s			0.015 [0.048]			0.05 [0.041]
Korea 2000s			0.01 [0.067]			0.029 [0.057]
Observations	691	691	691	814	814	814
R-squared	0.543	0.543	0.544	0.36	0.36	0.361

Source: Bosworth and Chodorow-Reich (2007) data, supplemented by World Bank, World Development Indicators. We are grateful to Barry Bosworth for sharing the data.

Note: The regression specifications follow Bosworth and Chodorow-Reich (2007); we have added Korea dummies. The sample covers the period from 1960 to 2004, and the data were converted to five-year averages before estimating the regression. The Korea dummy is a dummy variable that equals one if the observation corresponds to Korea and zero otherwise. We have also added Korea's decade dummies, which are defined similarly for each decade.

*** indicates statistical significance at the 1-percent level.

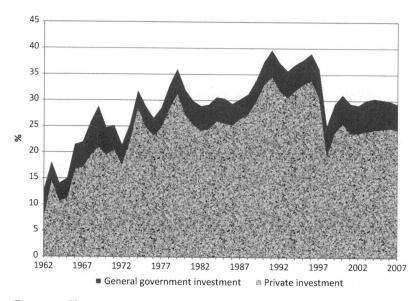

Figure 2.1. Changes in Investment Rate
The investment rate is obtained by dividing domestic investment by the aggregate GDP. Data are collected from Bank of Korea.

counting for only 2.6 percent, labor for 2.8 percent, and TFP for 3.7 percent. Evidently sharp increases in TFP preceded and, implicitly, precipitated the higher rates of investment and capital-stock growth in the 1970s. That sharp increase in productivity presumably raised the return to capital, which in turn elicited the higher rate of investment. Thus the story of the 1960s is not a story of Korea making a greater effort to increase savings and, through higher savings, to accelerate the growth of investment. Savings remained low, and while investment was higher, it was still well below the levels of later years. Rather, the story is first and foremost one of economic reforms leading initially to an increase in productivity, and only then to a higher rate of investment (and eventually a higher rate of savings).

The key reforms in the 1960s began with a major devaluation of the won, together with measures designed to promote exports. These were followed by a rise in interest rates that temporarily relaxed repressed financial conditions. More generally, the entire government apparatus was directed by President Park to focus on economic growth.[14]

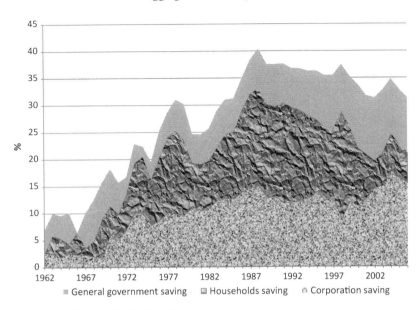

Figure 2.2. Changes in Saving Rate
The saving rate is obtained by dividing gross savings by the aggregate GDP. All the data are collected from Bank of Korea.

The picture changes as one moves through the 1970s, 1980s, and 1990s (see Figure 2.3). From 1971 to 2005 as a whole, capital formation contributed far more than total factor productivity to the economy's growth. But the relative importance of the two factors varied over time. The contribution of TFP growth declined significantly in the 1970s. This was the period of the Heavy and Chemical Industry Drive, during which, for military as well as economic reasons, the government channeled resources into these capital-intensive industries. In the 1980s, when Korea ended the Heavy and Chemical Industry Drive, reined in inflation, and instituted a series of liberalization measures, TFP growth accelerated, helping to boost the return to capital and contributing to the high and rising rate of investment.

In the 1990s TFP growth slowed, while investment remained more than 35 percent of GDP. This was when the chaebol went on a wild foray into new businesses. The return on capital fell sharply—and along with it, capital's share of national income (see Table 2.1, rightmost column; capital's share is [1 - labor's share])—and quite remarkably, given the

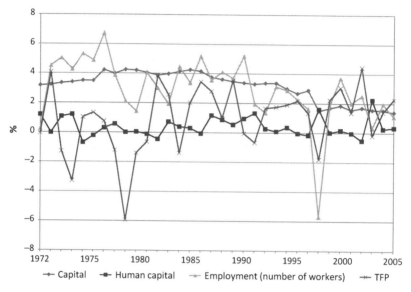

Figure 2.3. Sources of Growth, 1971–2005
Assuming a translog production function and a constant returns to scale technology, we decompose the growth rate of aggregate output into the sum of the growth rates of employment, total factor productivity (TFP), capital, and human capital. For the construction of each series, see the text.

rapid growth of the capital stock itself. The low productivity of many of these investments, together with large-scale short-term borrowing in foreign currency, also helped to set the stage for the financial crisis of 1997–1998 (see Figure 2.4).[15] Although TFP growth recovered following the crisis to levels comparable to earlier periods, the rate of return to capital recovered only to the lower levels of the first half of the 1990s. What happened after 1998 to reduce the return on capital and thereby limit investment and growth is one major question we hope to answer.

We can shed more light on the roles of capital intensity and efficiency improvements using the approach of Kumar and Russell (2002), who break down the growth of output per worker into the contributions of increasing capital intensity and technical efficiency, as above, but then go on to decompose those improvements in efficiency into those owing to changes in technology (efficiency-enhancing outward shifts in the worldwide technological frontier), and those owing to changes in national efficiency (as a country catches up to that worldwide technologi-

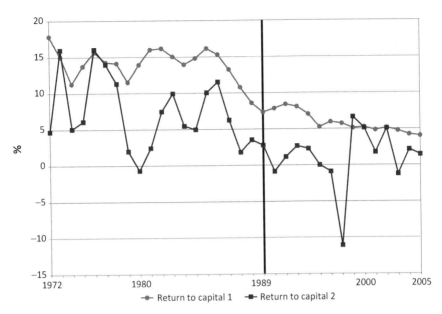

Figure 2.4. The Return to Capital in Korea

The estimates of return to capital are derived in two ways. "Return to capital 1" does not rely on the steady-state condition and is directly calculated from the growth rate of capital. "Return to capital 2" utilizes the steady-state condition that the growth rate of capital is the same as the growth rate of aggregate output. More specifically, **Return to Capital 1** $= \text{MPK} - \delta = v_k \dfrac{\dfrac{\Delta K}{K} + \delta}{\dfrac{I}{Y}} - \delta$ where MPK is the marginal product of capital, v_K is the elasticity of output with respective to capital, K is physical capital, ΔK is the change in physical capital, δ is depreciation rate, and Y is aggregate output. In the steady state, we can further represent the return to capital by expressing the growth rate of capital as (n + g), giving **Return to Capital 2** $= v_k \dfrac{(n+g+\delta)}{\dfrac{I}{Y}} - \delta$. Vertical line denotes break point in growth process identified on the basis of a Chow test.

cal frontier). The worldwide production frontier is estimated using cross-country data, and the decomposition is then implemented at the individual-country level—in this case, for Korea. The data are taken from Penn World Table, Version 6.2, with capital stock series constructed using the perpetual inventory method. Where Kumar and Russell's estimates end in 1990, we bring ours up through 2003.

The results are presented in Table 2.4. The patterns are consistent with what we found before, although the story they tell is now a bit more

Table 2.4. Percentage Change of Tripartite Decomposition Indices, 1971–1989 and 1989–2003

| Year | Output per worker | Period | Percentage change in output per worker | Contribution to percentage change in output per worker | | |
				Change in efficiency	Change in technology	Capital deepening
1971	$7,497					
1989	$19,134	1971–1989	93.7% (3.7)	38.4% (1.8)	4.1% (0.2)	77.2% (3.2)
2003	$33,784	1989–2003	56.9% (3.3)	20.2% (1.3)	24.2% (1.6)	18.2% (1.2)

Source: All variables, including real GDP, measured in 2000 international dollars, obtained from Penn World Table 6.2.

Note: The number of workers is retrieved by calculating real GDP per capita times the population and dividing by real GDP per worker. Capital stock data are constructed via the perpetual inventory method, using the real investment series. Tripartite decomposition indices are computed by using the method explained in Kumar and Russell (2002). Numbers in parentheses are annualized percentage changes.

complex. Capital deepening is far and away the most important factor contributing to Korean growth in the years from 1971 to 1989, although convergence toward the worldwide technological frontier is also important, explaining about half as much of the growth of output per worker as does capital accumulation. Growth in this period involved considerably more than brute-force capital accumulation, in other words, although it is with capital deepening that explanation should start.

In the period from 1990 to 2003, in contrast, catch-up became as important as capital deepening. In addition, there was an even larger contribution from outward shifts in the worldwide technology frontier in sectors relevant to Korea. Note also that the absolute contribution of catch-up slowed in the later period as Korea drew closer to the worldwide technology frontier. After 1989 efficiency improvements evidently required considerably more than just emulating practices that were already well established in the rest of the world. Increasingly they required Korea to keep pace with frontier technologies.

The Role of Labor Force and Education

A large share of the growth in the economy in the 1960s, 1970s, and 1980s can be explained, in a proximate sense, by the high rate of growth in the labor force and hours in nonagricultural employment.[16] This rapid

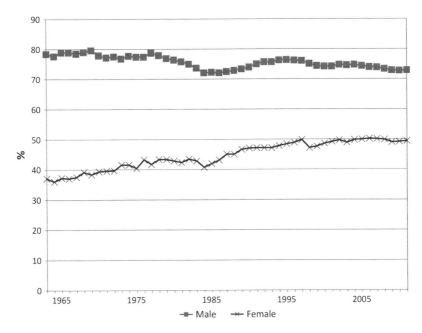

Figure 2.5. Share of Men and Women Employed
Data are from Korean Statistical Information Service.

increase was made possible mainly by migration out of agriculture.[17] By the 1990s, however, rural-to-urban migration had come to an end. At that point the growth of the labor force depended mostly on the rate of natural increase, which was declining as Korea experienced its demographic transition, and on the growing participation of women in the labor market. By 1985 the population growth rate had fallen to less than 1 percent.[18] Overall, the decline in the contribution of labor (not including human capital) accounted for a 2 percent drop in the GDP growth rate between the 1970s and 2000–2005.[19]

Also contributing to the growth of employment was a steady increase in the share of women in the labor force. By the end of 2009 some 10 million employed women made up 42 percent of the total labor force, up from 35 percent in the mid-1960s (see Figure 2.5). Equally important was the rapid demographic transition Korea experienced during the 1950s and 1960s. Korea, like many countries around the world, experienced a sharp drop in the crude death rate in the 1950s. But unlike many other developing countries, Korea's birth rate and the fertility rate of women of childbearing age also fell rapidly. The result was that by the early 1960s the population of children age four and under had stopped growing. Ten to fifteen years later those children constituted the new entrants into the Korean labor force. The labor force still grew, however, because the number of people entering the work force who were age four and under in 1960 was four times the number of those retiring from the labor force.

Koreans work a large number of hours per week and per year. No other country's employees work hours as long as those in Korea. However, from a growth accounting point of view what matters is whether the number of work hours per employee is rising or falling. In the case of Korea, the number of hours worked, while remaining very high by international standards, has been falling. This would thus show up in the growth accounting equation as a decline in the growth rate of labor. In Table 2.1 we separated out the role of declining labor hours. In the decades since 1971, declining hours lowered the GDP growth rate by 0.20 percent to 0.84 percent per year. If declining hours led to higher productivity per hour worked, GDP growth would rise, but this would probably show up in the growth accounting equation as an increase in total factor productivity rather than as an increase in the contribution to the growth of the labor force.

The standard growth accounting approach as implemented here suggests that human capital accumulation explains less than half a percent of the GDP growth rate. This is despite the fact that Korea in its high-growth period experienced an extraordinarily rapid increase in educational attainment (see Figure 2.6). In 1965 only 27 percent of the relevant age cohort was enrolled in high school in Korea and only 6.9 percent of the relevant age cohort was in universities or other tertiary-level institutions. By the 1990s virtually everyone of school age had achieved at least a secondary school education, up from less than 30 percent in the 1960s. After 2000, 87 percent of those of tertiary-school age were enrolled in a university or other tertiary-level school, far higher than the less than 10 percent that had prevailed in the 1960s and early 1970s and an unprecedented figure worldwide.[20]

Many analysts argue that the rapid expansion of education is central to Korea's high-growth story. It is thus perplexing that education does not play a larger role in these calculations. To illustrate the point, imagine that Korea had a population in 1961 where no one had education beyond three years of primary school. Assume further that in the subsequent

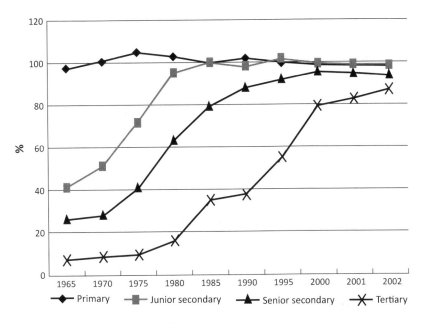

Figure 2.6. School Enrollment Rates, 1965–2002
Source: Lee (2005), 674.

three decades there was no increase in the level of education. According to our growth accounting calculations, the rate of growth of GDP would have fallen only from 8.5 to 8.0 percent per year. This conclusion is not plausible.

The likely explanation is that the standard growth accounting equation is incorrectly specified for a country like Korea. An economy starting out as far behind as Korea cannot simply build up capital and increase productivity with a work force that is illiterate and innumerate. Growth requires skilled workers to design, operate, and repair machinery; organize the labor force; and implement other measures contributing to the growth of TFP. Absent education, those skills would be lacking, and productivity would not increase. Growth would result mainly from increases in physical capital alone, but that physical capital would be poorly utilized and depreciate rapidly. The rate of return and incentive to invest would be depressed as a result.

To put the point another way, human capital is needed to ensure that capital and other inputs receive adequate returns. This points to what is distinctive about Korea. Almost uniquely among developing countries, it had a well-educated labor force already when high growth started. It then built on that base by rapidly expanding education at all levels.[21]

The conventional way of measuring the contribution of human capital is appropriate for a high-income country where marginal increases in education lead to marginal increases in labor productivity. In that setting, the technological and organizational capability for economic growth already exists but can be enhanced on the margin through further education. In such a country, it is appropriate to measure the contribution of education by the degree to which it increases the marginal productivity of labor, as measured by the increase in wages of that worker. In a country with few educated persons, in contrast, it simply will not be possible to develop the modern sector.[22] In this context, the contribution of additional education is more than marginal; it can lead to a fundamental (inframarginal) increase in technological and organizational capability and to sharp changes in the rate of growth. A growth accounting methodology suitable for analyzing marginal changes is not well designed to capture these inframarginal effects.

Thus, in the absence of a well-educated labor force, Korea might have been able to expand low-skilled, labor-intensive manufacturing. But it is unlikely that it could have then moved up the technology and business-organization ladders into more technologically and organizationally demanding industries and activities.

The Recent Period

Although recovery from the 1997–1998 crisis was rapid, Korea did not return to its earlier growth path once the crisis had passed. Gross capital formation as a percentage of GDP fell from the high levels of the early 1990s.[23] The rate of return did, however, recover to levels commensurate with the first half of the 1990s.[24] Tobin's q and the return on assets were the same in 2000–2007 as they had been in 1990–1997 (Table 2.5).[25] This increase in profitability as measured by Tobin's q accounted, to a substantial degree, for the recovery of investment to 1970s and 1980s levels (which were, as mentioned, somewhat lower than the exceptional levels scaled in the first half of the 1990s). This interpretation is also consistent with the regressions in Table 2.3, suggesting that there was little that was exceptional about Korea's investment rates.

Table 2.5. Emerging Asia: Median Corporate Soundness Indicators

	Korea	Indonesia	Malaysia	Philippines	Singapore	Thailand
Investment rate						
1990–1997	0.15	0.15	0.15	0.18	0.21	0.12
2000–2007	0.09	0.03	0.07	0.04	0.08	0.07
Profitability						
Operating margins (in percent)[a]						
1990–1997	6.8	13.7	12.7	10.9	7.3	8.4
2000–2007	5.5	7.1	5.9	6.6	5	6.3
Return on equity (in percent)						
1990–1997	3.9	9.8	10.8	8.8	6.1	8.7
2000–2007	7.2	7.6	5.7	4.7	7.1	10.3
Return on assets (in percent)						
1990–1997	4.9	7.4	7.2	5.2	3.9	5.9
2000–2007	4.9	5.9	4.1	4.3	4.5	6.9
Valuation						
Tobin's q						
1990–1997	1.3	1	3.3	1.8	3	1.8
2000–2007	1.3	0.8	1.6	1.1	1.7	1.4
Liquidity						
Current ratio[b]						
1990–1997	1	1.5	1.2	1.3	1.5	1.1
2000–2007	1.3	1.4	1.6	1.2	1.5	1.4

(continued)

Table 2.5. (Continued)

	Korea	Indonesia	Malaysia	Philippines	Singapore	Thailand
Quick ratio[c]						
1990–1997	0.7	1	0.8	0.8	1.1	0.6
2000–2007	0.9	0.8	1.1	0.8	1	0.8
Interest coverage ratio[d]						
1990–1997	1.3	3.1	6	3.2	5.4	2.5
2000–2007	3.2	2.4	3.8	2	5.8	5.5
Leverage and debt structure						
Debt to equity (in percent)						
1990–1997	186	76.5	39.4	35.4	41.8	103.2
2000–2007	54.6	63.5	37.1	37.2	33	42.6
Debt to assets (in percent)						
1990–1997	48.7	35.9	20	20.9	22.4	43.5
2000–2007	26.7	32.6	22.3	22.5	18.6	26.6
Short-term debt to total debt (in percent)						
1990–1997	54.5	58.4	66.8	52.8	54.7	75.7
2000–2007	64.8	50	69.9	50.9	63.5	63.9

Source: IMF, Republic of Korea: Selected Issues, IMF Country Report 08/296 (Washington, DC: International Monetary Fund, 2008).

[a] Operating earnings (earnings before interest and taxes) in percent of sales.
[b] Current assets to current liabilities.
[c] Cash and receivables to current liabilities.
[d] Operating earnings (earnings before interest and taxes) to gross interest expenses.

Total factor productivity growth, in contrast, accelerated relative to the pre-crisis 1990s, rising to levels not seen since the high-growth 1980s. But TFP growth in 2000–2005 was probably driven by very different factors than the high-TFP growth rates of the 1980s. We suspect that chaebol reform (as analyzed by Lim and Morck [forthcoming] in this series) was especially important in the recent period.

An even more important contributor in recent years has been research and development. Spending for R&D reached 3 percent of GDP in 2005, up from 2 percent in the early 1990s and less than 1 percent before 1983 (see Table 2.6). To shed light on its contribution, we regressed TFP growth on R&D, controlling for industry exports, capital intensity, and a measure of worker skill for 71 manufacturing industries in the period from 1992 to 2006.[26] The relationship between R&D and TFP growth at the industry level is both statistically significant and economically important (Table 2.7).[27] A 1 percent increase in expenditure on R&D as a percentage share of industrial value added raises TFP growth by 0.13 percent in the industry in question (Table 2.8).[28] Korean policymakers have attached priority to R&D spending; our results suggest that this emphasis is not misplaced.

Korea in International Context

Another perspective can be obtained by comparing growth accounting for Korea with that for other countries. Here we use the work of Bosworth and Collins (2003), which does not separate out Korea, and that of Hahn and Kim (2003), which does distinguish South Korea's experience. As shown in Tables 2.9 and 2.10, Korea's TFP and capital-stock growth rates are similar to those of other East Asian countries, and its TFP growth rate is considerably faster than in most of the countries of Southeast Asia (the exceptions being Singapore and Thailand). In sub-Saharan Africa, in contrast, TFP growth has been negative since the 1970s, and there has been little capital-stock growth. TFP growth in the Middle East has been marginally positive but the capital growth rate has been higher, due presumably to petroleum revenues. South Asia had little TFP growth and slow capital growth until the 1980s, but TFP and the capital growth rate then took off.[29] In Latin America there was substantial TFP and capital growth in the initial decades, but TFP growth on

Table 2.6. R&D Expenditures and Their Shares in GDP

	United States		France		Germany		Japan	
Year	Amount (million PPP $)	Percentage of GDP	Amount (million PPP $)	Percentage of GDP	Amount (million PPP $)	Percentage of GDP	Amount (million PPP $)	Percentage of GDP
1981	72,750	2.34	11,042	1.9	18,352	2.35	27,389	2.33
1982	81,166	2.51	12,530	1.99	19,959	2.42	31,046	2.42
1983	90,403	2.58	13,457	2.03	21,141	2.43	34,678	2.56
1984	102,875	2.64	14,787	2.12	22,559	2.43	38,329	2.64
1985	115,219	2.75	15,902	2.17	25,508	2.6	43,487	2.77
1986	120,562	2.72	16,512	2.15	26,951	2.63	45,215	2.73
1987	126,667	2.69	17,690	2.19	29,279	2.74	49,575	2.81
1988	134,202	2.65	19,107	2.19	31,255	2.73	54,979	2.82
1989	142,226	2.61	21,096	2.23	33,506	2.71	62,012	2.91
1990	152,389	2.65	23,372	2.32	35,180	2.61	69,620	2.99
1991	161,388	2.71	24,480	2.32	39,259	2.47	73,708	2.96
1992	165,835	2.64	25,465	2.33	39,114	2.35	74,939	2.92
1993	166,147	2.52	26,311	2.38	38,509	2.28	75,158	2.85
1994	169,613	2.42	26,790	2.32	38,684	2.18	76,040	2.79
1995	184,077	2.51	27,526	2.29	40,299	2.19	82,642	2.92
1996	197,792	2.55	28,194	2.27	41,515	2.19	83,209	2.81
1997	212,709	2.58	28,509	2.19	43,309	2.24	87,891	2.87
1998	226,934	2.61	29,289	2.14	45,199	2.27	91,093	3
1999	245,548	2.66	30,763	2.16	49,432	2.4	92,774	3.02
2000	268,121	2.75	32,920	2.15	52,284	2.45	98,775	3.04
2001	278,239	2.76	35,819	2.2	54,448	2.46	104,009	3.12
2002	277,066	2.66	38,153	2.23	56,657	2.49	108,166	3.17
2003	289,736	2.66	36,887	2.17	59,484	2.52	112,274	3.2
2004	300,840	2.59	38,025	2.15	61,393	2.49	117,495	3.17
2005	323,853	2.62	39,270	2.1	62,448	2.48	128,695	3.32
2006	348,658	2.66	41,508	2.1	66,716	2.54	138,782	3.39
2007	368,799	2.68	43,360	2.08	69,334	2.53		

Source: OECD, *Main Science and Technology Indicators* (Paris: Organization for Economic Cooperation and Development, October 2008). Data for Korea and Taipei from 1981 to 1990 are from Ha, Kim, and Lee (2009). We thank Joonkyung Ha for sharing the data.

Note: PPP = purchasing power parity. GDP is measured in millions of current PPP U.S. dollars, constructed by OECD.

China		Singapore		Taiwan		Korea	
Amount (million PPP $)	Percentage of GDP	Amount (million PPP $)	Percentage of GDP	Amount (million PPP $)	Percentage of GDP	Amount (million PPP $)	Percentage of GDP
					0.73	887	0.76
					0.68	1,275	0.96
					0.69	1,597	1.04
					0.73	2,078	1.21
					1.03	2,788	1.47
					1.01	3,509	1.64
					1.14	4,217	1.72
					1.24	5,151	1.84
					1.39	5,862	1.89
					1.66	6,576	1.87
7,556	0.73				1.70	7,325	1.84
8,897	0.74				1.78	8,354	1.94
9,796	0.7				1.76	9,911	2.12
10,242	0.64	878	1.09		1.80	12,041	2.32
10,462	0.57	1,018	1.14	5,373	1.72	13,681	2.37
11,619	0.57	1,343	1.37	5,863	1.74	15,282	2.42
14,648	0.64	1,592	1.48	6,643	1.82	16,637	2.48
16,171	0.65	1,941	1.81	7,387	1.91	14,789	2.34
20,464	0.76	2,216	1.9	8,199	1.98	15,793	2.25
27,029	0.9	2,473	1.88	8,834	1.97	18,494	2.39
31,570	0.95	2,771	2.11	9,337	2.08	21,280	2.59
39,445	1.07	3,004	2.15	10,428	2.18	22,507	2.53
46,945	1.13	3,119	2.11	11,676	2.31	23,969	2.63
57,670	1.23	3,668	2.2	13,131	2.38	27,936	2.85
71,063	1.33	4,248	2.3	14,528	2.45	30,618	2.98
86,758	1.42	4,783	2.31	16,553	2.58	35,886	3.22

Table 2.7. The Impact of R&D on Total Factor Productivity Growth at the Industry Level: Fixed Effects Estimates

Growth rate of TFP	[1]	[2]	[3]
Exports/value added	0.042***	0.042***	0.041***
	[0.013]	[0.013]	[0.013]
R&D intensity	0.130***	0.121***	0.121***
	[0.043]	[0.043]	[0.043]
Capital intensity		0.116***	0.119***
		[0.040]	[0.041]
Skill intensity			−0.053
			[0.061]
Observations	640	640	639
R-squared	0.11	0.12	0.12

Source: Calculations are based on UN Comtrade data and the Survey of Mining and Manufacturing (Korea National Statistical Office).

Note: TFP=total factor productivity. The dependent variable is the growth rate of total factor productivity at the manufacturing industry level. A total of 71 industries at the three-digit level were considered. Value-added and R&D data are obtained from Siwook Lee. Exports at the industry level are calculated by converting UN Comtrade data. R&D intensity is defined as the share of R&D expenditure in Value added; capital intensity is the logarithm of per-worker tangible fixed assets; skill intensity is the ratio of nonproduction workers to production workers. All the explanatory variables are one-period lagged. The sample period is 1992–2006. Time-fixed effects are included but not reported.

*** indicates statistical significance at the 1-percent level.

Table 2.8. The Impact of R&D on Total Factor Productivity Growth at the Industry Level: Arellano-Bond Estimates

Growth rate of TFP	[1]	[2]	[3]
Growth rate of TFP (−1)	−0.234***	−0.222***	−0.212***
	[0.046]	[0.046]	[0.047]
Exports/value added	0.120***	0.118***	0.119***
	[0.021]	[0.021]	[0.021]
R&D intensity	0.173***	0.172***	0.176***
	[0.051]	[0.051]	[0.051]
Capital intensity		0.098*	0.099*
		[0.057]	[0.057]
Skill intensity			0.068
			[0.123]
Observations	526	526	526

Note: See note for Table 2.7. The Arellano-Bond estimates reported use lagged levels and differences as instruments.

*** and * indicate statistical significance at the 1-percent and 10-percent level, respectively.

Table 2.9. Sources of Growth, Rest of World, 1960–2000

Region/period	Output	Output per worker	Contribution of		
			Physical capital	Education	Total factor productivity
World (84 countries)					
1960–1970	5.1	3.5	1.2	0.3	1.9
1970–1980	3.9	1.9	1.1	0.5	0.3
1980–1990	3.5	1.8	0.8	0.3	0.8
1990–2000	3.3	1.9	0.9	0.3	0.8
1960–2000	4.0	2.3	1.0	0.3	0.9
Industrial countries (22)					
1960–1970	5.2	3.9	1.3	0.3	2.2
1970–1980	3.3	1.7	0.9	0.5	0.3
1980–1990	2.9	1.8	0.7	0.2	0.9
1990–2000	2.5	1.5	0.8	0.2	0.5
1960–2000	3.5	2.2	0.9	0.3	1.0
China					
1960–1970	2.8	0.9	0	0.3	0.5
1970–1980	5.3	2.8	1.6	0.4	0.7
1980–1990	9.2	6.8	2.1	0.4	4.2
1990–2000	10.1	8.8	3.2	0.3	5.1
1960–2000	6.8	4.8	1.7	0.4	2.6
East Asia less China (7 countries)					
1960–1970	6.4	3.7	1.7	0.4	1.5
1970–1980	7.6	4.3	2.7	0.6	0.9
1980–1990	7.2	4.4	2.4	0.6	1.3
1990–2000	5.7	3.4	2.3	0.5	0.5
1960–2000	6.7	3.9	2.3	0.5	1.0
Latin America (22 countries)					
1960–1970	5.5	2.8	0.8	0.3	1.6
1970–1980	6.0	2.7	1.2	0.3	1.1
1980–1990	1.1	−1.8	0	0.5	−2.3
1990–2000	3.3	0.9	0.2	0.3	0.4
1960–2000	4.0	1.1	0.6	0.4	0.2

(continued)

Table 2.9. (Continued)

Region/period	Output	Output per worker	Physical capital	Education	Total factor productivity
			Contribution of		
South Asia (4 countries)					
1960–1970	4.2	2.2	1.2	0.3	0.7
1970–1980	3	0.7	0.6	0.3	−0.2
1980–1990	5.8	3.7	1.0	0.4	2.2
1990–2000	5.3	2.8	1.2	0.4	1.2
1960–2000	4.6	2.3	1.0	0.3	1.0
Africa (19 countries)					
1960–1970	5.2	2.8	0.7	0.2	1.9
1970–1980	3.6	1	1.3	0.1	−0.3
1980–1990	1.7	−1.1	−0.1	0.4	−1.4
1990–2000	2.3	−0.2	−0.1	0.4	−0.5
1960–2000	3.2	0.6	0.5	0.3	−0.1
Middle East (9 countries)					
1960–1970	6.4	4.5	1.5	0.3	2.6
1970–1980	4.4	1.9	2.1	0.5	−0.6
1980–1990	4	1.1	0.6	0.5	0.1
1990–2000	3.6	0.8	0.3	0.5	0
1960–2000	4.6	2.1	1.1	0.4	0.5

Source: Bosworth and Collins (2003).

Note: Regional averages are GDP weighted.

average was negative once the debt crisis took hold in the 1980s and the rate of growth of capital formation slowed.

These comparisons support the view that there is a substantial synergy between TFP and capital stock growth rates.[30] They suggest that what separates Korea from most other developing countries, therefore, is higher rates of growth of both TFP and the capital stock, not just one or the other.[31]

If instead of comparing Korea with other developing countries one compares it with advanced industrial countries, Korea (like most other countries in East Asia, and in South Asia since the 1980s) has a much higher rate of capital-stock growth but a similar rate of TFP growth.

Table 2.10. Alternative Estimates of Total Factor Productivity Growth (Percent per Annum)

Region and country	When labor input is adjusted by labor quality, as measured by educational attainment		Education as another input	
	Constant (= 0.35)	Different α across countries	Constant	Different
East Asia	1.00	0.63	0.87	0.84
Latin America	−0.52	−0.58	−0.46	−0.46
Middle East	0.42	0.28	0.23	0.22
South Asia	−0.12	−0.26	−0.32	−0.36
Sub-Sahara	−0.05	−0.07	−0.15	−0.15
Developed	0.77	0.64	0.74	0.75
Malaysia	0.53	0.31	0.46	0.48
Indonesia	0.59	0.39	0.36	0.36
Philippines	−0.58	−0.70	−0.34	−0.35
Singapore	1.31	0.88	0.95	0.99
South Korea	1.25	0.83	1.35	1.28
Taiwan	1.24	0.77	1.25	1.14
Thailand	1.54	1.08	1.18	1.05
Japan	2.09	1.77	1.60	1.68

Source: Hahn and Kim (2003), table 2.

Note: Hahn and Kim decompose the aggregate GDP growth rate, obtained from the purchasing power parity–adjusted real GDP series in Penn World Table 5.6, into accumulation of inputs of physical capital, human capital and labor, and total factor productivity growth.

If one focuses on the recent decade, when the country can be described as a middle- to high-income country, Korea's TFP growth rate is considerably faster than the advanced-country average. Whether the faster TFP growth rate of recent years is a temporary product of deep post-crisis reforms, a reflection of the effectiveness of Korean R&D spending, or simply represents further scope for catch-up, remains to be ascertained.[32]

In sum, the high-growth period from 1963 through 1995 reflected economic reforms that raised total factor productivity and returns to capital. Of particular importance were the market-opening reforms of the early 1960s and the market-liberalization reforms of the mid-1980s. Relatively high levels of educational attainment already achieved when these reforms were adopted made possible the increase in the return to capital.[33] The response of investors led to sustained rapid growth of the capital stock, which in turn sustained high growth even after the initial spurt of productivity from the reforms was spent. While external financing was critical for investment and capital-stock growth in the 1960s, domestic savings financed the bulk of Korean investment starting in the 1970s.[34]

The Financial Crisis and Economic Growth

The 1997–1998 financial crisis marked the end of the high-growth era. Although recovery from the crisis was at least as rapid as recovery from the earlier economic and political crisis that followed the late-1979 assassination of President Park, this time the growth rate seemed to decelerate once and for all.[35]

Korea is not the only country to experience this kind of deceleration. The growth rate in Taiwan over the comparable period was even lower (3.5 percent, down from 6.9 percent in the 1990s).[36] Japan's high-growth period had similarly come to an abrupt end in the early 1970s, coincident with the first OPEC oil shock. Japanese GDP growth from 1973 to 1979 averaged 3.2 percent. In the 1980s it averaged 4.3 percent.

Rapid growth appears to slow down in a variety of circumstances and in different ways. But we can be confident of one conclusion: no high-income economy grows at more than 4 percent a year on a sustained basis. Korea, Taiwan, and Japan all experienced per capita GDP growth at 5.5 to 6.7 percent a year (aggregate growth of 8 to 9 plus percent) in their decades of rapid growth but slowed down on reaching a per capita purchasing power parity GDP of around $14,000 in year 2000 prices—a level that falls well short of the high-income nations. In Japan the decline in the growth rate was sharp and abrupt. In Korea and Taiwan it was more gradual: growth decelerated in the first decade to 5.4 to 6.3 percent and in the next decade to 3.4 to 3.6 percent per year (levels similar to those in Japan).

Nor is East Asia's experience unique. All high-income countries have experienced periods when exceptionally rapid growth has come to an end. Put differently, although countries that initiated their growth later than the incumbent high-income economies, as well as countries that

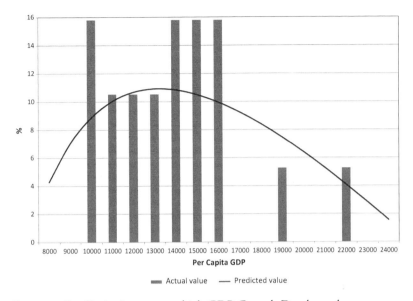

Figure 2.7. Per Capita Income at which GDP Growth Decelerated

This graph represents a sample of 20 sustained decelerations, with some countries represented by 2 different episodes of deceleration.

fell behind because of the impact of events such as World War II, frequently experienced periods of rapid growth as they caught up with the technological leaders, their high growth rates did not last forever. With few exceptions, the shift to slower growth occurred well before they reached parity with the highest per capita national incomes. Figure 2.7 and Table 2.11 show the per capita income (in purchasing power parity terms) at which the now-high-income countries slowed down. A slowdown of the growth rate is said to occur if the seven-year-average preslowdown growth rate is at least larger than 3.5 percent and the difference between the seven-year-average pregrowth rate and the seven-year-average post-slowdown growth rate is larger than 2 percent. (These calculations are restricted to countries that have achieved a per capita GDP of at least $10,000.)

Most countries slowed down at a point between $10,000 and $16,000 per capita in year-2000 purchasing power parity prices. Exceptions are the United States and countries experiencing a second slowdown (Japan, Hong Kong, and Singapore). The United States was the leading

Table 2.11. Episodes of Slowdown by Decade and Magnitude of Deceleration

Decade	Country	Year (t)	Growth before (t − 7 through t)	Growth after (t through t + 7)	Difference in growth	Per capita GDP at t (dollars)
1960s	Denmark	1964	5.0%	2.9%	−2.1%	13,800
	New Zealand	1965	4.1%	0.9%	−3.2%	14,073
	United States	1968	4.0%	1.5%	−2.5%	17,073
1970s	Denmark	1970	3.9%	1.5%	−2.4%	16,584
	Finland	1970	4.7%	2.3%	−2.4%	11,981
	Netherlands	1970	4.5%	2.0%	−2.4%	15,205
	Israel	1972	5.5%	1.2%	−4.3%	13,215
	Japan	1972	8.8%	2.8%	−6.0%	12,556
	Austria	1973	4.8%	2.7%	−2.0%	14,806
	Belgium	1973	4.7%	2.5%	−2.2%	14,371
	Greece	1973	7.4%	1.4%	−6.0%	10,747
	Netherlands	1973	3.6%	1.6%	−2.1%	16,294
	Spain	1974	5.5%	0.2%	−5.2%	11,703
	Finland	1974	5.3%	1.7%	−3.5%	14,308
	France	1974	4.1%	1.8%	−2.4%	15,487
	Italy	1974	4.3%	2.3%	−2.1%	13,494
	Belgium	1976	3.9%	1.3%	−2.6%	15,472
	Greece	1976	4.8%	0.1%	−4.7%	10,997
	Austria	1977	3.9%	1.6%	−2.4%	16,788
	Hong Kong	1978	6.5%	4.4%	−2.1%	11,761
	Ireland	1978	3.7%	0.8%	−2.9%	10,292
1980s	Singapore	1980	5.6%	2.8%	−2.8%	13,032
	Hong Kong	1982	7.4%	5.4%	−2.0%	14,519
	United Kingdom	1989	3.6%	1.4%	−2.2%	19,800
1990s	Puerto Rico	1990	4.8%	2.4%	−2.4%	15,087
	Portugal	1991	5.1%	2.1%	−3.0%	12,884
	Taiwan	1992	7.3%	5.1%	−2.2%	12,743
	Japan	1992	3.6%	0.6%	−3.0%	22,437
	Hong Kong	1994	4.6%	0.2%	−4.3%	26,602
	Korea, Rep. of	1995	7.1%	3.6%	−3.4%	13,297

(continued)

Table 2.11. (Continued)

Decade	Country	Year (t)	Growth before (t − 7 through t)	Growth after (t through t + 7)	Difference in growth	Per capita GDP at t (dollars)
	Malaysia	1996	6.3%	2.6%	−3.7%	10,099
	Singapore	1996	5.6%	0.1%	−5.5%	26,760
	Taiwan	1996	5.7%	3.1%	−2.6%	15,976
	Israel	1996	3.6%	0.3%	−3.4%	20,341
	Argentina	1997	5.0%	−0.8%	−5.8%	8,195
	Chile	1997	6.3%	2.0%	−4.3%	11,055
	Uruguay	1997	4.5%	−1.4%	−5.8%	10,858
	Norway	1997	3.8%	1.5%	−2.3%	31,292

Source: Data are from Penn World Table 6.2.

Note: Our analysis of growth slowdowns builds on a symmetrical analysis of growth accelerations by Hausmann, Pritchett, and Rodrik (2005). A slowdown of the growth rate is said to occur if the seven-year average pre-slowdown rate is greater than 3.5 percent and the difference between the seven-year average pre-slowdown rate and the seven-year average post-slowdown rate is larger than 2 percent. The sample is restricted to countries that have ever achieved a per capita GDP of $10,000.

economy in the last half of the twentieth century and thus was never in catch-up mode.[37] The timing of the U.S. slowdown was related to special circumstances: the aftermath of policies connected to the Vietnam War and the OPEC oil-price increases.[38] Not much can be generalized from its experience, in other words. The other cases were instances of a second slowdown that was also due to special circumstances that were ultimately reversed: the financial crisis that had a major impact on Hong Kong and Singapore, and the twelve years of stagnation in Japan following the bursting of the stock-market and real-estate bubbles.

We conclude that in countries that slowed down at per capita incomes between $10,000 and $16,000, the deceleration in the rate of growth cannot be explained by policy mistakes or international causes; rather, it is intrinsic to the process of catch-up and convergence.

Exactly what happens when a country reaches a per capita GDP of $10,000 can be gleaned from Table 2.12. There we regress an indicator variable for the date of a country's growth slowdown on per capita income and per capita income squared and, alternatively, per capita income relative to that of the lead country (denoted "ratio"), the manufacturing share of employment, the dependency ratio, and the fertility rate.

Table 2.12. Correlates of Growth Slowdowns (Dependent Variable Is Indicator of Year of Deceleration)

			Deceleration		
Per capita GDP	78.062** [25.759]		101.867** [38.648]	142.396** [39.291]	146.528** [41.121]
Per capita GDP squared	−4.113** [1.349]		−3.343* [1.415]	−7.440** [2.046]	−7.651** [2.142]
Ratio		17.998* [7.223]	−109.535 [91.881]		
Ratio squared		−14.872** [5.708]	36.905 [34.966]		
Dependency				−60.008* [23.514]	−62.432* [25.750]
Dependency squared				46.988* [21.363]	50.648* [23.186]
Fertility				0.962* [0.483]	0.465 [0.544]
Manufacturing employment share					85.107* [39.976]
Manufacturing employment share squared					−192.426* [83.380]
Pseudo *R*-square	0.21	0.20	0.24	0.28	0.33
Observations			265		
Countries			20		

Note: Regressions are estimated by probit. The estimated coefficients are marginal probabilities evaluated at sample means; numbers in parentheses are *t*-statistics. Year dummies are included but their coefficients are not reported. Per capita GDP is obtained from Penn World Table 6.2. Ratio is defined as the ratio of each country's per capita GDP to that of the frontier country, which is considered to be the U.S. Dependency is defined as dependents to working-age population. Dependency and fertility data are collected from World Bank, World Development Indicators. Manufacturing employment share is collected from the EU KLEMS database. A slowdown of the growth rate is said to occur if the seven-year average pre-slowdown growth rate is at least larger than 3.5 percent, the difference between the seven-year average pre-slowdown growth rate and the seven-year average post-slowdown rate is larger than 2 percent, and the country has achieved a per capita GDP of $10,000.

** and * indicate statistical significance at the 1-percent and 5-percent levels, respectively.

The regression results suggest that the timing of slowdowns is explained, in a proximate sense, by per capita income, or, more precisely, by the relationship between the level of GDP prevailing in a country and that prevailing in the country that defines the technological frontier.[39] This is the well-known "convergence" result in the cross-country econometric growth literature.[40] Other variables with explanatory power include the share of manufacturing, which typically rises rapidly before stabilizing, tracing out a logistic curve. Countries can grow very rapidly during their catch-up period, when the economy is dominated by manufacturing, but slow down sharply with the shift toward services.[41] Demography also plays a role, which makes sense since rapid growth rates are more easily achieved when a large proportion of the population participates in the work force. This typically occurs after the birth rate has begun to fall and there are fewer dependent children, but before the elderly share of the population begins to rise.[42]

No doubt additional variables also matter in particular countries. In Japan, Korea, and Taiwan, growth slowed when the rapid expansion of exports was no longer feasible, whether for domestic (supply-side) or foreign (demand-side) reasons. Taiwan's exports in current-dollar terms grew by 6.4 percent a year in the 1990s, down from 15.2 percent in the 1980s. Japan's export growth in yen terms fell from 16.6 percent a year in the 1960s to 5.3 percent in the 1980s.[43] In Korea the growth of exports fell from 15.2 percent per year in nominal-dollar terms in the 1980s to 8.7 percent per year in the 1990s.[44] All three economies had successfully pursued export-led growth strategies. But high rates of export growth could not last forever. With time, these economies had to depend more on domestic demand, and that transition turned out to be incompatible with maintenance of extraordinarily high rates of GDP growth.

None of these readily quantifiable changes provides a complete explanation for why growth slows when a country reaches this level of per capita income. The story for Europe is of countries falling behind the world leaders because of the impact of World War II and then closing the gap until they reached levels of income where sustained growth no longer received much impetus from "catching up." Those advanced countries that slowed by less than 1 percent were not directly affected by wartime destruction (Canada, New Zealand, Australia), discovered oil, or experienced a long period when government policies had a pronounced negative impact on growth followed by major pro-growth reforms (United

A Log per Capita* GDP

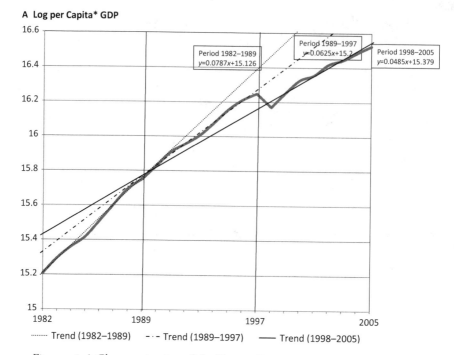

Period 1982–1989
y=0.0787x+15.126

Period 1989–1997
y=0.0625x+15.2

Period 1998–2005
y=0.0485x+15.379

········ Trend (1982–1989)   – ·· – Trend (1989–1997)   —— Trend (1998–2005)

Figure 2.8. A Characterization of the Korean Economy
(*A*) Log per capita GDP (in real terms). Data are from Bank of Korea. Real GDP is based on the aggregation of value-added of the industries, excluding two industries, agriculture and mining. Since the share of those two industries is shrinking, the growth rate of per capita GDP is scaled up by the decrease in the share, an amount equal to approximately 0.4 percent on an annual basis. The time trend is added by regressing of each series of the subsample on time. (*B*) Log capital/ labor ratio. Capital data are from Pyo, Chung, and Cho (2007). Labor represents the quantity of labor, that is, the number of employees multiplied by weekly average hours. (*C*) Log index of total factor productivity. Total factor productivity is derived from the translog production function assumed in the text. The index is constructed by normalizing log TFP in 1971 to one.

Kingdom). The exceptional nature of these cases reinforces the basic point: the slowdown in growth experienced around the time that GDP per capita exceeds $10,000 has much to do with the fact that the economy has caught up to the technological frontier. At that point it is no longer possible to simply adapt what is readily available elsewhere in order to produce at lower cost. Instead, countries must rely on technological innovation, an inherently slower and riskier process.[45]

While the slowdown in Korea is widely thought to have occurred after the crisis, there is in fact reason to think that the break point in the growth rate of per capita GDP occurred earlier. Figure 2.8 (*A*) plots per capita GDP of Korea from 1982 to 2005.[46] The figure suggests two

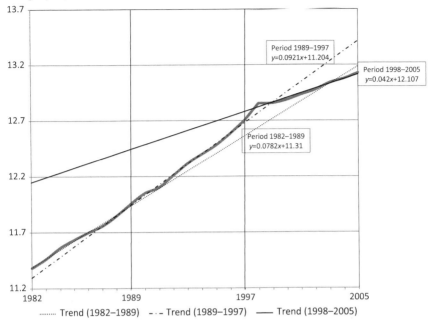

B Log Capital/Labor Ratio

Period 1989–1997
$y=0.0921x+11.204$

Period 1998–2005
$y=0.042x+12.107$

Period 1982–1989
$y=0.0782x+11.31$

········ Trend (1982–1989)   – · – Trend (1989–1997)   —— Trend (1998–2005)

Figure 2.8. A Characterization of the Korean Economy *(Continued)*

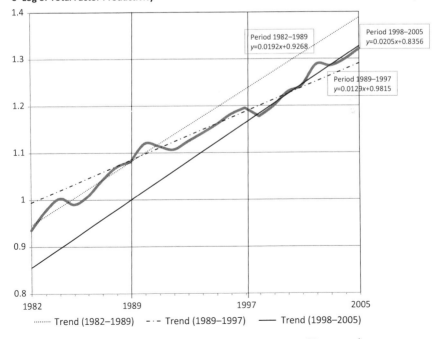

C Log of Total Factor Productivity

Period 1982–1989
$y=0.0192x+0.9268$

Period 1998–2005
$y=0.0205x+0.8356$

Period 1989–1997
$y=0.0129x+0.9815$

········ Trend (1982–1989)   – · – Trend (1989–1997)   —— Trend (1998–2005)

Figure 2.8. A Characterization of the Korean Economy *(Continued)*

breaks, one around 1989 and a second at approximately 1998. While 1998 is a natural choice given the financial crisis of that year, the break around 1989 does not correspond to any obvious historical event.[47] Nonetheless, the p-value of the Chow break-point test at year 1989 is 0.0006, which supports the existence of a break in the trend in per capita GDP around year 1989 at extremely high confidence levels.

The trend growth rates for 1982 to 1989 and 1989 to 1997 are 7.9 and 6.3 percent, respectively.[48] Since the Korean economy first took off in the 1960s, it had not averaged a per capita growth rate of less than 5 percent for such an extended period. This observation underscores the importance of understanding whether the post-1997 slowdown reflects a permanent reduction in potential growth or factors that might be overcome.

Strikingly, the trend in the capital/labor ratio in Figure 2.8 (*B*) also exhibits two structural breaks at the same two points in time. But unlike the trend in per capita GDP, the trend of the capital/labor ratio is higher in 1989–1997 than 1982–1989 (9.2 versus 7.8 percent). In 1998–2005, the trend rate of growth of the capital/labor ratio then fell to 4.2 percent. This has been pointed to as an important factor in the slow growth of the post-crisis period. If so, a question then arises: why had per capita income growth already slowed in the years from 1989 to 1997, despite the fact that the growth of the capital/labor ratio had, in fact, accelerated?

The answer lies in our index of total factor productivity in Figure 2.8 (*C*). Again two structural breaks are apparent. But the changes reveal a different pattern: trend TFP growth fell from 1.9 percent in 1982–1989 to 1.3 per cent in 1989 to 1997 before more than fully recovering to 2.1 per cent in 1998–2005. The trend of total factor productivity growth is highest in the period 1998–2005, precisely when the trend rate of per capita GDP growth is lowest.

Together these three series are consistent with the following story. Korean growth already showed a tendency to slow starting in the late 1980s, as easy approaches to boosting productivity (importing foreign technology, shifting labor from underemployment in agriculture to more productive employment in industry) approached exhaustion. An increase in investment rates (and in the capital/labor ratio) delayed what would have otherwise been a deceleration in the rate of growth. Thus, the fact that the warranted rate of growth had declined was not widely appreciated. But those higher investment rates, together with declining productivity growth, translated into a fall in the rate of return to capital.

Higher investment thus could not continue forever. The financial crisis of 1997–1998 was the occasion for a downward shift in the rate of investment, a recovery in the rate of TFP growth, and a decline in the trend rate of economic growth to lower but sustainable levels.

Cross-Country Econometric Studies of Growth

Scores of cross-country econometric studies consider the correlates of economic growth. Three, by Levine and Renelt (1992), Sala-i-Martin (1997), and Hoover and Perez (2004), are expressly concerned with identifying the subset of potential determinants that are robust. Levine and Renelt adopt the most restrictive approach—extreme bounds analysis—and identify few if any robust determinants of growth.[49] Hoover and Perez work with a general-to-specific methodology, dropping variables whose elimination does not worsen the fit of the equation.[50] They identify equipment investment, openness to foreign trade, political stability, and a set of cultural and religious variables as robust determinants of growth.[51] Finally, adopting a less restrictive extreme bounds analysis, Sala-i-Martin identifies a number of robust determinants: the initial level of per capita income, the investment rate (both equipment and nonequipment investment), the initial school enrollment rate, economic openness, the importance of primary products in exports, rule of law, reliance on private enterprise, the maintenance of an appropriate real exchange rate, and political stability.[52]

These analyses provide additional insight into why East Asia in general and South Korea in particular did so well in their first decades of sustained growth. The region ranked high in initial levels of education, investment, openness, maintenance of an appropriate exchange rate, and political stability. Like the rest of East Asia, South Korea had a high level of education when its rapid growth began.[53] Reforms then opened up the economy, and the maintenance of a competitive exchange rate, together with other policies, promoted exports.[54] Equipment investment was high starting in the 1970s. Korea also ranked high in terms of political stability (recall its relatively untroubled transition to democracy in 1987) and rule of law.[55] Like the rest of East Asia, it did not have much in the way of natural resources and therefore could not make the mistakes associated with natural resource–rich boom-and-bust economies.

None of these variables is especially helpful, however, for answering the central question of this study. To put the point concretely, none of the variables that lead to higher growth rates decline in value prior to or simultaneously with the decline in GDP growth rates.[56]

The one exception is the variable that measures the impact of the level of per capita income or per worker output at the beginning of the period of growth. In all cross-country econometric studies of growth, this variable has a large and statistically significant negative coefficient. Growth rates slow as per capita income rises, to put the point in the simplest possible way. Countries therefore converge toward a growth rate in the range of 2 to 4 percent as they rise to high-income status.

But these econometric studies imply that the decline in growth rates should be gradual, since convergence to high incomes is gradual. Actual experience, however, rarely displays such a smooth adjustment. More commonly there is a sharp drop to a new, lower growth rate, as noted above. In Japan the drop was probably precipitated by the OPEC oil-price increases, given Japan's heavy dependence on imported energy, and by the concurrent worldwide stagflation, particularly in Japan's major export markets. In Korea, enormous chaebol-initiated investment projects artificially supported growth for a time but also laid the foundation for the financial crisis that precipitated the sharp decline in growth.[57]

Thus, both growth accounting and cross-country regression suggest that it is normal for growth to slow when an economy exhausts the reservoir of surplus labor in the countryside and per capita income approaches that of already urbanized and industrialized nations. Inappropriate policy can no doubt cause the growth rate to fall further, just as good policy can have a modest influence in the opposite direction. Certainly that was the case in Japan during its twelve long years of near economic stagnation beginning in 1991. So far, however, nothing comparable has happened to slow growth any further in Korea.

Conclusion

Korea's high-growth decades, our growth accounting analysis suggests, were the product of rapid rates of capital accumulation, rapid rates of growth of the modern-sector labor force, and rapid increases in the productivity of those inputs. Rapidly rising TFP was in turn a result of comprehensive policy reforms in the 1960s and again in the 1980s. Those reforms and the resulting high productivity made possible high rates of return to capital, thereby encouraging investment. Cross-country regressions provide some guidance as to which policies and institutions mattered most for GDP and, by implication, productivity growth. In particular they highlight the importance of opening the economy and establishing an export orientation. While the two methodologies have difficulty in establishing the point formally, we are also convinced that Korea's relatively high levels of educational attainment when these reforms were introduced contributed to their effectiveness.

These two empirical perspectives also provide a clear picture of why growth slowed in the 1990s and never recovered fully to the high rates of earlier years. In part it slowed because the growth of the modern-sector labor force itself slowed as migration out of agriculture came to an end. And the rate of human capital accumulation slowed as almost all Koreans achieved at least a secondary education and an internationally unprecedented share of younger Koreans went on to university.[58]

Another factor was the difficulty of navigating the transition from export-led growth to a balanced-growth model where it was necessary to rely equally on domestic demand. Related to this, as we show in Chapters 3 and 4, is the fact that the service sector, together with construction, has generally performed less robustly than manufacturing. Given that high-income countries tend to rely more on services, this may be part of the explanation for why growth eventually slows—and for why it is slowing in Korea.

Cross-country comparisons shed further light on the factors underlying Korea's own slowdown. All countries slow down as per capita income rises. Among the now high-income countries, the slowdown from double-digit GDP growth rates appears to have occurred at a per capita income between $10,000 and $16,000 (in year-2000 purchasing power parity terms). When they reach this level, countries can no longer rely on adopting existing technology and must begin to sink the costs and take the risks associated with developing new technologies and organizational methods. Doing so is expensive—meaning that growth slows, other things equal—but unavoidable. The fact that Korea today spends 3 percent of GDP on research and development is an indication that business and the government realize that this change is, in fact, well under way. Indeed, the rise in total factor productivity growth in recent years may be a sign that this shift is already reaping returns.

Does it follow that Korea can do nothing to boost growth relative to the rates of the last decade? We know from Japan's twelve years of stagnation (1991–2002), not to mention the experience of other countries, that bad policies can slow growth markedly. By implication, more effective policies can raise the growth rate.[59] But there are limits. There is no evidence that future growth in Korea will again match the extraordinary rates of the 1960s, 1970s, and 1980s.

Appendix

Table 2.A1. Average Annual Growth Rate of Gross Domestic Product and Factors of Production

	Average annual growth rate				
Year	*GDP*	*Population*	*Total working hours*	*Capital*	*Human capital*
1971–1979	8.47%	1.65%	6.61%	10.39%	0.64%
(1971–1982)	(7.44%)	(1.63%)	(6.11%)	11.01%	(0.44%)
1982–1989	9.48%	1.09%	4.43%	12.58%	0.63%
1989–1997	7.32%	0.99%	3.11%	12.43%	0.57%
(1989–1998)	(5.86%)	(0.96%)	(1.71%)	(11.72%)	(0.74%)
1998–2005	5.75%	0.56%	2.31%	6.22%	0.50%
(1999–2005)	(5.29%)	(0.54%)	(1.66%)	(6.19%)	(0.57%)
1971–2005	7.10%	1.12%	3.82%	10.53%	0.57%

Note: For definitions and sources of variables, see note for Table 2.1.

Table 2.A2. Saving and Investment Rates for Korea (1962–2007)

	Saving			*Investment*	
	Corporation saving rate	*Household saving rate*	*General government saving rate*	*Private investment rate*	*General government investment rate*
1962	2.7	−0.1	4.3	7.4	5.4
1963	2.5	3.4	4.1	14.6	3.5
1964	1.8	3.5	4.3	10.7	3.4
1965	2.6	1.8	5.7	11.1	3.9
1966	2.3	4.1	5.5	16.8	4.8

(continued)

Table 2.A2. (Continued)

	Saving			Investment	
	Corporation saving rate	Household saving rate	General government saving rate	Private investment rate	General government investment rate
1967	2.3	1.3	6.5	17.1	4.9
1968	1.95	2.9	7.7	19.4	6.4
1969	1.9	7.1	6.8	21.0	7.8
1970	6.0	5.4	7.0	13.8	3.7
1971	5.0	4.9	5.9	13.3	3.1
1972	7.0	6.7	3.1	14.6	3.2
1973	10.0	9.3	3.6	20.1	3.0
1974	10.0	10.5	1.9	19.2	2.2
1975	7.7	8.5	3.2	17.1	2.7
1976	8.6	11.8	4.9	21.9	3.2
1977	10.1	14.0	4.7	24.6	3.7
1978	9.9	15.6	5.9	26.3	4.1
1979	9.6	13.9	6.7	25.5	3.9
1980	11.1	8.1	5.4	19.9	3.6
1981	10.4	8.5	5.5	19.6	3.5
1982	10.7	8.9	5.9	21.2	4.1
1983	12.3	9.8	6.8	22.9	4.4
1984	12.5	11.8	6.3	24.6	4.4
1985	12.4	12.3	6.1	24.6	4.6
1986	13.8	15.0	5.9	28.7	4.7
1987	14.6	17.5	6.3	32.8	4.7
1988	15.0	18.2	7.4	34.2	4.8
1989	12.8	17.3	7.5	32.0	4.3
1990	13.0	16.8	7.9	32.5	4.3
1991	11.9	18.5	7.3	32.4	4.8
1992	11.9	17.7	7.3	31.0	5.3
1993	12.4	16.7	7.8	31.0	5.2
1994	12.6	15.4	8.3	31.4	4.9
1995	13.8	13.3	9.1	31.7	4.5
1996	12.2	13.5	9.6	30.3	4.7

(continued)

Table 2.A2. (*Continued*)

	Saving			Investment	
	Corporation saving rate	Household saving rate	General government saving rate	Private investment rate	General government investment rate
1997	13.0	12.5	9.9	29.6	5.4
1998	8.6	19.8	8.9	28.6	8.6
1999	11.9	14.0	9.1	28.5	6.5
2000	11.2	10.6	11.8	27.8	6.0
2001	12.6	8.0	11.0	25.3	6.1
2002	14.5	5.1	11.7	24.8	5.5
2003	14.9	6.2	11.6	25.6	6.4
2004	17.2	7.4	10.2	27.7	6.8
2005	16.4	6.3	10.1	26.0	6.0
2006	15.4	5.6	10.2	25.2	5.3
2007	—	—	—	24.9	5.1

Source: Data for the 1960s are from Economic Planning Board, *Handbook of Korean Economy 1980.* Data for 1970–2007 are from Bank of Korea.

CHAPTER 3

The Changing Structure of Growth

Korea's economy has been experiencing rapid structural change. While the shift from manufacturing to services is an obvious aspect of this process, there have been equally dramatic changes within manufacturing: first, the shift from labor-intensive light industry to still-labor-intensive heavy industry, and more recently, the shift toward high-tech industries employing less labor per unit of output. In this sense, structural change within manufacturing is pushing labor into the service sector, in the phenomenon sometimes referred to as deindustrialization.[1]

Deindustrialization is a flashpoint in the debate over economic growth because workers leaving manufacturing do not automatically move into high-paying jobs in finance and consulting. Often they move into low-productivity jobs in, inter alia, retail and food services. This raises the question of whether structural change is creating a dual economy made up of relatively high-tech subsectors in services and manufacturing, employing highly skilled individuals, alongside relatively low-tech service sectors staffed by older, less-skilled workers who can no longer find employment that pays well.

Heightening the concern over the limited availability of high-paying manufacturing jobs is the increasing prevalence of temporary or non-regular employment. While this phenomenon is by no means unique to Korea, as of 2008 nonregular workers made up 26 percent of the labor force in Korea, roughly double the OECD average and up from 17 percent in 2001.[2] Not only are temporary workers easier to let go than regular employees, but they are also less likely to receive health and pension benefits. Their growing numbers reinforce the prevailing concern about the growth of a dual labor market.

Champions of service-sector growth point in response to the rapid development of the information and communications technology (ICT) sector, which is a source of high-paying jobs. Again, the relatively rapid growth of ICT is not unique to Korea, but in Korea as elsewhere it constitutes only a small fraction of economy-wide growth. The question is whether the rapid growth of ICT has the capacity, through spillovers, to raise the productivity of the economy as a whole or whether its productivity-enhancing effects will be largely limited to the ICT-producing sector itself.

Broad Sectoral Disaggregation

To get a grip on these questions, we start by disaggregating our sources-of-growth calculations into manufacturing (Table 3.1); construction (Table 3.2); electricity, gas, and water (Table 3.3); transport, post, and telecommunications (Table 3.4); and three service sectors (Tables 3.5–3.7). The tables are a reminder that the goods-producing sectors were the main source of dynamism in the high-growth period.[3] The rapid growth of these sectors was in turn made possible by a high rate of growth of total factor productivity, as emphasized in Chapter 2. TFP contributed more to industry output than capital except in the case of electricity, gas, and water, where the respective contributions were about equal. Increased employment, the remaining source of growth, was a substantial contributor only in transport, post, and telecommunications. Employment growth in manufacturing was slow—indeed, negative—starting in the 1980s.[4]

Service-sector performance was less robust. (We provide only an overview of service-sector performance here, deferring detailed treatment to Chapter 4.) Wholesale and retail trade (see Table 3.5) and social and personal services (see Table 3.7) together grew only half as fast as industry. For the period since 1970 as a whole, TFP growth in these subsectors was negligible. If one distinguishes subperiods, wholesale and retail trade showed substantial increases in productivity only in the 1980s and after the 1997–1998 financial crisis, two periods of significant policy reform.

Finance, insurance, real estate (FIRE), and business services were the only service subsectors displaying rapid output growth (see Table 3.6).

Table 3.1. Manufacturing Inputs and Outputs

Year	Average annual growth rate				Contribution to industry output					Labor income share
	Output	Capital	Human capital	Labor force	Capital	Human capital	Employment	Labor hours	TFP	
1971–1979	16.89%	12.52%	0.11%	10.61%	4.88%	0.09%	6.27%	0.00%	5.65%	0.61
(1971–1982)	(13.67%)	(12.68%)	(0.25%)	(7.79%)	(4.58%)	(0.19%)	(4.34%)	(0.27%)	(4.30%)	(0.64)
1982–1989	12.48%	12.39%	0.52%	5.77%	3.77%	0.37%	4.74%	-0.78%	4.38%	0.70
1989–1997	7.41%	10.75%	0.87%	-1.35%	2.70%	0.65%	-0.63%	-0.43%	5.12%	0.75
(1989–1998)	(5.67%)	(9.54%)	(1.05%)	(-3.01%)	(2.40%)	(0.77%)	(-1.74%)	(-0.51%)	(4.75%)	(0.75)
1999–2005	7.98%	4.33%	0.97%	0.09%	1.37%	0.67%	0.55%	0.51%	5.90%	0.68
(1998–2005)	(9.65%)	(3.99%)	(0.64%)	(1.19%)	(1.27%)	(0.44%)	(0.74%)	(0.05%)	(7.16%)	(0.68)
1971–2005	10.48%	10.00%	0.60%	3.15%	3.15%	0.43%	2.07%	-0.20%	5.02%	0.69

Note: TFP = total factor productivity. The sample period, 1971–2005, is divided into four subsample periods, excluding the crisis years, so that period one refers to 1971–1979, period two to 1982–1989, period 3 to 1989–1997, and period 4 to 1998–2005. The results for subsample periods that include the crisis years are reported in parentheses. Output is real value added at the 2000 year constant price of manufacturing obtained from National Accounts, Bank of Korea. Employment and labor hours are the number of employees and the average weekly hours, respectively, taken from Korea's *Annual Report on the Economic Active Population Survey* and the *Yearbook of Labor Statistics* (Geneva: International Labour Organization), respectively. The construction of human capital follows the lifetime-labor-income method of Jorgenson and Fraumeni (1989, 1992a, 1992b). Physical capital stock is net fixed capital stock by industry, constructed by Pyo, Chung, and Cho (2007). To construct the income share of the total labor force (i.e., labor income share), we add compensation for self-employed and family workers to that for employees on payroll.

Table 3.2. Construction Inputs and Outputs

	Average annual growth rate				Contribution to industry output						
Year	Output	Capital	Human capital	Labor force	Capital	Human capital	Employment	Labor hours	TFP	Labor income share
1971–1979	13.08%	15.11%	0.29%	10.45%	5.93%	0.20%	6.64%	−0.23%	0.54%	0.61
(1971–1982)	(10.04%)	(15.24%)	(0.37%)	(7.71%)	(5.50%)	(0.26%)	(4.81%)	(−0.04%)	(−0.48%)	(0.64)
1982–1989	9.52%	15.82%	0.29%	3.38%	4.18%	0.21%	3.44%	−0.83%	2.51%	0.73
1989–1997	8.63%	17.85%	0.12%	6.58%	3.31%	0.10%	5.91%	−0.53%	−0.16%	0.81
(1989–1998)	(6.50%)	(16.00%)	(0.20%)	(3.38%)	(2.96%)	(0.17%)	(2.89%)	(−0.22%)	(0.69%)	(0.82)
1999–2005	2.42%	1.93%	−0.16%	2.54%	0.17%	−0.14%	2.76%	−0.47%	0.09%	0.91
(1998–2005)	(0.89%)	(1.88%)	(−0.01%)	(1.65%)	(0.18%)	(−0.01%)	(1.52%)	(−0.01%)	(−0.78%)	(0.90)
1971–2005	7.11%	12.81%	0.23%	4.42%	3.46%	0.17%	3.34%	−0.24%	0.38%	0.76

Note: See note for Table 3.1.

Table 3.3. Electricity, Gas, and Water Inputs and Outputs

| Year | Average annual growth rate | | | | | Contribution to industry output | | | | | |
	Output	Capital	Human capital	Labor force	Capital	Human capital	Employment	Labor hours	TFP	Labor income share
1971–1979	15.74%	9.00%	0.16%	2.30%	5.23%	0.06%	1.41%	−0.51%	9.55%	0.43
(1971–1982)	(15.24%)	(9.53%)	(0.63%)	(0.02%)	(5.95%)	(0.18%)	(0.22%)	(0.03%)	(8.86%)	(0.39)
1982–1989	15.37%	10.23%	−0.54%	8.67%	7.79%	−0.18%	2.26%	−0.29%	5.79%	0.24
1989–1997	10.36%	10.51%	0.33%	3.70%	7.12%	0.12%	1.16%	0.03%	1.92%	0.32
(1989–1998)	(9.17%)	(9.80%)	(0.50%)	(0.55%)	(6.59%)	(0.20%)	(−0.15%)	(0.03%)	(2.50%)	(0.33)
1999–2005	7.50%	4.05%	−0.79%	0.25%	2.84%	−0.24%	0.73%	−0.76%	4.92%	0.31
(1998–2005)	(7.66%)	(4.56%)	(−0.69%)	(0.80%)	(3.13%)	(−0.21%)	(0.63%)	(−0.44%)	(4.55%)	(0.31)
1971–2005	12.10%	8.72%	0.08%	2.10%	5.92%	0.03%	0.62%	−0.13%	5.66%	0.33

Note: See note for Table 3.1.

Table 3.4. Wholesale and Retail Trade, Restaurants, and Hotels Inputs and Outputs

Year	Average annual growth rate				Contribution to industry output					
	Output	Capital	Human capital	Labor force	Capital	Human capital	Employment	Labor hours	TFP	Labor income share
1971–1979	7.35%	12.75%	0.66%	7.04%	2.83%	0.50%	5.65%	−0.22%	−1.41%	0.78
(1971–1982)	(6.11%)	(11.87%)	(0.34%)	(7.81%)	(2.79%)	(0.27%)	(5.69%)	(0.20%)	(−2.84%)	(0.76)
1982–1989	9.58%	10.60%	0.59%	1.55%	2.60%	0.43%	2.09%	−0.91%	5.37%	0.76
1989–1997	6.12%	15.78%	0.66%	4.81%	2.57%	0.53%	4.64%	−0.72%	−0.90%	0.84
(1989–1998)	(4.03%)	(14.26%)	(0.67%)	(3.80%)	(2.30%)	(0.55%)	(3.56%)	(−0.52%)	(−1.85%)	(0.85)
1999–2005	2.77%	3.48%	0.37%	−0.11%	0.21%	0.35%	0.18%	−0.27%	2.31%	0.94
(1998–2005)	(4.45%)	(3.44%)	(0.51%)	(0.67%)	(0.19%)	(0.49%)	(0.58%)	(0.08%)	(3.11%)	(0.94)
1971–2005	5.93%	10.51%	0.52%	3.99%	2.08%	0.42%	3.33%	−0.24%	0.34%	0.82

Note: See note for Table 3.1.

Table 3.5. Transport, Post, and Telecommunications Inputs and Outputs

Year	Average annual growth rate				Contribution to industry output					
	Output	Capital	Human capital	Labor force	Capital	Human capital	Employment	Labor hours	TFP	Labor income share
1971–1979	13.59%	6.17%	−0.45%	5.00%	1.73%	−0.32%	4.61%	−1.06%	8.62%	0.72
(1971–1982)	(11.24%)	(6.56%)	(−0.16%)	(4.46%)	(1.96%)	(−0.13%)	(3.65%)	(−0.50%)	(6.26%)	(0.70)
1982–1989	8.05%	7.74%	0.13%	4.64%	2.01%	0.06%	3.77%	−0.35%	2.56%	0.74
1989–1997	8.65%	7.89%	0.18%	3.73%	1.27%	0.13%	3.22%	−0.07%	4.11%	0.84
(1989–1998)	(7.49%)	(7.15%)	(0.52%)	(3.05%)	(1.14%)	(0.44%)	(2.74%)	(−0.19%)	(3.36%)	(0.85)
1999–2005	9.39%	5.43%	−0.10%	1.66%	0.51%	−0.07%	2.68%	−1.14%	7.41%	0.92
(1998–2005)	(9.80%)	(5.88%)	(0.01%)	(2.45%)	(0.59%)	(0.03%)	(2.71%)	(−0.48%)	(6.96%)	(0.92)
1971–2005	9.30%	6.82%	0.12%	3.71%	1.47%	0.09%	3.24%	−0.38%	4.87%	0.79

Note: See note for Table 3.1.

Table 3.6. Finance, Insurance, Real Estate, and Business Services Inputs and Outputs

	Average annual growth rate				Contribution to industry output					
Year	Output	Capital	Human capital	Labor force	Capital	Human capital	Employment	Labor hours	TFP	Labor income share
1971–1979	17.15%	13.03%	−0.72%	11.21%	6.81%	−0.34%	6.06%	−0.75%	5.37%	0.48
(1971–1982)	(14.97%)	(13.41%)	(−0.78%)	(10.79%)	(6.89%)	(−0.38%)	(5.52%)	(−0.38%)	(3.33%)	(0.49)
1982–1989	18.14%	15.25%	−0.23%	11.04%	6.71%	−0.14%	6.58%	−0.34%	5.33%	0.56
1989–1997	11.08%	12.24%	0.66%	10.83%	5.41%	0.38%	5.56%	0.47%	−0.73%	0.56
(1989–1998)	(9.45%)	(10.71%)	(0.96%)	(9.48%)	(4.73%)	(0.53%)	(4.79%)	(0.49%)	(−1.08%)	(0.55)
1999–2005	5.59%	6.62%	0.59%	5.36%	3.61%	0.25%	2.76%	−0.32%	−0.70%	0.45
(1998–2005)	(5.06%)	(4.62%)	(0.57%)	(5.02%)	(2.57%)	(0.25%)	(2.62%)	(−0.32%)	(−0.06%)	(0.46)
1971–2005	12.12%	11.26%	0.07%	9.31%	5.39%	0.04%	4.95%	−0.13%	1.87%	0.51

Note: Since the capital stock for real estate is dominantly large, to eliminate its impact we used the value-added and capital data for only the finance and insurance industries to derive the figures in this table. See also note for Table 3.1.

Table 3.7. Other Community, Social, and Personal Service Activities Inputs and Outputs

Year	Average annual growth rate				Contribution to industry output					Labor income share
	Output	Capital	Human capital	Labor force	Capital	Human capital	Employment	Labor Hours	TFP	
1971–1979	3.50%	3.48%	3.07%	0.35%	0.31%	2.72%	1.25%	−0.92%	0.16%	0.89
(1971–1982)	(3.84%)	(7.89%)	(2.26%)	(0.74%)	(0.74%)	(2.00%)	(1.10%)	(−0.42%)	(0.42%)	(0.90)
1982–1989	5.64%	17.92%	−0.35%	6.56%	2.14%	−0.28%	5.61%	−0.46%	−1.38%	0.88
1989–1997	4.96%	15.00%	−0.22%	3.80%	1.73%	−0.13%	3.60%	−0.14%	0.09%	0.89
(1989–1998)	(4.18%)	(14.12%)	(0.16%)	(3.54%)	(1.62%)	(0.18%)	(3.43%)	(−0.17%)	(−0.63%)	(0.89)
1999–2005	2.87%	7.17%	0.03%	4.96%	0.71%	0.29%	4.44%	−0.46%	−2.58%	0.90
(1998–2005)	(3.04%)	(7.16%)	(−0.09%)	(4.83%)	(0.71%)	(−0.09%)	(4.81%)	(−0.46%)	(−1.93%)	(0.90)
1971–2005	4.14%	11.45%	0.68%	3.52%	1.25%	0.61%	3.46%	−0.32%	−0.86%	0.89

Note: See note for Table 3.1.

They displayed rapid TFP growth in the 1970s and 1980s but negative productivity growth in the 1990s. The capital stock in these subsectors meanwhile grew rapidly in the 1990s before falling after the crisis. Clearly this deterioration in the performance of business services and FIRE is part of the explanation for the growth slowdown after 2000. But this should not be a surprise; the 1997–1998 crisis was first and foremost a crisis in the financial sector. With many financial institutions collapsing, it is understandable that the growth rate of this subsector slowed.

TFP growth in construction was never fast, although the growth of value added was (see Table 3.2). Construction was also the other place where growth slowed after the crisis. Again this is no surprise: construction and finance are closely linked; when one runs into trouble, as in 1997–1998, the other is adversely affected.[5]

The role of services in the slowdown in GDP growth in the 1990s was accentuated by the fact that by this time Korea had reached a point where the service sector loomed large in the economy. Manufacturing employment had grown rapidly from the 1960s into the 1980s before leveling off and then falling as a share of the total work force. Employment in services, in contrast, grew steadily from the early 1970s (see Figure 3.1).[6] We will explore later whether this decline in manufacturing employment represents "premature deindustrialization" or was simply a normal corollary of economic maturation. The point here is that the weak performance of the service sector came at a time when the activities comprising it had begun to play a large role in the economy.

The shift in output and employment away from agriculture and then manufacturing in favor of services is typical of middle- and high-income countries.[7] But the magnitude of the shift varies. In Japan, for example, services have never dominated to the same extent as in the United States and Western Europe. The pattern in Korea is more like that in Japan than other middle- and high-income countries. As shown in Figures 3. A1 and 3.A2 in the appendix to this chapter, the GDP shares of wholesale and retail trade and social and personal services were at the low end for a country with a per capital income of $10,000 to $15,000. FIRE services, which grew rapidly in the immediate pre-crisis years, were the only service subsectors with unusually high shares of GDP.

Shift-share analysis is a convenient way of gauging the importance for labor productivity of the shift first from low-productivity agriculture to higher-productivity manufacturing and then from higher-productivity

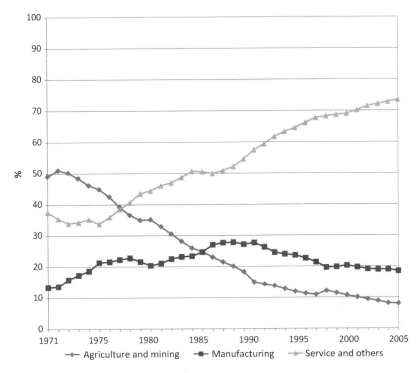

Figure 3.1. Shares of Employment by Industry, 1971–2005
The share of employment is calculated by dividing the number employed by the total employment. "Service and others" includes the industries other than agriculture, mining, and manufacturing industries. The share of manufacturing employment reached its peak at 27.8 percent in 1989. Data from Bank of Korea.

manufacturing to relatively low-productivity services. The growth of aggregate labor productivity can be expressed as:

$$\frac{\Delta P_t}{P_{t-1}} = \frac{\Sigma_{i=1}^{n}(\Delta P_t^i * S_{t-1}^i) + \Sigma_{i=1}^{n}(P_{t-1}^i * \Delta S_t^i) + \Sigma_{i=1}^{n}(\Delta P_t^i * \Delta S_t^i)}{P_{t-1}}$$

The first term is the "within effect" (the contribution of an individual sector's labor productivity growth to economy-wide productivity growth). The second term is the "static-shift effect" (the contribution via the shift in employment across sectors with different levels of productivity). The third term is the "dynamic-shift effect" (the contribution of relative employment shifts across sectors with different productivity

Table 3.8. Decomposition of Labor Productivity Growth, 1970–2007

			Shift effect		
Period	Growth of labor productivity	Within effect	Static shift effect	Dynamic shift effect	Total shift effect
1970–1981	3.2%	1.9%	1.6%	−0.3%	1.3%
1982–1989	5.8%	3.7%	2.3%	−0.2%	2.1%
1990–1997	4.5%	3.3%	1.5%	−0.2%	1.2%
1998–2007	3.3%	3.0%	0.5%	−0.2%	0.3%
Total	4.1%	2.9%	1.4%	−0.2%	1.2%

Source: Data are from Bank of Korea and annual reports on the Economically Active Population Survey, Statistics Korea.

Note: A total of nine (one-digit) industries are considered.

growth rates). In thinking about the contribution of structural change, we want to focus on the contribution of the second and third terms together.

The results suggest that structural change was important, but that it was not the dominant factor explaining Korean growth in this period. Observe in Table 3.8 that nearly two-thirds of the growth of labor productivity in Korea in the 1970s was attributable to the within effect (economy-wide increases in productivity holding sectoral shares constant). Manufacturing, with its relatively rapid productivity growth, accounted for most of this within effect (Table 3.9). Not only was this true in the 1970s, when manufacturing accounted for more than half of the total within effect, but it also was true in 1990 to 2007, when manufacturing accounted for fully three-quarters of the within effect. The exception is the 1980s, when manufacturing accounted for only about a quarter of the within effect. This makes sense insofar as the 1980s was a period of policy reform, when the pace of structural change accelerated in response to the removal of some of the excesses of the earlier Heavy and Chemical Industry Drive. The remaining quarter of the within effect is mainly accounted for by construction, wholesale and retail trade, and agriculture, which had relatively high productivity growth rates in comparison with other periods (Table 3.10).[8]

That labor productivity growth not accounted for by the within effect was due entirely to the shift between sectors with relatively low and high

Table 3.9. Decomposition of Labor Productivity Growth, 1970–2007: The Within Effect

Period	Total "within effect"	Agriculture, forestry & fishing	Mining	Manufacturing	Electricity & gas	Construction	Wholesale, retail, restaurants, & hotels	Transportation, storage, & communication	Finance, insurance, real estate, & business	Others
1970–1981	1.9%	0.5%	0.2%	1.0%	0.1%	-0.1%	0.0%	0.2%	-0.7%	0.7%
1982–1989	3.7%	0.8%	0.1%	1.0%	0.1%	0.7%	0.7%	0.2%	0.0%	0.0%
1990–1997	3.3%	0.4%	0.1%	2.1%	0.1%	0.2%	0.1%	0.3%	-0.2%	0.3%
1998–2007	3.0%	0.1%	0.0%	2.5%	0.2%	0.1%	0.3%	0.4%	-0.3%	-0.3%
Total	2.9%	0.5%	0.1%	1.6%	0.1%	0.2%	0.2%	0.3%	-0.3%	0.2%

Note: Decomposition of labor productivity growth in the within effect is derived by multiplying each industry's productivity growth by its labor share in the beginning period.

Table 3.10. Growth of Labor Productivity by Sector and Period

Industry sector	1970–1981 Average productivity growth (1)	(2)	Initial labor share	Change in labor share	1982–1989 Average productivity growth (1)	(2)	Initial labor share	Change in labor share
Agriculture, forestry, & fishing	3.2%	1.1%	50.9%	−16.6%	7.1%	2.9%	32.1%	−12.5%
Mining	6.0%	14.8%	1.1%	−0.3%	6.7%	9.3%	0.8%	−0.3%
Manufacturing	7.5%	5.2%	13.3%	7.1%	5.3%	4.5%	21.1%	6.7%
Electricity & gas	18.3%	40.8%	0.3%	−0.1%	7.6%	37.7%	0.2%	0.1%
Construction	−1.1%	−3.8%	2.9%	3.3%	7.7%	11.6%	5.8%	0.7%
Wholesale, retail, restaurants, & hotels	0.1%	0.3%	13.3%	6.4%	5.9%	2.9%	22.1%	−0.7%
Transportation, storage, & communication	6.1%	6.3%	3.4%	1.0%	4.0%	4.5%	4.2%	0.7%
Finance, insurance, & real estate	−4.8%	−44.7%	1.0%	1.7%	0.2%	0.8%	2.7%	2.3%
Others	2.2%	5.6%	13.6%	−2.5%	−0.1%	0.1%	11.1%	2.9%

Note: Since the static-shift effect in the formula is derived by calculating industry productivity growth relative to overall productivity, but not to its own productivity for industry, we report two measures of productivity growth. They are obtained by dividing the industry productivity change by (1) its own industry's initial productivity and (2) initial overall productivity. Initial labor share is each industry's labor share in the beginning year of the subperiod. Change in labor share refers to change in each industry's labor share during the entire subperiod.

levels of productivity. In other words, there was no contribution in this period from shifting labor into sectors where productivity was growing rapidly as opposed to those that had already reached relatively high productivity levels. In fact, this dynamic shift effect is negative: labor was already shifting away from the sectors with the fastest rates of productivity growth on average.[9]

The share of productivity growth accounted for by the static-shift effect then declined from 50 percent in 1970–1981 to 40 percent in 1982–1989 to 33 to 34 percent in 1990–2007. That the relative importance of this effect should decline over time makes sense: while Korea could still boost productivity growth by shifting labor to higher-productivity uses,

1990–1997				1998–2007			
Average productivity growth		*Initial labor share*	*Change in labor share*	*Average productivity growth*		*Initial labor share*	*Change in labor share*
(1)	*(2)*			*(1)*	*(2)*		
6.8%	3.0%	17.9%	−7.1%	3.2%	1.4%	12.0%	−4.7%
11.7%	33.0%	0.4%	−0.3%	2.8%	11.0%	0.1%	0.0%
8.7%	8.3%	27.2%	−5.8%	8.8%	13.0%	19.6%	−2.1%
7.2%	40.2%	0.4%	0.0%	6.4%	41.6%	0.3%	0.1%
1.6%	2.0%	7.4%	2.1%	0.9%	0.9%	7.9%	0.0%
0.5%	0.2%	21.8%	5.9%	2.9%	1.1%	27.9%	−3.5%
5.0%	5.0%	5.1%	0.4%	5.4%	6.4%	5.8%	0.6%
−1.2%	−3.6%	5.2%	3.8%	−1.5%	−2.9%	9.3%	4.2%
1.5%	1.8%	14.6%	1.0%	−1.9%	−1.8%	16.9%	5.5%

the contribution of such reallocation diminished as low-productivity agriculture emptied out in favor of high-productivity manufacturing.

To put these results in perspective, it is useful to compare them with a parallel analysis by the Ministry of Trade and Industry of Singapore (2008) and our own analysis of Taiwan.[10] In Taiwan, data for the 1970s are not available, but patterns in the subsequent period are strikingly similar. Compared with Korea, an even larger share of the growth of labor productivity is attributable to the within effect (economy-wide increases in productivity, holding sectoral shares constant): 83 percent in 1982–1989, 90 percent in 1990–1997, and 71 percent in 1998–2006. As in Korea, labor productivity growth not accounted for by the within effect was entirely due in all three periods to the shift between relatively low and high productivity sectors. And, as in Korea, the share of labor productivity growth accounted for by the static-shift effect tended to decline over time.

In Singapore, the static-shift effect accounted for only about 15 percent of the total growth of labor productivity in 1998–2007, less than half the share of such reallocation in Korea. This testifies to the contribution of restructuring to productivity growth in Korea in recent years. The overall rate of labor productivity growth is somewhat slower in Singapore: 1.9 percent per annum in 1999–2002 and 3.1 percent per annum in 2003–2007; the corresponding contributions of the static-shift effect are 0.4 percent and 0.3 percent. But whereas the contribution of the dynamic-shift effect is negative in Korea, it is zero in Singapore—a happier outcome. This presumably reflects the problems created by low productivity growth (in addition to low productivity levels) in services in Korea—a problem we examine in Chapter 4.

Explaining Sectoral TFP Growth Differences

We now disaggregate the economy further into 29 sectors. This allows us to ask whether there is a correlation between TFP and capital intensity, education intensity, and export intensity at the sectoral level.[11]

Figures 3.2 and 3.3 show the relationship between TFP, education, and capital intensity for the period from 1989 to 2005. Contrary to widespread presumption, there is little evidence that sector-specific TFP rises or falls with capital or education intensity.[12] Figures 3.4 through 3.8 show the manufacturing and service sectors separately. For manufacturing there is no clear relationship between TFP and either physical or human capital intensity. There is, however, some relationship between export intensity and TFP. While this is suggestive, it of course says nothing about the direction of causality, since while greater dependence on exports could apply pressure on producers to raise productivity, it is also possible that high TFP growth makes certain sectors more effective as exporters.

It is not possible to explore the correlation between service-sector TFP and exports because the service sector is so heavily domestically oriented.[13] But there are some interesting patterns in capital intensity. Strikingly, finance, insurance, and business services are the *least* capital intensive of the nine service sectors and have the highest TFP growth rates.[14] This

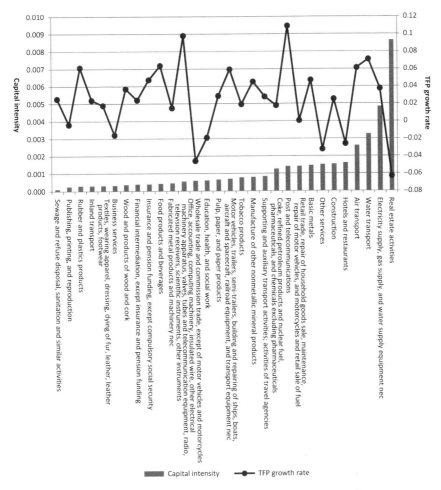

Figure 3.2. All Industries: Capital Intensity and Total Factor Productivity (TFP)
All variables are measured as averages over each period. Capital intensity is measured as a ratio of
capital to labor hours and TFP is derived from growth accounting.

makes for a *negative* correlation between capital intensity and TFP growth
in the service sector overall. This is in contrast to the positive relationship
between education intensity and TFP.

Only insurance displays positive TFP growth in both 1989–1996 and
1999–2005.[15] Finance, in contrast, experienced positive TFP growth only
in the 1999–2005 period. All three sectors, not surprisingly, had negative
TFP during the financial-crisis years 1997–1998, while business services,

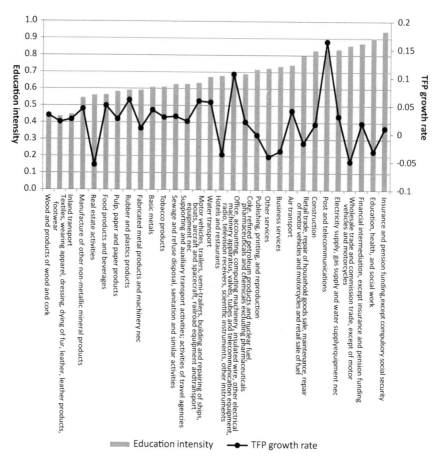

Figure 3.3. All Sectors: Education Intensity and TFP
All variables are measured as averages over each period. Education intensity is defined as the share of workers in each industry holding at least a two-year college degree, and total factor productivity is derived from growth accounting.

disturbingly, had negative productivity growth in the three periods. These data, like the more aggregated treatment earlier in this chapter, suggest that there is still substantial room for productivity improvement in business services, insurance, and finance.

The Emergence of High Tech

Another way of analyzing Korea's ability to make changes in the struc-ture of its economy that contribute to a high GDP growth rate and in-

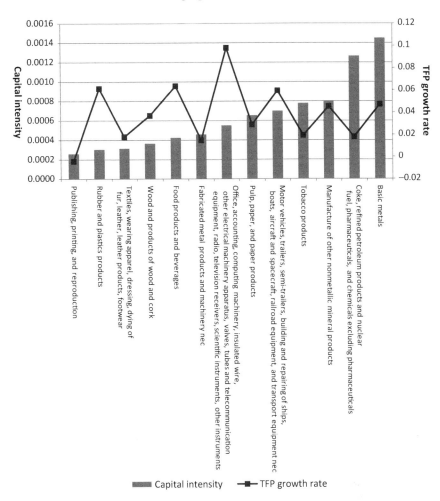

Figure 3.4. Manufacturing Capital Intensity and TFP

All variables are measured as averages over each period. Capital intensity is measured as the ratio of capital to labor hours, and total factor productivity is derived from growth accounting.

ternational competitiveness is to ask whether the country has succeeded in moving up the technology ladder from labor-intensive to capital- and technology-intensive industries.[16] Figures 3.9 and 3.10 document steady movement in this direction. The labor-intensive industries that fueled the first phase of Korea's export and growth boom already comprised a declining share of Korean manufacturing in the mid-1970s. The share of resource-based industries had begun declining even earlier.[17]

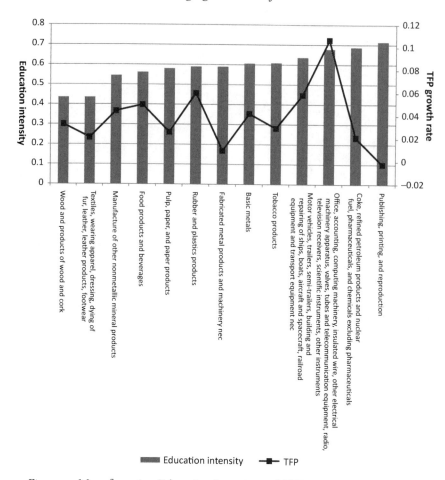

Figure 3.5. Manufacturing Education Intensity and TFP

All variables are measured as averages over each period. The measure of education intensity is defined as the share of workers in each industry holding at least a two-year college degree, and total factor productivity is derived from growth accounting.

The next phase of Korean industrialization involved the rise of the heavy and chemical industries (medium- and high-tech industries in Figures 3.9 and 3.10). The share of these sectors rose rapidly until the financial crisis of 1997–1998, after which their share in value added began declining (although their share in manufacturing employment continued to rise slightly). We will have more to say about these industries when we comment on the role of industrial policy later in this chapter.

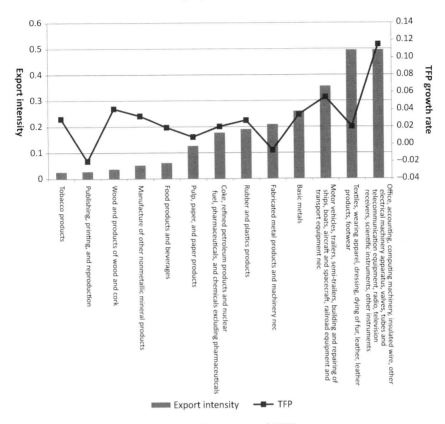

Figure 3.6. Manufacturing Export Intensity and TFP
All variables are measured as averages over each period. Export intensity is measured as a ratio of exports to output, and total factor productivity is derived from growth accounting.

High-technology industries went from just under 20 percent of all manufacturing value added in the mid-1990s to well over 40 percent of all manufacturing in 2005. It should be noted, however, that this rise in the high-technology share of value added was not matched by a commensurate rise in the share of high-tech employment. Employment in high tech hardly rose at all as a share of total manufacturing employment after the late 1980s. We will revisit this phenomenon, as well, later in the chapter.

It is useful to compare this change in the structure of Korean manufacturing with the structure of manufacturing in four other high-income countries: France, Germany, the United Kingdom, and Spain. Data for the comparators are presented in Figures 3.11 and 3.12. Strikingly,

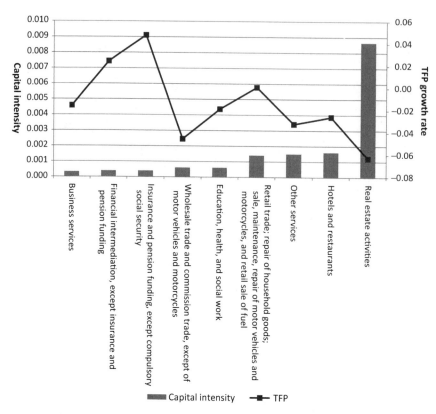

Figure 3.7. Services Capital Intensity and TFP
All variables are measured as averages over each period. Capital intensity is measured as a ratio of capital to labor hours and total factor productivity is derived from growth accounting.

the increase in high-tech value added and employment in all four countries is modest by Korean standards. This may indicate that Korea has been more successful at growing its high-tech sectors, or it may reflect the continuing excellence of these countries in medium-tech manufacturing.

A key question is, has high tech boosted productivity growth in the economy as a whole, or have the associated productivity gains essentially been confined to the high-technology sector itself? In the United States, initially the rise of ICT led to rapid productivity improvement mainly in the sector itself but not in the rest of the economy. As it is sometimes put, desktop computers were at first little more than efficient typewriters; the sector producing them learned to do so much more efficiently,

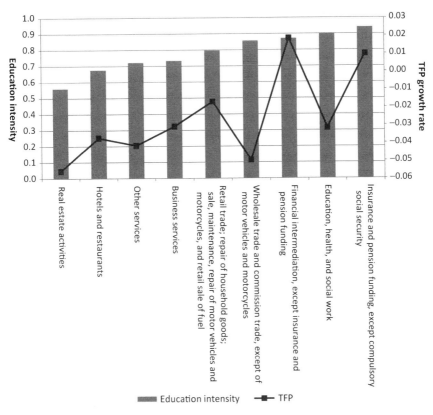

Figure 3.8. Services Education Intensity and TFP
All variables are measured as averages over each period. Education intensity is defined as the share of workers in each industry holding at least a two-year college degree, and total factor productivity is derived from growth accounting.

but this did little to enhance productivity elsewhere in the economy. But over time, production was reorganized to capitalize on the availability of new technology, at which point ICT began to exercise a major impact on productivity growth in other sectors. It is widely credited with being a major contributor to the rise in U.S. productivity and GDP growth in the second half of the 1990s.

Investment in ICT in various industrial and service subsectors is shown in Table 3.11. While most sectors have undertaken at least some ICT investment, the only ones displaying exceptionally high TFP growth are the ICT sectors themselves. The service sectors, while having invested substantially in ICT, show little evidence of robust TFP growth.[18]

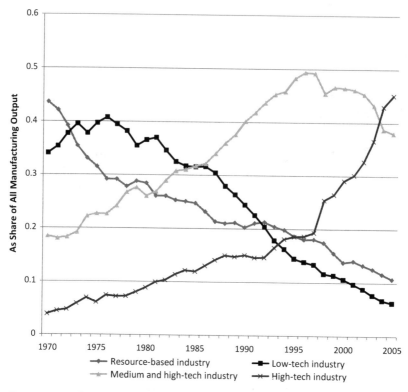

Figure 3.9. Evolution of Value-Added Shares of Manufacturing Industries by Technology
Technology classification of industries based on United Nations Industrial Development Organization (UNIDO). Calculations based on EU KLEMS data.

We can explore these relationships further with regression analysis. Our first specification regresses TFP growth on the growth of the ITC capital stock and a dummy variable distinguishing the pre– and post–financial crisis periods. The second substitutes real value added as the dependent variable. As additional controls we include other inputs, as in the standard production-function framework. We estimate these relationships using both fixed and random effects.

These regressions, in Tables 3.12 and 3.13, produce an insignificant coefficient on the ICT capital growth rate.[19] Several other specifications yield the same conclusion. ICT investment in Korea does not yet appear to be driving economic growth except in the ICT sectors themselves.

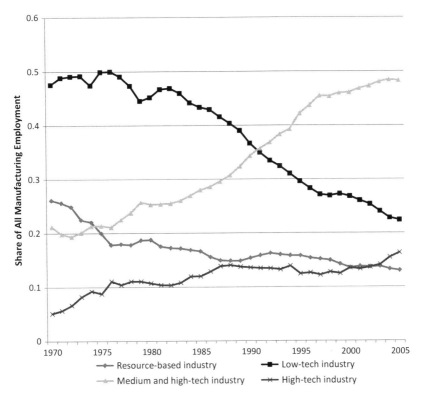

Figure 3.10. Evolution of Employment Shares of Manufacturing Industries by Technology
Calculations based on EU KLEMS data.

This finding has both optimistic and pessimistic interpretations. The pessimistic interpretation is that slower growth in Korea in recent years is partly a reflection of the fact that ICT investment is not yet being used in ways that have a significant impact on economy-wide performance. The more optimistic interpretation is that Korea can take better advantage of the ICT sector in the years ahead and that this should make possible a higher potential rate of growth.

The Role of Industrial Policy

Over the period for which we have data, Korean growth was led by the industrial sector. The rapid growth of industry was, in turn, a function

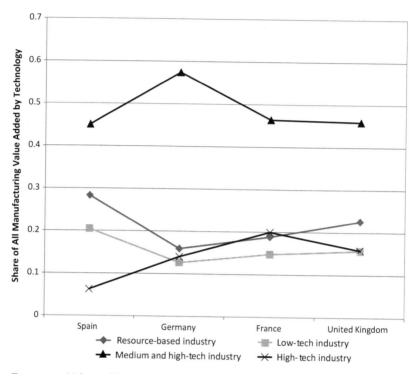

Figure 3.11. Value-Added Shares of Manufacturing Industries by Technology, for Selected Countries in 2005
Calculations based on EU KLEMS data.

of high rates of growth of TFP and rapid rates of capital formation. In Chapter 2 we argued that capital formation economy-wide was driven by high rates of return deriving from rapid productivity growth. This was true in particular for industry and even more for manufacturing.

An important question is whether industrial policy was a major reason for this performance or, to the contrary, whether it occurred despite the active role of government. In other words, did strategic interventions by the Korean authorities relax the constraints that previously limited rates of return, thereby eliciting higher rates of investment and thus more savings and growth? Or might those rates of return have been even higher and those other responses even more dramatic in the absence of industrial policy?

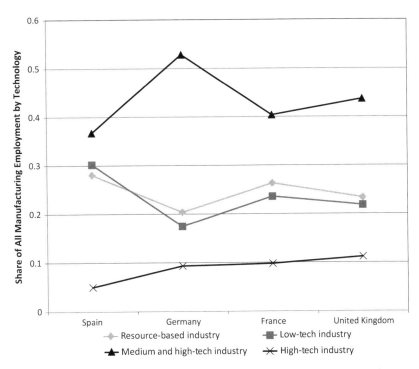

Figure 3.12. Employment Shares of Manufacturing Industries by Technology for Selected Countries in 2005.
Calculations based on EU KLEMS data.

Answering these questions requires more precision about what is meant by industrial policy. Industrial policy is often discussed as if it were a single set of similar policies carried out by successive governments. In fact, Korean industrial policy evolved from one administration and decade to the next. The focus in the wake of the Korean War was on recovery and reconstruction, based on large amounts of foreign aid. A few manufacturing firms produced labor-intensive goods for a protected domestic market; in addition, a few construction and transport firms undertook reconstruction projects and provided logistical support for United Nations troops (mainly Americans). To maximize foreign exchange earnings from the support of UN forces, the government maintained an overvalued exchange rate that made exporting unprofitable.[20]

Table 3.11. TFP Growth Rate and Share of ICT Investment in
Gross Investment

	TFP growth	ICT investment/ gross investment	Investment growth
Mining & quarrying	2.60%	4.20%	−11.00%
Food & beverages	0.00%	13.40%	2.50%
Tobacco	−1.50%	12.40%	11.30%
Textiles	2.10%	4.50%	−4.50%
Textiles, dyeing of fur, leather, & footwear	2.30%	13.80%	5.70%
Wood & cork	3.70%	2.40%	−3.20%
Pulp & paper	0.20%	6.30%	3.00%
Printing, publishing, & reproduction	−2.70%	17.20%	13.60%
Coke, refined petroleum, & nuclear fuel	5.90%	15.40%	−1.50%
Chemicals & chemical products	2.90%	9.30%	3.20%
Rubber & plastics	0.30%	14.60%	2.30%
Other nonmetallic minerals	2.90%	4.50%	0.80%
Basic metals	0.90%	7.10%	−1.00%
Fabricated metal	1.20%	5.70%	14.50%
Machinery not elsewhere classified	5.30%	19.30%	3.80%
Office, accounting, & computing machinery[a]	12.00%	42.20%	17.70%
Electrical machinery[a]	13.50%	30.40%	11.50%
Telecommunications equipment[a]	8.00%	30.30%	15.00%
Scientific instruments[a]	3.30%	18.80%	9.40%
Transport equipment	3.00%	15.20%	7.30%
Manufacturing not elsewhere classified; recycling	2.20%	12.60%	7.40%
Electricity, gas, & water supply	0.30%	19.20%	−1.40%
Construction	−0.30%	11.00%	0.90%
Wholesale & retail trade	−1.50%	11.80%	3.90%

Table 3.11. (Continued)

	TFP growth	ICT investment/ gross investment	Investment growth
Hotels & restaurants	−2.60%	3.10%	7.60%
Transport & storage	1.20%	2.40%	4.40%
Post & telecommunications[a]	13.70%	48.20%	6.70%
Financial intermediation & insurance	2.30%	49.30%	10.10%
Real estate	−3.90%	14.00%	14.40%
Renting & business activities	−3.20%	22.50%	13.00%
Education, health, & social work	−4.20%	21.80%	10.60%
Other services	−1.70%	5.80%	8.40%

Source: Data are from input-output table provided by Bank of Korea.

Note: ICT=information and communications technology; TFP=total factor productivity.

[a] An ICT-producing industry.

Table 3.12. ICT Capital as a Determinant of TFP Growth

	Fixed effects	Random effects
ICT capital growth rate	−0.064 [−0.778]	−0.072 [−1.036]
Other industries' ICT capital growth rate	0.189 [1.588]	0.203* [1.805]
Currency crisis dummy	−0.080*** [−4.046]	−0.080*** [−4.078]
R-squared	0.213	0.132

Note: ICT=information and communications technology; TFP=total factor productivity. The dependent variable is each industry's TFP growth rate. Other industries' ICT capital is the sum of ICT capital in the economy with its own industry ICT capital excluded. *t*-statistics in brackets.

*** and * indicate significance at the 1-percent and 10-percent levels, respectively.

Table 3.13. ICT Capital as a Determinant of TFP Growth with Additional Controls

	Fixed effects	Random effects
Labor input growth rate	0.163***	0.177***
	[4.28]	[4.73]
Capital growth rate	0.212***	0.234***
	[3.06]	[3.50]
Human capital growth rate	−1.923***	−1.923***
	[−3.69]	[−3.71]
ICT capital growth rate	−0.000	0.012
	[−0.00]	[0.19]
Other industries' ICT capital growth rate	−0.084	−0.083
	[−0.83]	[−0.83]
Currency crisis dummy	−0.091***	−0.088***
	[−4.34]	[−4.24]
R-squared	0.5037	0.4496

Note: ICT=information and communications technology; TFP=total factor productivity. The dependent variable is each industry's real value-added growth rate. *t*-statistics in brackets. *** indicates significance at the 1-percent level.

Following the fall of the Rhee government in 1960 and a brief democratic interlude, a military coup brought Park Chung Hee to power. Park could have maintained the overvalued exchange rate and import-substitution policies of the previous decade, financing essential imports with foreign aid and payments received for the logistical support of UN forces. Contemporary analyses suggested that this was the most likely and, indeed, most realistic option. But aid dependence would have placed Korea under pressure from the United States to return to a democratic political system. It would have meant that Korea was bound to grow slowly, since aid was bound to grow slowly. This was alarming to Park insofar as North Korea was perceived as doing well at rehabilitating and growing its economy.

The only escape was to find another way of funding essential imports. And the only way of doing that was by increasing exports. For that, devaluation of the currency was necessary, but not sufficient; there was still the question of what Korea would export. Exporting minerals was not feasible, since most of the mineral deposits on the Korean Peninsula were in the north. Exporting rice, as in the colonial period, implied an unacceptably high level of inequality because large-scale rice cultivation required large landholdings. And in any case, it was not clear that Korean agriculture could generate large surpluses.

The only way of increasing exports was by enhancing the competitiveness of Korean industry. Industrial policy in the 1960s therefore focused single-mindedly on promoting manufactured exports. A series of measures, in addition to a large devaluation, were used to provide incentives. Exporters were given tax breaks and concessionary financing. They were allowed generous wastage allowances that gave them more cotton than they needed to meet their export targets, permitting them to use what was left over for the protected domestic market. In effect, high domestic prices meant high profits that subsidized less profitable exports.

Implementation of this plan took place through monthly meetings between President Park and leading industrialists, in the presence of the relevant economic ministers. Korean industrialists were asked to set ambitious export targets. If they met their targets, the president was then receptive to removing other obstacles to their efforts. More often than not those obstacles were bureaucratic controls inherited from the past, which the president could eliminate simply by telling the relevant minister to fix the problem.

The result was that manufactured exports, mainly of labor-intensive textiles and shoes, grew rapidly in the 1960s. Exports rose from $55 million in 1962 to $882 million in 1970 and $1,676 million in 1972. Manufactured goods made up 78 percent of exports in 1970 and 85 percent in 1972. And, as was shown in Chapter 2, the large jump in economy-wide TFP in the 1960s was to a substantial degree related to the rapid gains in manufacturing output and competitiveness associated with the government's export-promotion policies. Investment and savings rates in the early 1960s were low, and growth largely depended on raising TFP. Export-oriented manufacturing was the only sector that can plausibly be described as a major contributor to this process.

There are not many studies of the effects of industrial policy in this early period. Some analysts argue that the interventions served only to offset the many inherited bureaucratic rules and barriers that had distorted the economy in the past. Rather than simply abolishing the offending rules and barriers, the government intervened to offset their impact. The net result, they suggest, is that government intervention created the equivalent of a market-driven regime with few price distortions. An early incarnation of this argument is made in Frank, Kim, and Westphal (1975).[21] The authors attempt to measure the impact of interventions in 1968 by estimating border prices. They conclude that the border prices of Korean products were very similar to world prices in 1968.[22] The implication is that Korean industrial policy did not make much of a difference.

The policies of the 1960s benefited all exporters; this was not a period when the government favored particular industries or firms. This changed, however, in the 1970s with the launch of the Heavy and Chemical Industry Drive. Policy as it affected heavy and chemical industries was turned over to a committee in the president's office. Based on a review of the experience of other countries, this committee drew up a plan spelling out which heavy industries should be built, how large they should be (in order to exploit economies of scale and to export part of their product), and where they should be located. Individual firms, usually chaebol, were then asked to carry out part of the plan. In return they received financing at favorable rates. Supporting infrastructure was also supplied by the government. A monopoly of the domestic market might be allowed for a learning period of a few years. These policies are often characterized as the essence of Korea's approach to industrial development. In reality they lasted for less than a decade, from 1972 to the assassination of President Park in 1979.

Most attempts to evaluate the effectiveness of Korean industrial policy focus on this period.[23] They seek to measure whether interventions supported industries that had relatively high and rapidly rising levels of TFP.[24] Some conclude that the Heavy and Chemical Industry Drive had a negative impact on Korean growth on the grounds that TFP growth in the heavy and chemical sectors was disappointing.[25] An example is Lee (1996), who analyzes four interventions in the years 1963 to 1983 in 38 industrial sectors (both heavy and chemical and other industries). As shown in Table 3.14, Lee finds that tariff and nontariff barriers had a negative impact on the growth of value added and TFP. They also had a negative impact on capital accumulation in the heavy and chemical industries. While tax incentives positively affected capital accumulation, their estimated impact on TFP and value-added growth was minimal.[26] Subsidized bank loans, arguably the most important tool in this period, had a positive impact on the growth of value added in the favored industries but a negative (if statistically insignificant) impact on capital accumulation and TFP. Overall, these estimates support the view that several

Table 3.14. Impact of Industrial Policy on Value Added, Growth Rate of Capital Stock, and Sector TFP in Korea, 1963–1983

	Dependent variables		
Independent variable	Value added	Capital accumulation	TFP
Log (initial value added)	−0.163	0.025	−0.153
	(−11.64)	(1.79)	(−10.2)
Log (initial capital)	0.172	−0.209	0.078
	(7.17)	(−12.30)	(4.33)
Nontariff barrier coverage rate	−0.092	−0.159	−0.167
	(−3.07)	(−5.68)	(−5.06)
Tariff rate	−0.118	−0.029	−0.113
	(−3.03)	(−0.76)	(−2.35)
Tax incentives	−0.084	0.499	0.074
	(−0.50)	(4.75)	(0.65)
Subsidized bank loans	0.092	−0.019	−0.123
	(10.76)	(−0.10)	(−0.68)
Estimation technique	3SLS	3SLS	3SLS
Number of observations	146	146	146

Source: Lee (1996), 401–402.

Note: TFP=total factor productivity. *t*-statistics appear in parentheses. 3SLS=equations estimated by three-stage least squares.

of the major interventions in the period when industrial policy was most active actually slowed TFP growth.

Yet another approach is to use micro data in cost-benefit calculations for important heavy-industry projects. Stern, Kim, Perkins, and Yoo (1995) start with the prices from the year a project was started and then redo the calculations using prices from a later year when the project was up and running. An unequivocal measure of successful intervention would be a project for which costs exceeded benefits at initial prices (suggesting that it would not have been undertaken) but where benefits exceeded costs at subsequent prices.[27] Pohang Iron and Steel Company (POSCO) and Hyundai Motor Company would no doubt have passed this test.[28] A number of other projects were successes in the sense that they had positive present value at both sets of prices, suggesting that they may well have been undertaken by private investors even in the absence of government intervention (Table 3.15). There were also a number of

Table 3.15. Classification of Industrial Projects

		Later-year prices	
		ERR ≥ P_k	ERR ≤ P_k
	ERR ≥ P_k	Quadrant I: Successful	Quadrant II: Unsuccessful
		Dong Yang Steel	Korea Heavy Machinery
		Hyundai Pipe	Korea Steel and Chemical
		Samsung Electronics	Boo-Kook Steel
Base-year prices	ERR ≤ P_k	Quadrant IV: Successful	Quadrant III: Unsuccessful
		POSCO[a]	—
		Hyundai Auto[a]	

Source: Stern, Kim, Perkins, and Yoo (1995), 122, with POSCO and Hyundai Auto examples added.
Note: ERR=economic rate of return; P_k=the opportunity cost of capital.
[a]Not based on detailed cost-benefit calculations.

cases in which heavy-industry firms were profitable at initial prices but ran into trouble subsequently, despite early government support. Thus, the conclusion from this approach is again mixed: industrial policy made a positive difference in some cases but not in others.

Another approach is to compare outcomes in Korea with outcomes in other countries with similar initial conditions and policies. For example, initial conditions in Taiwan were broadly similar, and there, too, most heavy-industry development was initially carried out by state-owned enterprises. However, the strategy in Taiwan differed in substantial respects, notably in that it relied less on interest-rate ceilings and directed credit, and that therefore large enterprises were less dominant. Hsueh, Hsu, and Perkins (2001) conclude that Korea's industrial policies were less successful than Taiwan's, on the grounds that Taiwan's exports of heavy industrial products grew faster. Again, support for the assertion that industrial policy was the key driver of Korean economic development in this period is, at best, mixed.

Korea began moving away from sectoral targeting in the 1980s. President Chun Doo Hwan was concerned with inflation, which had been fueled by the Heavy and Chemical Industry Drive. Chun was also less supportive of the chaebol, which had been major beneficiaries of earlier policies. But moving away from activist policy was not easy. Important industries required continued support in order to survive. The chaebol had taken them on because of government encouragement, with the implicit promise that if an initiative failed because of conditions not under the control of the private sector, then the authorities would intervene. The late 1970s and early 1980s thus saw a number of rescue and restructuring efforts for failing projects. The associated moral hazard had been kept in check in the Park years by the application of rigorous performance criteria (only reasonably high performers were helped). But that pressure dissipated in the 1980s as the chaebol grew and gained power—and as the government became as dependent on them as they were on the government.

In the late 1980s and early 1990s industrial policy moved further from its activist roots. With the advent of direct competitive elections for president, close ties with the chaebol became a political liability. As rising per capita incomes made Korea a candidate for OECD membership, the authorities had to prepare for the removal of trade restrictions and the liberalization of capital markets (both of which were obligations of OECD members), which in turn limited the scope for activist policy.

That said, liberalizing capital markets and the external accounts did not eliminate bureaucratic interventions. To start a new business, or even for an established business to carry out a major project, a firm still needed the cooperation of the government. Support from the president or from those purporting to speak for him was worth a great deal, and business was prepared to pay generously for that support. On the government's side, running for political office was expensive. The result was that businesses could cut through red tape and gain government support by funding politicians and their organizations. Where under President Park industrial policy decisions had been made mainly on the basis of technical criteria, under his successors, decisions were based more on political grounds.[29] Increasingly, industrial policy was driven by politics and rent-seeking rather than the pursuit of growth. Where the industrial policies of the 1960s and 1970s had produced the export boom and successful companies such as POSCO and Hyundai, the policies of the 1990s produced Hanbo Steel, whose bankruptcy, along with those of other politically favored companies, set the stage for the financial crisis of 1997–1998.

By the 1990s the industrial sector had developed beyond the point where government could provide much in the way of direction and leadership. Given the complex modern economy that Korea had become, central direction from the Blue House (the president's office) was no more feasible than, in the case of Russia, central direction from Gosplan. Industry's continued reliance on government support reflected not a need for government guidance but the fact, inherited from the past, that numerous bureaucratic decisions were required to do business, even though the regulations requiring those decisions no longer served a useful purpose.

The 1997–1998 financial crisis ushered in a very different attitude toward the chaebol and industrial policy. The first years of the Kim Dae Jung presidency marked a dramatic turn toward a more open economy that, among other things, removed a number of the barriers that had blocked inward foreign direct investment.[30] President Kim accepted virtually all of the conditions laid down by the International Monetary Fund (IMF) when its assistance was required to resolve the crisis. Indeed, in many cases the government went even further than the IMF called for in liberalizing the economy.

While it took steps to liberalize, however, the government also pursued major interventions, if only because crisis conditions left no choice. The crisis effectively bankrupted many banks and chaebol.[31] With the government being forced to intervene, the banks fell under the control of the government. If the government had not ordered the banks to roll over existing credits, large numbers of chaebol would have gone under. The government made it clear that surviving conglomerates should reduce their debt/equity ratio to 200 percent (down from the 400 to 500 percent typical of the pre-crisis period). It pressed them to divest subsidiaries and focus on core lines of business.

In other advanced economies such decisions are typically taken in the context of bankruptcy proceedings. Creditors force troubled firms to declare bankruptcy; stakeholders then resolve their differences under the supervision of the court, which has discretion within limits set by law and precedent. In Korea, however, the judicial system was not capable of administering complex bankruptcy restructurings. Restrictive regulation had tightly limited the number of lawyers. Few members of the bar, in any case, had training and experience in complicated economic cases. This left no choice but for the executive branch to manage bankruptcy restructurings just as it had managed earlier interventions in the industrial sector. In effect, bankruptcy proceedings became another form of activist policy run out of the Blue House.[32]

Eventually the financial crisis passed, and with it, the exceptional interventions of the late 1990s. Industrial policy now became much like industrial policy in other OECD countries. The Korean government is involved in key infrastructure projects, although it increasingly delegates responsibility to private firms. It has sought to upgrade the universities. It has negotiated free-trade agreements with Singapore, Chile, and the European Union, and has also concluded a free-trade agreement with the United States. Efforts to encourage FDI continue in the face of popular (and bureaucratic) resistance.[33] In short, industrial policy in Korea has converged with industrial policy in other high-income countries. The government seeks to provide a supportive environment for business in the form of efficient infrastructure, open markets, and high-quality human capital, but targeting of particular industries and to individual firms is largely a thing of the past.

An exception is the promotion of green growth. For some years Korea has been trying to reduce its use of energy, particularly carbon-based energy, and in recent years that effort has been explicitly tied to the worldwide effort to curb global warming.[34] Korea now sees low-carbon, environment-friendly industries as new engines of growth. In August 2008, President Lee Myung-Bak announced a "low carbon, green growth" strategy as a new vision to promote the nation's long-term growth. In response to the global crisis, the government in March 2009 proposed an economic stimulus package worth US$38.1 billion, of which 80 percent was to be allocated to environmental issues such as fresh water, waste, energy-efficient buildings, renewable energies, low-carbon vehicles, and the rail network.[35] In July 2009 the government announced its Five-Year Green Growth Plan (2009–2013), designed to serve as a medium-term plan for implementing the green-growth strategy. With total funding of US$83.6 billion, amounting to 2 percent of Korea's GDP, this five-year plan lists a series of operational policy initiatives designed to further encourage green growth.

This new strategy is intended as a departure from Korea's earlier five-year economic development plans. While previous plans focused on the accumulation of labor and capital, the new plan stresses new ideas, transformational innovations, and state-of-the-art technologies that promote growth through innovative activities. The government has selected 27 core technologies that have potential as new engines of growth, and it plans to provide tax benefits and low-interest financing to them through "green funds." The government will increase credit guarantees for green projects and launch a green private equity fund. How this turns out and, in particular, how much of a departure from earlier planning exercises it really represents, remain to be seen.

Ultimately, an assessment of the role of industrial policy must rest as much on qualitative as quantitative evidence.[36] Our assessment is that industrial policy played an important role in the early stages of Korea's growth but became a growing burden with the passage of time. In the 1960s, Park's policies of export promotion removed the earlier bias against manufacturing, allowing Korea to exploit its comparative advantage.[37] They also relaxed financing constraints that would have slowed and conceivably prevented the expansion of firms producing footwear, textiles, and other light manufactures for export in what was still a poor, low-savings economy. And they supplied some important collective goods—export marketing services, for example—that would have been beyond the reach of small manufacturers. These policies, by encouraging—and enabling—Korean manufacturers to begin to compete in international markets and continuing to support them only if they succeeded, forced manufacturers to move along their learning curves more quickly. One can imagine that Korea would have moved in this direction—eventually—had the government only devalued the exchange rate and left the rest to the market. But the take-off of light manufacturing would have been later and slower; indeed, it might have stalled out entirely over problems of financing and marketing. One can think of too many other countries that started out where Korea did but did not enjoy the same dynamic expansion of light manufacturing, where all the government did was devalue the exchange rate and leave the rest to the market.

Whereas our assessment of the industrial policies of the 1960s is positive, our view of their successors in the 1970s is more mixed. The Heavy and Chemical Industry Drive propelled Korea into steel, motor vehicles, and shipbuilding, where it eventually enjoyed a strong comparative advantage. It is possible to argue, as in Rodrik (1994), that the economy would never have made this transition in the absence of intervention. These different activities, it is argued, are strongly complementary. They produce different inputs, all of which are needed for the profitability of the others. Korea could not have had an internationally competitive shipbuilding industry in the absence of an internationally competitive steel industry, and vice versa. It could not have had an internationally competitive motor vehicle industry in the absence of an internationally competitive machine tool industry. But getting all these sectors up and running at the same time was beyond the capacity of the private sector; government intervention was needed to solve this coordination problem.

We are skeptical of this strong view. Inputs, from cold-rolled sheet metal to machine tools, could be imported from abroad—not least from neighboring Japan, which had developed many of the same sectors using technology broadly appropriate to Korea.[38] Imported inputs might have been somewhat less well tailored to Korean circumstances, but it is hard to imagine that they were so poorly suited to local conditions to have prevented the emergence of the heavy and chemical industries.

More likely, the government interventions supporting these sectors again pushed Korean industry into a set of activities to which it would have gravitated anyway, but much more quickly than would have been the case in the absence of intervention. Insofar as these activities were capital intensive, and therefore expensive, public support for investment may have made a very big difference indeed to the growth of these sectors. Insofar as many of these new sectors displayed low productivity growth in the start-up phase, as documented above, the need for finance in this initial period of low productivity and profits would have been greater still.[39] Again, the implication is that the industrial policies of the 1970s probably made a big difference for the pace, if not the direction, of Korea's transition from light to heavy manufacturing. And to the extent that the first mover has an advantage, the fact that Korea was one of the first movers into these sectors among developing countries positioned it for further growth. In selecting sectors to support, Korean policymakers got it right because it was possible for them to look to the experience of other countries with similar resource endowments, notably Japan, and emulate their example.

That said, the policies of this period also had a downside. They favored the chaebol, which became too big and politically influential to ignore. They contributed to the tendency toward excessive reliance on debt finance, a taste for expansionism on the part of the large conglomerates, and excessive reliance on government connections—three things that helped to set the stage for the 1997–1998 financial crisis. They slowed the development of dynamic small and medium-size enterprises.[40] And they fostered a mindset that attached excessive weight to government intervention. This became increasingly problematic with the transition to democracy, as a result of which bureaucrats lost whatever limited insulation from politics they had enjoyed previously, and the problem that industrial policy might be captured by industry became even more severe. Even today, the continuing tendency for government to attempt to direct resources, whether by selecting specific industries, like information technology and communications, as targets for increased R&D spending or by prioritizing green growth, reflects the powerful imprint left by this earlier experience. The ongoing political scandals associated with these initiatives are a reminder that past policies can outlive their usefulness.

Deindustrialization

A key structural change highlighted thus far is the steady decline in the share of industrial employment. This declining industrial employment share is often referred to as "deindustrialization of the labor force."[41] We use this terminology in what follows, although, as noted, deindustrialization in this sense does not imply that industrial value added is declining.[42]

Deindustrialization of the labor force characterizes all maturing countries. But a number of observers have raised red flags about it in Korea, arguing that its deindustrialization began too early in terms of per capita income or the manufacturing share of employment, proceeded too quickly, or was otherwise excessive. In Table 3.16 we compare the deindustrialization of the labor force in other OECD countries and Taiwan.[43] In the United States and the United Kingdom the decline in the share of the labor force in industry predated 1961. For the United States we were able to extend the sample period back to 1948 using data from the Bureau of Labor Statistics. These suggest that deindustrialization of the U.S. labor force began in 1953, when the share of employment in manufacturing reached 26.4 percent. Using Feinstein (1976), we extended the employment share in UK manufacturing back to 1938, when it equaled 32.5 percent, compared with 33.8 percent in 1948 and a peak of 35.9 percent in 1955. Thus, deindustrialization of the labor force appears to have set in at roughly the same stage of development in the United Kingdom, the technological leader in the nineteenth century, and the United States,

Table 3.16. Deindustrialization Experience of OECD Countries

		The share of manufacturing industry in employment			Per capita GDP (PPP 2000 U.S. dollars)		
Country	Starting year (t)	Annual % point increase (t − 8)[a]	Year t (%)[b]	Annual % point increase (t + 8)	Growth rate (t − 8)	Year t	Growth rate (t + 8)
United States[c]	1953	0.40	26.40	−0.44	1.00	$12,155	1.70
United Kingdom	1955	0.30	35.90	−0.09	2.41	$13,152	2.25
France	1964	0.17	26.20	−0.05	4.11	$15,182	4.18
Canada	1966	0.16	33.10	−1.40	1.48	$12,139	2.81
Norway	1966	0.17	23.60	−0.08	3.32	$11,850	3.49
Australia	1967	0.00	25.60	−0.49	2.30	$12,964	2.45
Netherlands	1969	—	25.50	−0.54	4.17	$14,531	2.36
Belgium	1970	—	31.20	−0.76	4.33	$12,532	3.06
Denmark	1970	0.20	25.90	−0.61	3.30	$16,584	1.50
Germany	1970	0.07	35.80	−0.51	—	$13,686	2.47
Sweden	1970	—	26.50	−0.37	3.44	$15,785	1.13
Japan	1973	0.37	26.20	−0.38	8.53	$13,438	2.06
Finland	1974	0.61	25.10	−0.19	4.74	$14,308	1.84
Ireland	1974	0.31	21.40	−0.14	4.30	$8,964	2.26
Austria	1977	0.06	23.30	−0.29	4.29	$16,788	1.76
Italy	1980	0.13	29.10	−0.57	3.35	$15,828	2.04
Portugal	1980	0.37	25.30	−0.15	2.74	$9,979	2.59
Spain	1980	0.10	23.10	−0.42	1.83	$12,049	2.10
Luxembourg	1985	—	22.70	−0.78	2.35	$22,728	5.57
Taiwan[d]	1987	0.75	35.20	−1.01	6.28	$9,396	5.99
Korea	1989	0.90	28.70	−0.91	7.77	$8,667	6.50
New Zealand	1989	—	21.20	−0.36	1.07	$17,381	1.35
Hungary	1992	—	26.10	−0.23	−0.66	$8,972	2.98
Iceland	1994	0.11	17.57	−0.41	0.31	$21,126	2.35
Poland	1995	0.02	21.10	−0.54	1.23	$6,776	3.84
Republic Slovak	1997	0.21	27.70	−0.46	−1.54	$8,895	3.45
Czech Republic	2003	0.23	28.20	—	1.96	$14,642	3.05
Average	—	0.26	26.22	−0.46	2.93	$13,317	2.88

(continued)

Table 3.16. (Continued)

Source: Per capita GDP is based on data obtained from Penn World Table 6.2. Other data obtained from OECD, Structural Analysis database (STAN) and International Sectoral Database (ISDB).

Note: PPP=purchasing power parity. While the STAN database covers 1971–2005, we extended the sample period back to 1961 by supplementing with the ISDB database. We granted priority to the STAN database for those years for which both data sets are available. For those years for which only the ISDB database is available, we adjusted the figures from the ISDB database by comparing the employment shares of the five closest overlapping years of both databases. For example, if the ISDB database covers 1961–1980, we calculated the average difference between the two databases for employment shares for 1971–1975 and then subtracted that average difference from the employment shares of the ISDB database.

[a] For some countries, due to data availability, the annual average is taken for less than eight years: United States for 1948–1953; United Kingdom for 1948–1955; France for 1960–1964; Canada for 1960–1966; Norway for 1962–1966; Australia for 1966–1967; Denmark for 1966–1970; Ireland for 1970–1974; Austria for 1976–1977; Portugal for 1977–1980; Spain for 1978–1980; Taiwan for 1985–1987; Greece for 1995–1996 and 1997–2003; Iceland for 1991–1994; Poland for 1992–1995 and 1996–2002; Republic Slovak for 1995–1997.

[b] We chose the earliest available year as the starting year for the Netherlands, Belgium, Sweden, Luxembourg, New Zealand, and Hungary. Share of manufacturing employment is still increasing in the Czech Republic, for which we selected the last available year as the starting year.

[c] U.S. figures are constructed with data provided by the Bureau of Labor Statistics.

[d] Since Taiwan does not belong to the OECD, data for Taiwan are obtained from the *Statistical Yearbook of the Republic of China*, which starts in 1985.

the technological leader in the twentieth. Most other advanced countries first experienced deindustrialization of the labor force in the 1970s. For the two developing economies, Taiwan and Korea, deindustrialization of the labor force began in 1987 and 1989, respectively.

Column four in Table 3.16 shows the share of employment in manufacturing at its peak (T); columns three and five, the average annual percentage point increases in the manufacturing employment share eight years before and after the peak. In most cases deindustrialization began before manufacturing's employment share reached 30 percent. Three exceptions are the United Kingdom, Germany, and Taiwan.[44] Since the United Kingdom was the first industrialized country, it experienced limited developing-country competition initially. It is not surprising, therefore, that its manufacturing-sector employment peaked at high levels.[45] Germany and Taiwan are both manufacturing-oriented countries. While Korea is also manufacturing oriented, the deindustrialization of its labor force began earlier, when the manufacturing employment share was still only 28 percent. That said, this is not significantly different from the point at which deindustrialization of the labor force commenced in most other countries in the sample. Viewed from this perspective, the evidence for the premature deindustrialization of the Korean labor force is less than overwhelming.

But when we compare the speed of industrialization as measured by the growth of the sector's employment share, Korea tops most other countries by a significant margin.[46] The average annual percentage point increase in manufacturing's employment share for eight years before the peak was 0.9 percent, whereas in most other countries it was less than or equal to 0.4 percent. Since Korea has been rapidly catching up with advanced countries, it is not surprising that the rate of growth of industrial employment should be high. The subsequent deindustrialization of the labor force is also unusually rapid. After passing the peak, manufacturing's employment share in Korea declined by 0.91 percent a year. This is the third highest figure in the sample, behind only Taiwan and Canada. Part of the explanation may lie in the rapid growth of competition from China and other emerging markets in the production of labor-intensive low- and medium-tech products, which has turned the terms of trade against manufacturing (which we analyze further in Chapter 5).

Column seven in Table 3.16 shows real per capita GDP when the share of manufacturing in employment peaked. At the peak in Korea, per capita GDP was barely half that of Italy or France.[47] This is another aspect of the phenomenon that worries the critics of deindustrialization in Korea. And it is another aspect in connection with which Chinese competition is invoked.

Average annual growth rates of per capita GDP at eight years before and eight years after the peak are presented in columns six and eight. Japan shows the largest decline in growth after the peak, from 8.5 to 2.1 percent.[48] Although Finland, which experienced deindustrialization of its labor force beginning in 1974, also displays a comparably large decline in the growth rate, other countries did not experience such rapid deceleration. Korea's growth rate declined after the peak by 1.3 percent, which is substantially less than the decline experienced by Japan or Finland. Again, this does not obviously suggest that deindustrialization in Korea has been excessive and damaging to economic growth.

A potential problem with these comparisons is that the relationship between growth and structural change may itself be changing. Deindustrialization may now be occurring at a lower level of per capita GDP as more services become tradable. Or it may be occurring earlier as more developing countries begin exporting manufactured goods. Following Eichengreen and Gupta (2009), we can look more closely at how Korea's pattern of industrialization and deindustrialization compares with that in other countries that underwent these transitions at similar points in

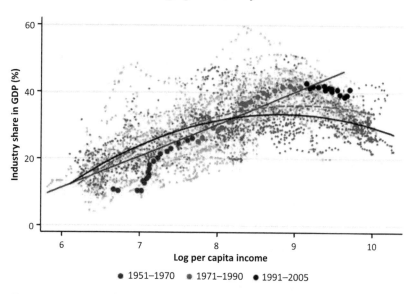

Figure 3.13. Output Share of Industry: Korea and Other Countries over Time
The graph is constructed based on data described in Eichengreen and Gupta (2011).

time. This involves taking data for a large sample of countries, starting in 1950, and observing the relationship between per capita GDP and the share of output in industry and services separately for the 1950s and 1960s, the 1970s and 1980s, and the post-1990 period. The analysis is necessarily done in terms of sector shares of GDP, because sector employment shares are not available for such a large sample of countries. Eichengreen and Gupta regress sector shares on GDP per capita and GDP per capita squared, separately for each subperiod. In Figure 3.13, the relatively straight curve shows the average share of manufacturing in GDP at different levels of income in the 1950s and 1960s. That the line is more or less straight reflects the small coefficient on the quadratic term; in other words, in this period there was not yet much deindustrialization over the relevant range. The tendency for the share of GDP accounted for by manufacturing to fall as incomes exceed the sample mean in the 1970s and 1980s is clearly evident in the broken line. The downward turn in the share of manufacturing then begins setting in even earlier after 1990, as indicated by the dark curve.

The same coding is used to distinguish the observations for Korea in the various subperiods. (These are the dark, medium, and very dark

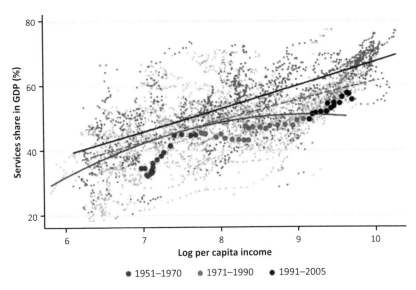

Figure 3.14. Output Share of Services: Korea and Other Countries over Time
The graph is constructed based on data described in Eichengreen and Gupta (2011).

circles.) In Figures 3.14 and 3.15, the dark circles are below the relatively straight curve, indicating that both the manufacturing and service sectors were still underdeveloped for much of the 1960s; Korea was still a predominantly agricultural economy. By 1970 the growth miracle then largely closed this gap for both industry and, interestingly, services. It was after 1980, after the Heavy and Chemical Industry Drive and the early 1980s export push, that Korea became more heavily industrialized than other countries with comparable per capita incomes and its service sector fell behind, both because the share of services in Korean GDP stagnated and because the share of services shifted up in other countries. After 1990 the share of GDP attributable to industry declines noticeably in Korea, but the dark circles for the country remain far above the corresponding black curve in Figure 3.13, suggesting that the country remained disproportionately industrial. The converse is of course true of services.

The slowdown in the growth rate may be a function of lower investment after the start of deindustrialization of the labor force if opportunities for profitable investment are fewer in services. The graphs in Figure 3.A3 in the appendix to this chapter show investment rates around the

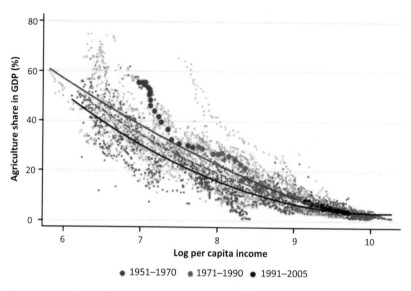

Figure 3.15. Output Share of Agriculture: Korea and Other Countries
The graph is constructed based on data described in Eichengreen and Gupta (2011).

time of deindustrialization.[49] Most countries did not experience a significant decline in investment with deindustrialization of the labor force. Four countries, the United Kingdom, France, Taiwan, and Korea, in fact show slight rises. However, the rise in Korea by far surpasses that in the other three countries. As emphasized above, this suggests that the investment boom in the decade leading up to the 1997–1998 financial crisis, when investment averaged 41 percent of GDP, was extraordinary for a country that had just begun deindustrialization of its labor force.[50] That investment rates fell subsequently is not obviously alarming, from this point of view.

In sum, deindustrialization of the labor force is a predictable concomitant of economic maturity. That said, in Korea the phenomenon appears to have commenced at a lower level of per capita income. We suspect that this reflects the increasing intensity of competition from lower-wage industrializing economies—China, in particular—and the tendency for the shift from manufacturing to services to occur earlier in more recent years, perhaps reflecting the greater tradability of service-sector output.

Conclusion

Disaggregating allows for a clearer picture of how Korea grew so rapidly between 1963 and 1997 and then slowed down. Its slowdown was associated with the shift away from rapidly growing manufacturing and toward slower growing services as the economy matured. Although some manufacturing industries continued to grow relatively rapidly, within manufacturing there was a shift away from the labor-intensive industries that had led the initial industrial boom, and then a further shift away from heavy industry toward high-tech industries in the late 1980s. All this is normal for an increasingly mature middle-income country.

High-tech sectors employ fewer people per unit of value added than had the labor-intensive industrial sectors. Thus Korea had a period when output in manufacturing continued to grow but employment in manufacturing began to fall, both as a share of the total labor force and in absolute terms. This fall in manufacturing employment began at an earlier stage in Korea than in other now-high-income countries, but this can be explained in part by the fact that deindustrialization of the labor force has tended to begin earlier in more recent years. Another factor in the precocious fall in manufacturing employment may have been the impact that China's rapid growth and opening up had on the speed with which Korean industry moved out of labor-intensive sectors in which Chinese producers enjoyed lower labor costs.

The alternative for workers unable to find jobs in manufacturing was services. While high-end services, such as finance, insurance, and business services, grew rapidly for a time, much of the labor expelled from manufacturing lacked the skills to move into these jobs. With large firms growing slowly in, among other areas, retail and wholesale trade, many of these workers ended up self-employed or in small businesses where there was little scope for high productivity growth and high personal income.

Thus the changing structure of the Korean economy from manufacturing to services is part of the explanation for slower growth in GDP, particularly after the 1997–1998 financial crisis. Most of this structural change had little to do with the financial crisis itself—it simply reflected structural changes that are common to all high-income countries.[51] With more than 70 percent of employment in Korea in the service sector, raising output and income growth now requires boosting service-sector productivity. It is to this problem we turn in Chapter 4.

Appendix

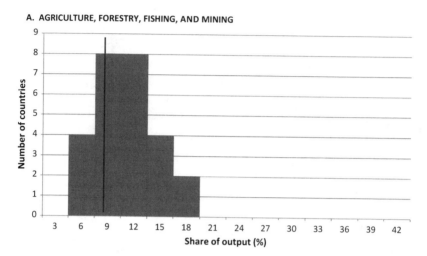

Figure 3.A1. Industry Output Shares in Selected Countries at $10,000 Per Capita GDP (1991 in Korea)

(*A–F*) The vertical line in each graph indicates the standing of Korea's share in the industry in question. Real GDP data (constant year-2000 prices) are from Penn World Table 6.2. Industry output data are from the EU KLEMS database. Fourteen countries were considered at the level of $10,000 per capita GDP (year evaluated in parentheses): Austria (1970), Belgium (1970), Finland (1970), Italy (1970), Japan (1970), United Kingdom (1970), Greece (1973), Ireland (1978), Portugal (1981), Korea (1991), Estonia (1998), Latvia (2002), and Lithuania (2002). Per capita GDP in countries evaluated in 1970 exceeded $10,000 but was less than $15,000.

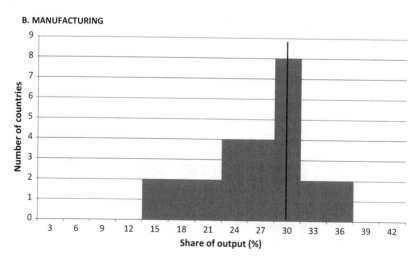

Figure 3.A1. (Continued)

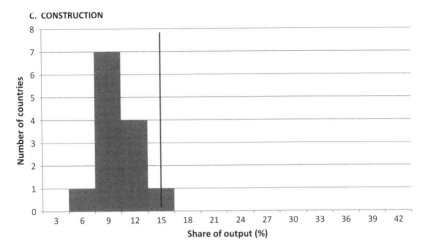

Figure 3.A1. *(Continued)*

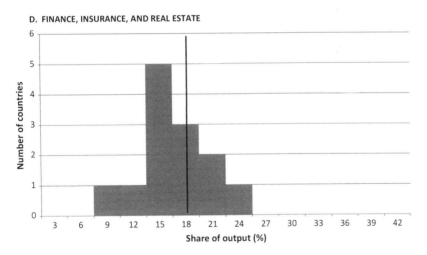

Figure 3.A1. *(Continued)*

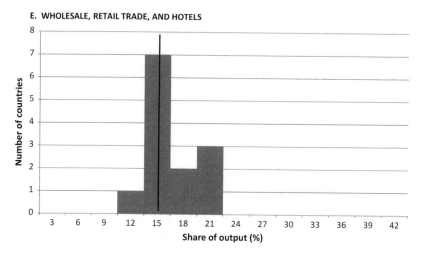

E. WHOLESALE, RETAIL TRADE, AND HOTELS

Figure 3.A1. (Continued)

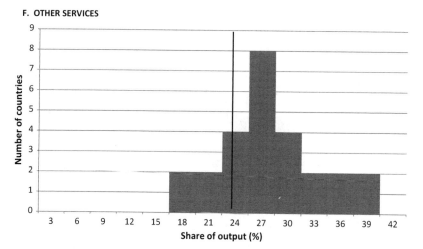

F. OTHER SERVICES

Figure 3.A1. (Continued)

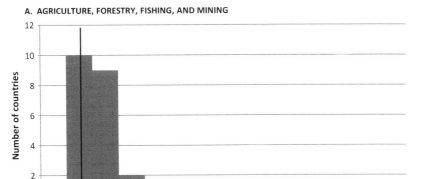

A. AGRICULTURE, FORESTRY, FISHING, AND MINING

Figure 3.A2. Industry Output Shares in Selected Countries at $15,000 Per Capita GDP (2000 in Korea)

(*A–F*) The vertical line indicates the standing of Korea's share in each industry in question. Real GDP data (constant year-2000 prices) are obtained from Penn World Table 6.2. Industry output data are from the EU KLEMS database. Twenty-one countries were considered at the level of $15,000 per capita GDP (year evaluated in parentheses): Denmark (1970), Luxembourg (1970), Netherlands (1970), Sweden (1970), United States (1970), Australia (1971), France (1973), Germany (1973), Austria (1974), Belgium (1976), United Kingdom (1978), Finland (1979), Italy (1979), Japan (1979), Spain (1990), Ireland (1995), Malta (1995), Portugal (1996), Korea (2000), Greece (2002), and the Czech Republic (2004). Per capita GDP in countries evaluated in 1970 exceeded $15,000 but was less than $20,000.

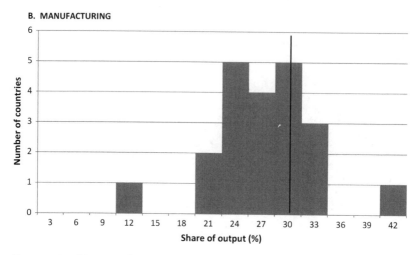

Figure 3.A2. (Continued)

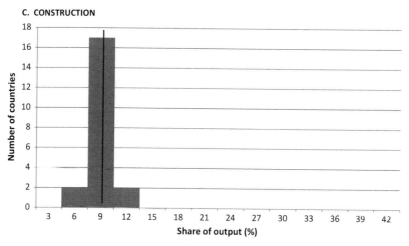

Figure 3.A2. (Continued)

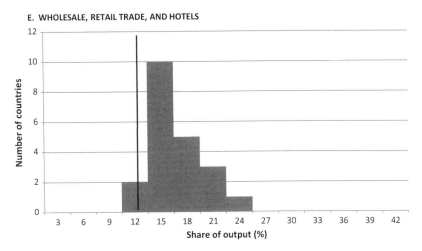

D. FINANCE, INSURANCE, AND REAL ESTATE

Figure 3.A2. (Continued)

E. WHOLESALE, RETAIL TRADE, AND HOTELS

Figure 3.A2. (Continued)

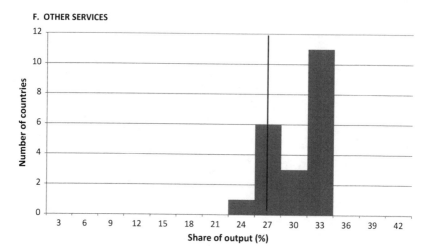

F. OTHER SERVICES

Figure 3.A2. (Continued)

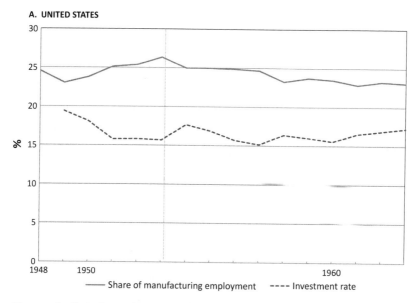

A. UNITED STATES

Share of manufacturing employment ---- Investment rate

Figure 3.A3. Deindustrialization and the Investment Rate

(A–I) The investment rate is defined as the ratio of domestic investment to GDP. Data are from Penn World Table 6.2. The vertical line indicates the break point of deindustrialization.

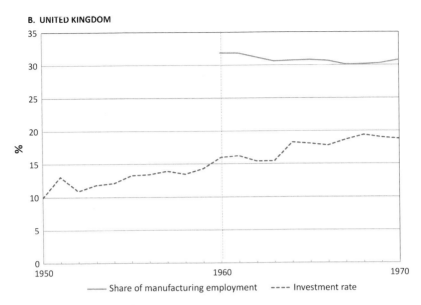

Figure 3.A3. (Continued)

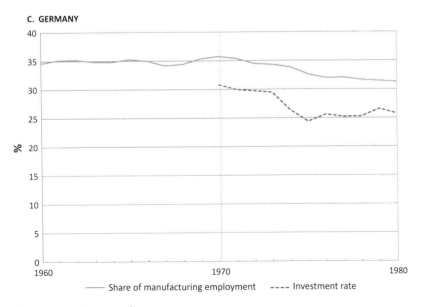

Figure 3.A3. (Continued)

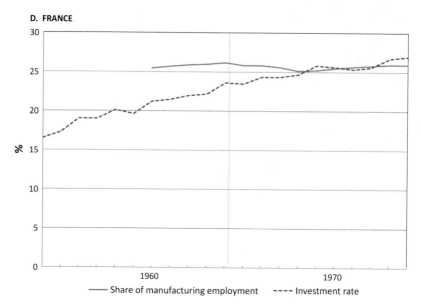

D. FRANCE

——— Share of manufacturing employment   - - - - Investment rate

Figure 3.A3. (Continued)

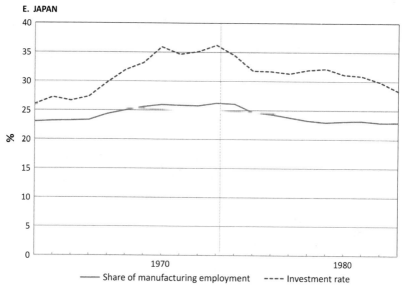

E. JAPAN

——— Share of manufacturing employment   - - - - Investment rate

Figure 3.A3. (Continued)

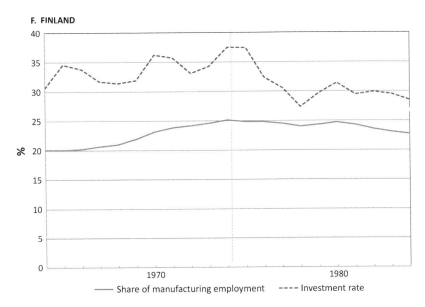

Figure 3.A3. (Continued)

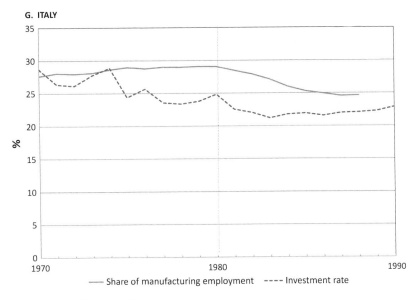

Figure 3.A3. (Continued)

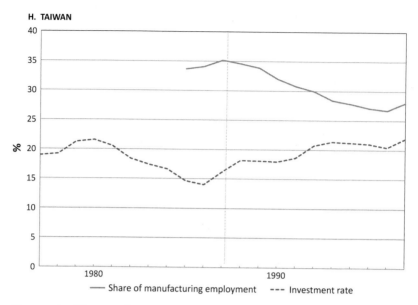

H. TAIWAN

——— Share of manufacturing employment   - - - Investment rate

Figure 3.A3. (Continued)

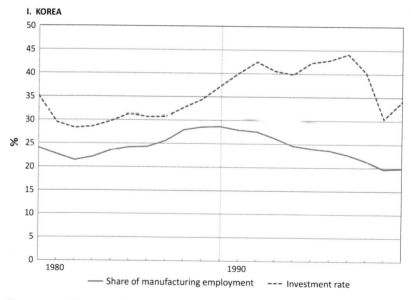

I. KOREA

——— Share of manufacturing employment   - - - Investment rate

Figure 3.A3. (Continued)

CHAPTER 4

The Service Sector and Economic Growth

Productivity growth in services has lagged behind that in manufacturing. This is a problem for the Korean economy as a whole, since services account for growing shares of output and employment as incomes rise.[1] It is for this reason that we provide a detailed analysis of service-sector performance.

The Service Sector in High-Income Countries

The growing share of GDP accounted for by services in middle- and high-income countries is evident in Figure 4.1. Although the service sector is not unimportant in low-income countries, over the past three decades its share in those countries has risen only slowly by the standards of the middle- and high-income countries.[2]

The service sector's value-added share of GDP has ranged from 64 percent to 70 percent in recent years (Figure 4.2). Nonetheless, Korea remains at the lower end of the range of shares for a country at its stage of development. As a result, the service-sector share of GDP was still lower in 2006–2010 than one would expect given the country's per capita income (Figure 4.3). That said, Korea is within two standard errors of the norm.[3] Other economies, such as Japan and Hong Kong, are significantly further from their corresponding norms, Japan with an atypically small service sector, Hong Kong with an atypically large one (see Table 4.1).[4]

Employment in services has risen even more strongly than output. The service sector's employment share was just 37.4 percent in 1971, but after declining at the beginning of the 1970s when the government pushed

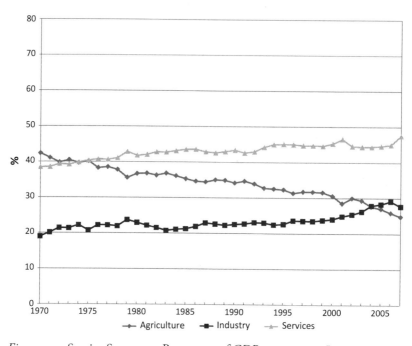

Figure 4.1a. Service Sector as a Percentage of GDP, 1970–2007, Low-income Countries

The definition of high-, middle-, and low-income countries follows *World Development Indicators;* data are from World Bank, *World Development Indicators* (various years).

resources into heavy industry, it rose strongly to 65.1 percent in 2005.[5] Since the service industry's share in employment was rising continuously, the disappointing performance of service industries in creating added value is an indication of the importance of low service-sector productivity for the performance of the economy.

It is sometimes said that services are unavoidably associated with low wages and unskilled employment. But, as Figure 4.4 shows, a very similar distribution of earnings is evident in manufacturing. To be sure, the service sector in Korea has a somewhat larger share of earnings at the bottom of the scale and also at the top, compared with other countries. This barbell profile is suggestive of two rather different service subsectors: traditional services, such as lodging, meal preparation, housecleaning, beauty and barber shops, parts of education, and health care, where wages and skill levels are relatively low, and modern services, like finance, in-

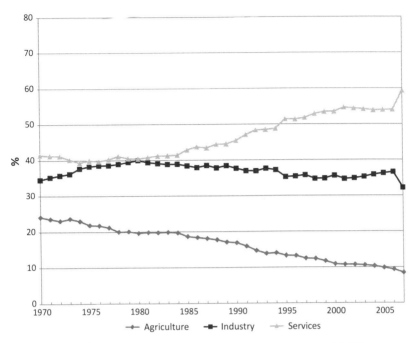

Figure 4.1b. Service Sector as a Percentage of GDP, 1970–2007, Middle-income Countries

surance, legal, communication, and business services, where both wages and skills are high.

Another common assertion is that it is intrinsically difficult to raise productivity in services. But, as Table 4.2 shows, some countries have in fact been able to achieve substantial gains. Labor productivity growth in services has exceeded 2 percent a year in the United States and a number of middle-income countries—Hungary, for example—with per capita incomes not that different from Korea's.[6] The U.S. story involved the reorganization of retail trade, wholesale trade, financial services, and telecommunications to take advantage of the productivity-enhancing capacity of new information and communications technologies. Hungary is an example of an economy that entered the period with a relatively backward financial system but was able to raise financial-sector productivity drastically, boosting service-sector productivity overall.[7] Both of these experiences have obvious implications for Korea.

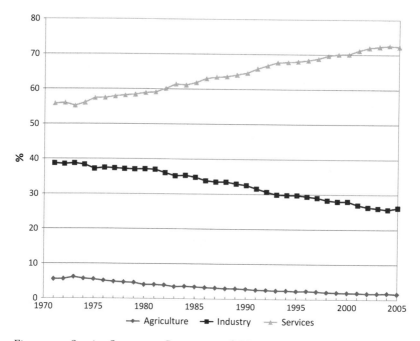

Figure 4.1c. Service Sector as a Percentage of GDP, 1970–2007, High-income Countries

Indeed, compared with other countries, Korea had one of the fastest rates of labor productivity growth across the service sector between 1999 and 2005. This favorable performance was driven by public administration, national defense, storage, and communications. At the same time, the rate of growth of labor productivity in the service sector was depressed by the disappointing performance of the education, health and social work, rental real estate, and business service subsectors.[8] The question is, why?

Sources of Low Service-Sector Productivity

Is the slow growth of service-sector productivity a result of policies and problems peculiar to Korea, or does it reflect the nature of the service sector, something not easily changed by government and business? In thinking about the answer, it is important to note that slow service-sector productivity growth is in fact common throughout the OECD countries. One popular explanation is that it is intrinsically difficult to raise productivity

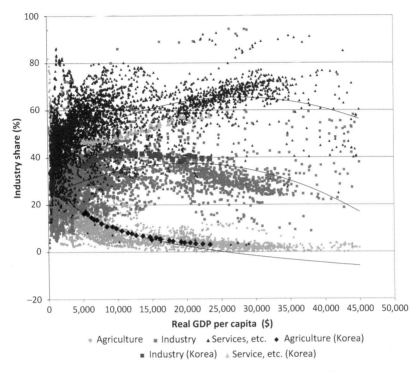

Figure 4.2. Agriculture, Industry, and Services as Percentages of GDP, 1970–2007
The sample covers 190 countries from 1980 to 2007. Real GDP per capita is denoted in PPP-adjusted constant 2005 international dollars, obtained from *World Development Indicators*. Countries whose real GDP per capita exceed $45,000 are truncated. Value added is used to calculate the industry share. Data are from World Bank, *World Development Indicators* (various years).

in services, owing to their labor intensity and the obstacles to mechanization. Innovation, in this view, is associated with investment in capital, making it a problem that the service sector is more labor intensive—and less capital intensive—than manufacturing.[9] Since output trends are similar in both sectors, while productivity necessarily rises more rapidly in manufacturing, a rising share of employment must be absorbed by the service sector. Baumol (1967) used this assumption to argue that rapid productivity growth in manufacturing and slow productivity growth in services would lead to a steady shift of labor into services.[10] The net result was that productivity in manufacturing would rise even further, while the productivity of labor in services would decline.

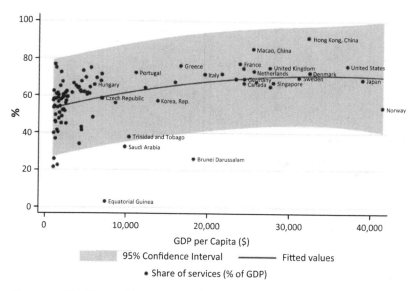

Figure 4.3. The Share of Services, 2006

The service sector is defined by *World Development Indicators* as industries corresponding to ISIC divisions 50–99: they include value added in wholesale and retail trade (including hotels and restaurants), transport, and government, financial, professional, and personal services, such as education, health care, and real estate services. Real GDP per capita is denoted in PPP-adjusted constant 2005 international dollars, obtained from the same source. The two standard-error bands around the quadratic regression line of the service share on GDP per capita are denoted by the shaded area. The data are from World Bank, *World Development Indicators* (various years).

Another argument is that technical change and mechanization are possible, but that service-sector firms, being small, are not in a position to devote significant resources to research and development or to risk introducing new techniques. Related to this is the hypothesis that service-sector innovations are not easily appropriated by innovators. It is suggestive in this connection that R&D expenditures in the service sector in Korea have fallen from 12 percent of overall R&D in 1998 to 7.1 percent in 2006, this in a period when the service sector has grown more important (Lee, Geon-woo, 2008). Revealingly, only 7 percent of Korean R&D circa 2006 was in services, in contrast to 25 percent in the OECD as a whole and more than 40 percent in countries like the United States. Moreover, much of that 7 percent is concentrated in a few activities, such as telecommunications and computer-related business services, where firms are larger.[11]

Table 4.1. Output and Employment Shares of the Service Sector

Country	Contribution to GDP (%)				Employment share (%)			
	1990	1995	2000	2005	1990	1995	2000	2005
Australia	63.7	67.6	69.6	69.9	69.3	72.2	73.3	75.0
Austria	64.2	66.9	67.0	68.6	54.9	60.5	63.8	66.7
Belgium	66.6	70.2	71.6	74.8	65.6	69.1	71.9	72.6
Canada	65.8	66.4	64.5	—	71.9	74.0	74.1	75.3
Czech Rep.	45.0	56.7	58.0	58.7	42.2	51.5	55.3	56.5
Denmark	70.4	71.5	70.6	73.0	66.6	68.5	70.2	72.7
Finland	60.3	62.8	62.8	65.7	61.0	64.9	66.3	69.4
France	69.5	71.8	74.3	77.0	—	—	—	71.5
Germany	61.2	66.6	68.5	69.7	—	60.8	64.1	67.8
Greece	65.6	70.9	73.1	76.6	48.3	56.3	60.0	65.1
Hong Kong, China	75.4	84.7	86.5	90.6	62.4	72.4	79.4	84.6
Hungary	46.4	60.6	62.5	65.5	—	59.3	59.7	62.6
Iceland	58.5	60.7	65.3	70.5	59.6	65.2	68.0	71.6
Ireland	56.6	55.3	53.9	61.9	56.4	59.9	62.9	65.6
Israel	—	—	—	—	67.5	67.6	73.0	75.6
Italy	64.4	66.4	68.8	71.2	59.3	59.9	62.8	65.1
Japan	57.8	63.6	65.8	68.6	58.2	60.4	63.1	66.4
Korea	**49.5**	**51.8**	**54.4**	**56.3**	**46.7**	**54.2**	**61.2**	**65.1**
Luxembourg	71.4	77.2	81.0	83.4	66.4	70.4	75.4	77.9
Netherlands	66.2	69.2	72.4	73.7	68.6	70.3	71.6	72.9
New Zealand	65.1	65.6	65.8	—	64.5	65.1	67.7	70.6
Norway	62.6	62.8	56.0	55.4	69.2	71.7	74.1	75.9
Portugal	62.3	65.9	68.6	72.2	47.6	56.6	52.9	57.5
Singapore	64.9	64.7	64.3	67.2	—	67.9	65.5	69.6
Spain	60.8	66.1	66.4	67.5	54.8	61.0	62.3	65.0
Sweden	65.9	67.0	69.5	70.6	67.2	71.0	73.0	75.7
Switzerland	64.1	66.5	69.6	70.3	63.6	67.6	70.4	73.2
United Kingdom	63.0	66.3	70.7	74.8	64.8	70.1	72.8	76.3
United States	70.1	72.1	74.6	76.0	70.7	72.9	74.3	77.8
G7	64.5	67.6	69.6	72.9	65.0	66.4	68.5	71.5
OECD	63.6	66.3	67.7	70.3	61.6	65.3	67.7	70.5

Source: Data from World Bank, World Development Indicators.

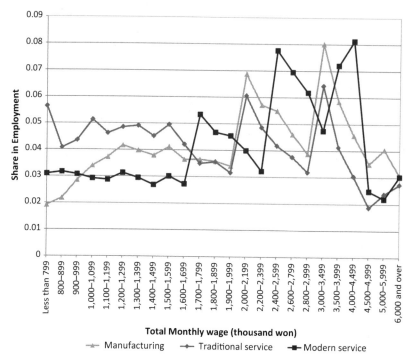

Figure 4.4. The Distribution of Manufacturing and Service Earnings in Korea (2007)

The traditional service sectors (restaurants and hotels, real estate and renting, health and social work, transport, wholesale and retail trade, and other services) are defined as those with mean earnings lower than in the manufacturing sector. The other service sectors are defined as the modern service sectors (business activities; culture and entertainment services; education, communication; financial intermediation; electricity, gas and water supply). The data are from Ministry of Employment and Labor of Korea, *Survey Report on Wage Structure in Korea.*

There is also a widely held view that competitive pressure on the service sector is weak because so much of its output is inherently nontraded. Sheltered from foreign competition, service-sector firms do not face the same pressure as manufacturers to shape up or go out of business. Productivity lags because of this insulation from the chill winds of (foreign) competition.

Finally there is the so-called catch-basin hypothesis. An advanced country competing with developing countries tends to lose low-skill manufacturing jobs and instead will specialize in highly skilled and more capital-intensive manufacturing sectors. But because those high-skill,

Table 4.2. Labor Productivity Growth by Industry, 1999–2005

Country	Total services	Education	Financial intermediation	Health & social work	Hotels & restaurants	Other community & social services	Public administration & defense	Real estate, renting, & business activities	Transport, storage, & communication	Wholesale & retail trade
Czech Rep.	2.21%	2.37%	2.38%	0.99%	−2.70%	−0.99%	−1.15%	0.19%	2.54%	5.60%
Denmark	1.40%	0.19%	6.16%	0.88%	−3.88%	−0.68%	0.62%	−1.57%	4.30%	1.93%
France	0.64%	−1.34%	2.42%	0.46%	−1.80%	2.01%	0.66%	−0.05%	2.22%	−0.05%
Germany	0.53%	−1.18%	−2.95%	1.25%	−2.67%	−1.14%	1.15%	−0.48%	1.85%	1.53%
Hungary	2.58%	3.33%	9.91%	2.73%	−4.79%	0.82%	0.75%	−2.07%	4.73%	2.75%
Ireland	2.19%	−1.34%	6.17%	−0.98%	−0.64%	2.99%	−1.93%	3.59%	3.24%	1.40%
Italy	−0.45%	0.46%	0.86%	0.49%	−4.50%	−4.58%	2.61%	−3.95%	2.89%	−1.35%
Japan	0.72%	0.66%	4.44%	−0.77%	−1.46%	0.30%	2.42%	−0.77%	2.85%	0.47%
Korea	**0.39%**	**−2.63%**	**5.51%**	**−7.36%**	**−0.82%**	**−5.20%**	**3.50%**	**−6.83%**	**8.59%**	**1.42%**
Netherlands	0.81%	−1.60%	2.31%	−0.75%	−2.43%	0.25%	0.96%	0.25%	4.24%	2.13%
Portugal	0.19%	−0.38%	8.56%	−0.28%	−2.33%	0.59%	0.04%	−2.70%	2.34%	−1.22%
Sweden	1.30%	−0.79%	4.08%	0.56%	−0.79%	1.25%	0.18%	−1.39%	2.66%	4.13%
United Kingdom	1.42%	−1.78%	4.96%	1.10%	0.83%	−0.81%	−0.24%	0.87%	2.27%	2.58%
United States	2.35%	0.01%	2.97%	1.97%	2.52%	0.94%	0.00%	2.29%	5.57%	4.22%

Source: Data are from EU KLEMS database.

capital-intensive manufacturing sectors require less labor, the share of employment provided by manufacturing tends to decline as competition with less-advanced countries intensifies.[12] The displaced labor has to go somewhere, and somewhere turns out to be relatively low-wage, low-skill service jobs. In this view, competition with newly developing countries like China accelerated the decline of industrial employment and the rise of service-sector employment in Korea.[13] Services, meanwhile, act as a catch basin for otherwise unemployed labor leaving manufacturing. Put differently, much employment in services really reflects underemployment of individuals unable to find other work.

The best evidence for this interpretation is that a third of the Korean work force is self-employed or employed as unpaid family workers in small businesses. This is an extraordinarily high figure for a middle- to high-income economy.[14] It suggests that the Korean self-employed often are doing service jobs as an alternative to open unemployment. Low productivity growth is to be expected when those entering a sector do so not because they are well suited to such activities or are entrepreneurial, but because they have few alternatives.

Raising Service-Sector Productivity

The preceding arguments do not by themselves explain why the service sector in Korea has been unable to achieve the same reasonable ratios of productivity in services, relative to other countries, that it has in manufactures. If the intrinsically small size of service-sector providers is a problem, it must be a problem in other countries as well as in Korea. If the intrinsic nontradability of services is a problem, it must similarly be a problem for other countries. Factors such as these cannot explain, in other words, why the productivity gap between Korea and other advanced countries is larger for services than manufacturing.

However valid these arguments, they do not by themselves prove that the service sector is incapable of achieving faster productivity growth. For example, there is evidence that foreign investment is associated with organizational innovation and faster productivity growth in services. The presence of foreign affiliates is positively associated with productivity growth in retail and wholesale trade across OECD countries (Wolfl 2005). Retailing may be largely nontradable, but there is an enormous difference between a sector dominated by tiny retail outlets and one that includes the giant stores of Walmart and Carrefour. Restrictions on entry by the latter are likely to have a pronounced effect on the former.

Similarly, there is evidence from other countries that international trade in services, also a source of international competition, is a further prod for service-sector productivity growth. A variety of services are increasingly tradable as a result of advances in information and communications technology. Given this fact, there is every reason to think that foreign trade in services can now be just as much a spur to productivity growth in services as in manufacturing. International competition can spur efficiency improvements by ratcheting up the pressure on firms to upgrade in order to survive. This is something that Korea knows from the experience of its manufacturing sector, starting in the 1960s. In addition, greater tradability allows the economy to specialize in that subset of service sectors in which it has a comparative advantage—that is, where its relative efficiency is greatest—and import the rest.

The share and level of service-sector output that is exported is shown in Tables 4.3 and 4.4. Korea is toward the low end of this sample of high-income countries in terms of the share of services exported.[15] Its largest service exports are transportation, which accounts for roughly half of all Korean service-sector exports and one-third of all service-sector imports. (The sector breakdown of service-sector export and import data for 2006 is presented in Table 4.A1 in the appendix to this chapter.) The importance of transport services reflects mainly shipping of merchandise between third countries, not the shipping of Korea's own exports (only 18 percent of which were shipped by Korean companies in 2006).[16] In addition, Korea has two internationally competitive airlines, Korea Air and Asiana.

"Other business services" are the next largest service sector, accounting for a quarter of service-sector exports and a slightly larger share of service-sector imports. While Korean service exports in travel, royalties, and license fees are all substantial (each valued at US$2 billion or more), imports of these services are far larger. Clearly more Koreans travel abroad than foreigners visit Korea. Korea also has some exports of communications, insurance, computers and information, and cultural and recreational services, but the amounts are small, a few hundred million dollars each, and imports of services in these sectors are generally much larger than exports.[17] The few exceptions to the rule—for example, the spread of K-Pop, Korean pop music and culture—suggest that there is considerable scope for growth.

Table 4.3. Export Ratio of the Service Sector (%)

Country	1975	1985	1995	2005
			Export Ratio	
Canada	4.5	4.8	7.2	8.2
Czech Rep.	—	—	23.7	17.9
Denmark	13.8	15.3	13.6	27.1
France	9.5	11.1	8.3	8.1
Germany	5.3	8.0	5.3	8.9
Hong Kong, China	—	—	—	41.0
Hungary	—	9.5	22.6	20.6
Ireland	13.9	13.1	15.0	54.8
Italy	7.3	8.0	9.1	7.9
Japan	—	2.8	2.0	3.5
Korea	—	**9.3**	**9.5**	**11.4**
Netherlands	17.1	18.0	17.5	19.5
New Zealand	10.6	10.9	11.9	13.4
Portugal	15.0	15.4	12.6	13.2
Singapore	69.1	43.8	50.3	69.4
Sweden	8.4	10.2	10.7	19.5
United Kingdom	13.6	13.0	11.9	14.1
United States	2.5	2.8	4.4	4.4

Source: Data are from World Bank, World Development Indicators.
Note: Export ratio of the service sector is defined as service exports divided by services, value added.

(Note that Korea's exports of cultural, recreational, and personal services exceed its exports of computer- and construction-related services.) Thus, while Korea has been able to achieve a level of productivity in some services that makes at least selected services internationally competitive, the challenge is to raise the international competitiveness of other service sectors, particularly those such as computers and information technology, that will be of growing importance in Korea's economic future.[18]

The fact that Korea imports more services than it exports suggests that competition from abroad is pushing the domestic service sector to do better. At the same time there is little doubt that restrictive regulation limited the competition from foreign suppliers in many sectors, at least prior to the

Table 4.4. Services Trade, 2006 (US$ Billions)

Country	Export	(Rank)	Import	(Rank)	Trade balance
United States	418.8	(1)	342.8	(1)	76.0
United Kingdom	234.5	(2)	177.3	(3)	57.2
Germany	173.1	(3)	215.0	(2)	−41.9
France	118.5	(4)	108.0	(5)	10.5
Japan	117.3	(5)	135.6	(4)	−18.3
Italy	99.0	(7)	100.5	(7)	−1.5
Netherlands	82.3	(9)	79.5	(8)	2.7
Hong Kong, China	72.7	(11)	37.1	(22)	35.7
Ireland	69.2	(12)	78.5	(9)	−9.3
Canada	59.3	(14)	72.6	(11)	−13.3
Singapore	59.1	(15)	61.9	(14)	−2.9
Denmark	52.7	(16)	45.5	(18)	7.1
Sweden	50.4	(19)	39.8	(21)	10.6
Korea	**49.9**	**(20)**	**68.9**	**(12)**	**−19.0**
Israel	19.3	(32)	15.0	(36)	4.3
Portugal	17.8	(33)	11.6	(40)	6.2
Czech Rep.	13.3	(37)	11.8	(38)	1.5
Hungary	13.3	(38)	11.7	(39)	1.6
New Zealand	8.1	(46)	7.8	(50)	0.3

Source: Data are from World Bank, World Development Indicators.

financial crisis of 1997–1998 and subsequent reforms (Kim and Kim 2003). The question is whether, or to what extent, those restrictive measures limiting foreign competition were subsequently eliminated or simply disguised.

Dealing with Regulatory Barriers

Prior to 1997–1998 Korea had numerous sector-specific regulations limiting foreign competition and restricting the entry of foreign firms and their affiliates into the service sector.[19] Its trade in services is significantly less than one would expect of a country with its characteristics, as already noted.[20] Similarly, the amount of foreign investment in the service sector is relatively small: foreign affiliates account for 19 percent of service-sector turnover and 10 percent of service-sector employment, on average in the OECD economies, but only 8 percent and 4 percent, respectively, in Korea (OECD 2008).

In addition there are a variety of regulatory limits on domestic competition. Of 543 categories of services, almost a third are characterized by significant entry barriers, according to the OECD, which consistently places Korea toward the top of advanced countries in terms of the restrictiveness of product market regulation of the nonmanufacturing sector.[21]

Much of this regulation is designed to shelter small and medium-size enterprises (SMEs), which are the main option for workers unable to find employment in manufacturing, as noted above. Table 4.5 shows that productivity in SMEs, as measured by value added per person employed, is less than half that in large firms. This is important in the aggregate, since some 80 percent of service-sector output is accounted for by SMEs.[22] Moreover, the growth of labor productivity over this period was considerably higher among large firms (5.1 percent) than SMEs (3.0 percent). This problem is only likely to worsen insofar as service-sector output becomes increasingly tradable and small firms find it difficult to export, and as service-sector productivity growth comes to depend increasingly on R&D and small firms find it prohibitively expensive to undertake such investments.

A major political reason for why SMEs are insulated from competition is that upwards of a third of Korea's workers are either self-employed or employed as unpaid family workers in small businesses, as noted above. While this partly reflects the natural decline in manufacturing employment as the economy matures, it is also a function of Korea's early retirement age of 55, which pushes employees out of career employment at an age when it is typically too late for retraining but when workers are still healthy and potentially productive.

The productivity differential by firm size is evident in virtually every subsector except business services and health care and social services. It is most pronounced in wholesale and retail trade, hotels and restaurants, telecommunications, and financial services. Interestingly, however, the salaries paid by SMEs are not lower, and their operating profits are actually higher. That SMEs are less productive, pay equivalent wages, and yet are more profitable suggests that they enjoy considerable rents. Put another way, heavy regulation exacts a toll on large firms. The exception is the financial sector, where large firms not only dominate but also enjoyed a rise in productivity growth over the period from 2001 to 2005 of

Table 4.5. Comparison of Small and Medium-Size Enterprises to Large Firms in Service Sectors, 2005

Industry	Value added per person (million won)		Operating profit/sales (%)		Salary/sales (%)		SMEs share of output (%)	SMEs share of employment (%)
	SMEs	Large firms	SMEs	Large firms	SMEs	Large firms		
Wholesale and retail trade	35.5	89.2	10.8	6.5	5.6	4.6	84.4	95.1
Hotels and restaurants	17.2	34.5	28.1	5.5	15.6	21.2	92.0	97.1
Telecommunications	161.0	377.7	17.3	13.4	8.2	6.3	80.7	91.1
Financial intermediation	72.9	175.6	18.9	17.2	10.9	7.5	18.9	40.8
Business services	34.1	37.6	12.3	8.7	28.7	32.7	70.8	72.3
Education	21.8	33.1	34.1	23.0	33.5	32.1	87.1	92.7
Health and social services	36.0	38.2	36.7	15.5	27.4	36.8	96.8	97.7
Personal and other services	20.4	31.9	26.9	5.2	17.5	25.7	89.4	95.1
Total service sector	**29.4**	**65.1**	**14.6**	**10.4**	**10.2**	**10.7**	**79.1**	**90.9**

Source: Data are from the Korean Small and Medium Business Administration.

Note: SMEs=small and medium-size enterprises.

19 percent per year, while among SMEs it rose by only 4.4 percent. This anomaly in the structure of the financial sector reflects the major government-led restructuring of large banks and other financial institutions that took place following the 1997–1998 financial crisis.

It is not as if the Korean government has failed to recognize the problem. It introduced a variety of measures deregulating the service sector as a result of the Uruguay Round of trade negotiations. Indeed, limited measures liberalizing foreign direct investment in the service sector had already been introduced in the first half of the 1990s in conjunction with the country's accession to the OECD (see Chapter 6). Then it made a series of industrial policy–style plans to upgrade the service sector. In December 2006 the government produced its "Plan for Strengthening Competitiveness of the Service Industry." In June 2007 it produced the "Second Plan for Strengthening the Competitiveness of the Service Industry." The first plan focused mainly on broad-brush deregulation and tax cuts, while the second plan recommended a range of subsector-specific initiatives. To reduce the trade deficit in tourism, for example, it recommended building low-cost golf courses and capping green fees. Creating more yacht harbors was also recommended. This approach is not entirely reassuring, as it has more in common with some of Korea's earlier interventionist industrial policies than with a more market-driven approach to raising service-sector productivity.

A recent study by the OECD (2008) acknowledges that there has been progress in reforming the service sector but argues that much remains to be done. In particular, entry barriers remain high. To remedy this, it emphasizes strengthening competition policy by expanding the investigatory powers of the Korea Fair Trade Commission and making more use of criminal penalties for violators. It recommends removing the many exemptions from competition law for SMEs. Finally it points to a variety of subsector-specific policies that need to be changed. An example is the capping of total enrollment in law schools at 2,000, when the number of lawyers in Korea per capita is a quarter of the OECD average.[23]

Another strategy is to capitalize on the country's existing service-sector strengths by developing its relatively high-productivity subsectors—financial services, for example—still further. Labor productivity in large financial firms rose strongly between 2001 and 2005, as we have noted. This strong productivity growth reflected not only the government-led restructuring of large banks and other financial institutions following the financial crisis, but also the elimination of a number of restrictive regulations that had previously depressed productivity and the application of new information technology.

A further major effort to reform financial services got under way in 2008. The Financial Services Commission, in the first phase in 2008, reviewed all regulations in the financial sector to see to what extent they were consistent with global standards. The second phase saw an attempt to harmonize regulations across different segments of the financial-services industry while retaining the distinction between banking, securities, and insurance. The Capital Markets Consolidation Act of 2009 also calls for further deregulation. It integrates seven related laws encompassing 420 provisions governing capital markets and investment-services industries. In addition, it is designed to reduce the firewalls between different investment services, thus allowing financial firms to provide a broader range of services. The third phase of regulatory reform to be carried out by the Financial Services Commission may move Korea toward a system of universal banking.[24]

Financial deregulation of this type must be undertaken with caution, as illustrated by the global credit crisis of 2008–2009, which reflected, in part, precipitous deregulation in countries like the United States. Big bang–style deregulation that breaks down most of the barriers between different types of financial firms may be part of the government's strategy for making Korea a financial hub for North Asia, but this emphasis, as opposed to strict regulations ensuring the transparency of financial assets and transactions, should be reexamined in light of the experience with the deregulation of financial services in the United States and the global credit crisis.[25] Pursued judiciously, however, deregulation of barriers to competition, combined with more transparency and oversight where required, can stimulate financial-sector innovation and productivity growth.

Sector-Specific Problems

The problems of service sectors exhibiting slow productivity growth are varied. In education, for example, they reflect a combination of tradition and entrenched interests. Education is conservative in most countries; it is slow to be reorganized in ways that promise to boost productivity. In Korea, in addition, there are specific problems at the university level. Governance procedures make reform difficult. University presidents and deans are typically elected by faculty for terms of two to four years, which is not long enough to exercise change-oriented leadership. Opponents of reform can simply wait out ambitious administrators.

With health care there is a consumer-protection argument for regulation. That said, regulations that overly restrict competition by, for instance, limiting the number of qualified medical practitioners or setting unrealistically high standards clearly harm productivity. The entire population is supposed to be covered by the Korean national health insurance system, which requires every medical institute to give medical treatment at government-assigned prices. Under this system, some services that should be provided more extensively as a way of enhancing outcomes and reducing costs are undersupplied because they are underpriced relative to cost. For-profit hospitals are strictly prohibited, and only individual medical doctors are allowed to form partnerships. Even in the latter case, advertisement of medical treatments is heavily regulated by the government.

This problem of heavy regulation is, if anything, even more acute in accounting, engineering, legal services, architecture, consulting, development, R&D, marketing, and advertising. It is reflected in the relatively slow growth of business services: although their share in GDP rose from 4 percent to 5 percent between 1993 and 2006, in the same period it rose from 6.5 to 8.7 percent in the OECD—twice as fast, and from what were already higher levels.[26]

Legal services are an extreme case. Korea has fewer lawyers per capita than in any other OECD country. For years entry into the profession was so restricted that only graduates of Seoul National University, the top university, were able to pass the bar. In recent years there have been efforts, responding to pressure from the business community, to increase the number of lawyers and law schools. Nonetheless the government decided in 2008 to limit enrollment in the by-then 25 law schools to 2,000 students.[27] The justification for these restrictions is typically based on the need to maintain quality, but the result is that the supply of lawyers falls far short of demand. In past years this meant that businesses generally did without lawyers and courts in settling disputes. Korea is by no means alone in this regard; throughout Asia the lack of lawyers practicing business-related law was often cited as a virtue because disputes could then be settled by informal means.[28] But this view became untenable as economies became more complex and business more global.[29] In effect, the argument for maintaining quality became a mechanism for maintaining a chronic shortage of a badly needed service.

Conclusion

While there has been progress in reforming the service sector, much remains to be done. Entry barriers remain high, and product market regulations are still restrictive. There is a need to strengthen competition policy by expanding the investigatory powers of the Korea Fair Trade Commission. To this end, it would help to remove or scale back the many exemptions from the competition law for SMEs. A further priority should be to reform a variety of subsector-specific policies, an example of which is the cap on enrollment in law schools, which in effect restricts competition in the legal profession. Korea also still has lower levels of foreign participation in the service sector than is typical of a high-income country; this is another place where deregulation could remove obstacles to competition.

To be sure, not all deregulation is helpful. In particular, Korea should take care in deregulating its financial sector. It should draw appropriate lessons from the 2008–2009 crisis (and from its own 1997–1998 crisis) about what can happen when financial deregulation is precipitous and remaining regulations are poorly enforced.

Beyond deregulation, there are two related approaches to accelerating service-sector growth. One is to encourage the high-tech end of the service sector, activities such as finance, insurance, and business services. Given that these are human-capital-intensive activities, there is no reason why Korea cannot be internationally competitive in their provision. The public and private sectors both are already taking steps in this direction, but aside from finance, where Korea is a net exporter, there is relatively little to show for these efforts so far.

A second way of boosting productivity is by reorganizing delivery to better capitalize on the productivity-enhancing potential of new information and communications technology. Korea has not yet moved from the stage where ICT is widely but not very efficiently used to the stage where sectors other than ICT itself make full use of the potential of this technology. Although it took the United States the better part of a decade to complete this transition, the result was acceleration in the growth of total factor productivity in financial services, wholesaling, and retailing. Now there are similar hopes for using ICT to boost productivity in additional services, such as health care and education. The fact that Korea has yet to move very far down this path creates scope for significant productivity enhancement through this mechanism.

Appendix

Table 4.A1. Service Trade by Sector, 2006 (US$ Millions)

(a) Transportation

Country	Export	(Rank)	Import	(Rank)	Trade balance
United States	68,484.0	(1)	92,785.0	(1)	−24,301.0
Germany	41,610.0	(2)	52,082.5	(2)	−10,472.4
Japan	37,652.1	(3)	42,838.7	(3)	−5,186.6
Denmark	33,185.7	(4)	23,869.7	(6)	9,316.0
United Kingdom	30,734.7	(5)	35,743.1	(4)	−5,008.4
France	26,215.0	(6)	29,444.0	(5)	−3,229.0
Korea	25,858.1	(7)	23,393.8	(7)	2,464.3
Netherlands	20,556.6	(8)	17,323.5	(10)	3,233.1
Spain	18,151.1	(9)	20,495.8	(9)	−2,344.6
Greece	17,970.8	(10)	8,768.7	(16)	9,202.1
Belgium	15,625.9	(11)	13,016.5	(12)	2,609.3
Italy	15,494.1	(12)	22,461.6	(8)	−6,967.4
Norway	15,229.2	(13)	9,355.2	(15)	5,874.0
Canada	10,692.4	(14)	16,920.6	(11)	−6,228.2
Austria	10,290.5	(15)	9,726.0	(14)	564.5
Sweden	9,624.1	(16)	5,172.8	(17)	4,451.3
Poland	6,969.0	(17)	4,237.9	(20)	2,731.1
Australia	6,356.3	(18)	11,321.8	(13)	−4,965.5
Switzerland	4,694.5	(19)	3,106.8	(22)	1,587.7
Turkey	4,230.0	(20)	4,308.0	(19)	−78.0
Portugal	3,990.3	(21)	3,556.8	(21)	433.4
Czech Rep.	3,730.5	(22)	2,744.3	(23)	986.2
Ireland	2,928.0	(23)	2,539.1	(26)	388.9
Finland	2,752.4	(24)	4,435.0	(18)	−1,682.6
Luxembourg	2,679.4	(25)	1,193.9	(29)	1,485.5
Hungary	2,389.1	(26)	2,413.0	(27)	−23.9
Mexico	1,913.1	(27)	2,683.5	(24)	−770.5
Slovak Rep.	1,903.4	(28)	1,279.6	(28)	623.8
New Zealand	1,663.4	(29)	2,593.9	(25)	−930.6
Iceland	829.3	(30)	762.1	(30)	67.2

Source: Data are from OECD, International Trade in Services Statistics.

Table 4.A1. Service Trade by Sector, 2006 (US$ Millions)

(b) Travel

Country	Export	(Rank)	Import	(Rank)	Trade balance
United States	106,736.0	(1)	77,028.0	(1)	29,708.0
Spain	51,070.1	(2)	16,642.0	(10)	34,428.1
France	46,298.0	(3)	31,162.7	(4)	15,135.4
Italy	38,054.8	(4)	23,039.9	(6)	15,014.9
United Kingdom	33,695.2	(5)	63,094.1	(3)	−29,398.9
Germany	32,730.8	(6)	73,882.9	(2)	−41,152.1
Australia	17,840.0	(7)	11,669.7	(12)	6,170.3
Turkey	16,853.0	(8)	2,743.0	(25)	14,110.0
Austria	16,628.2	(9)	9,308.3	(16)	7,319.9
Canada	14,632.0	(10)	20,549.9	(7)	−5,917.9
Greece	14,246.7	(11)	2,989.1	(24)	11,257.6
Mexico	12,176.6	(12)	8,108.3	(17)	4,068.4
Netherlands	11,336.4	(13)	17,010.8	(9)	−5,674.5
Switzerland	10,634.7	(14)	9,876.5	(14)	758.2
Belgium	10,214.0	(15)	15,427.7	(11)	−5,213.6
Sweden	8,469.4	(16)	9,554.0	(15)	−1,084.7
Japan	8,467.8	(17)	26,877.3	(5)	−18,408.6
Portugal	8,341.2	(18)	3,293.1	(22)	5,048.2
Poland	7,221.3	(19)	5,759.9	(20)	1,461.4
Denmark	5,584.7	(20)	7,410.7	(18)	−1,826.0
Ireland	5,341.6	(21)	6,832.0	(19)	−1,490.3
Korea	5,322.4	(22)	18,241.0	(8)	−12,918.6
Czech Rep.	5,006.5	(23)	2,656.1	(26)	2,350.4
New Zealand	4,750.1	(24)	2,529.1	(27)	2,221.1
Hungary	4,261.6	(25)	2,131.6	(28)	2,130.1
Luxembourg	3,616.4	(26)	3,126.5	(23)	490.0
Norway	3,596.4	(27)	11,521.6	(13)	−7,925.2
Finland	2,372.4	(28)	3,416.5	(21)	−1,044.0
Slovak Rep.	1,514.8	(29)	1,055.6	(30)	459.2
Iceland	442.7	(30)	1,075.2	(29)	−632.5

Source: Data are from OECD, International Trade in Services Statistics.

(continued)

Table 4.A1. Service Trade by Sector, 2006 (US$ Millions)

(c) Communication Services

Country	Export	(Rank)	Import	(Rank)	Trade balance
United Kingdom	7,834.7	(1)	7,304.1	(1)	531.8
United States	6,578.0	(2)	5,163.0	(3)	1,415.0
Germany	4,415.8	(3)	6,285.0	(2)	−1,869.2
Netherlands	3,994.9	(4)	3,481.0	(5)	5,13.9
France	3,720.8	(5)	2,088.7	(7)	1,632.1
Italy	3,158.8	(6)	4,585.1	(4)	−1,426.3
Canada	2,301.7	(7)	1,955.3	(8)	346.5
Belgium	2,037.3	(8)	1,594.5	(10)	442.8
Sweden	1,602.3	(9)	1,753.5	(9)	−151.3
Spain	1,411.3	(10)	2,239.3	(6)	−829.2
Luxembourg	1,362.0	(11)	1,338.6	(11)	23.4
Austria	1,353.6	(12)	1,098.9	(12)	254.7
Switzerland	1,100.5	(13)	801.6	(14)	298.9
Denmark	801.4	(14)	762.8	(16)	38.8
Portugal	679.2	(15)	470.6	(20)	208.6
Australia	640.8	(16)	656.6	(18)	−15.8
Ireland	523.1	(17)	959.7	(13)	−436.6
Mexico	466.4	(18)	107.3	(28)	359.1
Korea	466.3	(19)	778.3	(15)	−312.0
Czech Rep.	436.4	(20)	453.0	(22)	−16.6
Japan	435.9	(21)	732.6	(17)	−296.6
Finland	429.0	(22)	539.4	(19)	109.1
Turkey	416.0	(23)	296.0	(26)	120.0
Hungary	388.7	(24)	410.6	(23)	−22.0
Norway	387.9	(25)	298.6	(25)	89.3
Poland	385.1	(26)	456.0	(21)	−70.9
Greece	384.6	(27)	359.1	(24)	25.5
Slovak Rep.	254.6	(28)	97.8	(29)	156.8
Iceland	11.7	(29)	45.9	(30)	−34.2
New Zealand	—	—	195.2	(27)	—

Source: Data are from OECD, International Trade in Services Statistics.

Table 4.A1. Service Trade by Sector, 2006 (US$ Millions)

(d) Construction Services

Country	Export	(Rank)	Import	(Rank)	Trade balance
Japan	8,990.6	(1)	6,201.3	(2)	2,789.4
Germany	8,040.0	(2)	6,773.0	(1)	1,267.0
France	4,161.1	(3)	1,772.6	(4)	2,388.5
Italy	2,391.0	(4)	2,525.3	(3)	−134.2
Netherlands	2,294.2	(5)	1,201.4	(6)	1,092.8
Spain	2,184.1	(6)	1,312.2	(5)	871.9
Belgium	2,164.0	(7)	898.2	(8)	1,264.5
Poland	1,219.7	(8)	723.8	(10)	495.9
United Kingdom	1,210.5	(9)	973.4	(7)	237.1
Austria	966.0	(10)	766.5	(9)	199.5
Turkey	936.0	(11)	57.0	(22)	879.0
Sweden	662.8	(12)	619.1	(11)	43.6
Portugal	551.0	(13)	133.8	(20)	417.2
United States	477.0	(14)	300.0	(14)	177.0
Norway	370.8	(15)	49.1	(24)	321.7
Finland	348.7	(16)	327.4	(13)	21.3
Luxembourg	337.6	(17)	490.8	(12)	−153.2
Denmark	322.2	(18)	188.8	(16)	133.3
Greece	301.6	(19)	142.4	(18)	159.1
Hungary	255.7	(20)	138.7	(19)	117.0
Czech Rep.	213.0	(21)	173.3	(17)	39.6
Canada	199.2	(22)	97.9	(21)	100.5
Korea	126.1	(23)	3.1	(27)	122.9
Australia	97.1	(24)	0.0	(28)	97.1
Slovak Rep.	85.4	(25)	223.6	(15)	−138.2
Ireland	0.0	(27)	10.0	(26)	−10.0
Iceland	0.0	(27)	18.2	(25)	−18.2
New Zealand	—	—	49.3	(23)	—

Source: Data are from OECD, International Trade in Services Statistics.

(continued)

Table 4.A1. Service Trade by Sector, 2006 (US$ Millions)

(e) Insurance Services

Country	Export	(Rank)	Import	(Rank)	Trade balance
Ireland	11,027.0	(1)	8,990.9	(3)	2,036.0
United States	9,276.0	(2)	33,581.0	(1)	−24,305.0
United Kingdom	6,468.7	(3)	1,766.1	(10)	4,702.6
Switzerland	5,217.3	(4)	227.5	(24)	4,989.8
Canada	3,456.6	(5)	4,869.7	(4)	−1,413.1
Germany	3,196.4	(6)	2,376.0	(7)	819.2
Luxembourg	2,051.5	(7)	1,229.5	(11)	822.0
Italy	1,673.5	(8)	2,795.0	(6)	−1,121.5
Japan	1,575.3	(9)	4,568.4	(5)	−2,993.1
Mexico	1,262.9	(10)	9,278.2	(2)	−8,015.3
Austria	1,017.4	(11)	979.8	(12)	37.6
Belgium	932.1	(12)	518.1	(19)	414.0
Sweden	872.6	(13)	313.5	(21)	559.1
France	811.7	(14)	2,339.6	(8)	−1,528.0
Spain	759.0	(15)	1,938.2	(9)	−1,180.5
Australia	530.1	(16)	677.7	(17)	−147.6
Netherlands	511.3	(17)	884.7	(15)	−373.3
Korea	365.6	(18)	908.8	(14)	−543.2
Norway	321.7	(19)	146.1	(28)	175.6
Denmark	284.9	(20)	535.8	(18)	−251.1
Greece	265.4	(21)	934.0	(13)	−668.6
Turkey	229.0	(22)	850.0	(16)	−621.0
Portugal	118.0	(23)	234.2	(23)	−116.3
Poland	95.4	(24)	395.4	(20)	−300.0
Finland	66.5	(25)	191.9	(27)	−125.4
New Zealand	27.2	(26)	215.9	(25)	−189.4
Hungary	14.5	(27)	212.8	(26)	−198.3
Slovak Rep.	10.8	(28)	114.6	(29)	−103.8
Czech Rep.	10.1	(29)	240.9	(22)	−230.8
Iceland	9.7	(30)	41.5	(30)	−31.8

Source: Data are from OECD, International Trade in Services Statistics.

Table 4.A1. Service Trade by Sector, 2006 (US$ Millions)

(f) Financial Services

Country	Export	(Rank)	Import	(Rank)	Trade balance
United Kingdom	52,301.6	(1)	10,753.6	(3)	41,550.6
United States	42,814.0	(2)	14,297.0	(2)	28,517.0
Luxembourg	33,768.1	(3)	17,596.7	(1)	16,171.5
Switzerland	11,691.0	(4)	1,280.0	(12)	10,411.0
Germany	8,385.0	(5)	5,408.1	(4)	2,976.9
Ireland	7,762.8	(6)	4,704.3	(5)	3,058.4
Japan	6,151.4	(7)	2,988.8	(9)	3,162.5
Spain	3,881.4	(8)	4,159.9	(6)	−278.5
Belgium	3,609.2	(9)	3,451.1	(8)	158.1
Korea	2,557.2	(10)	616.0	(17)	1,941.2
Italy	1,972.1	(11)	1,022.4	(16)	949.6
Canada	1,895.3	(12)	2,861.5	(10)	−966.2
Sweden	1,814.7	(13)	1,038.6	(15)	776.1
Netherlands	1,440.8	(14)	1,925.1	(11)	−484.3
France	1,357.4	(15)	3,729.6	(7)	−2372.2
Austria	796.6	(16)	610.9	(18)	186.9
Norway	758.4	(17)	1,181.8	(13)	−423.3
Australia	756.0	(18)	451.8	(20)	304.2
Czech Rep.	389.3	(19)	1,085.9	(14)	−696.6
Turkey	277.0	(20)	524.0	(19)	−247.0
Portugal	247.7	(21)	259.8	(25)	−12.1
Poland	214.9	(22)	371.6	(22)	−156.6
Denmark	206.7	(23)	333.8	(24)	−127.1
Hungary	160.5	(24)	245.3	(26)	−84.8
Slovak Rep.	144.6	(25)	339.2	(23)	−194.7
Greece	105.2	(26)	140.5	(28)	−35.3
New Zealand	79.1	(27)	75.2	(29)	4.5
Finland	74.0	(28)	173.1	(27)	−99.1
Iceland	0.9	(29)	18.5	(30)	−17.6
Mexico	0.0	(30)	373.5	(21)	−373.5

Source: Data are from OECD, International Trade in Services Statistics.

(continued)

Table 4.A1. Service Trade by Sector, 2006 (US$ Millions)

(g) Computer and Information Services

Country	Export	(Rank)	Import	(Rank)	Trade balance
Ireland	21,009.0	(1)	666.1	(19)	20,342.8
United Kingdom	11,949.0	(2)	4,889.5	(3)	7,058.3
United States	10,096.0	(3)	11,092.0	(1)	−996.0
Germany	9,596.8	(4)	9,149.0	(2)	447.9
Canada	4,033.1	(5)	2,019.6	(8)	2,013.5
Spain	3,961.7	(6)	2,093.7	(7)	1,869.2
Netherlands	3,895.5	(7)	3,739.3	(4)	156.1
Sweden	3,567.2	(8)	2,245.1	(6)	1,322.1
Belgium	2,845.2	(9)	1,977.1	(10)	868.1
Luxembourg	2,207.6	(10)	667.7	(18)	1,539.9
France	1,948.2	(11)	1,978.3	(9)	−30.1
Austria	1,505.4	(12)	1,062.5	(15)	441.6
Finland	1,476.5	(13)	1,117.7	(14)	358.8
Norway	1,238.5	(14)	1,200.2	(13)	38.4
Denmark	1,216.1	(15)	1,490.9	(12)	−274.6
Australia	1,049.0	(16)	921.7	(16)	127.3
Japan	966.5	(17)	3,125.6	(5)	−2,160.0
Czech Rep.	884.8	(18)	538.4	(22)	346.4
Italy	873.1	(19)	1,698.6	(11)	−825.5
Hungary	485.4	(20)	542.7	(21)	−57.3
Poland	408.6	(21)	584.2	(20)	−175.6
Korea	239.9	(22)	773.4	(17)	−533.5
Greece	203.3	(23)	253.8	(25)	−50.5
Portugal	186.4	(24)	300.5	(23)	−114.1
New Zealand	183.5	(25)	269.8	(24)	−86.9
Slovak Rep.	170.3	(26)	200.0	(26)	−29.7
Iceland	89.0	(27)	17.1	(27)	72.0
Turkey	11.0	(28)	14.0	(28)	−3.0

Source: Data are from OECD, International Trade in Services Statistics.

Table 4.A1. Service Trade by Sector, 2006 (US$ Millions)

(h) Royalties and License Fees

Country	Export	(Rank)	Import	(Rank)	Trade balance
United States	62,378.0	(1)	26,432.0	(1)	35,946.0
Japan	20,104.2	(2)	15,496.3	(3)	4,607.1
United Kingdom	13,584.7	(3)	9,952.1	(4)	3,631.4
Netherlands	10,943.0	(4)	8,625.4	(6)	2,317.6
Switzerland	7,681.4	(5)	8,860.0	(5)	−1,178.7
France	6,228.5	(6)	3,298.0	(10)	2,930.5
Germany	5,877.3	(7)	7,838.0	(7)	−1,960.8
Sweden	3,982.8	(8)	1,671.4	(14)	2,311.4
Canada	3,244.1	(9)	7,317.8	(8)	−4,073.7
Korea	2,010.6	(10)	4,487.3	(9)	−2,476.7
Denmark	1,672.2	(11)	1,311.3	(17)	360.7
Belgium	1,515.4	(12)	1,066.3	(19)	449.1
Italy	1,092.7	(13)	1,820.3	(13)	−727.6
Finland	1,066.3	(14)	1,293.4	(18)	−227.1
Ireland	1,026.2	(15)	20,779.4	(2)	−19,753.2
Spain	938.4	(16)	2,502.7	(11)	−1,564.3
Norway	758.3	(17)	551.4	(21)	206.9
Hungary	624.1	(18)	1,051.7	(20)	−427.7
Australia	609.2	(19)	2,205.6	(12)	−1,596.4
Austria	535.7	(20)	1,321.0	(15)	−785.3
Luxembourg	374.8	(21)	163.9	(28)	211.0
Mexico	170.9	(22)	502.6	(24)	−331.7
New Zealand	122.6	(23)	487.0	(25)	−364.4
Slovak Rep.	89.5	(24)	106.4	(29)	−16.9
Portugal	81.6	(25)	348.6	(27)	−267.1
Greece	66.6	(26)	405.1	(26)	−338.5
Poland	38.3	(27)	1,311.9	(16)	−1,273.5
Czech Rep.	30.6	(28)	524.4	(23)	−493.8
Iceland	0.0	(29)	4.2	(30)	−4.2
Turkey	0.0	(30)	531.0	(22)	−531.0

Source: Data are from OECD, International Trade in Services Statistics.

(continued)

Table 4.A1. Service Trade by Sector, 2006 (US$ Millions)

(i) Other Business Services

Country	Export	(Rank)	Import	(Rank)	Trade balance
United States	79,636.0	(1)	46,663.0	(2)	32,973.0
United Kingdom	63,935.8	(2)	34,764.5	(5)	29,171.3
Germany	53,673.1	(3)	51,066.3	(1)	2,608.1
Netherlands	36,140.7	(4)	34,884.9	(4)	1,255.8
Italy	31,379.7	(5)	36,395.1	(3)	−5,015.4
Japan	30,695.0	(6)	29,768.1	(7)	926.9
France	24,821.2	(7)	28,263.5	(8)	−3,442.3
Spain	21,567.1	(8)	24,465.0	(9)	−2,897.9
Ireland	18,688.2	(9)	32,677.0	(6)	−13,988.8
Sweden	18,068.8	(10)	13,699.6	(11)	4,369.2
Belgium	17,608.0	(11)	13,681.4	(12)	3,926.5
Canada	13,915.3	(12)	11,613.6	(13)	2,300.9
Korea	13,070.6	(13)	19,904.9	(10)	−6,834.3
Austria	12,611.3	(14)	6,789.3	(15)	5,822.1
Switzerland	9,679.2	(15)	1,086.7	(26)	8,592.5
Norway	9,552.0	(16)	5,804.0	(16)	3,748.0
Finland	8,778.9	(17)	3,874.3	(18)	4,905.0
Denmark	8,145.4	(18)	7,960.9	(14)	184.5
Australia	4,002.3	(19)	2,823.9	(22)	1,178.5
Luxembourg	3,885.7	(20)	3,889.4	(17)	−3.8
Poland	3,764.2	(21)	3,846.4	(19)	−82.2
Hungary	3,529.1	(22)	3,477.5	(20)	51.5
Portugal	3,105.0	(23)	2,235.9	(23)	869.0
Czech Rep.	2,426.1	(24)	3,136.9	(21)	−710.8
Greece	1,795.0	(25)	1,655.0	(24)	140.1
Slovak Rep.	910.2	(26)	957.4	(27)	−47.2
New Zealand	820.3	(27)	1,242.5	(25)	−422.2
Iceland	377.0	(28)	527.3	(30)	−150.3
Turkey	289.0	(29)	723.0	(29)	−434.0
Mexico	0.0	(30)	950.0	(28)	−950.0

Source: Data are from OECD, International Trade in Services Statistics.

Table 4.A1. Service Trade by Sector, 2006 (US$ Millions)

(j) Personal, Cultural, and Recreational Services

Country	Export	(Rank)	Import	(Rank)	Trade balance
United States	11,357.0	(1)	1,008.0	(9)	10,349.0
United Kingdom	3,736.7	(2)	1,372.3	(6)	2,365.7
Canada	2,284.1	(3)	2,215.3	(3)	68.8
France	1,752.5	(4)	2,703.4	(2)	−950.9
Spain	1,236.9	(5)	1,913.1	(4)	−676.2
Hungary	1,067.6	(6)	845.8	(12)	221.8
Turkey	997.0	(7)	106.0	(26)	891.0
Netherlands	900.1	(8)	988.0	(10)	−88.0
Italy	884.4	(9)	1,570.6	(5)	−686.2
Germany	769.0	(10)	2,875.3	(1)	−2,106.3
Belgium	555.7	(11)	495.5	(16)	59.0
Australia	506.8	(12)	852.4	(11)	−345.6
Norway	464.8	(13)	594.9	(15)	−130.0
Mexico	382.7	(14)	325.8	(19)	56.9
Denmark	369.8	(15)	1,199.3	(8)	−829.7
Korea	368.5	(16)	680.3	(14)	−311.8
Luxembourg	327.5	(17)	427.2	(18)	−99.7
Sweden	268.1	(18)	147.5	(22)	120.6
Austria	257.2	(19)	752.7	(13)	−495.5
Portugal	254.5	(20)	469.5	(17)	−215.0
Ireland	230.8	(21)	140.5	(23)	90.3
Slovak Rep.	154.1	(22)	119.1	(25)	35.0
Greece	153.5	(23)	227.0	(21)	−73.0
New Zealand	153.0	(24)	40.2	(28)	112.8
Poland	147.6	(25)	232.7	(20)	−85.1
Japan	140.2	(26)	1,301.0	(7)	−1,160.8
Czech Rep.	121.1	(27)	132.8	(24)	−11.8
Finland	23.8	(28)	26.3	(29)	−2.5
Iceland	12.2	(29)	13.8	(30)	−1.7
Switzerland	2.7	(30)	84.0	(27)	−81.3

Source: Data are from OECD, International Trade in Services Statistics.

(continued)

Table 4.A1. Service Trade by Sector, 2006 (US$ Millions)

(k) Government Services Not Included Elsewhere

Country	Export	(Rank)	Import	(Rank)	Trade balance
United States	21,016.0	(1)	34,469.0	(1)	−13,453.0
Germany	6,178.3	(2)	1,735.0	(4)	4,443.4
United Kingdom	3,814.2	(3)	4,925.6	(2)	−1,111.3
Belgium	2,302.0	(4)	863.1	(10)	1,437.6
Japan	2,158.2	(5)	1,653.5	(5)	504.7
Netherlands	2,087.7	(6)	812.2	(12)	1,275.5
Canada	1,582.4	(7)	902.7	(8)	678.8
Korea	1,488.2	(8)	849.6	(11)	638.6
Italy	1,402.5	(9)	2,329.6	(3)	−927.1
Switzerland	1,238.4	(10)	157.8	(21)	1,080.7
France	886.9	(11)	1,048.7	(6)	−161.8
Spain	794.1	(12)	415.2	(17)	377.6
Denmark	694.8	(13)	899.5	(9)	−204.6
Australia	649.9	(14)	619.0	(14)	30.9
Ireland	530.6	(15)	70.3	(26)	460.4
Sweden	453.8	(16)	138.2	(22)	315.5
Austria	435.3	(17)	106.6	(23)	328.7
Luxembourg	327.5	(18)	30.3	(29)	297.2
Turkey	314.0	(19)	1,034.0	(7)	−720.0
Norway	213.9	(20)	729.4	(13)	−515.0
Portugal	184.9	(21)	298.4	(19)	−113.5
Finland	120.5	(22)	57.1	(28)	63.4
Hungary	104.2	(23)	189.1	(20)	−84.9
New Zealand	97.3	(24)	99.2	(24)	−1.9
Greece	91.0	(25)	467.0	(16)	−376.0
Poland	61.6	(26)	411.8	(18)	−350.3
Iceland	59.0	(27)	20.2	(30)	38.8
Czech Rep.	34.9	(28)	75.8	(25)	−40.9
Slovak Rep.	33.1	(29)	69.3	(27)	−36.3
Mexico	20.4	(30)	503.7	(15)	−483.3

Source: Data are from OECD, International Trade in Services Statistics.

CHAPTER 5

Exports and Economic Growth

To say that exports have a place of prominence in the literature on Korean economic growth is to put an understated gloss on the point. In the 1950s, when the country was desperately poor, it exported only small amounts of tungsten, iron ore, raw silk, dried seaweed, fish, and rice. The beginnings of the growth miracle in the 1960s are associated in both the scholarly and popular minds with the Park government's shift to export-led growth. The Heavy and Chemical Industry Drive of the 1970s saw the beginnings of the move from labor-intensive consumer-goods exports (textiles, apparel, footwear, and toys) to more capital- and technology-intensive producer goods (shipbuilding, cold-rolled steel, and electronic components). The country's successful adjustment and recovery following the debt crisis of the early 1980s is then ascribed to the decision to devalue and boost exports as a way of strengthening the balance of payments.[1]

Although exports continued to expand strongly through the first half of the 1990s, experts increasingly questioned whether this expansion was built on a firm foundation. In the conventional analysis, much export growth was accounted for by large conglomerates that expanded their capacity through borrowed funds but were financially vulnerable, owing to high gearing. These chaebol pushed aggressively into the production and export of high-tech products. They concentrated on products, like semiconductors, characterized by short product cycles and volatile demand, exposing themselves and the Korean economy to the risk of deteriorating market conditions. Meanwhile, Korea's traditional labor-intensive exports came under pressure from lower-cost producers, notably China. The 1997–1998 financial crisis then brought these chickens home to roost.

The days when exports might grow at an annual rate of 15 percent, as in the 1970s, seemed clearly past.

While this conventional account contains important insights, we challenge it in significant ways. For the period prior to democratization and the financial crisis, our analysis is consistent with accounts emphasizing Korea's much-better-than-average export performance and assigning considerable weight to exports in explaining Korean economic growth. For the subsequent period, however, our interpretation diverges from the existing literature. Where that literature tends to paint a gloomy picture of the country's international competitiveness—saying that the export sector is being hollowed out or that Korean manufacturers are losing the competitive edge—we find that Korea's merchandise exports have held up relatively well.

We argue that the break point in Korean export performance, when the rate of growth of aggregate exports slowed, was not the financial crisis, nor the recent period when China emerged as a serious competitor. Rather, the break came between the 1970s and the 1980s. Table 5.1 shows export growth in different decades. It is clear that the downshift occurred between the 20 percent or higher growth rate for exports in the 1960s and 1970s and the growth rate of about 10 percent since the 1980s. (For those wanting to date the shift more precisely, a Chow test locates it in 1979, as shown in Figure 5.1.) Although the 1990s were exceptional, first because

Table 5.1. Rate of Growth of Exports (Constant Prices)

Decade	Average real export growth rate
1950s	9.8%
1960s	29.0%
1970s	18.7%
1980s	10.3%
1990s	14.5%
2000s	10.4%

Source: Calculations based on export data from Bank of Korea.

Note: Data for the most recent decade are for the period 2000–2007.

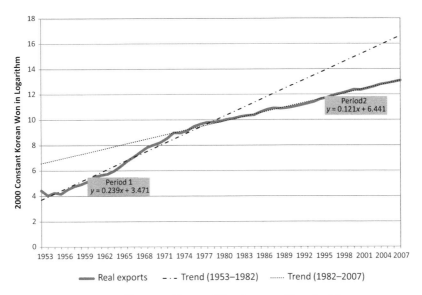

Figure 5.1. Exports in Constant Korean Won in 2000 (Log Scale)
The break point in 1979 is identified by performing Chow tests and selecting the year generating the lowest *F* value. Export data from Bank of Korea.

of the high-tech boom and then because of the collapse of domestic demand during the financial crisis, that does not change the point. This reading suggests that the slowing growth of merchandise exports relative to the high rates achieved in the miracle-growth years of the 1960s and 1970s is simply the consequence of the maturation of the Korean economy and its corollary, slower growth overall. Our analysis of exports in this chapter is consistent with our analysis of Korean economic growth in earlier chapters.

A similar picture emerges from analysis of the diversification of merchandise exports. While the share of exports accounted for by a limited number of medium- and high-tech products has been rising since the mid-1990s, export diversification remains broad compared with the situation in a variety of otherwise comparable countries. The same is again true of the extensive margin—that is, of the number of products exported. Korea performed well on this margin in the 1970s and especially the 1980s, as exports from the heavy and chemical industries and then various high-tech sectors increasingly supplemented the country's traditional labor-intensive exports. Its performance on the extensive margin was less exceptional in the 1990s, but this again appears to be a simple case of reversion to the mean. Note that this evidence is inconsistent with qualitative evidence that the chaebol in particular concentrated disproportionately on exporting a relatively narrow line of products and underinvested in diversification.

A related conclusion follows for the technological sophistication of exports. Korean exports may have been markedly more sophisticated than would have been predicted on the basis of the country's level of economic development in the 1960s, 1970s, and 1980s, but this has not been true more recently. However, Korea's performance on this dimension, while less exceptional than before, remains respectable. Indeed the sophistication of merchandise exports today is almost exactly what one would expect from Korea's per capita income and the behavior of other countries.[2] Once again this appears to be less failure than a reversion to the mean. In all these respects, then, our analysis of merchandise exports in this chapter is of a piece with our analysis of the larger growth process.

So why are observers of Korean export performance so pessimistic? One possibility is that the linkages from exports to aggregate growth have become weaker. An increase in foreign sales may appear to do less to boost domestic output and employment because a growing share of the value of those sales is accounted for by imported inputs—by parts and components sourced from countries like China. But to the extent that this effect is present, and we present some evidence for it below, this too is an entirely predictable consequence of economic maturation. As incomes rise and labor becomes more expensive, it is entirely normal that the production of labor-intensive inputs into the products of the country's export industries should be transferred abroad. This is one way in which a higher-income country maintains its international competitiveness. But the consequence is that a given increase in foreign sales adds less to domestic production and employment than in the past. The good news is that the external constraint—the balance of payments— does not inhibit domestic growth. The bad news, as it were, is that more output and employment growth must be generated in other sectors.

This brings us to a second reason for concern: the underperformance of the service sector, including exports of services. Viewed from a comparative international perspective, the one place where contemporary Korea stands out is in its low level of exports of services.[3] Where exports of services represent more than 10 percent of GDP in the typical OECD country and average 23 percent (Hong Kong and Singapore included) or 12 percent (Hong Kong and Singapore excluded) of GDP in the newly industrializing economies of East Asia, in Korea they are a mere 6 percent of GDP. This may be understood as a legacy of history: Korea's concentration on exports of merchandise at the expense of services reflects the government's earlier growth-and-development strategy, which privileged manufacturing. The question is whether this specialization is viable going forward, especially in light of growing competition from countries like China. And if this historical legacy has now become a historical burden, the question becomes: How quickly can it be overcome?

Analytical Considerations

A large body of literature documents the role of exports in Korea's high-growth period.[4] Krueger's *The Developmental Role of the Foreign Sector and Aid* (1982) is a classic of the genre. She builds the case for exports as an engine of growth by describing the evolution of policies, documenting the impact of those policies on relative prices, and emphasizing the temporal association of exports with the acceleration in economy-wide growth. As Krueger would be the first to admit, however, correlation is not causation. That is to say, export growth surely benefited from economic growth just as it benefited it, in turn.

For those troubled by this observation, there is also an econometric literature seeking to identify the causal connection running from exports to growth. One strand analyzes cross-country data. The most sophisticated study here is by Frankel and Romer (1999). Following much of the modern empirical literature on economic growth, the authors regress growth rates on the export ratio and a battery of controls. Their innovation is to use geographical variables (distance from a country's major markets, whether the country is landlocked, and so on, which are interpreted, as in the gravity model, as a proxy for transport and transactions costs) as instruments for the export variable. The effect of trade on per capita incomes is positive and significant. While the point estimates suggest sizable effects—raising the trade/GNP ratio by 1 percentage point increases per capita incomes by 0.5 percent to 2 percent—the effects are not estimated precisely. This suggests considerable uncertainty about magnitudes, both in general and for individual countries. Questions have also been raised (e.g., in Rodriguez and Rodrik 2000) about whether the geographical variables are really valid instruments (specifically, whether they satisfy the exclusion restriction), since they can also affect incomes directly through their association with disease burdens, institutional development, and natural resource endowments.

In addition, there are a number of rigorous if conceptually limited econometric studies of the causal role of exports in the Korean case, in particular. An early article by Viovodas (1974) estimated a positive coefficient on exports in an equation for capital-goods imports and argued that this was an important channel for growth in the 1960s. But while the author controlled for other possible determinants of capital-goods imports, he did not control for reverse causation. With this causality problem in mind, Darrat (1986) applied Granger causality tests to export and growth data starting in 1960 and found no significant causality running in either direction. Eyanayake (1999) and Awokuse (2006) applied cointegration, error correction, and vector autoregression methods, also to data since 1960, and concluded that the causality between exports and growth ran in both directions. But upon expanding the range of time series analyzed to include not just exports and growth but also investment, Feasel, Kim, and Smith (2001) concluded the opposite: while their vector autoregressions provided evidence of short-run impacts of exports and investment, these dissipated after four years. In other words, there was no durable impact of exports on the rate of growth.

Evidently such findings are sensitive to method and choice of estimator. In addition, they may suffer from omitted-variables bias. Still and all, these conflicting results have done little to undermine the presumption that the shift toward exports played a role in initiating and sustaining economic growth in the pre-1987 period.

The role of exports in Korean growth since 1987 has been analyzed less thoroughly. In part this reflects the fact that the influence of exports on the rate of growth is more straightforward in a less-developed country with a relatively small domestic market—such as South Korea before, say, 1987—than in a more mature economy with a larger home market, like that which developed in Korea subsequently. In a poor economy there will be a limited local market for industrial products, and expanding manufacturing production (where learning by doing is the norm) and manufacturing employment (to move underemployed rural residents off the land and into higher-paid urban jobs) requires expanding exports.

Where few capital goods are produced locally, it is necessary to export labor-intensive consumer goods to gain access to imported machinery and technology.[5] And with limited competitive pressure, exporting is a way to expose domestic firms to the chill winds of competition. Exporting helps to solve the hold-up problems that may otherwise deter investment in manufacturing when there exists only one or just a handful or domestic purchasers of a firm's output and only one or very few domestic suppliers of key inputs. Where the government provides tax breaks, import-duty drawbacks, and preferential loans to get a critical mass of manufacturing firms up and running, export performance offers a measure by which the authorities can gauge the continued worthiness of the recipients of their largesse. Each of these positive aspects of the export-growth connection was evident in South Korea from the second half of the 1960s through the first half of the 1980s.

But in the larger and more advanced economy that South Korea has become, it is less clear how much importance should be ascribed to exports as an engine of growth.[6] In an economy with a larger domestic market, there will be more manufacturing firms and more competition. Exports, while still useful for forcing firms to meet the market test, will no longer be as essential. Trade will no longer be essential for solving hold-up problems. The larger market will mean that fewer industries are constrained by limited domestic demand. There will be more production of capital goods. If the government needs a gauge of how firms or industries are doing, their balance sheets will provide an alternative to exports. And as the economy matures there will be a tendency for employment in services to expand relative to employment in industry. Many (if not all) services are nontradable; they can be neither exported nor imported.[7]

In such an economy, export growth is better seen as an indicator of economic performance, rather than a determinant. When productivity rises strongly and wage growth is contained, the favorable evolution of unit labor costs will be reflected in strong export growth. When a country succeeds in moving up into the production of more technologically sophisticated goods, this will be reflected in higher export unit values. But it is other domestic fundamentals—productivity growth, wage costs, technological upgrading—and not exports per se that are the motors of growth. This is the main way in which exports are viewed and analyzed in this chapter: as an indicator rather than a determinant of the economy's growth performance.

That said, there still may be circumstances in which exports matter in addition to, rather than instead of, these other factors. In some sectors, such as semiconductors, shipbuilding, and motor vehicles, minimum efficient scale is very high and can be attained only by exporting. Inadequate export competitiveness can stymie the development of such industries, and firms can become world leaders only by competing with other world leaders in global markets.

Not only are efforts at pinpointing the role of exports in Korean growth since 1987 hampered by the absence of an adequate analytical framework, but they also are complicated by the fact that the economy has experienced sharp shocks and structural changes. Most recently, the rise of China has reshaped many of Korea's export industries. Parts and components previously produced at home are now assembled in China before being reexported to their final market. In other cases, Korea's own exports of final goods are built with parts and components fabricated in China. Foreign direct investment by Korean firms, not just in China but in the United States and other countries, points to the question of whether FDI and exports are substitutes or complements. Corporate and financial restructuring in the wake of the 1997–1998 financial crisis, the further opening of the Korean economy that followed this event, and the rise of broadband and the Internet all have important implications for the structure of Korean exports and their connection to economic growth. These shocks and structural changes provide identifying variation, but they also hinder efforts at generalization.

Benchmarking Korea's Export Performance

We benchmark Korean export performance by comparing it with that of other countries. Duran, Mulder, and Onodera (2008) analyze the role of exports in economic growth in six East Asian countries (Indonesia, Malaysia, the Philippines, Singapore, Thailand, and Vietnam), eight Latin American economies (Argentina, Brazil, Chile, Colombia, Costa Rica, Ecuador, Mexico, and Peru), and China.[8] Our benchmarking exercise follows their template.

Figure 5.2 shows how the East Asian six and China have succeeded in partially closing the per capita income gap, measured in constant international prices, since the mid-1970s. Measured at purchasing power parity (PPP), China overtook this particular sample of six East Asian economies

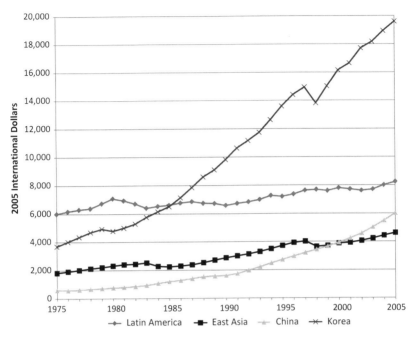

Figure 5.2. GDP per Capita, Purchasing Power Parity (International Dollars, 2005)

The values for Latin America (Argentina, Brazil, Chile, Colombia, Costa Rica, Ecuador, Mexico, and Peru) and East Asia (Indonesia, Malaysia, Philippines, Singapore, Thailand, and Vietnam) are weighted average of purchasing power parity GDP per capita, with population used as weights. Data from Penn World Table 6.3.

around the turn of the century. But it is the series for South Korea that stands out. By this measure, Korea first surpassed the eight Latin American economies in terms of per capita incomes at PPP in the mid-1980s. With Korea continuing to outperform Latin America, its living standards so measured are now fully three times those in Latin America.

To what extent did trade policy and export orientation contribute to this differential performance? A first cut at the answer considers the contribution of exports to GDP growth from an accounting perspective. Figure 5.3 shows that the contribution of net exports was larger in East Asia than Latin America in the 1990s and since the turn of the century, although it was smaller in the 1980s, the decade of the Latin American debt crisis, when the economies of the region attempted to export their way out of their debt-induced slump. Strikingly, the contribution of net

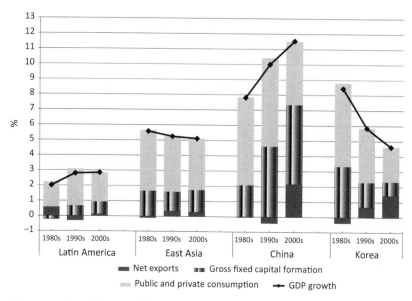

Figure 5.3. Contribution of Net Exports, Fixed Investment, and Consumption
Regional figures are weighted averages of individual countries belonging to the region, with each country's purchasing power parity GDP in 1990 as weights. Calculations based on UN Department of Economic and Social Affairs (DESA), National Accounts Main Aggregates database, for all countries except Korea, for which we used data from National Accounts, Bank of Korea. Source: Duran, Mulder, and Onodera (2008), fig. 3, with Korea's values added.

exports has been even larger in South Korea than in the East Asian six, both in the 1990s and since the turn of the century. Despite the fact that Korea has grown at only half of China's rate since the turn of the century, the contribution of net exports to the growth of aggregate expenditure has been similar. Note that the contribution of net exports to Korean growth was smaller in earlier periods, reflecting the fact that the country was in chronic deficit (and importing capital).

The importance of net exports, in comparison with China and the East Asian six, in contributing to the growth in demand for Korean products, especially since the turn of the century, reflects not so much the unusually rapid growth of gross exports as it does the relatively slow growth of imports (Figure 5.4).[9] This makes sense insofar as consumer demand in Korea was depressed starting in 2003 by a crisis in the credit card industry.

The exceptionally strong contribution of trade to the growth of spending on Korean products reflects the exchange-rate-cum-macroeconomic-

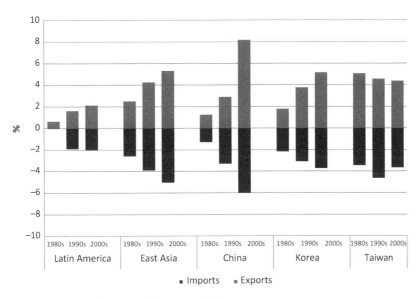

Figure 5.4. Contribution of Exports and Imports

Regional figures are weighted averages of individual countries belonging to the region, with each country's purchasing power parity GDP in 1990 as weights. Calculations based on UN DESA, National Accounts Main Aggregates database. Data for Korea are from National Accounts, Bank of Korea; data for Taiwan are from *Statistical Abstract of National Income in Taiwan Area, Republic of China,* May 2007. Source: Duran, Mulder, and Onodera (2008), fig. 3, with Korea and Taiwan added.

policy mix and relatively early liberalization of the trade regime. Central to Korea's development strategy starting in the mid-1960s was a highly competitive (some would say undervalued) exchange rate that favored exports over other activities. To be sure, the real exchange rate may not have been equally favorable throughout. Qualitative accounts suggest that the real rate depreciated strongly in the early 1980s, as Korea used currency devaluation and fiscal retrenchment to adjust to its debt crisis, and then appreciated with the wage explosion that coincided with democratization in 1987. It was argued by, among others, the International Monetary Fund that the exchange rate was fairly valued in the first half of the 1990s, when unit labor costs and productivity moved in tandem, that it became undervalued in the wake of the financial crisis, and that it may then have grown overvalued as the economy recovered at the turn of the decade.

To analyze these claims, we construct a measure of the real exchange rate (RER)—following Prasad, Rajan, and Subramanian (2006); Rodrik

(2007); and Eichengreen (2008)—as the nominal exchange rate (e) relative to purchasing power parity: RER = e/PPP. Next, we compute the "normal" or equilibrium RER for a large sample of countries, regressing RER on per capita GDP and a vector of time dummies. The extent of real over- or undervaluation is then the difference between the actual RER and the fitted value. We can think of this as indicating whether relative prices favored traded goods (which depend on the market exchange rate) or nontraded goods (which are included in the PPP price level), taking into account how per capita incomes affect the demand and supply (and therefore the relative price) of nontradables.[10]

The resulting series is presented in Figure 5.5.[11] It confirms the existence of substantial real depreciation in the first half of the 1960s with the shift toward export-led growth, followed by secular appreciation. That secular appreciation is interrupted and modestly reversed in the first half of the 1980s, reflecting the sharp devaluation and adjustment undertaken in response to debt problems, first in Korea and then globally. But real appreciation resumes thereafter. Starting in 1989 Korea's real exchange rate is stronger than would be predicted on the basis of this comparison with other countries, consistent with a picture of growing problems of international competitiveness. In other words, these estimates suggest that the period of strong undervaluation was over by the first half of the 1990s and that other factors (artificially?) held up Korean exports. In the second half of the 1990s, when the financial crisis resulted in a sharp depreciation of the nominal exchange rate, there is also some depreciation of the real exchange rate, creating a more favorable environment for exports. But it is striking that the real exchange rate continues to appear at least modestly overvalued in the wake of the financial crisis. That overvaluation is even more pronounced when we adjust for Korea's demographic structure.[12]

Strikingly, this analysis suggests that Korean exporters had already lost the advantage of an unusually favorable RER by 1987. The Korean RER is right on the zero line or even slightly below it, depending on the inclusion or exclusion of additional controls. Qualitative accounts point to the wage explosion that coincided with the transition to democracy. Our results confirm that this brought the era of the undervalued won to an end. This was about the time when commentators, such as Dornbusch and Park (1987), emphasized the importance of real undervaluation and competitive labor costs in initiating and sustaining Korean economic

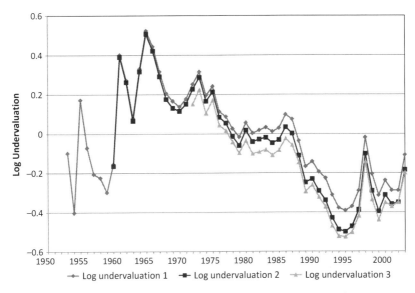

Figure 5.5. Undervaluation of Real Exchange Rate (Annual Estimates)

This figure plots three log undervaluation indices of the real exchange rate following Rodrik (2007), except that we use annual data instead of data for five-year periods. The first index, log undervaluation 1, is constructed by subtracting the Balassa-Samuelson adjusted rate from the actual real exchange rate. The Balassa-Samuelson adjusted rate is obtained by regressing the actual real exchange rate on purchasing power parity-adjusted per capita GDP. Log undervaluation 2 and log undervaluation 3 are obtained in a similar manner except that the Balassa-Samuelson adjusted rate is augmented by including demographic factors (population ages 0–14 and 65 and over) and the degree of democracy, respectively. The exchange rate is from Penn World Table 6.2; the real exchange rate is obtained by dividing the exchange rate by purchasing power parity. The demography variable is from World Bank, *World Development Indicators* (various years).

growth. The irony is that, just as they made the point, the phenomenon was coming to an end.

The other striking result is the suggestion of a progressively worsening problem of price competitiveness in the first half of the 1990s, peaking in 1995.[13] It is tempting to link this shift in relative prices to the country's growing current account deficit and to the financial crisis that eventuated in 1997. This conclusion is very different from IMF analyses at the time, which, as noted, concluded that there was no problem of overvaluation.

We can similarly assess Korea's commercial policy by comparing it with other emerging markets. The effective tariff, shown in Figure 5.6, is calculated as the average tariff multiplied by the share of imports coming

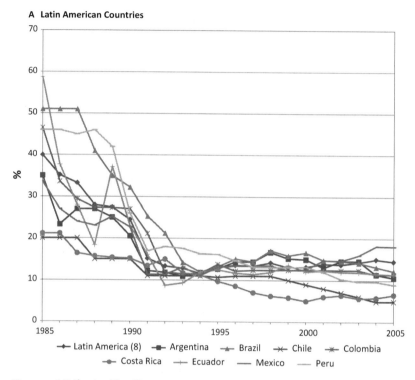

Figure 5.6. Effective Tariff
Source: Based on Duran, Mulder, and Onodero (2008), fig. 4. We thank the authors for providing the data.

from countries not participating with the subject country in a regional, bilateral, or plurilateral free trade agreement.[14] Although Korea is not renowned for its openness to imports, of the other East Asian countries considered here (see Figure 5.6 [*B*]) only Malaysia had reduced its effective tariffs on imports to equally low levels by the mid-1980s. Subsequent tariff reductions are more modest but still noticeable. Korea has been criticized for limiting foreign access to its markets, but any such bias is not evident in the data on tariff protection.[15] The temporary move up in 1996 reflects a shift in the composition of Korean imports toward lower-tech products, owing to the slowdown in the global semiconductor industry and an increase in rates on agricultural products, among others, taken in anticipation of the need for reductions following the country's accession to the World Trade Organization (WTO).[16]

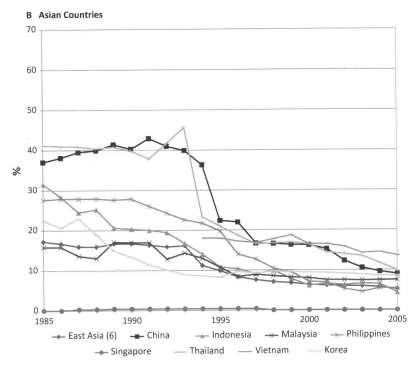

Figure 5.6. Effective Tariff *(Continued)*

Table 5.2 shows frequency coverage ratios of nontariff barriers (NTBs) for various product categories in 2001. Korea stands out relative to other emerging markets for its high level of agricultural protection. This is not surprising given that it is a land-poor economy and a net importer of land-intensive goods. More striking is the relatively extensive nontariff protection enjoyed by the chemical industry. Aside from that, NTBs in Korea are relatively unexceptional: their average coverage puts the country more or less in the middle of the pack.

Having considered policies, we now consider outcomes. Table 5.3 shows trade/GDP and export/GDP ratios starting in 1970. Since 1980 (but not in 1970, given that the shift to export-led growth dated only from the mid-1960s), Korea stands out in comparison with Latin America and even China, though not relative to the other six East Asian countries. Table 5.4 then shows export growth by decade. Korea's high growth rate in the 1970s, the decade of the Heavy and Chemical Industry Drive, reflects in

Table 5.2. Coverage of Nontariff Barriers by Sector, Selected Countries

Product category (SITC)	Brazil	Chile	Mexico	Peru	China	Indonesia	Malaysia	Philippines	Singapore	Thailand	Vietnam	Korea
Primary products (0–4, 68)	3.54	1.22	2.41	0.88	6.46	4.40	3.02	0.74	0.61	6.32	0.43	9.29
Agriculture products (0–2, 4)	3.76	1.43	2.54	1.03	7.30	3.40	3.53	0.76	0.72	6.67	0.41	10.76
Mining products (3, 68)	2.50	0.00	1.67	0.00	1.51	10.80	0.00	0.61	0.00	4.22	0.54	0.60
Manufactures (5–8 less 68)	3.91	0.17	0.80	0.03	8.00	1.1	2.41	1.92	0.13	3.30	1.23	0.37
Iron and steel (67)	0.49	0.00	0.00	0.00	44.85	1.90	7.97	0.00	0.00	0.00	21.74	0.00
Chemicals (5)	0.87	0.00	0.14	0.00	3.90	1.60	0.75	4.67	0.00	0.24	0.12	1.25
Other semi-manufactures (61–64, 66, 69)	2.20	0.00	0.08	0.00	1.36	1.20	0.90	0.60	0.00	1.47	0.41	0.16
Machinery and transport equipment (7)	8.14	0.73	2.25	0.07	14.02	1.90	4.29	1.92	0.56	1.39	0.00	0.00
Textile and clothing (65, 84)	5.36	0.00	0.00	0.06	2.85	0.00	0.30	0.00	0.00	13.50	0.00	0.38
Other consumer goods (81–83, 85, 87–89)	6.85	0.00	1.57	0.00	5.05	0.00	4.31	2.65	0.00	0.00	0.00	0.00
Other products (9)	0.00	0.00	0.00	0.00	0.00	0.00	0.00	8.33	0.00	0.00	0.00	0.00
ALL PRODUCTS (0–9)	3.88	0.41	1.16	0.22	7.62	1.80	2.54	1.68	0.24	3.97	1.03	2.37

Source: Bora, Kuwahara, and Laird (2002).

Note: SITC=Standard International Trade Classification. Indonesia data from Duran, Mulder, and Onodera (2007). Data are for 2001 for most countries.

Table 5.3. Trade/GDP and Export/GDP Ratios, 1970–2005

	Openness	1970	1980	1990	2000	2005
Latin America	Trade/GDP	21.8%	21.2%	24.8%	50.0%	62.7%
(8 countries)	Exports/GDP	9.0%	8.0%	13.2%	24.5%	32.0%
East Asia	Trade/GDP	71.6%	83.0%	102.2%	159.3%	185.7%
(6 countries)	Exports/GDP	36.8%	41.1%	50.7%	83.6%	97.8%
China	Trade/GDP	2.8%	43.8%	33.4%	50.8%	92.3%
	Exports/GDP	2.8%	25.7%	18.4%	25.5%	51.7%
Korea	Trade/GDP	19.1%	46.7%	57.0%	110.8%	152.0%
	Exports/GDP	7.2%	23.1%	28.0%	65.7%	94.2%

Source: UN Department of Economic and Social Affairs, National Accounts Main Aggregates database.

Note: Openness is measured by (1) total trade (exports plus imports) divided by GDP and (2) exports divided by GDP. Trade and GDP data are based on the current nominal U.S. dollar prices in each year.

part the low level from which exports started.[17] The rate of growth of exports in the most recent decade (actually 2000–2008, given data limitations) is almost exactly the same as in the 1980s. It is also quite respectable by international standards, running significantly behind only China (a well-known special case) and Argentina (which suffered from output- and export-growth stagnation in previous years and adopted a grossly undervalued exchange rate following its 2001–2002 financial crisis).[18] The decade that most stands out (besides the 1970s) is, interestingly, the 1990s—that is, before, during, and after the financial crisis.[19]

We use the now-standard framework for analyzing trade flows, the gravity model, to ask whether Korea's exports to various destinations are easily understood in terms of the country's observable characteristics, or whether they are, in some sense, unusually high. We regress the log of exports on source- and destination-country GDP, source- and destination-country GDP per capita, distance between trading partners, common language, and whether or not the countries in question are landlocked. We also include a Korea dummy to see whether these characteristics fully explain the extent of Korea's trade or if there is something exceptional about the country's performance.

The results suggest that Korea is exceptional all through the second half of the twentieth century, but in different ways in different subperiods. In Table 5.5 the dummy variable for Korea in the 1960s is negative, indicating

Table 5.4. Export Growth by Decade

Country	1970s	1980s	1990s	2000s
Latin America				
Argentina	4.7%	4.9%	6.4%	6.9%
Brazil	9.5%	7.2%	5.6%	7.6%
Chile	9.8%	5.9%	8.8%	5.9%
Colombia	6.1%	5.9%	5.4%	5.2%
Costa Rica	5.8%	6.2%	10.3%	5.7%
Ecuador	13.1%	5.1%	5.6%	5.5%
Mexico	8.0%	7.5%	12.5%	4.4%
Peru	3.0%	−2.0%	8.3%	7.9%
East Asia				
China	16.7%	5.5%	14.4%	15.6%
Indonesia	7.2%	2.5%	6.4%	7.4%
Korea	18.7%	10.3%	14.5%	9.4%
Malaysia	9.7%	10.3%	11.7%	4.8%
Philippines	9.2%	3.4%	7.2%	5.2%
Singapore	13.3%	5.8%	8.1%	8.3%
Taiwan	17.3%	7.6%	5.4%	3.7%
Thailand	9.1%	12.9%	10.1%	6.4%
Vietnam	3.7%	5.6%	14.6%	10.8%
Worldwide	6.2%	5.2%	7.0%	5.6%

Source: Calculations based on UN National Accounts Main Aggregates database. Data for Taiwan are from Macro Statistics Database, National Statistics, Republic of China (Taiwan).

Note: Real export growth rate is calculated in constant 1990 U.S. dollars. Ten-year averages are reported for each decade except the 2000s, which covers the period 2000–2008.

fewer exports than predicted, and the effect is statistically significant at the 99 percent confidence level. There are then a series of significant positive coefficients on this dummy starting in the 1970s. The point estimates are large. A coefficient of one, like that for the 1970s, suggests that Korea exports nearly three times as much as its characteristics and the average behavior of other countries would lead one to expect.[20] The magnitude of the effect rises further from the 1970s to the 1980s and 1990s, and the point estimates for the 1980s and after are significantly different from those that come before.[21] There is then a slight drop in the magnitude of the coeffi-

Table 5.5. Level of Korea's Trade Is Not Wholly Explained by Arguments of Standard Gravity Model

	(1) *Korea dummy*	(2) *Korea decade dummy*
GDP in reporter country	0.775** (0.006)	0.771** (0.006)
GDP in partner country	0.560** (0.006)	0.557** (0.006)
Per capita GDP in reporter country	0.525** (0.010)	0.519** (0.010)
Per capita GDP in partner country	0.367** (0.010)	0.362** (0.010)
Distance	−1.213** (0.023)	−1.213** (0.023)
No. of landlocked	−0.513** (0.032)	−0.518** (0.032)
No. of island	−0.099** (0.037)	−0.099** (0.037)
Land border dummy	1.150** (0.115)	1.149** (0.115)
1 for common language	0.335** (0.047)	0.332** (0.047)
Dummy for common colonizer post-1945	0.593** (0.062)	0.583** (0.062)
Dummy for same nation/perennial colonies	0.854 (1.191)	0.868 (1.191)
Dummy for pairs ever in colonial relationship	2.202** (0.151)	2.214** (0.151)
Dummy for pairs currently in colonial relationship	−0.085 (0.124)	−0.088 (0.124)
Strict currency union	0.478** (0.059)	0.474** (0.059)
RTA dummy	0.489** (0.032)	0.496** (0.032)
Product of land areas	0.114** (0.006)	0.115** (0.006)
Korea dummy	0.943** (0.033)	—
Korea 1960s dummy	—	−0.819** (0.116)

(continued)

Table 5.5. (Continued)

	(1) Korea dummy	(2) Korea decade dummy
Korea 1970s dummy	—	0.727** (0.062)
Korea 1980s dummy	—	1.118** (0.046)
Korea 1990s dummy	—	1.091** (0.044)
Korea 2000s dummy	—	0.944** (0.061)
R-squared	0.61	0.60

Note: The dependent variable is bilateral real exports. Real exports are obtained by dividing current U.S. dollar values, collected from the IMF's Direction of Trade Statistics database, by the U.S. consumer price index (CPI). All explanatory variables (other than the dummies) are expressed in logarithms. GDP is collected from the World Bank's World Development Indicators database and deflated by the U.S. CPI; real per capita GDP is obtained from Penn World Table 6.2. Other country variables are from Rose (2000). RTA dummy takes one if the pair countries have formed regional trade agreement. Panel data estimation techniques with random effects were applied to 474,755 country pairs for the period 1960–2004. Robust standard errors are in parentheses. Intercepts and time-fixed effects are included but not reported. In column 2, the coefficients on the dummy variables for the 1980s, 1990s, and 2000s do not differ significantly from one another at the 5 percent level.
** indicates statistical significance at the 5-percent level.

cient for the most recent decade, although the extent to which Korean exports still outperform the international average, given the country's characteristics, remains striking. This is our first bit of evidence that popular pessimism about Korea's export competitiveness tends to be exaggerated.

To be sure, if the country's exports were concentrated in a small number of products for which demand is relatively volatile, then the preceding would not be reassuring. However, a more diversified export portfolio makes for greater macroeconomic stability and thus higher investment and growth rates, other things being equal (De Piñeres and Ferrantino 1997). A diversified export portfolio may also enable a country to more fully capture cross-industry learning spillovers and to capitalize on the existence of backward and forward linkages (Riedel 1976). Figure 5.7 shows that Korea's exports are, in fact, reasonably well diversified. It reports the Herfindahl-Hirschman Index (HHI) of squared product shares

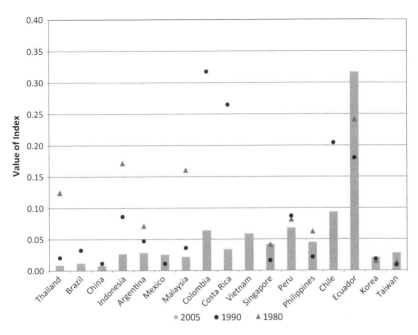

Figure 5.7. Export Diversification, 1980–2005
Diversification is measured by the Herfindahl-Hirschman Index. Source: Duran, Mulder, and
Onodera (2008), fig. 6, with Korea and Taiwan added. Calculations based on UN Comtrade data.

as a measure of export diversification.[22] In 1980 Korea already stood out
for its relatively diversified export bundle, reflecting not only the continued dominance of labor-intensive exports but also the increasing importance of the exports of the heavy and chemical industries. Say what you
will about the merits and demerits of the Heavy and Chemical Industry
Drive, it seems to have delivered a relatively well-diversified export portfolio, something that may have eased adjustment in the difficult circumstances of the early 1980s.[23]

The cross-country literature can be used to infer the difference this
relatively high level of export diversification made for economic growth.
Al-Marhubi (2000) regresses the average annual rate of growth of real
GDP per capita over the period from 1961 to 1988 on the HHI of export
concentration.[24] His estimates imply that reducing the degree of export
concentration circa 1990 from 0.095 (Indonesia's level) to 0.022 (the
value observed for Korea), would have increased annual average growth
by two-tenths of a percentage point, not a negligible amount.

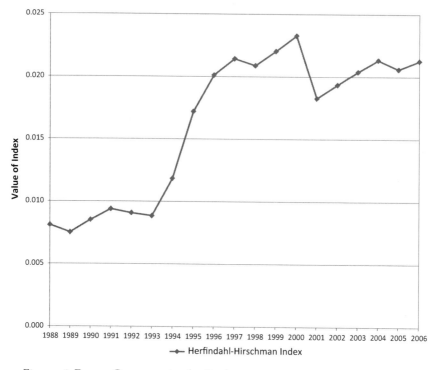

Figure 5.8. Export Concentration by Product, 1988–2006
Product classification based on the six-digit level of *Harmonized Commodity Description and Coding System,* 1992. Calculations based on UN Comtrade data.

Figure 5.8 shows the diversification of Korean exports, again as measured by the HHI, at a higher level of resolution. There is some evidence that the concentration of exports in a small number of important products has been rising over time. The products responsible are semiconductors, computer-related products, consumer electronics, electrical machinery, automobiles, and ships. It may be that the rising concentration of Korean exports of these products reflects the receding role of industrial policy, which in earlier periods continually pushed Korean producers into new sectors. The trend may simply reflect the comparative advantage of an increasingly mature middle-income country and the capacity of a more financially developed economy, which can use financial markets to partially insure against risks, to specialize more extensively along lines of comparative advantage.

We can also analyze how well Korea has done in terms of increasing the range and variety of its exports to different markets (that is, in developing the extensive margin of its exports). Following Bergin and Lin (2008), the extensive margin is defined as the varieties that the source country exports relative to all varieties the destination country imports, where varieties are weighted by their importance in world exports to the destination country. In Table 5.6 this measure of the extensive margin is regressed on the standard arguments of the gravity model along with dummy variables for Korea. Precise results vary, depending on estimator (in particular, whether we control for both country and year fixed effects). Controlling for only country fixed effects, there is again evidence of an inverted-U-shaped pattern. That is, Korea underperformed for a country of its characteristics on the extensive margin in the 1960s. This is consistent with our gravity-model-theoretic coefficients for the total volume of exports.[25] It is also not surprising, given Korea's prior history of exporting only a narrow range and small amount of mainly agricultural- and resource-based products and that significant opening of trade occurred only around the middle of the decade. The country's performance on the extensive margin turns positive in the 1970s, with exports from the heavy and chemical industries supplementing exports by labor-intensive sectors, and even more so in the 1980s with the emergence of the first high-tech exports. But there is reversion to the mean in the 1990s, when the government moderated the pressure of policy to force the economy upstream and the pace of aggregate growth slowed.[26] All this is consistent with our earlier picture of reversion to the mean in recent years. It is not consistent with prevailing pessimism about Korean export performance.

A related perspective would consider not the diversity of export products but the diversity of export destinations, on the grounds that a more diversified portfolio of destinations better insulates industry from foreign shocks. Figure 5.9 shows that Korea has become less dependent on a small number of export markets over time. It suggests that the significant increase in the geographical diversification of Korean exports was concentrated at the start of the period. It is associated with a decline in the U.S. share—what with the 1991 recession in the United States being superimposed on the secular downward trend in the dominance of the U.S. market—and the concurrent emergence of Singapore, Indonesia, Thailand, and, above all, China as increasingly significant export markets.

Table 5.6. Extensive Margin of Korea's Trade Is Not Wholly Explained by the Arguments of Standard Gravity Model

	Logarithm of the extensive margin				
Dependent variable	Country fixed effects		Country fixed effects		Country fixed effects+year fixed effects
Currency union	0.595**	0.595**	0.527**	0.527**	0.526**
	(0.042)	(0.042)	(0.042)	(0.042)	(0.042)
Exchange rate volatility	−0.464**	−0.466**	−0.251**	−0.251**	−0.246**
	(0.046)	(0.046)	(0.047)	(0.047)	(0.047)
Log-relative real per capita GDP	1.619**	1.613**	1.613**	1.613**	1.599**
	(0.013)	(0.014)	(0.014)	(0.014)	(0.014)
Log-relative population	1.434**	1.435**	1.383**	1.383**	1.387**
	(0.011)	(0.011)	(0.012)	(0.012)	(0.012)
Log distance	−0.794**	−0.794**	−0.790**	−0.790**	−0.791**
	(0.006)	(0.006)	(0.006)	(0.006)	(0.006)
Common language	0.451**	0.451**	0.451**	0.451**	0.450**
	(0.010)	(0.010)	(0.010)	(0.010)	(0.010)
Border	0.430**	0.430**	0.420**	0.420**	0.418**
	(0.026)	(0.026)	(0.026)	(0.026)	(0.026)
Free trade agreement	−0.078*	−0.077*	−0.037	−0.037	−0.034
	(0.036)	(0.036)	(0.036)	(0.036)	(0.036)
Currently in colonial relationship	−0.007	−0.007	−0.05	−0.05	−0.053
	(0.102)	(0.102)	(0.101)	(0.101)	(0.101)

	(1)	(2)	(3)	(4)	(5)	(6)
Ever in colonial relationship	0.768**	0.768**	0.768**	0.791**	0.791**	0.792**
	(0.027)	(0.027)	(0.027)	(0.027)	(0.027)	(0.027)
Korea dummy		0.006			0.027	
		(0.025)			(0.025)	
Korea 1960s			−0.431**			−0.475**
			(0.075)			(0.075)
Korea 1970s			0.088			−0.056
			(0.048)			(0.048)
Korea 1980s			0.110*			0.329**
			(0.051)			(0.051)
Korea 1990–1995			0.032			0.096
			(0.056)			(0.056)
Korea 1996–2000			−0.016			−0.013
			(0.058)			(0.058)
Observations	176,094	176,094	176,094	176,094	176,094	176,094
R-squared	0.29	0.29	0.29	0.3	0.3	0.3

Note: The dependent variable is a bilateral measure of the extensive margin of exports, constructed following Bergin and Lin (2008). Log relative real GDP per capita is the log of real GDP per capita of the exporter relative to all countries exporting to the same importer. Log relative population is calculated in the same manner. Both variables are collected from Penn World Table 6.2. Exchange rate volatility is the standard deviation of the monthly bilateral exchange rate changes in the corresponding year, where the exchange rate is from the IMF's International Financial Statistics database. All other variables are from Rose (2000). The Korea dummy equals unity when Korea is the exporter. The Korea decade dummy is the interaction of the Korea dummy and the decade dummy.

** and * indicate statistical significance at the 1- and 5-percent levels, respectively.

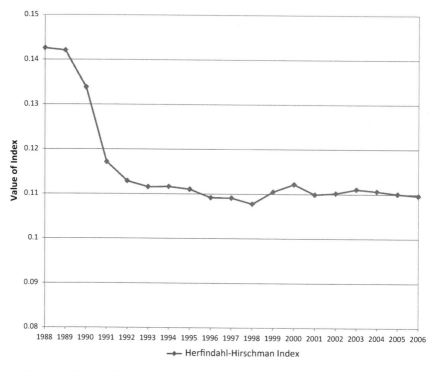

Figure 5.9. Export Concentration by Market, 1988–2006

Markets measured by countries of export destinations. Higher value indicates that Korea's exports are more dependent on a small number of export markets. Calculations based on data from International Monetary Fund, *Direction of Trade Statistics Yearbook, 2008.*

Table 5.7 lists the top countries, in descending order, accounting for the top 70 percent of Korean exports at five-year intervals, starting in 1987. The list lengthens with time, indicative of increased export-market diversification. The share of exports destined for the United States declines from more than a third in 1988 to barely a sixth in 2006, by which time China overtakes the United States as the single most important destination for Korean exports. The same is true of the Japanese market, whose share of Korea's exports declines from a fifth to less than a tenth over the period. Singapore and Hong Kong are significant Asian destinations all through the period, reflecting Singapore's role as both an importer and an exporter of electronic components and products, and Hong Kong's role as an entrepôt for trade with China. One also sees the addition to the list of a number of Asian countries, reflecting Korea's growing involvement in intra-Asian trade.

Table 5.8 shows the shares of Korea's exports of manufactures destined for different national and regional markets, comparing it with Japan, China, East Asia as a whole, the United States, and the European Union. Table 5.8c, on manufacturing imports, shows that intra–East Asian trade accounts for a growing share of the region's trade and that what is true of the region as a whole is also true of Korea, to a slightly lesser extent. The export percentages, in Table 5.8b, are lower for both East Asia and Korea, reflecting the fact that more final-goods exports continue to be destined for the United States, the European Union, and other extraregional markets. There is little about the Korean figures that stands out relative to the East Asian norm.

We can also ask whether Korean firms are encountering stiffer competition in their principal export markets by constructing an HHI for each product and each export market. Following Hennessy and Lapan (2007), the summary indicator of the intensity of export-market competition is then the sum of Herfindahl indices across all products and markets, weighted by the export shares of each market. The results suggest increasing overlap between Korea's exports and the exports of other countries active in the same markets, suggesting that competition is becoming more intense (Figure 5.10). The most noticeable increase is in the second half of the 1990s. The main countries responsible for the increase in overlap in this period are China, Thailand, Malaysia, Singapore, Japan, Germany, the United Kingdom, and the United States (Figure 5.11). We see here the other leading producers of consumer electronics, semiconductors, computer-related equipment, electrical machinery, and automobiles that are increasingly important to Korea's export basket. Of course, insofar as this suggests that international competition is becoming more intense, this effect is by no means limited to the case of Korea.

Finally, it is worth looking more closely at competition from China, since this is so often emphasized as a factor affecting the profitability and fortunes of Korean companies. Figure 5.12 confirms that Chinese competition is increasingly evident in the Korean market itself: the share of Korea's imports originating in China has risen steadily from essentially zero in the mid-1980s to nearly one-fifth today. Figure 5.13 shows that China is, similarly, increasingly present in the foreign markets to which Korean companies export; the figure shows China's and Korea's shares in the imports of the markets to which Korea exports.[27] (Shares are weighted

Table 5.7. Principal Destinations of Korean Exports (Countries Accounting for 70 Percent of Total Exports)

	1988		1991		1994		1997	
Destination	Share (%)	Destination	Share (%)	Destination	Share (%)	Destination	Share (%)
United States	35.4	United States	25.7	United States	20.4	United States	15.2
Japan	19.8	Japan	17.1	Japan	13.3	Japan	10.3
Hong Kong	5.9	Hong Kong	6.6	Hong Kong	7.9	China	9.4
Germany	3.9	Germany	4.4	China	6.1	Hong Kong	8.1
United Kingdom	3.2	Singapore	3.7	Germany	4.3	Singapore	4.0
Canada	2.8	Liberia	2.9	Singapore	4.1	Germany	3.3
		United Kingdom	2.4	Indonesia	2.5	Malaysia	3.0
		Canada	2.3	Panama	1.9	United Kingdom	2.8
		Indonesia	1.9	Thailand	1.8	Indonesia	2.5
		Thailand	1.8	United Kingdom	1.8	Philippines	1.8
		Netherlands	1.6	Liberia	1.8	Thailand	1.6
				Malaysia	1.6	Australia	1.5
				Canada	1.4	Switzerland	1.4
				Mexico	1.3	Panama	1.3
						Russia	1.2
						Brazil	1.2
						Vietnam	1.1
						Liberia	1.1

Source: Data from IMF, Direction of Trade Statistics database, 2008.

2000		2003		2006	
Destination	Share (%)	Destination	Share (%)	Destination	Share (%)
United States	21.9	China	18.1	China	21.3
Japan	11.9	United States	17.7	United States	13.3
China	10.7	Japan	8.9	Japan	8.1
Hong Kong	6.2	Hong Kong	7.6	Hong Kong	5.9
Singapore	3.3	Germany	2.9	Germany	3.1
United Kingdom	3.1	Singapore	2.4	Singapore	2.9
Germany	3.0	United Kingdom	2.1	Mexico	2.0
Malaysia	2.0	Malaysia	2.0	United Kingdom	1.7
Indonesia	2.0	Indonesia	1.7	India	1.7
Philippines	2.0	Australia	1.7	Russia	1.6
Netherlands	1.5	Philippines	1.5	Malaysia	1.5
Australia	1.5	India	1.5	Indonesia	1.5
Canada	1.4	Canada	1.4	Australia	1.5
		Vietnam	1.3	Italy	1.3
				Thailand	1.3
				Philippines	1.2

Table 5.8a. Direction of Manufacturing Trade: Exports Plus Imports

Region/country	Year	East Asia	China	Japan	Korea	United States	European Union	Other	World value ($ billion)
East Asia	1992	50.1%	8.9%	12.1%	3.9%	20.7%	15.8%	13.3%	999.9
	1996	53.1%	10.6%	12.8%	4.7%	18.6%	13.6%	14.7%	1,987.4
	2000	53.8%	12.0%	11.8%	4.7%	20.2%	14.4%	11.6%	2,106.8
	2006	59.2%	18.3%	10.0%	5.7%	14.5%	13.1%	13.2%	3,846.1
China	1992	65.8%	—	13.4%	2.2%	10.4%	12.0%	11.8%	106.8
	1996	56.5%	—	21.1%	7.2%	14.9%	14.1%	14.6%	231.2
	2000	53.8%	—	18.0%	7.1%	17.3%	17.0%	12.0%	316.5
	2006	53.4%	—	12.8%	8.4%	15.3%	15.2%	16.1%	1,146.7
Japan	1992	37.1%	5.2%	—	6.6%	26.1%	19.4%	17.5%	302.2
	1996	44.1%	9.2%	—	7.1%	24.2%	13.9%	17.8%	528.4
	2000	46.3%	11.3%	—	6.7%	26.4%	16.8%	10.5%	489.4
	2006	54.7%	22.2%	—	7.8%	18.6%	14.6%	12.1%	645.4
Korea	1992	43.5%	3.2%	22.3%	—	24.3%	14.8%	17.4%	96.3
	1996	46.2%	7.7%	18.8%	—	19.8%	13.3%	20.7%	205.7
	2000	48.9%	10.1%	17.5%	—	22.7%	13.9%	14.6%	199.4
	2006	55.6%	22.2%	14.4%	—	13.4%	13.5%	17.6%	359.7

United States	1992	36.7%	4.6%	14.5%	3.7%	—	21.5%	41.7%	548.6
	1996	35.5%	5.6%	12.6%	3.7%	—	19.1%	45.4%	979.9
	2000	35.9%	8.1%	10.9%	3.7%	—	21.1%	43.0%	1,204.9
	2006	37.0%	15.7%	7.5%	3.0%	—	21.3%	41.7%	1,603.4
European Union	1992	9.8%	1.4%	3.8%	0.8%	7.6%	57.4%	25.2%	1,674.6
	1996	10.0%	1.6%	2.9%	0.9%	7.8%	54.3%	27.8%	2,644.8
	2000	11.2%	2.7%	3.2%	1.0%	10.2%	56.5%	22.1%	2,657.9
	2006	12.4%	5.1%	2.4%	1.2%	8.3%	56.0%	23.3%	4,328.5
World	1992	24.1%	3.7%	7.6%	2.0%	13.8%	39.1%	23.1%	3,977.3
	1996	25.8%	4.7%	7.2%	2.5%	13.8%	34.7%	25.7%	7,292.5
	2000	28.0%	6.4%	7.2%	2.6%	17.8%	30.2%	24.0%	8,411.4
	2006	31.2%	11.2%	5.6%	3.0%	13.5%	29.7%	25.6%	1,3945.5

Source: Calculations based on UN Comtrade data (Standard International Trade Classification, Rev. 3).

Note: Regions or countries in the first column are exporters and those across are importers.

Table 5.8b. Direction of Manufacturing Trade: Exports

Region/country	Year	East Asia	China	Japan	Korea	United States	European Union	Other	World value ($ billion)
East Asia	1992	43.2%	7.5%	5.0%	3.2%	23.7%	16.0%	17.0%	579.7
	1996	51.6%	10.0%	8.5%	4.1%	20.5%	12.9%	14.9%	1,025.8
	2000	47.1%	10.0%	7.1%	3.6%	22.9%	15.2%	14.8%	1,201.5
	2006	51.1%	15.9%	6.2%	3.8%	16.8%	14.0%	18.1%	2,226.4
China	1992	66.3%	—	8.3%	1.5%	11.0%	9.3%	13.5%	53.2
	1996	53.4%	—	18.9%	4.6%	18.7%	13.2%	14.7%	119.8
	2000	43.3%	—	13.8%	3.2%	23.4%	16.6%	16.6%	173.4
	2006	38.0%	—	8.4%	3.8%	21.2%	17.3%	23.5%	662.2
Japan	1992	37.3%	3.6%	—	6.0%	25.2%	17.7%	19.8%	224.9
	1996	47.7%	6.0%	—	8.0%	24.0%	13.1%	15.2%	308.1
	2000	44.5%	7.0%	—	6.8%	26.5%	16.5%	12.5%	329.8
	2006	51.8%	16.4%	—	8.1%	19.2%	13.7%	15.3%	412.2
Korea	1992	39.3%	2.9%	12.0%	—	23.9%	12.3%	24.5%	54.2
	1996	52.2%	9.5%	11.6%	—	15.6%	10.0%	22.2%	100.0
	2000	45.8%	11.3%	9.2%	—	20.1%	13.7%	20.5%	117.1
	2006	51.4%	23.2%	7.3%	—	11.3%	12.5%	24.8%	220.2

United States	1992	23.4%	1.4%	8.0%	3.0%	—	22.5%	54.2%	258.6
	1996	28.5%	1.7%	10.0%	4.2%	—	18.9%	52.6%	458.9
	2000	25.3%	1.8%	7.4%	3.6%	—	21.7%	52.9%	529.3
	2006	23.9%	4.3%	5.4%	3.3%	—	21.6%	54.5%	657.0
European Union	1992	6.7%	0.8%	1.9%	0.7%	7.1%	55.2%	30.9%	864.4
	1996	8.6%	1.0%	2.1%	1.0%	7.2%	52.9%	31.3%	1,393.3
	2000	7.4%	1.2%	1.8%	0.7%	10.0%	56.6%	26.1%	1,380.6
	2006	7.5%	2.1%	1.5%	0.8%	8.8%	55.0%	28.8%	2,306.7
World	1992	19.7%	2.8%	3.6%	1.7%	14.3%	37.3%	28.7%	2,009.9
	1996	24.2%	3.8%	5.3%	2.4%	13.9%	33.5%	28.4%	3,649.6
	2000	22.6%	4.1%	4.3%	2.0%	19.0%	29.7%	28.7%	4,200.8
	2006	24.0%	7.0%	3.6%	2.1%	15.3%	28.7%	31.9%	7,135.1

Source: Calculations based on UN Comtrade data (Standard International Trade Classification, Rev. 3).

Table 5.8c. Direction of Manufacturing Trade: Imports

Region/country	Year	East Asia	China	Japan	Korea	United States	European Union	Other	World value ($ billion)
East Asia	1992	59.7%	10.9%	21.9%	4.9%	16.6%	15.7%	8.0%	420.2
	1996	54.6%	11.3%	17.4%	5.4%	16.6%	14.3%	14.5%	961.6
	2000	62.7%	14.7%	18.1%	6.1%	16.5%	13.2%	7.5%	905.3
	2006	70.4%	21.5%	15.3%	8.3%	11.3%	11.9%	6.4%	1,619.7
China	1992	65.3%	—	18.5%	3.0%	9.9%	14.6%	10.2%	53.6
	1996	59.8%	—	23.4%	10.0%	10.8%	15.0%	14.5%	111.5
	2000	66.4%	4.0%	23.0%	11.7%	9.8%	17.4%	6.4%	143.1
	2006	74.5%	12.4%	18.8%	14.7%	7.2%	12.3%	6.0%	484.5
Japan	1992	36.4%	9.6%	—	8.3%	28.7%	24.1%	10.8%	77.3
	1996	39.1%	13.5%	—	5.8%	24.5%	15.0%	21.3%	220.3
	2000	50.0%	20.4%	—	6.4%	26.0%	17.5%	6.5%	159.6
	2006	59.9%	32.3%	—	7.2%	17.7%	16.2%	6.2%	233.1
Korea	1992	48.8%	3.6%	35.6%	—	24.8%	18.0%	8.4%	42.1
	1996	40.5%	6.0%	25.5%	—	23.7%	16.5%	19.3%	105.7
	2000	53.4%	8.2%	29.2%	—	26.4%	14.1%	6.1%	82.3
	2006	62.0%	20.7%	25.6%	—	16.7%	15.1%	6.2%	139.5

United States	1992	48.7%	7.4%	20.3%	4.3%	—	20.7%	30.6%	290.0
	1996	41.6%	9.0%	14.8%	3.3%	—	19.4%	39.0%	521.0
	2000	44.2%	13.1%	13.6%	3.8%	—	20.5%	35.3%	675.7
	2006	46.1%	23.6%	9.0%	2.9%	—	21.1%	32.9%	946.3
European Union	1992	13.1%	2.0%	5.8%	0.9%	8.2%	59.7%	19.1%	810.2
	1996	11.6%	2.3%	3.8%	0.8%	8.6%	55.9%	23.9%	1,251.6
	2000	15.3%	4.2%	4.7%	1.2%	10.5%	56.4%	17.8%	1,277.3
	2006	18.0%	8.5%	3.3%	1.6%	7.7%	57.2%	17.0%	2,021.8
World	1992	28.6%	4.6%	11.7%	2.4%	13.2%	40.9%	17.3%	1,967.5
	1996	27.4%	5.6%	9.1%	2.5%	13.7%	35.9%	23.0%	3,642.9
	2000	33.4%	8.7%	10.0%	3.1%	16.7%	30.7%	19.2%	4,210.6
	2006	38.8%	15.7%	7.7%	4.0%	11.5%	30.7%	19.0%	6,810.4

Source: Calculations based on UN Comtrade data (Standard International Trade Classification, Rev. 3).

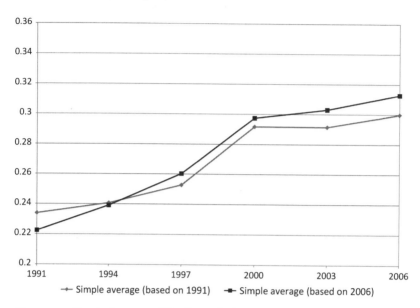

Figure 5.10. Simple Average of Similarity Index
The average competition index, based on the top ten most competitive countries, 1991 and 2006.
Calculations based on UN Comtrade data.

by the relative importance of different national markets for Korea's export sales.) The excess of China's share over Korea's widens steadily. Figure 5.14 shows that circa 1990 China was a consequential competitor in markets for Korea's ten most important exports only in the case of the declining labor-intensive products—footwear and children's toys. By 1995 it has surfaced as a consequential competitor in cargo vessels, iron and steel, and telecommunications equipment (transmitters, televisions, cellular handsets, and the like). By 2005 Chinese competition is evident across the board, although China has attained significant market shares relative to Korea only in optical instruments and electronic components (and, to a lesser extent, oceangoing vessels).

The Technological Sophistication of Exports

In addition to the diversity of exports, their technology content also serves as an indicator of the economy's success in moving into the production of more sophisticated exports. Doing so insulates the economy against competitive pressure from lower-wage economies like China.

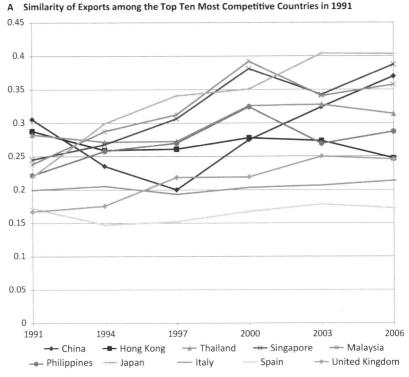

A   Similarity of Exports among the Top Ten Most Competitive Countries in 1991

Figure 5.11. Similarity of Exports of Korea's Principal Competitors
The export similarity index is constructed by following Hennessy and Lapan (2007) to measure how similar are export shares of destination countries and commodities for each competitor country. (*A*) Similarity of exports among the top ten most competitive countries in 1991. (*B*) Similarity of exports among the top ten most competitive countries in 2006. Calculations based on UN Comtrade data.

Some observers argue, in addition, that medium- and high-tech products offer more scope for learning by doing, and hence for productivity growth, and that they are less subject to declining terms of trade insofar as demand for such products is elastic with respect to income.

Figure 5.15 divides exports into high-, medium-, and low-tech manufactures (as well as into resource-based manufactures and exports of natural resources themselves).[28] It shows a shift in the technology content of South Korea's exports since the 1980s. Two decades ago the country was a large net exporter of low-tech products, ran balanced trade in medium-tech products, and was a net importer of high-tech products.[29]

B   Similarity of Exports among the Top Ten Most Competitive Countries in 2006

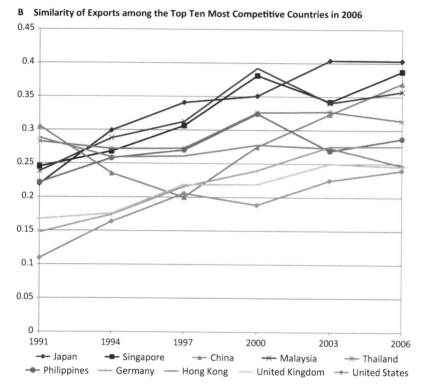

Figure 5.11. (Continued)

By 2004–2006, in contrast, Korea had become a very large net exporter of medium- and high-tech products. Comparably pronounced shifts are not evident in Latin America, China, or even the other East Asian countries.[30] (Taiwan is the exception that proves the rule.) Figure 5.15 suggests that in 1979–1980 Korea still relied heavily on exports of low-tech manufactures; by 2004–2006, in contrast, the portion of the bar representing exports of low-tech manufactures has almost disappeared. Note how this remains the most important segment of Chinese exports; thus, by moving up market Korea has succeeded in insulating itself, at least in part, from Chinese competition.[31] Again, this conclusion is not consistent with the "hollowing-out" story nor with the pessimistic interpretation of Korean export performance.

Figure 5.16 adds an important point. It suggests that the medium- and high-technology share of Korean exports was already high by emerging-

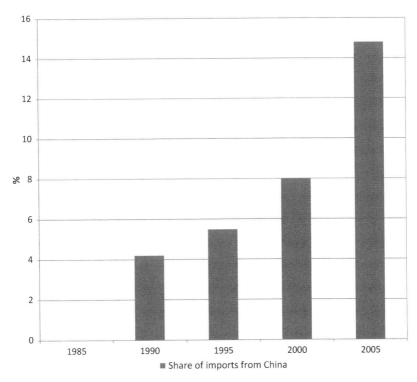

Figure 5.12. Share of Korea's Imports from China
Share of imports from China is calculated by dividing Korea's imports from China by total Korean imports. Data from International Monetary Fund, Direction of Trade Statistics database. The value in 1991 is used for 1990 because the 1990 data are missing.

market standards in 1990. Of the countries in our comparison group, only Singapore and Taiwan had equally high shares of medium- and high-tech products in its total exports at this relatively early date. This presumably reflects the fact that in the 1980s those governments were already making efforts to push producers up the technological ladder, with subsidies and tax breaks for R&D and technologically sophisticated investments. In other words, South Korea is a successful exporter of medium- and high-tech products because it had already started down this road fully three decades ago.

Within many of these medium- and high-tech industries, however, Korean exporters appear to occupy the bottom end of the market. We can see this by analyzing data on the unit value of exports to one particular

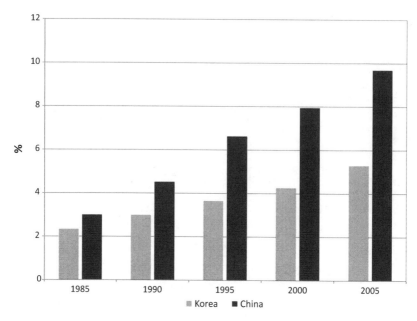

Figure 5.13. Shares of Korea and China in the Total Imports of Countries to Which Korea Exports

Korea's share is defined as the average share of imports from Korea in the total imports of countries to which Korea exports. China's share is defined similarly for the same countries to which Korea exports. Korean exports are used as weights in calculating both averages. Calculations based on International Monetary Fund, Direction of Trade Statistics database.

market, the United States, for which finely disaggregated data are available, where unit values are taken as a measure of technology content. Then, following Schott (2008), we regress the log unit value for each country-product observation on a vector of country characteristics (real GDP per capita, skill abundance, whether the exporter is landlocked, distance from the United States), controls (the ad valorem U.S. tariff rate and ad valorem trade cost), and dummy variables for Korea interacted with various years. We estimate this relationship over the period from 1972 to 2005.[32] The results take as given the industry composition of exports—and the division between high-, medium-, and low-tech—and ask whether, within those categories, Korea is exporting high-value or low-value goods.

The estimates, in Table 5.9, indicate that relative export unit values rise with skill abundance at an increasing rate. Landlocked countries and countries far from the U.S. market tend to export high-unit-value goods,

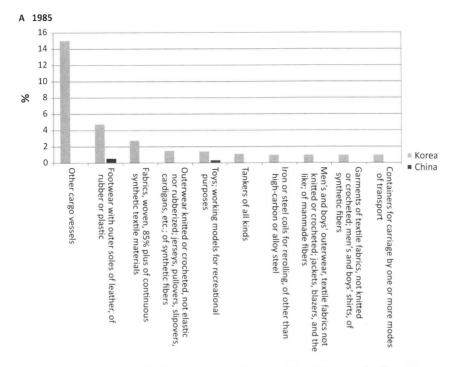

Figure 5.14. Korean and Chinese Market Shares in World Exports for Ten Most Important Export Products of Korea, Selected Years
(A) 1985. (B) 1990. (C) 1995. (D) 2000. (E) 2005. Calculations based on UN Comtrade data, rev. 2.

reflecting high transport costs. The most important results concern the dummy variables for Korea, which distinguish successive decades as before. Except in the 1980s, when the dummy for Korea is indistinguishable from zero, the coefficients in question are consistently negative. These results suggest that while Korea has been moving up the technology ladder into the production and export of increasingly sophisticated goods, it continues to occupy the bottom end of the niches in question. It exports Hyundais, not BMWs. When we add a vector of year dummy variables for the decade dummy variables for Korea, we confirm that this phenomenon postdates the 1980s and find that it has grown increasingly pronounced over time. The coefficients on the annual dummy variables are plotted in Figure 5.17.[33]

Our interpretation of this pattern is as follows. The further Korea has stretched into the production of high-tech products, the greater has

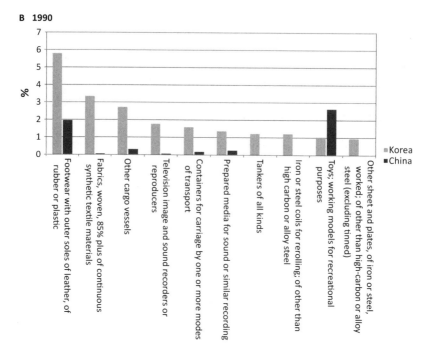

Figure 5.14. Korean and Chinese Market Shares in World Exports for Ten Most Important Export Products of Korea, Selected Years *(Continued)*

been its tendency to concentrate on the low end of the markets in question. The tendency for Korea to export low-end high-tech products does not appear to be simply a function of government policies like the Heavy and Chemical Industry Drive, which pushed the economy into relatively sophisticated high-tech industries before it was ready. Rather, it appears that the continuing strategic decisions of the chaebol may have worked in this direction. Table 5.10 shows that Korea's focus on the low end of the market for various kinds of high-tech products is associated with a growing share of exports accounted for by the chaebol (for present purposes, we take "large firms" and "chaebol" as synonymous).[34] This may be a long-term legacy of Korea's policies in the 1970s and after, which encouraged the chaebol to enter capital-intensive high-tech activities—for example, chip fabrication—in contrast to Taiwan, where small producers with freer access to credit specialized in higher-end, more

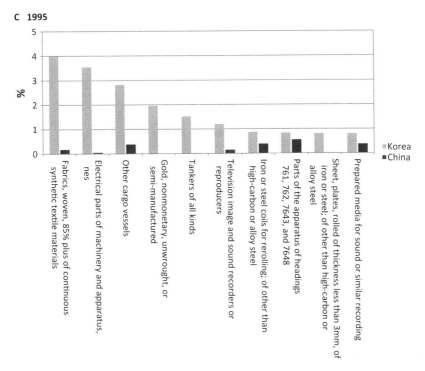

Figure 5.14. Korean and Chinese Market Shares in World Exports for Ten Most Important Export Products of Korea, Selected Years *(Continued)*

human-capital-intensive segments of the same sectors, such as software design.

A final approach to gauging the sophistication of Korea's exports follows Hausmann, Hwang, and Rodrik (2007). This involves assigning an average income level (per capita GDP in purchasing-power-parity terms) to each commodity export as a function of the incomes of the countries observed to export that good.[35] The average income level is constructed by weighting the incomes of the countries exporting that commodity by their shares in global exports of the commodity in question. We do this for a sample of 90 countries for which complete data are available for the period 1962 to 2000. We can then compare the income level associated with Korea's portfolio of exports with its actual per capita GDP. The resulting comparison can be thought of as a summary measure of the

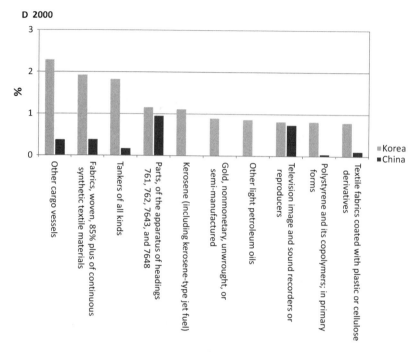

Figure 5.14. Korean and Chinese Market Shares in World Exports for Ten Most Important Export Products of Korea, Selected Years *(Continued)*

sophistication of Korean exports relative to what would be expected of a country at its stage of economic development.

In Figure 5.18 *(A)* we see that the income level associated with Korea's export basket exceeded its actual GDP by nearly a factor of two throughout the 1960s and 1970s. By successfully exporting labor-intensive products in the 1960s and a combination of labor-intensive goods and the products of the heavy and mechanical industries in the 1970s, Korea succeeded in both periods in exporting goods associated with higher income countries. Strikingly, in the 1980s, precisely when the country began moving into higher-tech exports, the gap between the income level typically associated with those exports and Korea's own income level began to diminish. By the mid-1990s and on the eve of the financial crisis, Korea was producing exactly the kinds of exports that one would predict on the basis of its income level and the behavior of other countries.

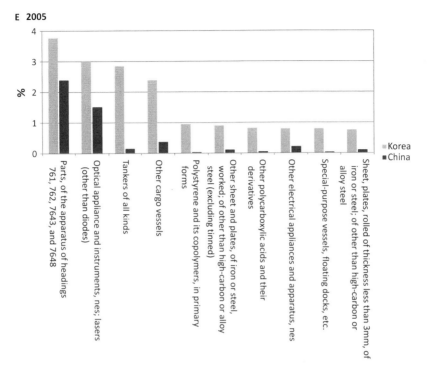

Figure 5.14. Korean and Chinese Market Shares in World Exports for Ten Most Important Export Products of Korea, Selected Years *(Continued)*

Whether or not this is disturbing is a matter of interpretation. The most obvious interpretation, it seems to us, is that Korea is now squarely on the trajectory predicted for a country with a per capita GDP in the $15,000 to $20,000 range. Its exports are neither more nor less sophisticated than one would have predicted. Again, to the extent that there is angst about the country's export performance, this reflects the extent to which it outperformed expectations, not just in terms of the volume of exports but also in terms of their sophistication, in the earlier period of "miracle growth."

The comparison with Taiwan is also reassuring. Just like Korea, the products Taiwan exported all through the 1960s and 1970s were associated with countries with higher per capita incomes. Like Korea, the gap closed in the 1980s; indeed, it closed somewhat earlier in Taiwan. This suggests that Taiwan now exports products that are typically associated

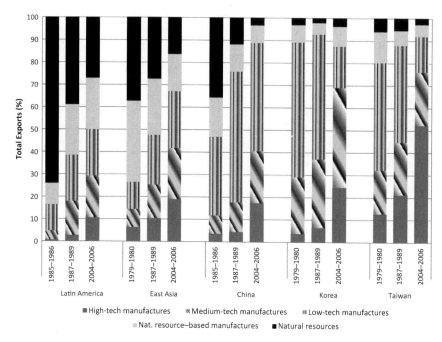

Figure 5.15. Export Composition by Technology Content, 1970s to 2000s, as Percent of Total Exports
Technology classification follows Lall (2000). The countries included in the regions vary depending on availability of data. Source: Duran, Mulder, and Onodera (2008), fig. 7, with Korea and Taiwan values added. Calculations based on UN Comtrade data.

with lower per capita incomes than its own. There is a sense in which Korean observers should be reassured by the comparison.

Has the Export–Economic Growth Link Loosened? Is China the Cause?

Overall, then, Korean exports have been holding up relatively well, significantly better than one would expect of a country with South Korea's characteristics. The export basket is diverse, and many of its constituents have a relatively high technology content. The economy, including its exports, may be growing more slowly than before, but there is little evidence that this slowdown is being driven by a loss of international competitiveness. In particular, there is little sign in the aggregate data that the rise of neighboring China as an export powerhouse is having a negative impact.

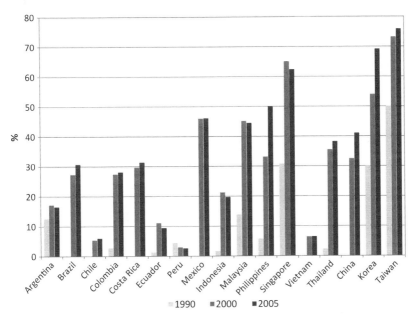

Figure 5.16. Share of Medium- and High-Tech Products in Exports, 1990, 2000, and 2005
Technology classification follows Lall (2000). Source: Duran, Mulder, and Onodera (2008), fig. 8, with Korea and Taiwan values added. Calculations based on UN Comtrade data.

This last conclusion is not entirely surprising. Since the late 1970s Korea has been an important producer and exporter of not just consumer goods but also capital goods. And China has a voracious appetite for capital equipment. Moreover, Korean firms have capitalized on the presence of abundant supplies of low-cost labor in neighboring countries, to which it exports parts and components (P&C) that are then assembled into final products and sold onward into third markets. This has been an important way for Korea to maintain its international competitiveness in the face of rising domestic labor costs.

Clearly, this is not an entirely happy story for workers in assembly operations in Korea who see their jobs moving offshore and for whom finding new jobs in expanding sectors is not easy. Figure 5.19 shows how employment shares in the textile, apparel, and leather industries in manufacturing changed in the past fifteen years. Table 5.11, based on survey data for Korean companies, confirms that the number of textile- and

Table 5.9. Korea's Relative Export Unit Values Are Not Wholly Predicted by the Standard Gravity Model

	(1) OLS	(2) Robust Clustering
Log (real per capita GDP)	−0.594**	−0.594
	(0.063)	(0.680)
Log (real per capita GDP) squared	0.047**	0.047
	(0.003)	(0.040)
Log (skill abundance)	−0.360**	−0.360*
	(0.024)	(0.147)
Log (skill abundance) squared	0.117**	0.117*
	(0.007)	(0.057)
Korea 1970s	0.218**	0.218**
	(0.060)	(0.073)
Korea 1980s	0.041	0.041
	(−0.025)	(−0.073)
Korea 1990s	−0.546**	−0.546**
	(0.021)	(0.060)
Korea 2000s	−0.752**	−0.752**
	(0.027)	(0.057)
Log (distance)	5.986**	5.986**
	(0.109)	(1.617))
Log (distance) squared	−0.358**	−0.358**
	(0.007)	(0.099)
Landlocked	0.301**	0.301**
	(0.008)	(0.065)
Constant	−0.974**	−0.974**
	(0.002)	(0.033)
Product-year fixed effects	Yes	Yes
Robust cluster	—	Yes
R-squared	0.04	0.04
Sample	511,843	511,843

Note: Column 1 reports ordinary least squares (OLS) estimates, and column 2 reports robust standard errors (SE) adjusted for clustering at the export country level. The dependent variable is log unit value of U.S. imports, disaggregated by source country and product. Unit values are derived by dividing total values by quantity in the UN Comtrade database. Per capita GDP is obtained from the Penn World Table 6.2. Skill abundance is capital as constructed by Barro and Lee (2000), with missing values filled in by affine interpolation. Geographical distance and landlocked values are from Rose (2000). Four Korea dummies are included (decades represent data for 1978–1979, 1980–1989, 1990–1999, and 2000–2004).

** and * indicate statistical significance at the 1- and 5-percent levels, respectively.

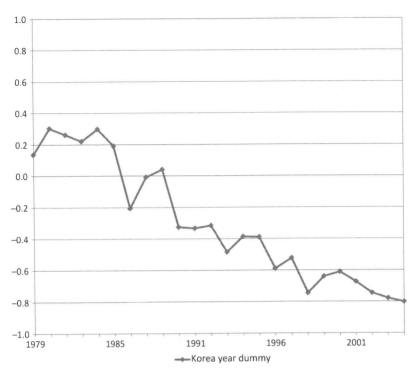

Figure 5.17. Value of the Dummy Variable for South Korea in Export Unit Value Equation

The Korea dummy is estimated from the same equation reported in Table 5.9 except that the decade dummies are replaced by year dummies.

apparel-manufacturing firms moving production offshore is especially high. The employment share in textiles shrank from 11.7 percent of the labor force (340,000 workers) in 1991 to 4.9 percent (142,000 workers) in 2006. The employment shares of the apparel and leather industries also fell dramatically, from 7.2 and 6.2 percent, respectively, in 1991 to 3.9 and 1.0 percent in 2006. Total employment expanded enormously, of course, over this period. But no doubt there were adjustment costs and distributional consequences.

The question is whether the positive impact of Korea's growing integration into regional supply chains and production networks on the profitability of firms producing traded goods also shows up as a positive impact on the growth of output, investment, and employment. Table 5.12

Table 5.10. Exports by Enterprise Size

Year	Total exports ($ thousand)	SMEs	LEs	Public sectors & etc.
1985	30,283,122	27.8%	68.2%	4.1%
1986	34,714,470	35.2%	60.8%	4.0%
1987	47,280,927	37.7%	57.6%	4.7%
1988	60,696,388	37.9%	61.9%	0.2%
1989	62,377,174	41.8%	58.1%	0.2%
1990	65,015,730	42.1%	57.7%	0.1%
1991	71,870,121	39.9%	59.9%	0.2%
1992	76,631,515	40.0%	59.9%	0.1%
1993	82,235,866	42.8%	57.1%	0.1%
1994	96,013,237	42.4%	57.4%	0.2%
1995	125,057,988	39.6%	60.2%	0.2%
1996	129,715,137	41.8%	58.1%	0.1%
1997	136,164,204	41.8%	58.1%	0.1%
1998	132,313,143	42.6%	57.3%	0.1%
1999	143,685,459	34.1%	65.7%	0.2%
2000	172,267,510	36.9%	63.1%	0.1%
2001	150,439,144	42.9%	57.0%	0.1%
2002	162,470,528	42.0%	57.9%	0.1%
2003	193,817,443	42.2%	57.8%	0.1%
2004	253,844,672	35.6%	64.3%	0.1%
2005	284,418,743	32.4%	67.5%	0.1%
2006	325,464,705	32.0%	67.9%	0.1%

Source: Korean Small and Medium Business Administration.
Note: SMEs=small and medium-size enterprises; LEs=large enterprises. Total exports include only merchandise exports. SMEs are defined as companies with fewer than 300 employees or capitalization of less than 8 billion won.

documents the growing importance of trade in parts and components (P&C) in East Asia. We follow Athukorala (2006), using Revision 3 of the United Nations' Comtrade database and classifying as P&C exports and imports 225 specific subsectors of Standard International Trade Classification 7 (SITC7; machinery and transport equipment) and SITC8 (miscellaneous exports). As of 2006, East Asia (including Japan)

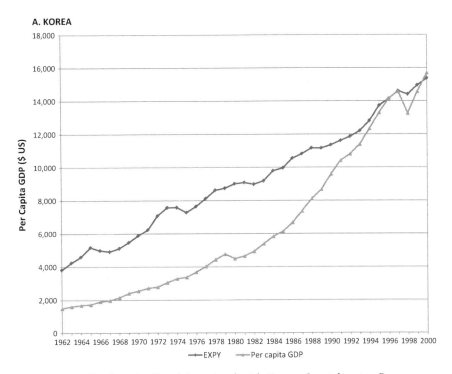

Figure 5.18. Productivity Level Associated with Export Specialization Pattern and Actual Per Capita GDP

Here we construct EXPY, the productivity level associated with a country's export specialization pattern, originally developed by Hausmann, Hwang, and Rodrik (2007). To calculate the new EXPY, we selected countries that have no missing data for the entire sample period, 1962–2000, which yielded a sample of 90 countries. (*A*) EXPY and actual per capita GDP for Korea. (*B*) EXPY and actual per capita GDP for Taiwan. Calculations based on world trade data from the Center for International Data at the University of California, Davis, and Penn World Table 6.2.

accounted for fully 42 percent of global trade in P&C, up from 36 percent in 2000 and only 29 percent in 1992. Not surprisingly, the region has a strongly positive balance of trade in P&C, whose value quadrupled in current dollar terms over the period. South Korea's share of global trade in P&C rose in step with the East Asian pattern, expanding from 2.4 percent of the global total in 1992 to 3.8 percent in 2006. Its balance therefore shifted from slightly negative to strongly positive. There is nothing unusual here. Table 5.13 shows the share of P&C manufacturing in exports and imports, by country and region. In Korea the P&C share of exports rose from 21 percent in 1992 to 33 percent in 2006, matching

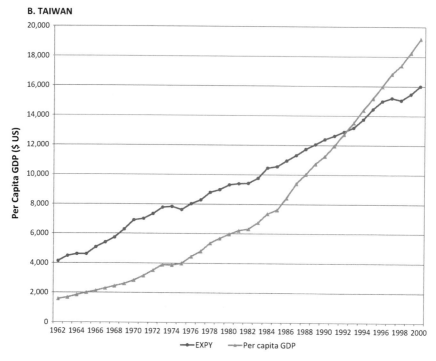

Figure 5.18. Productivity Level Associated with Export Specialization Pattern and Actual Per Capita GDP *(Continued)*

the movement of the East Asian average. For the world as a whole, in contrast, the P&C share started at roughly the same place in 1992 but then rose much more slowly. Evidently, the rapid growth of P&C trade is a distinctively East Asian phenomenon but not a distinctively Korean one. The final columns of Tables 5.13a and 5.13b show the contribution of P&C to total export growth. Again, there is very little that is unusual about Korea viewed from an East Asian perspective.

Table 5.14 looks at the share of P&C in regional manufacturing trade flows. From 25 percent of Korea's exports of manufactures to other East Asian countries, parts and components have risen to 40 to 45 percent since the turn of the century, with the entire rise occurring since the middle of the 1990s. That increase has clearly been driven by exports to China. This is the same pattern evident in Japan, in East Asia generally, and, for that matter, in the rest of the world.[36] Korea stands out as a relatively dramatic case in this general phenomenon only because exports of parts and com-

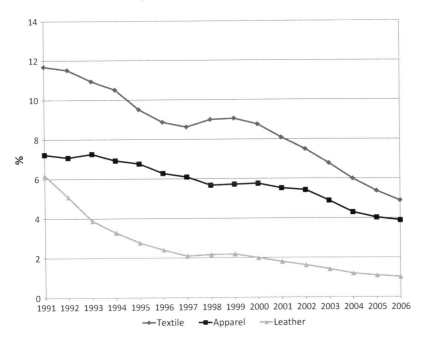

Figure 5.19. Employment Shares of Textile, Apparel, and Leather Industries in the Manufacturing Sector
Data from Korean Statistical Information Service.

ponents to China as a share of Korea's total manufacturing exports was low by international standards in the early 1990s.

A few unusual features of Korea's intraindustry trade emerge when we look within P&C trade, as in Table 5.15. Machinery and equipment dominates P&C exports in every country considered, but it is even more dominant in Korea than elsewhere (the only countries with a higher machinery and equipment share in P&C being Singapore and, interestingly, the Philippines). Roughly a third of this, in the Korean case, is exports of parts and components going into the production of household electrical equipment (household appliances and consumer electronics, two categories that increasingly overlap). Exports of electronic components as a share of total P&C trade is even more important for Singapore, Malaysia, and Taiwan, as is well known, and also, again, for the Philippines. Korea stands out for its relatively large share of telecommunications equipment, reflecting notable successes of Korean companies with products like cell phones, which they nonetheless produce using regional supply chains.

Exports and Economic Growth

Table 5.11. Percentage of Firms with Offshore Production in 2007, by Industry

Industry	Percentage of offshoring firms
Manufacture of food products and beverages	11.1
Manufacture of textiles	43.9
Manufacture of sewn wearing and fur apparel	62.5
Tanning and dressing of leather, manufacture of luggage and footwear	36.4
Manufacture of pulp, paper, and paper products	7.1
Manufacture of chemicals and chemical products	9.6
Manufacture of rubber and plastic products	23.1
Manufacture of other nonmetallic mineral products	17.5
Manufacture of basic metal products	7.1
Manufacture of fabricated structural metal products	27.5
Manufacture of other machinery and equipment	34.1
Manufacture of computers and office machinery	33.3
Manufacture of other electrical machinery	14.3
Manufacture of electronic components, computer, radio, television, and communication equipment and apparatuses	37.3
Manufacture of medical, precision, and optical instruments, watches, and clocks	20.0
Manufacture of motor vehicles, trailers, and semitrailers	34.1
Manufacture of other transport equipment	28.6
Other manufactures	11.8

Source: Lee and Lee (2009).

Note: Data from Korean Gallup survey, 2007, which covers 500 companies in the Korean manufacturing industry. The percentage of offshoring firms is defined as the proportion of firms in each industry that practices offshore sourcing.

Even if a negative impact of China on Korea is not evident in the aggregate, the growing importance of trade in P&C and of vertical intraindustry trade suggests that important effects may be hiding at a more disaggregated level. We explore this by extending the methodology of Hahn and Choi (2008). Those authors regress the rate of growth of production at the industry level (using panel data on Korean output from the Survey of Mining and Manufacturing, published by the Korea National Statistical Office) on exports of consumption goods, capital goods, and intermediate

Table 5.12. Trade in Parts and Components, 1992–2006

	Exports				Imports				Trade balance ($ billion)			
	1992	1996	2000	2006	1992	1996	2000	2006	1992	1996	2000	2006
East Asia	29.0%	36.5%	36.3%	42.2%	23.9%	31.5%	29.5%	37.2%	31.8	46.9	82.1	123.1
China	0.8%	1.3%	2.2%	7.3%	2.4%	2.6%	4.2%	11.6%	−7.0	−9.9	−23.4	−74.0
Hong Kong	3.0%	3.6%	3.7%	5.8%	3.5%	4.3%	4.2%	6.1%	−1.5	−4.5	−6.7	−2.0
Indonesia	0.1%	0.2%	0.4%	0.3%	0.8%	0.8%	0.3%	0.2%	−3.0	−4.7	1.1	0.9
Japan	13.9%	13.6%	10.4%	7.9%	3.3%	4.5%	4.1%	3.7%	52.0	71.9	76.1	84.4
Korea	2.4%	3.4%	3.7%	3.8%	2.8%	3.1%	2.9%	2.5%	−1.1	3.1	9.0	26.8
Malaysia	2.1%	3.0%	3.1%	2.4%	2.5%	3.6%	3.1%	2.7%	−1.0	−3.7	0.1	−2.9
Taiwan	3.0%	3.9%	5.1%	6.3%	3.0%	3.1%	3.4%	2.6%	0.6	6.7	20.3	72.8
Philippines	0.2%	1.1%	1.8%	1.3%	0.4%	1.4%	1.4%	1.4%	−1.2	−1.9	4.7	−1.3
Singapore	2.7%	5.1%	4.7%	5.8%	3.6%	5.7%	4.5%	4.9%	−3.2	−3.4	2.5	21.9
Vietnam	0.0%	0.0%	0.1%	0.1%	0.0%	0.1%	0.1%	0.2%	−0.1	−0.6	−0.7	−1.6
Thailand	0.9%	1.2%	1.4%	1.2%	1.5%	2.1%	1.4%	1.4%	−2.7	−6.1	−0.9	−1.9
United States	20.0%	19.5%	17.8%	11.8%	16.7%	17.2%	15.5%	11.7%	20.7	22.0	27.4	11.5
European Union	40.1%	32.7%	20.9%	25.2%	39.2%	31.0%	26.1%	24.5%	16.4	20.5	−61.6	30.7
Other countries	10.8%	11.3%	25.0%	20.7%	20.2%	20.4%	28.9%	26.6%	−38.9	−65.7	−45.9	−93.3
Worldwide value ($ billion)	477.5	777.4	1,199.0	1,916.0	447.5	753.7	1,197.0	1,844.0				
Share of parts and components in world manufacturing trade	23.8%	21.3%	28.5%	26.9%	22.8%	20.7%	28.4%	27.1%				

Source: Calculations based on UN Comtrade data (Standard International Trade Classification, Rev. 3).

Notes: We follow Athukorala (2005) in classifying trade in parts and components. European Union includes the fifteen countries in the EU as of 1986.

Table 5.13a. Share of Parts and Components in Manufacturing Exports and Imports: Exports

Country/region	Share of parts and components				Export growth			Contribution of parts and components to exports growth		
	1992	1996	2000	2006	1992–1996	1996–2000	2000–2006	1992–1996	1996–2000	2000–2006
East Asia	23.9%	27.7%	36.2%	36.3%	14.3%	4.0%	10.3%	32.5%	86.1%	36.4%
China	6.9%	8.2%	15.2%	21.1%	20.3%	9.3%	22.3%	9.1%	31.4%	22.6%
Hong Kong	15.4%	18.4%	26.7%	43.0%	12.8%	1.9%	7.5%	22.6%	135.9%	71.5%
Indonesia	4.2%	5.1%	15.5%	15.3%	21.3%	-2.9%	3.1%	5.8%	-88.3%	14.0%
Japan	29.6%	34.5%	37.9%	37.0%	7.9%	1.7%	3.7%	47.8%	85.8%	33.3%
Korea	21.3%	26.8%	37.4%	33.3%	15.3%	4.0%	10.5%	33.1%	99.7%	28.7%
Malaysia	43.3%	39.6%	56.3%	50.9%	23.6%	2.3%	5.5%	37.5%	234.2%	37.0%
Taiwan	22.1%	29.5%	43.5%	50.5%	11.7%	7.7%	8.9%	41.8%	82.9%	60.1%
Philippines	23.3%	50.5%	76.9%	71.4%	40.6%	11.5%	3.4%	54.5%	121.9%	47.2%
Singapore	38.9%	47.1%	58.8%	59.8%	22.8%	3.3%	11.2%	52.1%	142.5%	60.8%
Vietnam	0.9%	2.2%	13.5%	10.3%	57.4%	1.9%	18.2%	2.2%	196.3%	8.9%
Thailand	23.9%	21.3%	29.3%	31.2%	24.0%	5.1%	4.8%	19.8%	64.8%	36.7%
United States	36.9%	33.0%	40.3%	34.5%	14.3%	3.6%	3.6%	28.0%	88.4%	10.5%
European Union	22.2%	18.2%	22.3%	20.9%	11.9%	-0.2%	8.6%	12.0%	-423.4%	19.0%
Other countries	16.8%	11.3%	22.2%	20.4%	23.0%	8.6%	9.7%	8.1%	49.6%	18.2%
Worldwide	23.8%	21.3%	23.5%	26.9%	14.9%	3.5%	8.8%	18.4%	76.7%	24.5%

Source: Calculations based on UN Comtrade cata (Standard International Trade Classification, Rev. 3).

Note: Export and import growth rates are based on the nominal U.S. dollar values.

Table 5.13b. Share of Parts and Components in Manufacturing Exports and Imports: Imports

Country/region	Share of parts and components				Export growth			Contribution of parts and components to exports growth		
	1992	1996	2000	2006	1992–1996	1996–2000	2000–2006	1992–1996	1996–2000	2000–2006
East Asia	25.4%	24.6%	39.0%	42.4%	20.7%	–1.5%	9.7%	24.1%	210.0%	46.5%
China	20.0%	17.7%	34.8%	44.2%	18.3%	6.3%	20.3%	15.7%	97.1%	47.2%
Hong Kong	17.3%	19.4%	31.0%	43.6%	15.5%	–0.6%	7.8%	21.8%	496.1%	64.5%
Indonesia	20.3%	18.8%	20.0%	17.9%	16.1%	–17.0%	6.3%	17.3%	17.8%	13.6%
Japan	18.9%	15.5%	30.6%	29.0%	26.2%	–8.0%	6.3%	13.9%	25.8%	25.5%
Korea	29.8%	22.4%	42.3%	33.3%	23.0%	–6.3%	8.8%	18.0%	49.7%	20.7%
Malaysia	40.9%	41.8%	61.2%	59.6%	22.3%	–2.2%	5.3%	42.3%	170.6%	55.4%
Taiwan	35.5%	33.4%	41.3%	41.0%	15.3%	8.3%	3.0%	31.0%	61.4%	39.3%
Philippines	28.9%	39.5%	62.6%	70.3%	34.7%	–0.8%	5.4%	41.9%	642.7%	90.2%
Singapore	37.6%	43.7%	53.8%	60.7%	20.4%	0.4%	6.7%	48.1%	762.7%	74.4%
Vietnam	6.6%	9.8%	15.6%	13.3%	34.1%	4.6%	15.8%	10.5%	45.1%	11.9%
Thailand	30.2%	28.3%	36.2%	35.7%	22.4%	–3.9%	6.5%	27.2%	18.4%	34.7%
United States	25.8%	24.8%	27.5%	22.8%	14.6%	6.5%	5.6%	23.6%	36.6%	10.9%
European Union	21.6%	18.7%	24.4%	22.4%	10.9%	0.5%	7.7%	13.3%	306.5%	18.9%
Other countries	20.2%	16.9%	25.6%	22.0%	17.7%	9.9%	8.3%	13.9%	43.3%	16.7%
Worldwide	22.7%	20.7%	28.4%	27.1%	15.4%	3.6%	8.0%	18.4%	78.4%	24.9%

Source: Calculations based on UN Comtrade data (Standard International Trade Classification, Rev. 3).

Note: Export and import growth rates are based on the nominal U.S. dollar values.

Table 5.14. Share of Parts and Components Content in Manufacturing Trade Flows

Exporter/ importer	Year	East Asia	China	Japan	Korea	United States	EU	Other	World-wide
East Asia	1992	26.20%	18.80%	19.60%	32.40%	28.50%	21.30%	14.20%	23.90%
	1996	28.70%	19.40%	20.20%	28.00%	34.20%	27.40%	15.80%	27.70%
	2000	42.70%	35.90%	34.80%	43.30%	34.10%	32.40%	22.70%	36.20%
	2006	46.50%	50.70%	34.30%	39.50%	28.60%	26.80%	22.10%	36.30%
China	1992	8.00%	—	6.10%	6.00%	4.60%	3.10%	6.00%	6.90%
	1996	10.30%	—	8.70%	9.90%	6.60%	5.20%	5.20%	8.20%
	2000	22.10%	—	16.90%	23.40%	9.30%	11.40%	9.60%	15.20%
	2006	32.30%	—	23.70%	29.80%	15.60%	16.20%	11.60%	21.10%
Japan	1992	31.00%	13.20%	—	33.40%	38.80%	26.20%	18.50%	29.60%
	1996	34.30%	20.90%	—	29.20%	43.60%	34.00%	21.60%	34.50%
	2000	40.90%	33.10%	—	36.50%	40.30%	35.00%	26.00%	37.90%
	2006	38.20%	38.90%	—	27.60%	40.50%	36.60%	28.80%	37.00%
Korea	1992	26.70%	7.50%	20.60%	—	27.30%	18.20%	8.10%	21.30%
	1996	25.10%	10.20%	27.40%	—	49.60%	34.10%	11.50%	26.80%
	2000	44.30%	26.40%	47.70%	—	44.60%	36.00%	15.90%	37.40%
	2006	42.10%	41.10%	29.50%	—	34.90%	17.20%	22.40%	33.30%
United States	1992	40.10%	25.40%	35.10%	38.90%	—	37.90%	35.20%	36.90%
	1996	36.80%	22.30%	30.30%	33.10%	—	34.80%	30.30%	33.00%
	2000	49.80%	34.80%	41.10%	53.10%	—	39.00%	36.30%	40.30%
	2006	45.50%	43.70%	33.00%	42.50%	—	29.90%	31.50%	34.50%
EU	1992	22.70%	30.60%	14.70%	19.40%	27.50%	21.50%	22.00%	22.20%
	1996	22.00%	22.40%	15.30%	21.30%	24.80%	17.00%	17.90%	18.20%
	2000	30.40%	35.50%	18.40%	29.90%	24.90%	20.80%	22.30%	22.30%
	2006	29.90%	33.00%	16.70%	22.70%	22.10%	19.50%	21.00%	20.90%
Worldwide	1992	26.80%	20.70%	21.70%	30.60%	27.70%	21.50%	22.60%	23.80%
	1996	26.40%	18.80%	18.80%	24.70%	26.50%	17.90%	18.40%	21.30%
	2000	40.20%	35.10%	31.00%	41.80%	28.50%	24.00%	24.10%	28.50%
	2006	41.90%	45.70%	28.40%	35.00%	24.90%	21.50%	21.30%	26.90%

Note: See note to Table 5.12.
Source: Calculations based on UN Comtrade data (Standard International Trade Classification, Rev. 3).

				Importer			
East Asia	China	Japan	Korea	United States	EU	Other	World-wide
26.20%	6.30%	32.50%	21.70%	36.00%	19.30%	10.00%	25.40%
27.90%	9.60%	35.80%	26.00%	34.10%	20.10%	6.30%	24.60%
40.50%	19.50%	42.80%	41.00%	47.30%	30.40%	22.90%	39.00%
45.90%	36.30%	39.70%	49.00%	45.70%	29.60%	22.00%	42.40%
20.70%	—	21.60%	11.80%	20.00%	23.80%	10.80%	20.00%
20.30%	—	25.80%	12.80%	16.70%	17.00%	8.50%	17.70%
36.60%	49.20%	38.20%	27.60%	30.40%	36.10%	19.00%	34.80%
49.00%	56.80%	39.20%	45.70%	37.40%	29.20%	23.10%	44.20%
16.10%	3.70%	—	18.90%	32.60%	11.80%	7.80%	18.90%
17.10%	7.60%	—	28.50%	27.20%	11.00%	2.20%	15.50%
33.10%	15.00%	—	44.30%	39.70%	15.60%	15.40%	30.60%
31.90%	22.30%	—	42.30%	34.70%	16.60%	16.90%	29.00%
36.10%	4.00%	34.50%	—	34.70%	16.00%	8.90%	29.80%
28.60%	10.60%	30.00%	—	29.50%	17.80%	4.80%	22.40%
45.70%	27.90%	39.40%	—	48.30%	28.70%	17.60%	42.30%
35.90%	29.30%	27.10%	—	38.20%	23.30%	17.90%	33.30%
26.40%	3.10%	36.30%	23.90%	—	24.20%	25.90%	25.80%
33.40%	6.80%	41.70%	52.70%	—	22.10%	17.00%	24.80%
33.00%	10.00%	40.40%	46.50%	—	22.20%	23.80%	27.50%
24.70%	13.40%	38.50%	35.50%	—	19.30%	22.30%	22.80%
20.90%	2.80%	26.30%	17.40%	35.90%	21.70%	15.80%	21.60%
27.10%	6.10%	34.30%	40.00%	32.60%	17.90%	11.30%	18.70%
28.90%	10.70%	34.20%	36.60%	36.10%	22.00%	21.50%	24.40%
25.10%	14.60%	35.20%	27.90%	29.20%	21.30%	20.00%	22.40%
24.30%	4.80%	30.80%	20.80%	33.00%	20.80%	17.00%	22.70%
28.10%	8.20%	36.00%	32.50%	30.40%	17.60%	10.90%	20.70%
34.30%	13.90%	39.10%	38.40%	36.70%	22.20%	21.00%	28.40%
34.50%	22.10%	38.30%	40.30%	31.90%	21.30%	18.40%	27.10%

Table 5.15a. Percentage Composition of Parts and Components Exports and Imports, by SITC Categories, 2006: Exports

SITC Rev. 3	Description	EU	United States	China	Hong Kong	Indonesia	Japan
7	Machinery and equipment	94.50%	94.00%	96.20%	96.30%	96.80%	94.30%
713	Internal combustion engines	4.70%	2.30%	0.90%	0.30%	2.40%	5.10%
714	Engines and motors, nonelectric	4.30%	6.30%	0.20%	0.40%	0.30%	1.50%
723	Civil engineering/ constructors' equipment	2.20%	4.40%	1.20%	0.10%	4.30%	1.00%
724	Textile and leather machinery	0.70%	0.20%	0.40%	0.30%	0.20%	0.30%
728	Specialized industrial machinery	2.60%	2.10%	0.50%	0.30%	1.00%	1.80%
735	Parts and accessories for office machinery	0.70%	0.60%	0.30%	0.10%	0.10%	0.90%
737	Metalworking machinery	0.90%	0.40%	0.40%	0.10%	0.10%	0.50%
741	Heating and cooling equipment	1.40%	1.00%	1.20%	0.40%	1.20%	0.70%
742	Pumps for liquid elevators	1.00%	0.70%	0.40%	0.10%	0.20%	0.50%
744	Mechanical handling equipment	1.60%	1.00%	0.50%	0.10%	0.20%	0.60%
745	Nonelectrical machine tools and apparatus	1.70%	0.80%	0.60%	0.40%	0.40%	0.30%
749	Nonelectrical parts of machinery	1.00%	0.30%	0.20%	0.10%	0.20%	0.40%
759	Parts and accessories for office machinery	10.00%	9.20%	23.60%	24.70%	10.70%	10.40%
764	Telecommunication equipment, NES	5.50%	5.40%	22.50%	22.20%	11.80%	9.60%
771	Electrical power machinery	0.50%	0.30%	0.60%	2.00%	0.60%	0.30%
772	Apparatus for switching/ protecting electrical circuits	9.80%	6.30%	5.80%	6.90%	11.10%	8.60%

Korea	Malaysia	Taiwan	Philippines	Singapore	Vietnam	Thailand	World
98.20%	97.90%	99.00%	99.40%	98.50%	92.30%	95.10%	95.10%
0.70%	0.60%	0.30%	0.20%	0.80%	1.60%	2.90%	3.00%
0.20%	0.10%	0.10%	0.00%	0.70%	0.00%	0.60%	3.00%
1.40%	0.10%	0.00%	0.10%	2.60%	0.30%	0.30%	2.10%
0.50%	0.10%	0.20%	0.00%	0.10%	4.00%	0.30%	0.50%
1.40%	0.20%	0.30%	0.20%	0.90%	0.20%	0.30%	1.90%
0.30%	0.20%	0.30%	0.10%	0.30%	0.10%	0.10%	0.60%
0.30%	0.10%	0.10%	0.00%	0.20%	0.20%	0.20%	0.60%
1.00%	0.30%	0.20%	0.40%	0.20%	0.70%	1.40%	1.10%
0.20%	0.00%	0.10%	0.00%	0.20%	0.10%	0.10%	0.70%
0.20%	0.10%	0.10%	0.10%	0.30%	0.10%	0.20%	1.00%
0.10%	0.10%	0.30%	0.00%	0.20%	0.50%	0.10%	1.00%
0.10%	0.00%	0.10%	0.10%	0.70%	0.00%	0.20%	0.60%
12.00%	24.00%	14.10%	14.00%	16.50%	31.30%	16.40%	12.20%
20.00%	6.40%	7.10%	2.40%	4.60%	5.00%	6.70%	9.00%
0.50%	0.10%	0.30%	0.10%	0.20%	1.30%	0.40%	0.50%
2.50%	6.40%	3.10%	3.50%	4.00%	6.50%	6.20%	7.90%

(continued)

Table 5.15a. (Continued)

SITC Rev. 3	Description	EU	United States	China	Hong Kong	Indonesia	Japan
776	Household electrical equipment, NES	11.20%	23.40%	20.90%	34.20%	13.20%	27.40%
778	Thermionic, cold cathodes or photo cathode valves and tubes	2.50%	1.90%	5.20%	2.40%	12.90%	3.50%
784	Electrical machinery/ apparatus, NES	22.10%	14.90%	6.40%	0.10%	17.10%	17.00%
785	Motorcycles and cycles	0.70%	0.20%	1.40%	0.10%	4.60%	1.00%
792	Aircrafts and associated equipment	3.60%	9.10%	0.70%	0.20%	2.40%	1.30%
	Other	5.80%	3.30%	2.40%	0.90%	1.70%	1.80%
8	Miscellaneous manufac-tured articles	5.50%	6.00%	3.80%	3.70%	3.20%	5.70%
821	Furniture and parts thereof	0.80%	0.90%	0.60%	0.00%	0.30%	0.40%
846	Clothing accessories of textile fabrics	0.10%	0.10%	0.10%	0.40%	0.10%	0.00%
874	Measuring, analyzing, and checking equipment	2.20%	2.90%	0.60%	0.40%	1.40%	2.90%
881	Photographic equip-ment, NES	0.30%	0.20%	0.20%	0.80%	0.00%	0.40%
891	Arms and ammunition	0.20%	1.10%	0.00%	0.00%	0.00%	0.00%
	Other	2.00%	0.90%	2.20%	2.00%	1.40%	1.90%

Note: This table is a replication of Athukorala (2005), table 3. We have updated the original table year from 2000 to 2006. Calculations based on UN Comtrade data (Standard International Trade Classification [SITC], Rev. 3).

goods to China; on the intensity of Chinese competition in the Korean market; and on the intensity of Chinese competition with Korea in third markets, using the standard controls (the capital and skill intensity of the industry, and so on).[37] In supplementary regressions, Hahn and Choi also use industry-level investment as the dependent variable, reflecting concerns that Chinese competition may be depressing investment in Korean manufacturing. Chinese import competition in the Korean market is measured as China's share of total imports of the products of the industry in question times the share of Korean import products that China exports

Korea	Malaysia	Taiwan	Philippines	Singapore	Vietnam	Thailand	World
38.90%	55.30%	66.80%	70.60%	60.80%	12.60%	36.20%	25.20%
3.10%	1.30%	1.30%	0.20%	1.20%	4.10%	3.40%	2.50%
12.90%	0.90%	2.00%	5.80%	1.30%	16.50%	10.90%	14.60%
0.10%	0.10%	1.60%	0.10%	0.40%	6.00%	2.20%	0.60%
0.60%	0.90%	0.10%	1.20%	1.70%	0.10%	5.10%	3.00%
1.00%	0.40%	0.40%	0.20%	0.40%	1.20%	1.00%	3.60%
1.80%	2.10%	1.00%	0.60%	1.50%	7.70%	4.90%	4.90%
0.60%	0.10%	0.20%	0.00%	0.00%	2.20%	0.60%	1.00%
0.10%	0.00%	0.00%	0.00%	0.00%	0.20%	0.00%	0.10%
0.50%	1.70%	0.20%	0.10%	0.90%	0.10%	0.10%	1.80%
0.10%	0.10%	0.10%	0.10%	0.20%	2.80%	0.50%	0.30%
0.20%	0.00%	0.00%	0.00%	0.00%	0.00%	0.00%	0.20%
0.50%	0.20%	0.40%	0.40%	0.40%	2.40%	3.60%	1.50%

to Korea. Chinese export competition in third markets is measured as China's global export market share as a fraction of China and Korea's combined global export market share (where the Chinese and Korean home markets are excluded from these global totals).[38]

We updated the Hahn-Choi model from 2003 through 2006.[39] With the growing amount of attention paid to Chinese competition, extending the sample increases the likelihood of picking up any effect on Korean manufacturing production and investment that may be present. Given that much of the attention devoted to this question focuses on the employment

Table 5.15b. Parts and Components Trade by Type: Imports

SITC Rev. 3	Description	EU	United States	China	Hong Kong	Indonesia	Japaɪ
7	Machinery and equipment	93.80%	93.10%	98.10%	97.10%	96.70%	92.30
713	Internal combustion engines	4.00%	4.30%	0.90%	0.60%	11.70%	1.70⬤
714	Engines and motors, nonelectric	3.60%	4.00%	0.40%	1.00%	2.90%	3.80⬤
723	Civil engineering/ constructors' equipment	1.80%	2.10%	0.50%	0.10%	9.20%	1.10%
728	Specialized industrial machinery	1.70%	1.60%	0.50%	0.30%	3.20%	1.80⬤
735	Parts and accessories for office machinery	0.70%	0.50%	0.30%	0.10%	0.60%	0.90⬤
737	Metalworking machinery	0.50%	0.40%	0.60%	0.20%	1.10%	0.40⬤
741	Heating and cooling equipment	1.20%	1.20%	0.40%	0.40%	2.30%	1.40%
742	Pumps for liquid elevators	0.90%	0.80%	0.10%	0.10%	2.00%	0.40%
744	Mechanical handling equipment	1.60%	1.30%	0.20%	0.10%	1.10%	0.60%
745	Nonelectrical machine tools and apparatus	1.20%	0.90%	0.20%	0.30%	1.10%	0.70%
759	Parts and accessories for office machinery	13.60%	16.10%	8.70%	22.00%	1.30%	11.40%
764	Telecommunication equipment, NES	6.00%	7.70%	11.70%	16.30%	5.30%	10.70%
771	Electrical power machinery	0.30%	0.40%	0.50%	1.10%	0.30%	0.40%
772	Apparatus for switching/ protecting electrical circuits	7.40%	7.30%	6.90%	6.40%	6.90%	5.90%
775	Electro-diagnostic apparatus	0.30%	0.30%	0.20%	0.50%	0.20%	0.40%
776	Household electrical equipment, NES	12.20%	13.10%	56.90%	43.90%	3.00%	36.60%

Korea	Malaysia	Taiwan	Philippines	Singapore	Vietnam	Thailand	World
94.50%	97.30%	95.90%	97.70%	97.50%	93.50%	97.20%	95.00%
2.20%	0.50%	0.70%	0.20%	1.20%	3.10%	3.30%	3.00%
0.80%	0.30%	0.90%	0.10%	2.30%	0.30%	1.10%	2.80%
0.40%	0.30%	0.10%	0.20%	3.00%	1.20%	0.40%	1.50%
2.40%	0.40%	2.80%	1.90%	1.50%	1.50%	0.50%	1.50%
0.70%	0.30%	0.90%	0.20%	0.30%	0.90%	0.10%	0.50%
0.60%	0.20%	0.40%	0.00%	0.20%	1.30%	0.30%	0.50%
0.60%	0.30%	0.60%	0.20%	0.40%	2.50%	0.70%	1.00%
0.40%	0.10%	0.20%	0.10%	0.20%	0.30%	0.20%	0.60%
0.30%	0.30%	0.60%	0.10%	0.40%	0.60%	0.30%	0.90%
0.40%	0.10%	0.30%	0.10%	0.30%	1.10%	0.30%	0.80%
7.00%	14.60%	7.70%	14.00%	13.60%	14.40%	17.20%	13.10%
6.50%	4.60%	4.70%	3.60%	6.40%	6.70%	5.90%	9.00%
0.60%	0.20%	0.20%	0.60%	0.20%	0.90%	0.20%	0.40%
7.20%	5.20%	5.50%	2.00%	4.10%	14.00%	8.80%	7.40%
0.20%	0.20%	0.10%	0.00%	0.00%	0.10%	0.10%	0.30%
53.20%	63.90%	61.90%	71.10%	55.10%	20.20%	40.70%	28.10%

(continued)

Table 5.15b. (Continued)

SITC Rev. 3	Description	EU	United States	China	Hong Kong	Indonesia	Japan
778	Thermionic, cold cathodes or photo cathode valves, etc.	2.70%	2.50%	2.60%	2.40%	2.80%	1.90%
784	Electrical machinery/ apparatus, NES	22.50%	21.10%	4.20%	0.30%	20.40%	6.70%
785	Motorcycles and cycles	1.00%	0.60%	0.10%	0.10%	8.00%	0.50%
792	Aircrafts and associated equipment	5.10%	3.10%	0.50%	0.20%	1.50%	2.40%
799	Other	5.80%	3.70%	1.70%	0.80%	11.80%	3.00%
8	Miscellaneous manufactured articles	6.20%	6.90%	1.90%	2.90%	3.30%	7.70%
821	Furniture and parts thereof	1.50%	2.80%	0.20%	0.00%	0.30%	1.20%
846	Clothing accessories of textile fabrics	0.00%	0.00%	0.00%	0.30%	0.10%	0.00%
848	Clothing accessories other than textile fabrics	0.00%	0.00%	0.00%	0.00%	0.00%	0.00%
874	Measuring, analyzing, and checking equipment	1.90%	1.90%	0.80%	0.50%	1.20%	3.60%
881	Photographic equipment, NES	0.30%	0.20%	0.10%	0.50%	0.00%	0.40%
899	Other	2.40%	2.00%	0.80%	1.60%	1.60%	2.40%

Note: This table is a replication of Athukorala (2005), table 3. We have updated the original table year from 2000 to 2006. Calculations based on UN Comtrade data (Standard International Trade Classification [SITC], Rev. 3).

effects of Chinese competition, we also estimate the model with employment at the industry level as the dependent variable. Hahn and Choi estimate this equation assuming random effects (that is, they allow the error term to vary by industry). We consider fixed-effects estimates as well (where the slope coefficient is allowed to vary by industry).

The results for output growth are shown in Table 5.16. Chinese import competition in the domestic market has a consistently negative

Korea	Malaysia	Taiwan	Philippines	Singapore	Vietnam	Thailand	World
2.40%	1.80%	1.40%	0.50%	1.40%	2.80%	1.70%	2.50%
5.50%	2.00%	2.50%	1.40%	1.50%	10.00%	10.50%	13.70%
0.10%	0.30%	1.00%	0.20%	0.40%	6.20%	0.70%	0.70%
1.00%	0.80%	1.50%	0.60%	3.90%	0.10%	2.10%	3.00%
2.10%	0.90%	1.90%	0.50%	1.40%	5.40%	2.10%	3.70%
5.50%	2.70%	4.10%	2.30%	2.50%	6.50%	2.80%	5.00%
0.60%	0.20%	0.10%	0.00%	0.00%	0.50%	0.40%	1.10%
0.00%	0.00%	0.00%	0.10%	0.10%	0.40%	0.10%	0.10%
0.00%	0.00%	0.00%	0.00%	0.00%	0.10%	0.00%	0.00%
2.60%	2.00%	2.10%	0.20%	1.70%	0.70%	0.60%	1.70%
0.30%	0.30%	0.70%	1.30%	0.20%	1.30%	0.30%	0.30%
1.90%	0.20%	1.20%	0.70%	0.40%	3.40%	1.40%	1.80%

impact on domestic output at the industry level. Chinese export competition in third markets also has a negative impact on the output of Korean industry, although the statistical significance of this coefficient varies depending on the composition of the vector of controls (compare column 2 with columns 3 and 4 in the table). Table 5.17 allows these effects to vary between the pre-crisis (1992–1997) and post-crisis (1999–2006) periods. The results suggest that the adverse effects of Chinese

Table 5.16. Impact of China on Output Growth: Between Effects (1992–2006)

Growth rate of real production	[1]	[2]	[3]	[4]
Capital intensity	−0.013	−0.022	−0.002	−0.009
	[0.013]	[0.014]	[0.014]	[0.016]
Skill intensity	0.033	0.036	0.013	0.022
	[0.024]	[0.023]	[0.024]	[0.026]
Import competition	−0.210***	−0.139*	−0.123*	−0.136*
	[0.070]	[0.076]	[0.071]	[0.073]
Export competition		−0.113**	−0.002	0.003
		[0.052]	[0.055]	[0.055]
Capital goods share			0.101***	0.113***
			[0.023]	[0.028]
Intermediate goods share				0.026
				[0.031]
Number of groups	67	67	63	63
R-squared	0.17	0.23	0.36	0.37

Source: Estimates are based on Hahn and Choi (2008), with updated and extended calculations. All data are obtained from the Survey of Mining and Manufacturing, Statistics Korea, except for deflators collected from Bank of Korea and trade data collected from the UN Comtrade database.

Note: The dependent variable is the growth rate of output in 67 manufacturing industries at the three-digit level. Nominal industrial production is deflated by the sector GDP deflator obtained from Bank of Korea. Capital intensity is the natural logarithm of real tangible fixed assets per worker. Skill intensity is the natural logarithm of the ratio of the numbers of nonproduction workers and production workers. Import competition is the product of value share and product share, following Schott (2002). Export competition is computed as the relative market share of China to that of Korea for the same industry products in the world exports market. Capital-goods and intermediate-goods shares are defined as the shares of those goods exports out of total exports in each industry. Classification of capital goods and intermediate goods follows Eichengreen, Rhee, and Tong (2007).

***, **, and * indicate statistical significance at the 1-, 5-, and 10-percent levels, respectively.

export competition have been felt most intensively in the more recent (post-crisis) period, whereas the impact of Chinese import competition in the Korean market itself was more evident in the earlier (pre-crisis) period.

The decline in domestic investment since the crisis has been widely discussed. Table 5.18 therefore estimates a similar model for the rate of growth of investment. All specifications suggest that this decline has been particularly pronounced in industries experiencing more intense Chinese

Table 5.17. Pre-crisis and Post-crisis Impacts of China on Output Growth (1992–2006)

Growth rate of output	[1]	[2]	[3]	[4]
Before crisis × capital intensity	0.012 [0.016]	0.006 [0.017]	0.024 [0.017]	0.014 [0.020]
After crisis × capital intensity	−0.014 [0.012]	−0.022* [0.012]	−0.006 [0.013]	0.001 [0.014]
Before crisis × skill intensity	0.034 [0.030]	0.035 [0.030]	0.013 [0.031]	0.024 [0.033]
After crisis × skill intensity	0.014 [0.018]	0.015 [0.018]	−0.005 [0.019]	−0.014 [0.020]
Before crisis × import competition	−0.300*** [0.107]	−0.236** [0.116]	−0.234** [0.117]	−0.264** [0.120]
After crisis × import competition	−0.131** [0.052]	−0.094* [0.054]	−0.068 [0.058]	−0.061 [0.058]
Before crisis × export competition		−0.074 [0.052]	0.047 [0.058]	0.06 [0.059]
After crisis × export competition		−0.099** [0.045]	−0.032 [0.048]	−0.038 [0.048]
Before crisis × capital goods share			0.127*** [0.031]	0.147*** [0.037]
After crisis × capital goods share			0.092*** [0.020]	0.075*** [0.024]
Before crisis × intermediate goods share				0.038 [0.038]
After crisis × intermediate goods share				−0.034 [0.027]
Observations	841	841	763	763
R-squared	0.15	0.16	0.19	0.19

Note: Standard errors in brackets. This estimation is based on Hahn and Choi (2008), with updated and extended calculations. Before-crisis period is defined as 1992–1997 and the after-crisis period as 1999–2006.
***, **, and * indicate statistical significance at the 1-, 5-, and 10-levels, respectively.

competition in the home market. In contrast, there is little sign that more intense Chinese competition in third markets has had a negative impact on investment growth rates.

Tables 5.19 and 5.20 consider the impact on employment growth. The basic specifications in Table 5.19 show that Chinese competition has had an

Table 5.18. Pre-crisis and Post-crisis Impacts of China on Investment Growth (1992–2006)

Growth rate of real investment	[1]	[2]	[3]	[4]
Before crisis × capital intensity	0.013 [0.023]	−0.001 [0.024]	0.008 [0.026]	0.039 [0.030]
After crisis × capital intensity	−0.032* [0.018]	−0.029 [0.019]	−0.021 [0.020]	−0.016 [0.021]
Before crisis × skill intensity	0.035 [0.038]	0.039 [0.038]	0.03 [0.039]	−0.002 [0.042]
After crisis × skill intensity	−0.028 [0.027]	−0.028 [0.027]	−0.024 [0.028]	−0.031 [0.030]
Before crisis × import competition	−0.212 [0.157]	−0.123 [0.164]	−0.085 [0.171]	0.001 [0.177]
After crisis × import competition	−0.188** [0.073]	−0.198*** [0.077]	−0.180** [0.082]	−0.174** [0.082]
Before crisis × export competition		−0.125* [0.069]	−0.061 [0.077]	−0.08 [0.078]
After crisis × export competition		0.031 [0.066]	0.05 [0.073]	0.047 [0.073]
Before crisis × capital goods share			0.071* [0.042]	0.025 [0.048]
After crisis × capital goods share			0.028 [0.030]	0.016 [0.035]
Before crisis × intermediate goods share				−0.101* [0.051]
After crisis × intermediate goods share				−0.024 [0.038]
Observations	709	709	650	650
R-squared	0.07	0.07	0.08	0.08

Note: Standard errors in brackets. This estimation is based on Hahn and Choi (2008), with updated and extended calculations. The before-crisis period is defined as 1992–1997 and the after-crisis period as 1999–2006.

***, **, and * indicate statistical significance at the 1-, 5-, and 10-percent levels, respectively.

adverse impact on employment growth in Korea, with larger negative effects felt in industries experiencing more intense Chinese competition. Direct competition in the domestic Korean market appears to have had the larger negative impact on employment, just as in the case of investment. Table 5.20 shows that the basic result carries over—indeed, it is

Table 5.19. Impact of China on Employment Growth: Between Effects
(1992–2006)

Growth rate of employment	[1]	[2]	[3]	[4]
Capital intensity	−0.008 [0.009]	−0.015 [0.009]	−0.014 [0.011]	−0.017 [0.012]
Skill intensity	−0.007 [0.017]	−0.003 [0.016]	−0.018 [0.018]	−0.013 [0.021]
Import competition	−0.272*** [0.054]	−0.202*** [0.056]	−0.274*** [0.059]	−0.280*** [0.060]
Export competition		−0.108*** [0.036]	−0.068 [0.042]	−0.064 [0.043]
Capital goods share			0.025 [0.018]	0.033 [0.022]
Intermediate goods share				0.016 [0.024]
Number of groups	67	67	63	63
R-squared	0.3	0.39	0.43	0.44

Note: Standard errors in brackets. The dependent variable is the growth rate of employment in 67 manufacturing industries at three-digit level. Additional data are drawn from Survey of Mining and Manufacturing, Statistics Korea.
*** indicates statistical significance at the 1-percent level.

strengthened—when the same equations are estimated assuming industry-fixed effects rather than random effects, although it is no longer clear whether Chinese competition in Korean or third markets has the larger adverse employment effect.

The questions left open by this analysis are the direction and the magnitude of the overall effect. We can summarize that aggregate impact using the Eichengreen, Rhee, and Tong (2006) approach, analyzing the impact of China's exports on the exports of other Asian countries. The set-up for this analysis is, once again, the workhorse gravity model of trade. We extend the model by adding China's exports to each market as an additional determinant of other Asian countries' exports to that market. The sample is made up of 13 Asian countries' exports to other Asian countries and extraregional markets (180 importing countries in all), where each bilateral flow is treated as an individual observation. Whereas the earlier Eichengreen, Rhee, and Tong analysis looked at data through 2002, here we bring the analysis up through 2005.

Table 5.20. Impact of China on Employment Growth: Fixed Effects (1992–2006)

Growth rate of employment	[1]	[2]	[3]	[4]
Capital intensity	−0.303***	−0.314***	−0.330***	−0.331***
	[0.020]	[0.020]	[0.021]	[0.021]
Skill intensity	0.064*	0.063*	0.058	0.057
	[0.033]	[0.033]	[0.036]	[0.036]
Import competition	−0.170**	−0.171**	−0.126	−0.122
	[0.074]	[0.074]	[0.088]	[0.088]
Export competition		−0.194***	−0.239***	−0.228***
		[0.062]	[0.068]	[0.068]
Capital goods share			0.002	−0.031
			[0.066]	[0.069]
Intermediate goods share				−0.076
				[0.048]
Observations	896	896	818	818
R-squared	0.29	0.3	0.31	0.31

Note: Standard errors in brackets. The dependent variable is the growth rate of employment in 67 manufacturing industries at three-digit level. Additional data are drawn from Survey of Mining and Manufacturing, Statistics Korea.

***, **, and * indicate statistical significance at the 1-, 5-, and 10-percent levels, respectively.

The key step is addressing the endogeneity of China's exports. Failing to do this would almost guarantee a positive coefficient on China's exports. In other words, a positive shock to, say, the U.S. economy, which increased its demand for imports from Korea would almost certainly also increase its demand for imports from China, other things being equal. (Think of that shock as an increase in demand pressure in the United States.) We address this problem by using the distance between China and the market to which the exports are destined (as suggested by the gravity model) as an instrument for China's exports. Note that the distance in the second-stage equation is the distance not from China to the importing market but from the competing Asian exporter to the importing market.

Basic results are presented in Table 5.21a, while the first-stage estimates, with the predicted negative coefficient on China's distance from the final market, are shown in Table 5.21b. Although the ordinary least squares (OLS) estimates presented for comparison suggest that an in-

Table 5.21a. Impact of China's Exports on Asian Countries' Exports to Third Markets (1990–2005)

	OLS		IV	
China's exports	0.493*** [0.009]	0.493*** [0.009]	−0.158*** [0.040]	−0.162*** [0.040]
China's exports × Korea dummy		−0.049*** [0.014]		−0.058*** [0.015]
GDP of importing country	0.431*** [0.012]	0.435*** [0.012]	1.066*** [0.040]	1.075*** [0.040]
GDP per capita of importing country	−0.003 [0.014]	−0.004 [0.014]	−0.168*** [0.018]	−0.170*** [0.018]
GDP of exporting country	0.716*** [0.010]	0.716*** [0.010]	0.729*** [0.011]	0.730*** [0.011]
GDP per capita of exporting country	0.454*** [0.011]	0.456*** [0.011]	0.450*** [0.012]	0.452*** [0.012]
Product of land areas	0.001 [0.006]	0.001 [0.006]	−0.018*** [0.006]	−0.018*** [0.006]
Distance	−0.632*** [0.020]	−0.638*** [0.020]	−1.126*** [0.036]	−1.137*** [0.037]
Dummy for common language	0.376*** [0.026]	0.381*** [0.026]	0.561*** [0.030]	0.568*** [0.030]
No. of landlocked 0/1/2	−0.539*** [0.026]	−0.542*** [0.026]	−0.734*** [0.030]	−0.738*** [0.030]
No. of islands 0/1/2	−0.489*** [0.019]	−0.494*** [0.019]	−0.464*** [0.021]	−0.470*** [0.021]
Land border dummy	0.760*** [0.094]	0.750*** [0.094]	0.319*** [0.104]	0.304*** [0.104]
Dummy for common colonizer post-1945	0.903*** [0.033]	0.904*** [0.033]	1.027*** [0.037]	1.029*** [0.037]
Dummy for pairs ever in colonial relationship	0.786*** [0.104]	0.769*** [0.104]	0.564*** [0.112]	0.543*** [0.112]
RTA dummy	0.797*** [0.054]	0.793*** [0.054]	0.747*** [0.058]	0.741*** [0.058]
Transparency of host country	0.107*** [0.008]	0.109*** [0.008]	0.260*** [0.012]	0.262*** [0.012]
Observations	21,916	21,916	21,916	21,916
R-squared	0.794	0.794	0.764	0.764

Note: Standard errors in brackets. We follow the Eichengreen, Rhee, and Tong (2006) approach. OLS = ordinary least squares; IV = instrumental variables. The dependent variable is real exports of each Asian country to a third country. Real exports are obtained by dividing current U.S. dollar values, collected from the IMF's Direction of Trade Statistics database, by the U.S. consumer price index (CPI). All explanatory variables (other than the dummies) are expressed in logs. GDP is collected from the World Bank's World Development Indicators and deflated by the U.S. CPI; real per capita GDP obtained from Penn World Table 6.2. Other country variables are from Rose (2000). RTA dummy takes one if the pair countries have formed regional trade agreement. Robust standard errors are in brackets.

*** indicates statistical significance at the 1-percent level.

Table 5.21b. First-Stage Estimation: Determinants of China's Exports to Third Markets (1990–2005)

	OLS
GDP of importing country	0.947**
	[0.006]
GDP per capita of importing country	−0.241**
	[0.010]
GDP of exporting country	0.021**
	[0.008]
GDP per capita of exporting country	−0.042**
	[0.008]
Product of land areas	−0.021**
	[0.004]
Distance	−0.063*
	[0.024]
Dummy for common language	0.317**
	[0.020]
Number of landlocked 0/1/2	−0.370**
	[0.019]
Number of islands 0/1/2	0.048**
	[0.015]
Land border dummy	−0.172*
	[0.073]
Dummy for common colonizer post-1945	0.306**
	[0.026]
Dummy for pairs ever in colonial relationship	−0.346**
	[0.079]
RTA dummy	0.057
	[0.041]
Transparency of host country	0.232**
	[0.006]
China's distance to importing countries	−0.851**
	[0.024]
Observations	21,916
R-squared	0.831

Note: Standard errors in brackets. OLS=ordinary least squares. The dependent variable is real exports of China to a third country. The first-stage estimation is used to form instrumental variables for the instrumental variables estimation in Table 5.21a.

** and * indicate statistical significance at the 1- and 5-percent levels, respectively.

crease in China's exports leads to an increase in other Asian countries' exports to the same market, reflecting the existence of reverse causality, the instrumental variables estimates yield a more plausible negative coefficient on China's exports. That negative coefficient is large; it is statistically significant at any imaginable confidence level. The result confirms that China's exports crowd out the exports of other Asian economies.

In the second of each pair of regressions, we interact China's exports (where appropriate we use the fitted value from the first stage) with a dummy variable for Korea. This gives us the additional "Korea effect"— whether China has a larger or smaller impact on Korea's exports than on the exports of other Asian economies. The small negative coefficient on this interaction tells us that Korea has suffered a slightly greater loss of exports as a result of Chinese competition than the average for twelve other Asian exporters in the sample.

One suspects that this difference reflects the fact that Korea exports a higher ratio of capital goods and intermediates to consumer goods than other Asian countries, and that China competes less intensively in markets for capital goods. Table 5.22 therefore disaggregates exports into consumer goods, intermediates, and capital goods and runs separate regressions for each. (The discussion here focuses on the instrumental-variables estimates.) The coefficients on China's exports confirm that the largest negative effect is felt by other Asian exporters of consumer goods; exporters of capital goods and intermediates experience somewhat smaller losses of their own exports with the growth of China's exports of those same product categories. The additional Korea effect is negative in the case of consumer goods. This suggests that Korea suffers even larger losses than other Asian countries when China begins muscling into world markets for these products.

For intermediates, in contrast, the coefficient on this interaction term is zero; the impact of Chinese competition on Korea is no different than its impact on other Asian countries. But the coefficient in question is strongly positive for capital goods. In other words, Korea suffers much less than other Asian countries from Chinese competition in markets for capital goods. Evidently Korea and China produce rather different capital goods that are relatively imperfect substitutes for one another. Shipbuilding illustrates the point. Korean shipbuilders specialized increasingly in high-value-added ships: in 2007 they were producing 72 percent of all liquid natural gas carriers and 67 percent of mega-container ships. China, in

Table 5.22. Impact of China's Exports on Asian Countries' Exports to Third Markets, Disaggregated by Commodity Type (1990–2005)

	OLS					
	Consumer goods		Intermediates		Capital goods	
China's exports	0.295**	0.295**	0.335**	0.335**	0.395**	0.396**
	[0.009]	[0.009]	[0.009]	[0.009]	[0.012]	[0.012]
China's exports × Korea dummy		−0.005		0.005		0.016**
		[0.003]		[0.004]		[0.004]
GDP of importing country	0.526**	0.527**	0.629**	0.628**	0.421**	0.418**
	[0.013]	[0.013]	[0.014]	[0.014]	[0.018]	[0.018]
GDP per capita of importing country	0.110**	0.109**	−0.232**	−0.232**	0.094**	0.095**
	[0.017]	[0.017]	[0.018]	[0.018]	[0.023]	[0.023]
GDP of exporting country	0.605**	0.607**	0.798**	0.797**	0.731**	0.725**
	[0.013]	[0.013]	[0.013]	[0.014]	[0.017]	[0.017]
GDP per capita of exporting country	0.462**	0.466**	0.301**	0.297**	1.044**	1.030**
	[0.014]	[0.014]	[0.014]	[0.015]	[0.018]	[0.019]
Product of land areas	0.034**	0.033**	−0.074**	−0.072**	−0.006	−0.001
	[0.007]	[0.007]	[0.007]	[0.008]	[0.010]	[0.010]
Distance	−0.752**	−0.754**	−0.878**	−0.877**	−0.586**	−0.578**
	[0.024]	[0.024]	[0.025]	[0.025]	[0.033]	[0.033]
Dummy for common language	0.334**	0.342**	0.470**	0.462**	0.681**	0.653**
	[0.032]	[0.032]	[0.034]	[0.034]	[0.042]	[0.042]
Number of landlocked 0/1/2	−0.609**	−0.612**	−1.259**	−1.256**	−0.697**	−0.689**
	[0.033]	[0.033]	[0.035]	[0.035]	[0.045]	[0.045]
Number of islands 0/1/2	−0.501**	−0.515**	−0.917**	−0.903**	−0.570**	−0.516**
	[0.024]	[0.026]	[0.025]	[0.028]	[0.032]	[0.035]
Land border dummy	0.526**	0.517**	0.207	0.216	0.585**	0.619**
	[0.116]	[0.117]	[0.124]	[0.125]	[0.150]	[0.150]
Dummy for common colonizer post-1945	0.882**	0.875**	1.274**	1.281**	0.818**	0.842**
	[0.042]	[0.042]	[0.045]	[0.045]	[0.056]	[0.056]
Dummy for pairs ever in colonial relationship	0.921**	0.912**	0.615**	0.624**	0.743**	0.772**
	[0.132]	[0.132]	[0.141]	[0.141]	[0.167]	[0.167]
RTA dummy	0.585**	0.587**	1.017**	1.015**	1.514**	1.509**
	[0.067]	[0.067]	[0.071]	[0.071]	[0.087]	[0.087]
Transparency of host country	0.170**	0.170**	0.164**	0.164**	0.111**	0.110**
	[0.009]	[0.009]	[0.010]	[0.010]	[0.012]	[0.012]
Observations	19,904	19,904	20,018	20,018	17,246	17,246
R-squared	0.716	0.716	0.698	0.698	0.676	0.676

Source: Disaggregated trade data are collected from UN Comtrade.

Note: Standard errors in brackets. This is a similar estimation to the one reported in Table 5.21a except that we report the results at disaggregated levels. OLS=ordinary least squares; IV=instrumental variables; RTA=regional trade agreement. For other information, see note for Table 5.21a.

** and * indicate statistical significance at the 1- and 5-percent levels, respectively.

	IV				
Consumer goods		Intermediates		Capital goods	
−0.579**	−0.583**	−0.305**	−0.304**	−0.415**	−0.407**
[0.043]	[0.043]	[0.046]	[0.046]	[0.062]	[0.062]
	−0.009**		0.002		0.011*
	[0.004]		[0.004]		[0.005]
1.398**	1.404**	1.263**	1.262**	1.223**	1.214**
[0.044]	[0.044]	[0.046]	[0.046]	[0.063]	[0.063]
−0.165**	−0.166**	−0.434**	−0.433**	−0.164**	−0.162**
[0.022]	[0.022]	[0.023]	[0.023]	[0.031]	[0.031]
0.623**	0.626**	0.809**	0.808**	0.748**	0.744**
[0.013]	[0.013]	[0.014]	[0.014]	[0.017]	[0.018]
0.465**	0.473**	0.299**	0.298**	1.024**	1.014**
[0.014]	[0.014]	[0.015]	[0.015]	[0.019]	[0.019]
0.001	−0.002	−0.097**	−0.097**	−0.041**	−0.038**
[0.007]	[0.007]	[0.008]	[0.008]	[0.010]	[0.010]
−1.388**	−1.394**	−1.340**	−1.339**	−1.183**	−1.173**
[0.039]	[0.039]	[0.041]	[0.041]	[0.056]	[0.056]
0.523**	0.539**	0.609**	0.605**	0.823**	0.803**
[0.034]	[0.034]	[0.036]	[0.037]	[0.044]	[0.045]
−1.250**	−1.258**	−1.741**	−1.739**	−1.295**	−1.285**
[0.045]	[0.045]	[0.049]	[0.049]	[0.065]	[0.065]
−0.529**	−0.557**	−0.927**	−0.922**	−0.577**	−0.540**
[0.024]	[0.026]	[0.026]	[0.029]	[0.033]	[0.036]
−0.078	−0.098	−0.224	−0.22	0.06	0.087
[0.123]	[0.123]	[0.132]	[0.132]	[0.159]	[0.159]
1.092**	1.080**	1.418**	1.420**	0.975**	0.991**
[0.044]	[0.044]	[0.047]	[0.047]	[0.059]	[0.059]
0.801**	0.784**	0.552**	0.555**	0.664**	0.685**
[0.135]	[0.135]	[0.145]	[0.145]	[0.172]	[0.172]
0.754**	0.758**	1.136**	1.136**	1.618**	1.614**
[0.069]	[0.069]	[0.074]	[0.074]	[0.090]	[0.090]
0.282**	0.283**	0.248**	0.248**	0.219**	0.217**
[0.011]	[0.011]	[0.012]	[0.012]	[0.015]	[0.015]
19,904	19,904	20,018	20,018	17,246	17,246
0.702	0.702	0.679	0.679	0.657	0.657

contrast, continues to specialize in small container ships and other small-capacity, low-complexity vessels.

China's own imports are also an increasingly important part of the equation. Again we use a modified gravity-model framework to analyze their determinants, asking how the growth of China's GDP has affected its imports from other Asian countries, and how the answer differs for consumer goods, capital goods, and intermediates. The second column of Table 5.23 tells the tale for the more recent period, from 1997 to 2005. China has a strong income elasticity of demand for imports. The elasticity for Korea is at the upper end of the range of estimated coefficients. Only the point estimate for Japan, another exporter of sophisticated capital and intermediate goods, is higher. Table 5.24 undertakes the same exercise for the three categories of exports. The results confirm that the elasticity of China's imports with respect to GDP is much higher for capital goods than for either intermediates or consumables.

Overall, the results suggest that Korea (like Japan), as an exporter of relatively sophisticated capital goods both to third markets and to China itself, is hurt the least and on balance is probably even helped, in terms of overall export demand, by the rise of China.

To gauge the overall effect, consider the following thought experiment. The regression for China's exports tells us that a 10 percent increase in Chinese GDP is associated with a 15.4 percent increase in China's own exports; according to the disaggregated trade data, this breaks down into a 23.7 percent increase in its exports of capital goods, a 16.0 percent increase in its exports of consumer goods, and a 14.4 percent increase in its exports of intermediates. We can then combine those results with our estimates of how China's export growth affects the third-market exports of Korea and how its income growth affects its imports from Korea. We use the parameters estimated over the full period from 1990 to 2005, with the trade data disaggregated into capital goods, intermediate goods, and consumer goods. For China's import demand, we use the different income elasticities for different exporting countries. The income elasticities are 1.4 percent for the aggregate exports of Korea, 2.6 percent for Korea's capital goods exports, 1.2 percent for Korea's consumer goods exports, and 1.2 percent for Korea's intermediate goods exports.

Given this, a 10 percent rise in Chinese incomes leads to a 1.1 percent increase in Korea's aggregate exports; this is consistent with the conjecture of a positive net effect, as suggested above. On the other hand, at the disag-

Table 5.23. China's Imports from Asian Countries, Disaggregated by Exporting Country

	1990–2005	*1997–2005*
China's GDP × Japan dummy	1.334** [0.289]	3.295** [0.487]
China's GDP × Korea dummy	1.379** [0.254]	3.111** [0.428]
China's GDP × Singapore dummy	1.224** [0.234]	2.748** [0.376]
China's GDP × Indonesia dummy	1.568** [0.260]	3.178** [0.460]
China's GDP × Malaysia dummy	1.400** [0.228]	2.939** [0.386]
China's GDP × Philippines dummy	1.483** [0.237]	3.024** [0.414]
China's GDP × Thailand dummy	1.458** [0.240]	3.043** [0.414]
China's GDP × Bangladesh dummy	1.453** [0.240]	2.918** [0.428]
China's GDP × Cambodia dummy	1.396** [0.186]	2.606** [0.324]
China's GDP × Sri Lanka dummy	1.302** [0.206]	2.646** [0.354]
China's GDP × Pakistan dummy	1.511** [0.245]	3.038** [0.435]
China's GDP × Vietnam dummy	1.528** [0.228]	2.972** [0.404]
China's GDP × India dummy	1.617** [0.300]	3.355** [0.540]
GDP of exporting country	−0.646 [0.997]	−3.769* [1.847]
GDP per capita of exporting country	2.904* [1.188]	3.053 [2.064]
Observations	205	117
R-squared	0.95	0.98

Note: Standard errors in brackets. The dependent variable is China's real imports from Asian countries. We drop the distance variable since it is not statistically significant, as explained in Eichengreen, Rhee, and Tong (2006).

** and * indicate statistical significance at the 1- and 5-percent levels, respectively.

Table 5.24. China's Imports from Asian Countries, Disaggregated by Commodity Type (1990–2005)

	Capital goods	Consumer goods	Intermediates
China's GDP×Japan dummy	2.516** [0.628]	1.113** [0.414]	1.190** [0.371]
China's GDP×Korea dummy	2.589** [0.548]	1.167** [0.361]	1.153** [0.323]
China's GDP×Singapore dummy	2.716** [0.514]	1.218** [0.338]	0.721* [0.303]
China's GDP×Indonesia dummy	2.431** [0.541]	1.118** [0.357]	1.501** [0.320]
China's GDP×Malaysia dummy	2.618** [0.489]	1.164** [0.322]	1.086** [0.289]
China's GDP×Philippines dummy	2.500** [0.496]	1.124** [0.327]	1.271** [0.293]
China's GDP×Thailand dummy	2.548** [0.508]	1.195** [0.335]	1.243** [0.300]
China's GDP×Bangladesh dummy	2.375** [0.497]	1.075** [0.328]	1.339** [0.294]
China's GDP×Cambodia dummy	2.418** [0.391]	1.118** [0.257]	1.018** [0.231]
China's GDP×Sri Lanka dummy	2.434** [0.434]	1.087** [0.286]	0.934** [0.256]
China's GDP×Pakistan dummy	2.339** [0.509]	1.082** [0.336]	1.383** [0.301]
China's GDP×Vietnam dummy	2.466** [0.475]	1.223** [0.313]	1.381** [0.280]
China's GDP×India dummy	2.300** [0.617]	1.081** [0.407]	1.703** [0.365]
GDP of exporting country	1.965 [2.016]	1.22 [1.330]	−3.545** [1.192]
GDP per capita of exporting country	−0.865 [2.473]	−0.011 [1.625]	5.785** [1.456]
Observations	179	182	182
R-squared	0.91	0.91	0.93

Source: Disaggregate trade data are collected from UN Comtrade.

Note: Standard errors in brackets. This is the same estimation as in Table 5.23 except the regression is made at disaggregate levels.

** indicates statistical significance at the 1-percent level.

gregated level, a 10 percent increase in Chinese income leads to 2.1 percent decline in Korea's capital goods exports, a 6.6 percent decline in Korea's consumer goods exports, and a 0.2 percent increase in Korea's intermediate goods exports. If we recalculate using the disaggregated figures, we get a 4.1 percent decrease in Korea's capital goods exports. The aggregate and the disaggregated figures are not consistent with each other because of different sources of data: the aggregate figures are drawn from the IMF's Direction of Trade Statistics, while the disaggregated analysis uses UN Comtrade data. The prudent conclusion would seem to be that the net effect on Korea can be either positive or negative, but either way it is small.

Finally, it is possible that, owing to the growing foreign content component, a given increase in exports is having a smaller impact than before on the growth of Korean output and employment. We explore this using input/output (IO) tables that we have assembled back to the 1970s. (The most recent IO table currently available is for 2003.) Inverting the matrix of IO coefficients, we can back out the implications for production, value added, and employment of an impulse to exports.

Table 5.25 shows the worker requirement coefficient of exports—how many additional employees are required, by sector, due to a given impulse to exports. (We also show the worker requirement coefficient for total final demand and the value-added multipliers for exports in Tables 5.26 and 5.27.) We see, not surprisingly, that worker requirement coefficients have declined over time—this is simply the flip side of the increase in labor productivity documented elsewhere in this volume. Averaging across the entire economy, these worker requirement coefficients fall by roughly half between each successive five-year period.

But when we split the sample at 1990, the year when Korea's trade with China first reached significant levels, we reach a different conclusion. Between 1973 and 1990 the worker requirement coefficients associated with consumption, investment, and exports fell by 54.5 percent, 50 percent, and 43.5 percent, respectively. Relative to the other components of final demand, the role of exports in employment creation was getting larger. Between 1990 and 2003, in contrast, the same worker requirement coefficients fell by 51.2 percent, 45.3 percent, and 60.5 percent, respectively. In this period, in contrast to the preceding one, the role of exports contributing to employment creation was getting smaller.[40]

The main explanation for why the employment-creation role of exports declined in the second period appears to be that export industries started

Table 5.25. Worker Requirement Coefficients of Exports, by Industry

	1970	1975	1980	1985	1990	1995	2000	2003
Total	—	69.0	64.5	47.0	39.0	26.6	17.2	15.4
Agriculture, forestry, and fishing	—	20.0	24.1	13.2	8.4	4.1	3.0	2.3
Mining and quarrying	—	1.5	0.9	0.7	0.3	0.1	0.0	0.0
Manufacturing	—	26.7	19.5	17.2	17.0	11.8	6.6	6.5
Electricity, gas, and water supply	—	0.2	0.2	0.2	0.1	0.1	0.1	0.1
Construction	—	0.2	0.3	0.4	0.2	0.1	0.1	0.1
Services	—	20.4	19.5	15.4	12.9	10.4	7.4	6.5
Dummy sectors	—	0.0	0.0	0.0	0.0	0.0	0.0	0.0

Source: Data are collected from input/output tables for various years, constructed by Bank of Korea.

Note: Worker requirement coefficients are calculated from nominal values and then deflated by GDP deflators.

Table 5.26. Worker Requirement Coefficients of Total Final Demand (Consumption + Investment + Exports), by Industry

	1970	1975	1980	1985	1990	1995	2000	2003
Total	—	88.3	67.4	52.5	41.4	31.4	21.3	19.8
Agriculture, forestry, and fishing	—	37.8	21.5	13.4	7.7	4.5	2.8	2.2
Mining and quarrying	—	1.0	0.7	0.6	0.2	0.1	0.0	0.0
Manufacturing	—	17.6	14.6	12.0	11.4	7.5	4.1	3.7
Electricity, gas, and water supply	—	0.2	0.2	0.2	0.2	0.1	0.1	0.1
Construction	—	3.7	3.6	3.2	3.1	2.5	1.6	1.8
Services	—	28.0	26.6	23.2	18.9	16.7	12.7	12.0
Dummy sectors	—	0.0	0.0	0.0	0.0	0.0	0.0	0.0

Source: Data are from input/output tables for various years, constructed by Bank of Korea.

Note: Worker requirement coefficients are calculated from nominal values and then deflated by GDP deflators.

Table 5.27. Value-Added Multipliers of Exports, by Industry

	1970	1975	1980	1985	1990	1995	2000	2003
Total	0.785	0.679	0.679	0.689	0.729	0.729	0.674	0.686
Agriculture, forestry, and fishing	0.119	0.093	0.121	0.093	0.071	0.041	0.032	0.025
Mining and quarrying	0.039	0.018	0.012	0.010	0.009	0.006	0.003	0.003
Manufacturing	0.299	0.317	0.287	0.326	0.376	0.415	0.367	0.396
Electricity, gas, and water supply	0.020	0.009	0.016	0.024	0.015	0.014	0.014	0.015
Construction	0.011	0.003	0.005	0.007	0.007	0.004	0.004	0.004
Services	0.287	0.236	0.237	0.231	0.253	0.250	0.252	0.243
Dummy sectors	0.009	0.003	0.000	−0.001	−0.002	0.000	0.002	0.000

Source: Data are from input/output tables for various years, constructed by Bank of Korea.

Note: Worker requirement coefficients are calculated from nominal values and then deflated by GDP deflators.

using more imported intermediate inputs as trade in P&C increased—intermediate inputs sourced from, inter alia, China. Even though consumption and investment goods also use imported intermediates, they play a less important role there, relatively speaking. This is especially the case for consumption goods because service sectors, a major component of consumption good output, use mainly domestic inputs.[41]

There is more evidence of an effect when we look at Chinese competition for Korean exports in particular. We again compute the change between 1990 and 2003 in worker requirement coefficients associated with each two-digit industry, but now relate it to a measure of competition from Chinese exports of the products of that same industry, computed as the market share of China relative to that of Korea for the same industry products in the world exports market. Figure 5.20 confirms the existence of a strong negative relationship: where Chinese competition has intensified, the additional employment owing to an increase in Korean exports of the products of the same industry has declined especially dramatically. This presumably reflects the tendency for these export sectors to move

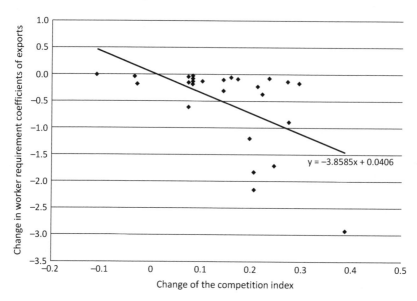

Figure 5.20. Changes in Competition Index versus Worker Requirement Coefficients of Exports, 1990–2003

into the production of more technology- and capital-intensive products and away from the kind of labor-intensive products in which China specializes. Note that an equally strong negative relationship is not evident for consumption and investment, or for total final demand. Evidently this is an effect associated with exports, and with competition from China in particular. It points to, if not exactly an export competitiveness problem, then a very specific source of social and political discomfort with the performance of Korea's export sector.[12]

Exports of Services

If merchandise trade is not the problem, why is there such angst about Korea's international competitiveness? As we have suggested, there may be a reluctance to accept the fact that a mature economy necessarily grows more slowly than an industrializing one, and that this observation applies to export industries just as it does the rest of the economy. But to the extent that there is a problem, it is located in trade in services—since, as we showed in a previous chapter, this is where there is evidence of a productivity problem.

Table 5.28. Trade in Services, Korea and Its Competitors, Selected Years

	Openness	1980	1990	2000	2005
Latin America	Trade of services/GDP	7.5%	8.8%	9.2%	9.0%
(8 countries)	Exports of services/GDP	3.1%	4.0%	4.2%	4.3%
East Asia	Trade of services/GDP	21.4%	22.6%	28.8%	34.6%
(5 countries)	Exports of services/GDP	11.1%	12.1%	13.0%	15.9%
China	Trade of services/GDP	2.2%	2.9%	5.5%	7.1%
	Exports of services/GDP	1.2%	1.7%	2.5%	3.3%
Korea	Trade of services/GDP	9.2%	7.5%	12.5%	13.2%
	Exports of services/GDP	4.0%	3.7%	6.0%	5.8%
OECD	Trade of services/GDP	11.3%	13.0%	19.1%	19.6%
	Exports of services/GDP	5.9%	6.7%	9.7%	10.2%

Source: Data are collected from World Bank, World Development Indicators.
Note: Service trade denotes the sum of exports and imports of services. The reported values are simple averages. East Asia and OECD exclude Vietnam and Luxembourg, respectively, because data are not available.

Table 5.28 shows trade and exports of services (as a share of GDP) for Korea and its competitors. As an exporter of services, Korea lags far behind the OECD. It also lags behind the East Asian average. It can be argued that the East Asian average is elevated by Singapore and Hong Kong, which are big exporters of financial services, but this is precisely the point. Singapore long specialized in producing the kind of medium- and high-tech manufactures in which Korea continues to specialize, while Hong Kong specialized in entrepôt trade. Both have moved into trade in financial and other services faster than Korea. The question is whether these differences reflect special country characteristics (Singapore and Hong Kong both have very limited land with which to support the growth of exports of manufactures) or the failure of Korea to keep up.

To see whether Korea underperforms as an exporter of services, we estimate a gravity model for services exports in the manner of Walsh (2006). The sample we analyze includes 27 OECD countries and up to 50 of their trading partners. Like Walsh, we augment the gravity equation with a measure of the coverage of restrictions on services trade constructed by the Australian Productivity Commission. The dependent variable is bilateral real service exports. In Table 5.29, the first two columns pool annual data for the years 1999 to 2005 and estimate the relationship using OLS. The

Table 5.29. Korean Service Exports Are Not Wholly Explained by the Conventional Arguments Variables of the Gravity Model

	OLS		Panel	
		Korea dummy		*Korea dummy*
GDP in source country	0.862**	0.865**	0.891**	0.895**
	(0.011)	(0.011)	(0.024)	(0.024)
GDP in partner country	0.731**	0.733**	0.656**	0.658**
	(0.010)	(0.010)	(0.019)	(0.0119)
Per capita GDP in source country	1.345**	1.363**	1.130**	1.131**
	(0.048)	(0.049)	(0.079)	(0.079)
Per capita GDP in partner country	0.304**	0.310**	0.458**	0.464**
	(0.019)	(0.019)	(0.040)	(0.040)
Distance	−0.863**	−0.837**	−0.790**	−0.764**
	(0.016)	(0.016)	(0.034)	(0.035)
No. of landlocked	−0.250**	−0.246**	−0.274**	−0.273**
	(0.029)	(0.029)	(0.060)	(0.060)
No. of islands	0.334**	0.301**	0.272**	0.235**
	(0.029)	(0.029)	(0.068)	(0.068)
Land border dummy	0.269**	0.293**	0.361**	0.385**
	(0.059)	(0.059)	(0.126)	(0.125)
1 for common language	0.886**	0.916**	0.834**	0.861**
	(0.041)	(0.042)	(0.098)	(0.098)
Dummy for common colonizer post-1945	3.397**	3.408**	3.060**	3.069**
	(0.294)	(0.293)	(0.593)	(0.591)
Dummy for pair ever in colonial relationship	0.537**	0.500*	0.532**	0.501**
	(0.066)	(0.066)	(0.157)	(0.157)
RTA dummy	0.132**	0.126**	0.083	0.075
	(0.040)	(0.040)	(0.086)	(0.086)
Log of product of land area	−0.034**	−0.042**	−0.021	−0.039*
	(0.006)	(0.006)	(0.013)	(0.013)
Korea export dummy		−0.861**		−0.843**
		(0.086)		(0.195)
Korea import dummy		1.179**		1.412**
		(0.182)		(0.469)
R-squared	0.63	0.63	0.63	0.63
Observations	20,128	20,128	20,128	20,128

Table 5.29. (Continued)

Note: Standard errors in parentheses. OLS=ordinary least squares. The dependent variable is bilateral real service imports of the source country from the partner country. Real imports are obtained by dividing current U.S. dollar values, collected from the OECD's statistics on international trade in services (OECD 2007), by the U.S. consumer price index (CPI). We collected data on four categories of services (government, travel, transport, and other commercial services) and estimated the gravity equation by pooling the data. GDP and per capita GDP are from World Bank, World Development Indicators, and converted into real terms by dividing by the U.S. CPI. The Korea dummy is set to one if Korea is a partner country and zero otherwise. Other country-specific explanatory variables are obtained from Rose (2000). The RTA dummy takes one if the pair countries have formed a regional trade agreement. All the explanatory variables except the dummy variables are expressed as logarithms. The first two columns report pooled regressions on annual data for the period 1999–2005. In the next two columns, we used panel data estimation techniques with random effects. Standard errors of the estimated coefficients are reported in parentheses. Intercepts and time-fixed effects are included but not reported.

** and * indicate statistical significance at the 1- and 5-percent levels, respectively.

next two columns apply panel-data techniques assuming random effects. The key coefficient, on the dummy variable for Korea, is significantly negative. A coefficient of -0.85 suggests that Korea's exports of services are 53.3 percent lower than would be predicted on the basis of the average international performance of a country with its characteristics. This obviously is a considerable shortfall.

Following Walsh, we also estimate equations for four categories of services: government, travel, transport, and other commercial services.[43] As shown in Table 5.30, the indicator for South Korea enters negatively in all four columns. This confirms that the country underperforms in terms of exports of services across the board. The largest negative coefficient, for what this is worth, is on exports of miscellaneous commercial services.[44] Why does Korea underperform so dramatically as an exporter of services? For the same reasons that productivity in the service sector is low generally—reasons that we address in Chapter 4 and Chapter 8.

Conclusion

Korean export performance has held up well despite the challenges of the financial crisis, extensive post-crisis restructuring, the emergence of China, and the slower growth that is the entirely normal consequence of economic maturation. During the high-growth period, Korean exports were exceptional in a number of ways. They grew unusually rapidly. They were unusually sophisticated. They were unusually well diversified. Korea was precocious in developing the extensive as well as the intensive margins.

Table 5.30. Korean Service Exports Are Not Wholly Explained by the Conventional Arguments of the Gravity Model: Seemingly Unrelated Regressions

	Government services not incl. elsewhere	Korea dummy	Transportation	Korea dummy	Travel	Korea dummy	Other commercial services	Korea dummy
GDP in source country	0.767** (0.026)	0.759** (0.026)	0.827** (0.022)	0.817** (0.022)	0.805** (0.026)	0.793** (0.025)	0.861** (0.023)	0.771** (0.025)
GDP in partner country	0.632** (0.022)	0.616** (0.022)	0.791** (0.019)	0.769** (0.019)	0.653** (0.022)	0.623** (0.022)	0.937** (0.020)	0.891** (0.021)
Per capita GDP in source country	1.181* (0.208)	1.300** (0.207)	0.969** (0.155)	1.217** (0.163)	1.545** (0.205)	1.704** (0.201)	2.573** (0.161)	3.065** (0.165)
Per capita GDP in partner country	0.183** (0.043)	0.196** (0.043)	0.165** (0.036)	0.180** (0.036)	0.152** (0.043)	0.180** (0.042)	0.494** (0.039)	0.524** (0.038)
Distance	-0.398** (0.036)	-0.367** (0.037)	-0.740** (0.031)	-0.709** (0.031)	-0.911** (0.036)	-0.848** (0.036)	-0.853** (0.034)	-0.821** (0.033)
No. of landlocked	-0.274** (0.078)	-0.275** (0.078)	-0.674** (0.065)	-0.678** (0.065)	0.067 (0.078)	0.072 (0.076)	-0.184** (0.070)	-0.229** (0.069)
No. of islands	0.031 (0.058)	0.005 (0.058)	0.361** (0.048)	0.356** (0.048)	0.511** (0.058)	0.448** (0.057)	0.312** (0.053)	0.2435* (0.055)
Land border dummy	-0.306* (0.121)	-0.263* (0.121)	0.227* (0.102)	0.272** (0.102)	0.136 (0.121)	0.226 (0.119)	0.132 (0.111)	0.100 (0.109)
1 for common language	0.680** (0.084)	0.683** (0.085)	0.846** (0.071)	0.827** (0.072)	0.884** (0.084)	0.902** (0.083)	0.603** (0.078)	0.755** (0.078)

Dummy for pair ever in colonial relationship	0.415**	0.386**	0.565**	0.558**	0.966**	0.889**	0.663**	0.577**
	(0.114)	(0.114)	(0.097)	(0.097)	(0.114)	(0.112)	(0.103)	(0.101)
RTA dummy	0.048	0.065	0.014	0.044	0.489**	0.516**	0.100	0.137
	(0.080)	(0.080)	(0.068)	(0.068)	(0.080)	(0.079)	(0.073)	(0.072)
Log of product of land area	−0.001	−0.002	−0.087**	−0.084**	0.084**	0.084**	−0.092**	−0.073**
	(0.013)	(0.013)	(0.011)	(0.011)	(0.013)	(0.013)	(0.012)	(0.012)
Nontariff barrier	1.771	1.145	0.556	0.240	−0.875	−2.727**	0.246	−13.518**
	(0.957)	(1.026)	(0.412)	(0.422)	(0.903)	(0.954)	(1.091)	(1.079)
Korea export dummy		−0.503**		−0.271		−1.070**		−1.169**
		(0.166)		(0.141)		(0.163)		(0.150)
Korea import dummy		1.107**		1.202**		2.177**		4.118**
		(0.291)		(0.238)		(0.284)		(0.414)
R-squared	0.65	0.66	0.77	0.77	0.73	0.75	0.81	0.82
Observations	2,246	2,246	2,246	2,246	2,246	2,246	2,246	2,246

Note: Standard errors in parentheses. The regressions reported here are estimated by seemingly unrelated regressions. The measure of nontariff barriers is the Australian Productivity Commission's trade-restrictive index. For other variable definitions, see the note to Table 5.29. See also Table 5.A5 in the appendix to this chapter.

** indicates statistical significance at the 1-percent level.

Over time, however, there has been predictable reversion to the mean. The technology content of exports is now exactly what one would expect of a country with Korea's per capita GDP. Similarly, performance on the extensive margin is now exactly what one would expect of an economy with its per capita GDP. At the same time, on a number of dimensions—the overall rate of growth of exports and the diversification of the export bundle, for example—Korea continues to perform better than other countries at a similar stage of economic development. Anxiety over Korean export performance seems to us exaggerated.

If there are grounds for concern, they lie in two places. First, in exports, because Korea underperforms as an exporter of services, and second, in China, as the rise of China may make it more difficult for Korea to maintain its export competitiveness and increase employment on that basis.

To be sure, the sources of export competitiveness have changed. Public policy, including the maintenance of a real exchange rate that is exceptionally favorable to exports, plays a smaller role. Product and process innovation within manufacturing itself is more important. But this does not change the point that Korea continues to export more than other countries with similar characteristics. While the extent of that outperforming has declined since the first half of the 1990s, the magnitude of the decline is slight. Korea continues to export more high-tech products than most other countries with similar characteristics. While it tends to occupy the bottom end of many of those high-tech markets, there is nothing new about this behavior; rather, it is part of a long-standing pattern, reflecting the country's precocious move into those technologically sophisticated sectors and the chaebol's dominance of many export lines. It does not change the fact that Korea's move upmarket into the production of more technologically sophisticated exports has been rapid by international standards. It does not diminish the extent to which this has helped to insulate the country from competition from other lower-cost economies.

If Korean manufacturing has not lost its competitiveness, then what is the problem? The problem, internationally as domestically, is the service sector. Korea is experiencing the same shift from manufacturing to services evident in all maturing economies. As we have emphasized, this does not bode well for the future, given that the increasingly traded nature of services is one of the most important characteristics distinguishing the twenty-first-century environment in which the economy must compete.

Appendix

Table 5.A1. Determinants of the Real Exchange Rate

	ln RER1 (5-year)	ln RER2 (5-year)	ln RER3 (5-year)	ln RERI	ln RER2	ln RER3
Real per capita GDP	−0.240*** [0.012]	−0.181*** [0.019]	−0.239*** [0.022]	−0.232*** [0.005]	−0.166*** [0.008]	−0.231*** [0.010]
Population age 0–14 (% of total)		−0.002 [0.004]	−0.011** [0.004]		−0.000 [0.002]	−0.010*** [0.002]
Population age 65 and up (% of total)		−0.031*** [0.008]	−0.040*** [0.009]		−.030*** [0.003]	−0.037*** [0.004]
Democracy			0.008 [0.010]			0.013*** [0.004]
Observations	1,339	1,157	912	7,000	6,092	4,592
R-squared	0.3008	0.3290	0.3683	0.2782	0.3041	0.3623

Note: Standard errors in brackets. This table is an appendix to Figure 5.5. RER=real exchange rate. The first three columns are based on five-year time averages, while the next three columns utilize annual observations covering the period 1950–2004. The demographic variables are defined as the share of population age 0 to 14 and the share of the population 65 and older. Index of democracy is obtained from Freedomhouse, http://www.freedomhouse.org.

*** and ** indicate statistical significance at the 1-percent and 5-percent levels, respectively.

Table 5.A2. Classification of Industries by Technology

Low-Technology Manufactures	Medium-Technology Manufactures	High-Technology Manufactures
611 LEATHER	266 SYNTHETIC FIBERS TO SPIN	524 RADIOACTIVE ETC MATERIAL
612 LEATHER ETC MANUFACTURES	267 OTHER MAN-MADE FIBERS	541 MEDICINAL,PHARM PRODUCTS
613 FUR SKINS TANNED,DRESSED	512 ALCOHOLS,PHENOLS ETC	712 STEAM ENGINES,TURBINES
642 PAPER,ETC,PRECUT,ARTS OF	513 CARBOXYLIC ACIDS ETC	716 ROTATING ELECTRIC PLANT
651 TEXTILE YARN	533 PIGMENTS,PAINTS,ETC	718 OTH POWER GENERATG MACHY
652 COTTON FABRICS,WOVEN	553 PERFUMERY,COSMETICS,ETC	751 OFFICE MACHINES
654 OTH WOVEN TEXTILE FABRIC	554 SOAP,CLEANSING ETC PREPS	752 AUTOMTIC DATA PROC EQUIP
655 KNITTED,ETC FABRICS	562 FERTILIZERS,MANUFACTURED	759 OFFICE,ADP MCH PTS,ACCES
656 LACE,RIBBONS,TULLE,ETC	572 EXPLOSIVES,PYROTECH PROD	761 TELEVISION RECEIVERS
657 SPECIAL TXTL FABRC,PRODS	582 PROD OF CONDENSATION ETC	764 TELECOM EQPT,PTS,ACC NES
658 TEXTILE ARTICLES NES	583 POLYMERIZATION ETC PRODS	771 ELECTRIC POWER MACHY NES
659 FLOOR COVERINGS,ETC	584 CELLULOSE DERIVATIVS ETC	774 ELECTRO-MEDCL,XRAY EQUIP
665 GLASSWARE	585 PLASTIC MATERIAL NES	776 TRANSISTORS, VALVES, ETC.
666 POTTERY	591 PESTICIDES,DISINFECTANTS	778 ELECTRICAL MACHINERY NES
673 IRON,STEEL SHAPES ETC	598 MISCEL CHEM PRODUCTS NES	792 AIRCRAFT ETC
674 IRN,STL UNIV,PLATE,SHEET	653 WOVN MAN-MADE FIB FABRIC	871 OPTICAL INSTRUMENTS
675 IRON,STEEL HOOP,STRIP	671 PIG IRON ETC.	874 MEASURNG,CONTROLNG INSTR
676 RAILWY RAILS ETC IRN,STL	672 IRON,STEEL PRIMARY FORMS	881 PHOTO APPARAT,EQUIPT NES

677 IRN,STL WIRE(EXCL W ROD)
679 IRN,STL CASTINGS UNWORKD
691 STRUCTURES AND PARTS NES
692 METAL TANKS,BOXES,ETC
693 WIRE PRODUCTS NON ELECTR
694 STL,COPPR NAILS,NUTS,ETC
695 TOOLS
696 CUTLERY
697 BASE MTL HOUSEHOLD EQUIP
699 BASE METAL MFRS NES
821 FURNITURE,PARTS THEREOF
831 TRAVEL GOODS,HANDBAGS
842 MENS OUTERWEAR NOT KNIT
843 WOMENS OUTERWEAR NONKNIT
844 UNDER GARMENTS NOT KNIT
845 OUTERWEAR KNIT NONELASTC
846 UNDER GARMENTS KNITTED
847 TEXTILE CLTHNG ACCES NES
848 HEADGEAR,NONTXTL CLOTHNG
851 FOOTWEAR
893 ARTICLES OF PLASTIC NES
894 TOYS,SPORTING GOODS,ETC

678 IRN,STL TUBES,PIPES,ETC
711 STEAM BOILERS & AUX PLNT
713 INTRNL COMBUS PSTN ENGIN
714 ENGINES AND MOTORS NES
721 AGRIC MACHY,EXC TRACTORS
722 TRACTORS NON-ROAD
723 CIVIL ENGNEERG EQUIP ETC
724 TEXTILE,LEATHER MACHNRY
725 PAPER ETC MILL MACHINERY
726 PRINTG,BKBINDG MACHY,PTS
727 FOOD MACHRY NON-DOMESTIC
728 OTH MACHY FOR SPCL INDUS
736 METALWORKING MACH-TOOLS
737 METALWORKING MACHNRY NES
741 HEATING,COOLING EQUIPMNT
742 PUMPS FOR LIQUIDS ETC
743 PUMPS NES,CENTRFUGES ETC
744 MECHANICAL HANDLING EQU
745 NONELEC MACHY,TOOLS NES
749 NONELEC MACH PTS,ACC NES
762 RADIO BROADCAST RECEIVRS
763 SOUND RECORDRS,PHONOGRPH

(continued)

Table 5-A2. (Continued)

Low-Technology Manufactures	Medium-Technology Manufactures	High-Technology Manufactures
895 OFFICE SUPPLIES NES	772 SWITCHGEAR ETC,PARTS NES	
897 GOLD,SILVERWARE,JEWELRY	773 ELECTR DISTRIBUTNG EQUIP	
898 MUSICAL INSTRUMENTS,PTS	775 HOUSEHOLD TYPE EQUIP NES	
899 OTHER MANUFACTURED GOODS	781 PASS MOTOR VEH EXC BUSES	
	782 LORRIES,SPCL MTR VEH NES	
	783 ROAD MOTOR VEHICLES NES	
	784 MOTOR VEH PRTS,ACCES NES	
	785 CYCLES,ETC MOTRZD OR NOT	
	786 TRAILERS,NONMOTR VEH,NES	
	791 RAILWAY VEHICLES	
	793 SHIPS AND BOATS ETC	
	812 PLUMBG,HEATNG,LGHTNG EQU	
	872 MEDICAL INSTRUMENTS NES	
	873 METERS AND COUNTERS NES	
	882 PHOTO,CINEMA SUPPLIES	
	884 OPTICAL GOODS NES	
	885 WATCHES AND CLOCKS	
	951 WAR FIREARMS,AMMUNITION	

Source: Lall (2000), appendix table 1, 34.

Note: This table is an appendix to Figure 5.15. Code numbers are Standard International Trade Classification three-digit codes, Rev. 2.

Table 5.A3. Exports, Imports, and Trade Balance by Technology Intensity, 1987–1989 and 2004–2006

Regions (selected countries)		Latin America			East Asia[a]			China			Korea		
		Exports	Imports	Balance	Exports	Imports	Balance	Exports	Imports	Balance	Exports	Imports	Balance
1987–1989	Commodities	36.7	9.8	26.9	37.0	14.3	22.7	9.7	5.3	4.5	2.1	7.5	-5.4
	Natural resource–based manufactures	21.4	18.3	3.1	34.1	24.5	9.6	10.1	11.4	-1.3	5.4	19.9	-14.4
	Low-tech	19.6	11.1	8.5	30.2	27.1	3.2	48.5	26.3	22.3	59.3	10.7	48.6
	Mid-tech	14.5	28.1	-13.6	20.4	52.1	-31.7	11.0	46.1	-35.1	32.5	29.7	2.8
	High-tech	2.5	10.0	-7.5	14.2	29.3	-15.2	3.7	8.5	-4.8	6.8	13.1	-6.3
	Total	94.7	77.3	17.3	135.9	147.2	-11.4	82.9	97.5	-14.5	106.2	80.8	25.3
2004–2006	Commodities	154.1	50.2	104.0	110.6	53.8	56.8	43.3	71.7	-28.4	14.3	60.7	-46.4
	Natural resource–based manufactures	130.9	95.5	35.4	117.9	92.3	25.4	105.1	164.2	-59.2	35.3	69.1	-33.7
	Low-tech	119.0	132.9	-13.9	162.8	108.6	54.1	649.0	123.2	527.0	73.7	61.8	11.8
	Mid-tech	106.0	186.4	-80.4	164.1	197.1	-33.2	310.5	330.0	-20.1	177.3	111.2	66.1
	High-tech	60.6	111.1	-50.5	136.3	205.9	-69.6	233.6	272.7	-39.1	97.4	69.8	27.7
	Total	570.6	576.1	-5.4	691.8	657.7	33.7	1341.5	961.8	380.2	397.9	372.6	25.5

Source: Calculations based on UN Comtrade data. Technology classification follows Lall (2000).

Note: [a] Vietnam is excluded from East Asia in 1987–1989.

Table 5.A4. Changes in Export Composition

Period & products		Argentina	Brazil	Chile	Colombia	Costa Rica	Ecuador	Mexico	Peru	Latin America (8 countries)
1987–1989	Commodities	42.3%	18.1%	66.6%	75.1%	50.3%	65.0%	33.4%	22.3%	38.8%
	Natural resource–based manufactures	21.4%	24.1%	29.3%	5.9%	12.5%	27.0%	22.0%	29.7%	22.6%
	Low-tech	21.3%	31.6%	1.7%	10.2%	26.5%	5.2%	20.0%	34.5%	20.7%
	Mid-tech	13.4%	23.2%	2.2%	8.0%	4.6%	2.1%	19.1%	10.2%	15.3%
	High-tech	1.5%	3.0%	0.1%	0.9%	6.2%	0.7%	5.5%	3.3%	2.6%
	Total	100.0%	100.0%	100.0%	100.0%	100.0%	100.0%	100.0%	100.0%	100.0%
2004–2006	Commodities	50.8%	23.6%	48.6%	34.1%	29.8%	46.6%	9.6%	10.8%	27.0%
	Natural resource–based manufactures	24.8%	26.0%	44.7%	11.4%	14.6%	27.1%	10.2%	11.9%	22.9%
	Low-tech	8.8%	19.3%	1.5%	25.1%	21.0%	15.0%	34.1%	30.2%	20.9%
	Mid-tech	12.1%	26.1%	4.9%	24.4%	23.2%	6.8%	23.4%	10.2%	18.6%
	High-tech	3.6%	5.0%	0.3%	5.1%	11.4%	4.5%	22.7%	36.9%	10.6%
	Total	100.0%	100.0%	100.0%	100.0%	100.0%	100.0%	100.0%	100.0%	100.0%

1987–1989	Commodities	51.0%	28.6%	22.3%	11.3%	35.5%	—	27.8%	11.7%	2.0%
	Natural resource–based manufactures	22.3%	33.9%	29.7%	26.3%	10.4%	—	24.1%	12.1%	5.1%
	Low-tech	18.9%	15.3%	34.5%	18.8%	40.5%	—	23.5%	58.5%	55.9%
	Mid-tech	7.1%	11.3%	10.2%	25.4%	7.0%	—	14.5%	13.2%	30.6%
	High-tech	0.8%	10.8%	3.3%	18.1%	6.5%	—	10.1%	4.4%	6.4%
	Total	100.0%	100.0%	100.0%	100.0%	100.0%		100.0%	100.0%	100.0%
2004–2006	Commodities	28.3%	20.6%	10.8%	3.8%	18.0%	21.6%	16.2% (16.0%)	3.2%	3.6%
	Natural resource–based manufactures	23.8%	12.8%	11.9%	16.8%	16.5%	6.8%	16.6% (17.0%)	7.8%	8.9%
	Low-tech	28.2%	21.6%	30.2%	17.2%	28.0%	65.3%	25.4% (23.5%)	48.4%	18.5%
	Mid-tech	13.3%	26.4%	10.2%	30.4%	24.8%	3.5%	22.8% (23.7%)	23.1%	44.6%
	High-tech	6.4%	18.6%	36.9%	31.8%	12.7%	2.9%	19.0% (19.7%)	17.4%	24.5%
	Total	100.0%	100.0%	100.0%	100.0%	100.0%	100.0%	100.0%	100.0%	100.0%

Source: Calculations based on UN Comtrade data. Technology classification follows Lall (2000).

Note: The data for Vietnam in 1987–1989 are not available. The values in parentheses for East Asia in 2004–2006 are based on five countries, excluding Vietnam.

Table 5.A5. Determinants of Service Exports by Sector

	Total		Government services not included elsewhere	
	OLS	Panel	OLS	Panel
GDP in source country	0.955**	0.905**	0.781**	0.804**
	(0.012)	(0.026)	(0.021)	(0.038)
GDP in partner country	0.756**	0.638**	0.571**	0.553**
	(0.010)	(0.020)	(0.018)	(0.032)
Per capita GDP in source country	0.595**	0.530**	0.862**	0.447
	(0.064)	(0.114)	(0.150)	(0.263)
Per capita GDP in partner country	0.244**	0.387**	0.150**	0.093
	(0.018)	(0.036)	(0.034)	(0.062)
Distance	−0.759**	−0.714**	−0.341**	−0.324**
	(0.017)	(0.037)	(0.028)	(0.051)
No. of landlocked	−0.131**	−0.077	−0.132*	−0.133
	(0.029)	(0.056)	(0.056)	(0.095)
No. of islands	0.410**	0.384**	−0.022	−0.036**
	(0.035)	(0.078)	(0.050)	(0.102)
Common land border	0.667**	0.805**	−0.063	0.026
	(0.067)	(0.152)	(0.102)	(0.178)
Common language	0.860**	0.776**	0.757**	0.787**
	(0.044)	(0.095)	(0.082)	(0.158)
Common colonizer post-1945	3.195**	2.685**	2.659**	2.481**
	(0.210)	(0.412)	(0.603)	(0.828)
Pair ever in colonial relationship	0.889**	0.930**	0.339**	0.207
	(0.066)	(0.138)	(0.112)	(0.224)
RTA dummy[a]	0.356**	0.519**	−0.012	0.032
	(0.046)	(0.106)	(0.075)	(0.127)
Log of product of land area	−0.070**	−0.031*	−0.022*	−0.039
	(0.007)	(0.014)	(0.011)	(0.020)
Nontariff barrier	−1.864**	−2.455**	1.654*	−0.102
	(0.379)	(0.687)	(0.751)	(1.247)
Korea dummy	−0.725**	−0.502*	−0.531**	−0.567*
	(0.107)	(0.254)	(0.134)	(0.263)
R-squared	0.79	0.79	0.65	0.64
Observations	9,575	9,575	3,534	3,534
Group		2,126		867

Note: Standard errors in parentheses. This table is an appendix to Table 5.30. Instead of applying the seemingly unrelated regression technique, here we estimated the gravity equation separately for the four categories of services imports (government, travel, transport, and other commercial services). We also estimated the gravity equation for total service imports.

[a] RTA = regional trade agreement.

** and * indicate the estimated coefficient is statistically significant from zero at the 1 percent and 5 percent levels.

	Transportation		Travel		Other commercial services	
	OLS	Panel	OLS	Panel	OLS	Panel
	0.933** (0.018)	0.967** (0.040)	0.885** (0.017)	0.942** (0.037)	0.943** (0.018)	0.946** (0.038)
	0.845** (0.016)	0.767** (0.032)	0.701** (0.015)	0.665** (0.030)	0.963** (0.016)	0.894** (0.033)
	0.577** (0.121)	0.399* (0.202)	1.719** (0.118)	1.593** (0.200)	2.299** (0.125)	2.368** (0.215)
	0.136** (0.031)	0.329** (0.066)	0.139** (0.029)	0.332** (0.063)	0.418** (0.031)	0.482** (0.066)
	−0.697** (0.026)	−0.609** (0.058)	−1.008** (0.025)	−1.002** (0.054)	−0.881** (0.029)	−0.844** (0.062)
	−0.502** (0.049)	−0.460** (0.112)	−0.193** (0.046)	−0.261** (0.098)	−0.187** (0.057)	−0.249* (0.119)
	0.427** (0.047)	0.358** (0.108)	0.650** (0.047)	0.588** (0.108)	0.386** (0.043)	0.339** (0.101)
	0.250** (0.090)	0.301 (0.210)	0.429** (0.086)	0.608** (0.188)	0.131 (0.117)	0.120 (0.249)
	1.022** (0.064)	1.015** (0.153)	0.824** (0.061)	0.753** (0.145)	0.625** (0.059)	0.630** (0.135)
	—	—	3.029** (0.384)	2.858** (0.908)	—	—
	0.414** (0.095)	0.474* (0.223)	0.887** (0.098)	0.888** (0.236)	0.773** (0.102)	0.761** (0.244)
	0.099 (0.058)	0.222 (0.130)	0.301** (0.056)	0.198 (0.127)	0.232** (0.072)	0.349* (0.145)
	−0.134** (0.010)	−0.115** (0.023)	0.040** (0.009)	0.036 (0.020)	−0.100** (0.010)	−0.086** (0.021)
	0.409 (0.454)	−0.282 (1.042)	1.017 (0.557)	1.967 (1.053)	3.555** (1.242)	5.209** (3.145)
	−0.644** (0.133)	−0.523 (0.317)	−1.241** (0.145)	−1.251** (0.328)	−1.002** (0.134)	−1.092** (0.302)
	0.73	0.72	0.73	0.73	0.79	0.79
	4,619	4,619	5,676	5,676	4,092	4,092
		832		1,118		863

CHAPTER 6

Foreign Direct Investment
and Economic Growth

If export performance has not been a problem for Korean economic growth, then perhaps foreign direct investment has. Observers worry that Korea is a relatively unattractive destination for foreign investment. Policies toward inward FDI have long been restrictive. Costs of production are increasingly high, and labor market regulation is extensive. There are more attractive low-cost locations—notably China—for foreign firms seeking to set up operations. Korea is therefore relatively unsuccessful in attracting foreign companies that bring with them capital and technologies conducive to economic growth. Meanwhile, outward foreign investment is high. Korean companies, those same observers worry, increasingly prefer to invest abroad, in China, where costs of production are lower, or in the United States, where market access is secured. Even if this behavior strengthens corporate earnings, it slows the growth of output and employment at home.

In examining foreign direct investment in this chapter, we confirm that inward FDI is indeed less than would be expected of a country with Korea's characteristics. This is true of inward FDI into manufacturing and services alike, although the shortfall is especially pronounced for the service sector. For many years this was the result of restrictive policies, because Korean officials and firms favored other modes of capital and technology transfer. But while overt restrictions on FDI have now been removed, Korea continues to underperform on this dimension. Foreign investors complain that the rules of the game are neither transparent nor equitably enforced. Family and personal connections continue to matter, handicapping foreign firms. Moreover, since the turn of the century China has emerged as an increasingly attractive destination for FDI. There is evidence of significant FDI diversion from Korea to China.

In contrast, statistical analysis rejects the view that Korea undertakes significantly more FDI abroad than would be expected of a country with its characteristics. While outflows were larger than would have been predicted for a country with Korea's characteristics in the 1980s and 1990s, this is no longer the case. Since 2001 Korea's FDI outflow has been right on target. Insofar as domestic investment has fallen, this is not the result of an unusually high level of outward FDI. If the country has an FDI problem, it is entirely on the inflow side.

But this is not an argument for across-the-board FDI inducement. Rather, it is an argument for regulatory reforms and incentives to encourage FDI in manufacturing industries that rely on highly skilled labor and service sectors such as finance, insurance, and real estate, where both international evidence and Korea's own experience point to the existence of substantial benefits.

Overview

Before 1960, Korea did not permit inward FDI. Japanese-owned companies dominated the Korean economy in the colonial period, rendering foreign ownership a politically delicate issue following Korean independence. The Foreign Capital Promotion and Inducement Act adopted in 1960 removed only select prohibitions; it was intended mainly to attract FDI from Korean expatriates living abroad. The Dow Chemical Company and the Chungju Fertilizer Company created a joint venture to produce polyethylene for domestic consumption. Other than this, however, FDI in this early period was essentially nil.

With the inauguration of the first five-year plan in 1962, this began to change. In 1963 the FDI law was amended to facilitate approval of foreign direct investments that might contribute to exports. Thirty-nine applications for FDI were approved in the five years of the first plan, though only half of the proposed inward foreign investment actually took place. More significant were the normalization of diplomatic relations with Japan in 1965 and the consolidation of existing rules into the more liberal Foreign Capital Inducement Law in 1966. As part of this consolidation, longer tax

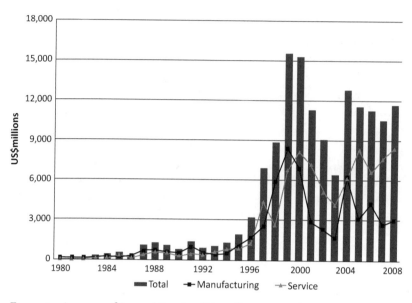

Figure 6.1. Amount of Inward Foreign Direct Investment (FDI) in Korean Manufacturing and Service Industries
Data from Ministry of Knowledge Economy.

holidays were extended to new foreign business ventures, foreign managers and technicians were exempted from Korean income taxes, and previous requirements for local participation (joint ventures) were removed. An Office of Investment Promotion was established in the Economic Planning Board to reduce red tape and speed processing of FDI applications. In 1970 the Masan free trade zone was established and a law preventing union activities in foreign-invested firms was adopted. The second five-year plan (1966 to 1971) saw a significant increase in the flow of FDI into labor-intensive sectors, particularly textiles and electronics subcontracting. The United States and, especially after 1968, Japan were the main sources of foreign investment. This was the "golden age" of foreign investment (see Figure 6.1).

With the shift to the Heavy and Chemical Industry Drive in 1973, policy toward foreign investment again turned more restrictive. The authorities encouraged domestic ownership and control of the heavy industries on which the growth strategy now focused.[1] Export, minimum-investment, and joint-venture requirements were imposed on foreign projects. FDI first surged ahead in the mid-1970s as the capital-intensive Heavy and Chemical Industry Drive was launched, but fell back as regulation began to bite. The provision of subsidized credit to the heavy and chemical industries gave domestic producers an alternative to joint ventures as a way of financing their expansion. Given the rapid growth of the economy and the record of successful technological upgrading in this period, it is hard to argue that the authorities' strategy, which relied on imported capital equipment and licensing rather than FDI for technology transfer, and on debt rather than equity finance, was an impediment to growth.[2]

But there is reason to think that this approach to technology transfer worked best for a country still relatively far from the technological frontier, which Korea gradually began to approach in the 1980s. In addition, relying on debt rather than equity finance heightened financial fragility.[3] Thus, the debt crisis of the early 1980s saw the beginnings of a shift toward more liberal FDI policies. In 1984 the government moved to a negative list system. Previously it had been necessary to secure approval for each individual FDI project; now any project not specifically prohibited or restricted was open to FDI. The government shortened the negative list in 1985 and 1987. Foreign investment was authorized in a growing number of industries, and majority-owned and wholly owned foreign firms were permitted for the first time. Electronics and electrical equipment, along with hotels and tourism, were among the most popular destinations for FDI, and Japan was the most important source.

By mid-1991, foreign investment was still prohibited or restricted in only 12 of 522 manufacturing industries distinguished by the Ministry of Finance.[4] Remaining restrictions applied mainly to nonmanufacturing sectors. South Korea was looking to join the Organization for Economic Cooperation and Development, and a relatively open FDI regime was a concomitant of membership. FDI receipts rose by 50 percent between 1987 and 1991 and 1992 and 1996, reflecting the strong growth of the economy and a favorable international environment. In December 1996, when accession to the OECD finally occurred, Korea amended its foreign investment law to bring it in line with international norms: starting in February 1997 friendly mergers and acquisitions (achieved with the consent of the board of directors) were allowed.

But foreign companies and governments continued to complain that the country was less open to foreign investment than it appeared to be.[5]

FDI amounted to barely one-quarter of 1 percent of GDP and one-half of 1 percent of domestic investment in the mid-1990s. For foreign finance Korea favored debt rather than equity—a preference that helped to set the stage for the 1997–1998 crisis.[6]

That crisis occasioned perhaps the most marked shift in FDI policy in the country's history. Further deregulation and financial liberalization—cornerstones of the International Monetary Fund program—were integral to the Kim Dae Jung government's efforts to restore investor confidence, attract capital back into the country, and raise the efficiency and productivity of the economy. It moved quickly to remove restrictions on cross-border mergers and acquisitions and land-ownership by foreigners. In April 1998 it removed restrictions on 22 categories of business, including rental real estate, securities trading, investment and trust companies, insurance related activities, and golf courses. The government extended new tax exemptions and concessions for foreign firms investing in factory sites. In November 1998 it adopted the Foreign Investment Promotion Act, which simplified procedures related to FDI and permitted, among other things, hostile takeovers by foreign investors. By the end of 1998, 1,117 of 1,148 subject sectors were completely opened to FDI, and another 18 sectors were partially opened.[7] In the service sector, foreigners were permitted to own financial, marketing, procurement, and public relations consulting firms. However, the activities of foreign law firms were still severely restricted, and professional engineers, architects, accountants, and management consultants were allowed to work only on a contractual basis for local firms. Still, this was a much more open FDI regime than what had existed before.

The new policy, in combination with depreciation of the won, which created fire-sale prices, induced a sharp increase in inward FDI, from less than $3 billion in 1997 to $5 billion in 1998 and more than $15 billion in both 1999 and 2000 (more than 3 percent of Korean GDP each year). Whereas most previous FDI in Korea had been destined for manufacturing, starting in 1999 the majority went into the service sector (Table 6.1). Foreign investors, mainly from the United States, acquired control of a substantial fraction of the financial services industry; for example, foreign-controlled banks accounted for 10 percent of the assets of the banking sector by 2000. In this period only China and Hong Kong among countries in the Asia-Pacific region attracted more foreign investment.[8]

Table 6.1. Inward Foreign Direct Investment to Korea

Year	Agriculture, fishing, & mining (%)	Manufacturing						Service			Total (million $)
		Total (%)	High-tech (%)	Medium-tech (%)	Low-tech (%)	Resource-based (%)	Total (%)	Finance & insurance (%)	Electricity & construction (%)		
1970	0.9	81.8	11.8	10.5	17.2	42.4	9.7	0.5	7.6	75.9
1971	0.4	72.3	11.8	26.8	26.7	7.1	24.2	0.0	3.1	40.2
1972	1.5	89.8	34.3	32.7	13.8	9.0	8.6	1.1	0.1	122.0
1973	0.8	62.2	11.4	34.8	11.6	4.5	31.9	0.3	5.1	318.2
1974	0.9	83.8	15.1	27.4	29.3	12.1	14.2	2.4	1.1	152.8
1975	0.3	82.0	1.4	12.1	49.1	19.4	16.8	0.3	0.9	207.3
1976	0.9	70.5	24.3	7.7	32.7	5.8	26.9	5.0	1.7	79.2
1977	0.6	46.4	7.7	5.8	22.2	10.6	48.4	20.9	4.7	83.6
1978	0.5	41.4	9.7	9.1	19.2	3.4	49.1	7.6	9.1	149.4
1979	0.4	51.1	11.2	5.8	18.3	15.8	36.1	26.2	12.4	191.3
1980	0.0	70.4	23.1	3.2	33.2	10.9	25.6	8.2	4.0	143.1
1981	0.8	83.8	28.6	6.0	40.1	9.1	5.9	2.0	9.5	153.2
1982	0.9	60.9	14.4	3.8	34.7	8.0	20.7	11.7	17.5	189.0
1983	0.6	38.9	20.8	2.7	11.2	4.1	54.8	1.7	5.8	269.4
1984	0.0	59.6	36.2	2.5	12.9	8.0	29.3	3.1	11.0	422.3
1985	0.2	32.9	5.5	5.5	14.8	7.0	64.9	3.4	2.0	532.2

(continued)

Table 6.1. (Continued)

Year	Agriculture, fishing, & mining (%)	Manufacturing					Service			
		Total (%)	High-tech (%)	Medium-tech (%)	Low-tech (%)	Resource-based (%)	Total (%)	Finance & insurance (%)	Electricity & construction (%)	Total (million $)
1986	0.5	72.5	15.7	7.1	32.4	17.2	26.4	2.9	0.6	354.7
1987	0.1	62.1	17.2	3.6	22.4	18.9	37.6	1.6	0.2	1,063.3
1988	0.5	54.1	16.9	3.6	24.8	8.8	44.7	7.3	0.6	1,283.8
1989	0.1	51.8	12.2	3.8	25.3	10.5	47.0	18.5	1.1	1,090.3
1990	0.1	64.8	11.9	6.2	28.3	18.4	35.0	15.6	0.2	802.6
1991	0.1	67.9	7.2	3.1	16.8	40.9	31.7	12.9	0.4	1,396.0
1992	0.2	57.7	9.6	3.6	23.1	21.4	42.1	4.5	0.0	894.5
1993	0.0	37.5	4.1	2.7	18.7	12.0	56.4	3.5	6.1	1,044.3
1994	2.2	37.3	4.6	5.1	18.7	8.8	59.9	14.1	0.6	1,316.5
1995	0.1	52.9	10.7	6.4	24.0	11.7	43.8	15.8	3.2	1,970.4
1996	7.3	52.2	3.3	2.6	25.8	20.6	38.2	6.4	2.4	3,203.6

Year									
1997	0.1	36.0	1.1	13.9	17.0	62.6	4.9	1.4	6,971.1
1998	0.9	65.9	1.2	18.6	30.3	29.3	6.3	4.0	8,858.0
1999	0.1	53.8	1.1	19.5	10.4	43.6	16.6	2.5	15,544.6
2000	0.0	45.1	0.9	26.8	3.9	53.2	12.6	1.7	15,256.0
2001	0.1	25.8	2.3	7.7	8.7	64.1	15.7	10.1	11,287.1
2002	0.2	25.7	1.1	17.4	2.0	56.3	11.3	17.8	9,094.6
2003	0.1	26.3	1.2	15.2	4.8	63.9	25.5	9.8	6,470.5
2004	0.0	48.6	0.4	17.7	7.8	48.0	25.2	3.4	12,792.0
2005	0.0	26.6	0.9	8.0	7.7	71.8	33.9	1.6	11,565.5
2006	0.0	37.8	2.8	11.0	5.6	58.9	26.9	3.3	11,243.4
2007	0.0	25.6	1.3	14.7	3.6	72.4	21.8	2.0	10,514.4

Source: Data are from Ministry of Knowledge Economy.

Note: Technology classification for the manufacturing sector follows Lall (2000).

Table 6.2. Motivations for Korean Foreign Direct Investment, by Period

	1968–1993	1994–1996	1997–2001	2002–2004	2005–2007
Securing or developing local or third-country markets	14.2%	4.2%	2.7%	12.9%	31.2%
Export promotion	26.8%	46.3%	46.0%	32.1%	24.6%
Utilizing local labor costs	3.9%	10.4%	4.9%	10.1%	8.8%
Avoiding trade barriers	0.6%	3.0%	4.2%	4.1%	1.5%
Securing raw materials	1.1%	2.0%	0.8%	0.7%	0.6%
Acquiring advanced technology or management know-how	0.6%	4.1%	2.8%	3.0%	1.6%
Developing natural resources	41.3%	10.5%	8.0%	8.7%	11.7%
Other factors	11.49%	19.5%	30.6%	28.3%	20.0%

Source: Data are from Export-Import Bank of Korea.

As recovery proceeded, FDI inflows fell back. To some extent this decline was natural once the won stabilized. At the same time, there have been more than a few complaints about bureaucratic obstacles to mergers and acquisitions (in the financial sector in particular), lack of clarity regarding the enforcement of laws, and the continuing importance of personal ties in the Korean business world. A famous example is that of Lone Star, a U.S. private equity fund, and Korea Exchange Bank (KEB). After Lone Star bought the credit card unit of KEB in 2003, it was accused by Korean prosecutors of having manipulated the prices of the unit's shares in an effort to depress the purchase price. This led to a lengthy court case, at the end of which Lone Star was acquitted but during which it was prohibited from selling its interest in KEB to HSBC Holdings, which sought a presence in Korea's retail banking markets. Even then the Financial Services Commission refused to let the sale go ahead, on the grounds that there were other cases, not involving Lone Star or HSBC, still pending. It is clear how such proceedings could have had a chilling effect on foreign investment.

Turning to outward FDI, this rose from low levels starting in the 1990s and then fell slightly, owing to the financial crisis, before picking up again in 2004. Table 6.2 presents a tabulation of motives for outward

FDI in various subperiods. It shows that prior to 1993 outward FDI had been prompted mainly by the search for secure supplies of natural resources—quite natural for a resource-poor economy—and, to a lesser extent, by the need to ensure access to foreign markets and to capitalize on lower labor costs abroad.

From the mid-1990s the picture is very different. Since then, security of market access, followed closely by the advantages of lower labor costs abroad, have come to dominate resource- and raw-materials-related motives. China has become the single most important destination for Korean FDI, surpassing the United States in 2002; by 2006 Korean FDI in China was double that in the United States (see Table 6.3). One suspects that Korean firms are investing in production facilities in China not simply to capitalize on that country's relatively low production costs (which, with the passage of time, are no longer so low), but mainly to capitalize on its proximity to the rapidly growing Chinese market.[9]

Inward FDI

It will be helpful to place Korea's performance in attracting FDI in comparative perspective. Table 6.4 shows that the inward FDI stock as of 1990, at 2 percent of GDP, was below that for all comparator countries—not only in East Asia but also in Latin America.[10] The same thing is evident in Figure 6.2. This exceptionally low figure for 1990 reflects the barriers Korea historically put in the way of foreign investors. After 1990 there was considerable liberalization of policy toward inward FDI, first in conjunction with Korea's accession to the OECD and then in response to the financial crisis. Especially after the crisis, the idea—espoused by the IMF and some but not all Korean leaders—was that foreign investors could come in and help reorganize and rehabilitate Korean firms, most obviously in the banking and financial sector. The result was a quadrupling of cumulative inward FDI as a share of GDP 1 between 1990 and 2006 (see Figure 6.2). Note also the comparison with Taiwan (see Table 6.4). Where Korea lagged far behind Taiwan in 1990 in terms of ability to attract inward FDI, that differential had essentially disappeared by 2006.

Korea's inward FDI has been disproportionately destined for the secondary and tertiary sectors, which was predictable, given its resource endowment and comparative advantage (Figure 6.3). Table 6.5 breaks down these FDI inflows further, by recipient sector.[11] As one would expect,

Table 6.3. Outward Foreign Direct Investment by Region and Sector

Period	Region	Agriculture, fishing, & mining (%)	Manufacturing					Service			Total annual average (million $)
			Total (%)	High-tech (%)	Medium-tech (%)	Low-tech (%)	Resource-based (%)	Total (%)	Finance & insurance (%)	Electricity & construction (%)	
1981–1985	Other Asia	25.2	45.6	0.6	2.0	1.5	41.5	28.5	22.8	0.7	17.8
	Europe	85.3	1.1		0.9		0.2	13.6		0.0	11.2
	US	4.4	13.7	4.5	7.7	1.4	0.1	79.7	48.0	2.2	25.3
	ROW	69.4	5.2		3.4	1.4	0.4	19.1	14.0	6.3	48.7
1986–1990	China	0.0	96.9	18.3	4.8	31.9	41.9	3.1			4.5
	Other Asia	27.8	40.9	2.6	11.8	17.5	9.0	31.0	24.6	0.4	153.4
	Europe	10.3	37.2	10.5	22.4	2.6	1.8	52.5	14.0	0.0	25.8
	US	7.3	42.3	2.1	32.0	4.7	3.5	48.4	8.5	2.0	181.7
	ROW	52.7	35.2	0.5	26.4	7.1	1.2	11.3	5.2	0.8	168.2
1991–1995	China	1.0	82.2	16.7	20.9	28.9	15.8	14.9	5.9	1.9	412.1
	Other Asia	5.6	62.7	19.3	16.2	16.6	10.7	30.9	16.2	0.9	580.6
	Europe	0.4	43.3	13.5	23.8	0.8	5.2	56.0	12.4	0.3	313.3
	US	1.6	34.3	8.8	19.3	2.6	3.6	61.2	2.9	2.9	450.6
	ROW	42.4	34.7	5.5	10.1	15.1	4.0	22.0	0.0	0.8	226.2

1996–2000	China	0.6	74.7	19.1	27.1	12.9	15.7	20.7	3.8	4.0	715.3
	Other Asia	1.7	48.2	10.5	18.5	11.8	7.4	46.7	4.1	3.4	1,068.2
	Europe	5.1	41.0	12.2	26.8	0.7	1.3	53.9	2.5	0.1	590.3
	US	1.8	49.9	28.0	18.9	1.9	1.1	47.3	1.5	1.1	1,255.5
	ROW	16.1	20.4	6.9	7.0	3.7	2.7	61.9	0.7	1.6	747.0
2001–2005	China	0.7	84.3	23.4	34.7	14.2	12.0	13.3	3.9	1.7	1,750.0
	Other Asia	8.8	44.1	13.5	11.2	12.7	6.7	44.8	1.5	2.3	939.0
	Europe	0.6	62.6	45.8	15.4	0.5	0.9	36.7	1.9	0.1	953.2
	US	2.0	37.4	22.0	11.5	1.8	2.2	57.8	1.0	2.7	1,150.6
	ROW	39.3	22.0	6.7	5.6	8.1	1.6	35.0	1.4	3.8	472.9
2006–2007	China	1.0	72.2	33.7	24.4	6.4	7.7	23.7	10.3	3.1	4,396.8
	Other Asia	8.1	31.9	5.9	13.9	6.0	6.1	48.2	5.3	11.9	4,236.0
	Europe	5.6	43.4	7.5	32.7	0.2	2.9	47.9	1.7	3.1	2,607.6
	US	8.0	18.4	3.1	11.3	0.7	3.2	71.3	1.3	2.3	2,609.6
	ROW	52.6	16.2	4.5	5.8	2.3	3.7	25.4	4.7	5.8	2,011.3

Source: Data are from Export-Import Bank of Korea.

Note: ROW = rest of the world. Technology classification of the manufacturing sector follows Lall (2000).

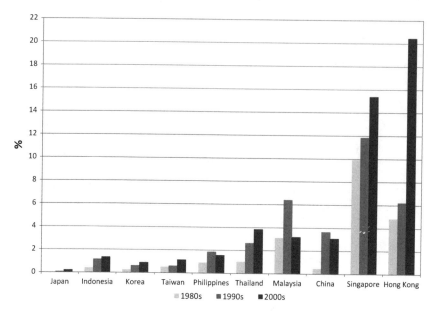

Figure 6.2. FDI Inflows as Percent of GDP, East Asia

Foreign direct investment flows and GDP are measured in current U.S. dollars, and the ratio is constructed by dividing the value of FDI flows by the value of GDP for each country. The simple average in the corresponding decade is reported. The value for 2000s is the average for the period between 2000 and 2008. Data from UNCTAD (2009).

inward FDI has been increasingly directed toward medium-technology and high-technology sectors. A growing share went into financial services following the liberalization measures adopted in the wake of the financial crisis. Interestingly, a growing share also appears to be directed toward other (nonfinancial) services (these are principally business services, real estate, and leasing), which may bode well for the productivity and exports of the service sector.

But the amount of Korean FDI remains strikingly low, Indonesia being the only comparator country where the FDI stock as a share of GDP was lower in 2006.[12] The question is, was this low FDI stock just a legacy of history—cumulative FDI as a share of GDP having started out so low in 1990 that even a relatively permissive regime could not raise it to levels of other countries in a mere fifteen years—or did Korea continue to place a variety of subtle and not-so-subtle obstacles in the way of aspiring foreign investors? While the arguments for FDI as a way of facilitat-

Table 6.4. Trends in Foreign Direct Investment, 1970–2008: Annual Averages in Dollars and as Percent of GDP

	Flows				Stock	
	1970–1979	1980–1989	1990–1999	2000–2008	1990	2008
	Millions of USD				Percent of GDP	
Latin America	2,117.54	5,839.32	32,693.68	68,505.49	9.4%	26.5%
Argentina	130.56	584.40	6,813.06	5,182.08	5.5%	23.0%
Brazil	1,269.84	1,721.42	9,921.66	23,738.64	7.8%	18.5%
Chile	59.06	481.18	3246.68	7,415.12	48.1%	59.5%
Colombia	53.04	478.51	1,807.02	5,374.31	7.3%	34.1%
Costa Rica	44.45	71.68	351.31	1,016.05	18.2%	36.8%
Ecuador	68.25	84.98	470.87	719.30	14.5%	22.2%
Mexico	447.35	2,388.25	8,507.47	2,2461.28	8.5%	31.1%
Peru	44.99	28.90	1,575.62	2,598.72	4.5%	23.5%
East Asia	1,291.89	4,520.20	22,609.74	40,739.13	14.5%	36.6%
Indonesia	437.95	338.31	2,156.70	2,455.85	7.0%	13.1%
Malaysia	326.19	964.74	4,815.83	4,579.97	22.6%	33.0%
Philippines	80.02	317.80	1,193.80	1,596.33	10.2%	12.7%
Singapore	301.30	1,906.81	8,476.46	18,460.22	82.6%	185.6%
Thailand	79.82	515.29	3,182.40	6,853.15	9.7%	38.5%
Taiwan	65.87	471.70	1,459.10	3,898.11	5.9%	11.6%
Vietnam	0.74	5.55	1,325.46	2,895.50	25.5%	53.2%
China	0.08	1,618.65	29,042.70	65,713.77	5.1%	8.7%
Korea	109.40	330.43	2,467.98	5,781.94	2.0%	10.7%

Source: Calculations based on data from UN Conference on Trade and Development.

ing the transfer of technological and organizational knowledge are compelling to economists, one can imagine that incumbents in the target sectors would not have welcomed the additional competition.

De jure impediments to inward FDI were surveyed by the OECD, which ranks countries from open (zero) to closed (one) by individual sector (OECD 2006). Table 6.6 summarizes its findings, comparing Korea (column 1) with the OECD and East Asian averages (columns 2 and 3). In de jure terms Korea looks relatively open. Having experienced one of the largest increases since 1998 in de jure openness to FDI among the countries

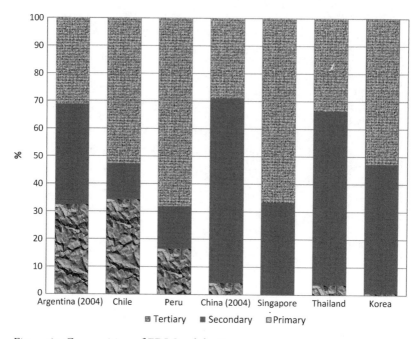

Figure 6.3. Composition of FDI Stock by Sector, 2005
Calculations based on data from Investment Map, www.investmentmap.org.

considered, Korea's summary value of 0.120 now indicates a greater openness than in the OECD (average value of 0.148). Korea's value is almost equal to that given for the United States. With the exceptions of Chile, Israel, and the Baltics, it appears far more open than the other middle-income countries considered by the OECD, telecommunications (fixed and mobile), transport (air and maritime), and the electricity sectors being partial exceptions. This assessment does not suggest that Korea continues to place unusually onerous barriers in the way of inward FDI.

De jure regulation is one thing; experience on the ground is another. Potential foreign investors continue to complain that regulation in Korea remains burdensome and that the playing field is not level. Evidence on this can be gleaned from the World Bank survey, "Doing Business: Comparing Regulations" (World Bank 2008a).[13] Table 6.7 compares Korea with the rest of the OECD and with the rest of East Asia. In most respects Korea again does not stand out relative to the OECD. For example, there are negligible differences between Korea and the rest of the OECD in the

Table 65. Foreign Direct Investment Inflows to Korea by Technology Classification

	1970s		1980s		1990s		2000s	
	Value (thousand $)	Share	Value (thousand $)	Share	Value (thousand $)	Share	Value (thousand $)	Share
Agriculture, forestry, fishing, & mining	1,005	0.71%	1,830	0.33%	39,638	0.94%	5,115	0.05%
Manufacturing								
Low-tech	26,302	18.52%	43,442	7.90%	582,873	13.88%	417,315	3.78%
Medium- to high-tech	48,139	33.90%	140,791	25.59%	884,847	21.07%	1,796,533	16.29%
High-tech	20,638	14.53%	120,991	21.99%	761,534	18.13%	1,543,692	14.00%
Electricity, gas, water supply, & construction	6,930	4.88%	15,034	2.73%	105,262	2.51%	604,298	5.48%
Wholesale, retail, hotels, & restaurants	22,757	16.03%	161,163	29.29%	1,053,879	25.09%	1,642,475	14.89%
Transport, post, & telecommunications	4,247	2.99%	2,671	0.49%	90,194	2.15%	548,789	4.98%
Financial institutions & insurance	9,982	7.03%	39,568	7.19%	456,209	10.86%	2,352,744	21.33%
Other services	2,990	2.11%	24,833	4.51%	229,700	5.47%	2,116,985	19.20%
All industries (thousand $)	$141,991		$550,138		$4,200,172		$11,027,947	

Source: Calculations based on data from Ministry of Knowledge Economy, http://www.mke.go.kr.

Note: Following OECD (2005), manufacturing industries are classified by three levels of technology: low, medium to high, and high. The values are average nominal foreign investment flows in U.S. dollars (in thousands) in four decades, except for the last column, which covers the period 2000–2007.

Table 6.6. Foreign Direct Investment Regulatory Restrictiveness Scores by
Country and Sector

		Korea	*OECD average*	*Non-OECD average*	*China*
Business services	Legal	0.075	0.221	0.271	0.300
	Accounting	0.075	0.196	0.175	0.425
	Architecture	0.050	0.094	0.148	0.100
	Engineering	0.050	0.094	0.075	0.100
	Total	0.063	0.152	0.175	0.231
Telecommunications	Fixed	0.400	0.198	0.229	0.550
	Mobile	0.400	0.143	0.206	0.450
	Total	0.400	0.184	0.223	0.525
Construction		0.050	0.074	0.098	0.150
Distribution		0.050	0.072	0.140	0.450
Finance	Insurance	0.050	0.135	0.206	0.350
	Banking	0.050	0.157	0.211	0.550
	Total	0.050	0.152	0.210	0.504
Hotels & restaurants		0.050	0.072	0.071	0.150
Transport	Air	0.350	0.443	0.461	0.550
	Maritime	0.450	0.280	0.246	0.550
	Road	0.050	0.106	0.188	0.150
	Total	0.333	0.299	0.305	0.466
Electricity		0.400	0.326	0.536	0.750
Manufacturing		0.050	0.076	0.119	0.400
TOTAL		0.120	0.148	0.189	0.405

Source: This table is reconstructed from OECD (2006), table 1.

Note: The index measures deviations from "national treatment"—i.e., discrimination against foreign investment—rather than the institutional environment more generally. The restrictiveness index is measured on a 0–1 scale, with 0 representing full openness and 1 a complete prohibition of foreign direct investment. Non-OECD countries include Argentina, Brazil, Chile, Israel, Estonia, Latvia, Lithuania, Romania, Slovenia, China, India, Russia, and South Africa.

number of procedures and number of days required to start a business. However, the cost of starting a business is somewhat higher. Part of the explanation may be in the cost of dealing with licenses (see Table 6.7).

Foreign investors also complain that the rigidity of Korea's labor market is a deterrent to doing business there. Layoffs are difficult. Labor disputes are unpredictable. About half of Korean and foreign CEOs surveyed by the OECD in 2003 pointed to labor-management problems as disincentives to investment.[14]

A final way of addressing the question of whether FDI has been a problem for Korea's economic growth is by analyzing recent FDI flows, asking if these are lower than would be predicted on the basis of Korea's observable characteristics and if such divergences are plausibly attributable to lack of transparency, red tape, and so on. Following Wei (1999), we regress the flow of FDI drawn from each of 30 source countries in each of 150 recipient countries and ask whether Korea stands out.[15] Our observations are annual and cover the period from 1985 to 2006. The dependent variable is the log of the FDI flow. This is regressed on the log GDP of the recipient, the log per capita GDP of the source, great-circle distance between the source and recipient countries, whether the source and recipient share a linguistic tie, and, finally, the measure of transparency.[16] A high numerical score denotes high transparency: in 2003 to 2005, for example, this measure equals 5.0 for Korea, compared with a sample average of 4.1 (but an OECD average of 7.1). We include a dummy variable for Korea to see whether the country's other characteristics fully explain its relatively low FDI share (in a statistical sense).

The results in Table 6.8 show that FDI increases with the size of the recipient and source countries, as measured by GDP, and with the economic transparency of the recipient. It is greater in country pairs with a bilateral or regional trade arrangement and when the countries are members of a currency union.[17] It declines with the distance between the two countries, when the recipient is landlocked, and when different languages are spoken in the source and destination countries.

Most important for our present purposes, the estimates in Table 6.8, column 2, suggest that Korea attracts less FDI than expected of a country with its characteristics. The dummy variable for observations where Korea is the destination of the FDI flow enters with a significantly negative coefficient even when its other economic characteristics (and those of the source) are taken into account. A point estimate of -0.61 suggests,

Table. 6.7. Survey Results: Ease of Doing Business, Korea Compared with OECD and East Asi

Economy					Korea		
Year			2004	2005	2006	2007	2008
Ease of doing business rank		All				27	30
		OECD				18/24	18/24
Starting a business	Rank	All				101	110
		OECD				21/23	21/24
	Procedures (number)		10	10	10	10	10
	Time (days)		17	17	17	17	17
	Cost (% of income per capita)		18	18	18	18	17
	Min. capital (% of income per capita)		348	332	309	300	296
Dealing with licenses	Rank	All				16	22
		OECD				4/23	7/24
	Procedures (number)				13	13	13
	Time (days)				56	34	34
	Cost (% of income per capita)				108	114	170
Employing workers	Rank	All				130	131
		OECD				18/23	18/23
	Difficulty of Hiring Index		11	11	11	11	11
	Rigidity of Hours Index		60	60	60	60	60
	Difficulty of Firing Index		40	40	40	40	40
	Rigidity of Employment Index		37	37	37	37	37
	Nonwage labor cost (% of salary)				14	14	13
	Firing costs (weeks of wages)		91	91	91	91	91
Registering property	Rank	All				65	68
		OECD				18/23	19/24
	Procedures (number)			7	7	7	7
	Time (days)			11	11	11	11
	Cost (% of property value)			6	6	6	6
Getting credit	Rank	All				32	36
		OECD				16/23	17/24
	Legal Rights Index			5	5	5	5
	Credit Information Index		5	5	5	5	5
	Public registry coverage (% adults)		0	0	0	0	0
	Private bureau coverage (% adults)		67		81	77	74

OECD					East Asia				
2004	2005	2006	2007	2008	2004	2005	2006	2007	2008
7	6	6	6	6	10	10	10	10	10
29	25	19	16	15	52	49	48	41	40
8	8	6	5	5	28	27	22	19	19
33	31	29	24	21	170	155	135	51	46
		14	14	14			21	21	21
		158	154	158			204	204	203
		66	64	57			258	227	208
22	22	24	24	26	31	31	30	28	27
40	40	40	37	38	16	16	16	16	16
28	28	27	27	27	27	27	27	27	27
30	30	30	30	31	25	25	24	23	23
		22	22	21			14	14	14
22	23	22	22	23	74	74	74	74	74
	5	5	5	5		5	5	5	5
	35	34	33	29		43	43	43	43
	5	5	4	5		5	5	5	5
	6	6	6	6		6	6	6	6
5	5	5	5	5	3	4	4	4	4
5	8	8	9	9	2	4	4	7	14
53	53	58	60	59	16	18	23	24	26

(continued)

Table. 6.7. (Continued)

Economy			2004	2005	Korea 2006	2007	2008
Protecting investors	Rank	All				62	64
		OECD				16/23	17/24
	Disclosure Index				7	7	7
	Director Liability Index				2	2	2
	Shareholder Suits Index				7	7	7
	Investor Protection Index				5	5	5
Paying taxes	Rank	All				106	106
		OECD				22/23	23/24
	Payments (number)				48	48	48
	Time (hours)				290	290	290
	Profit tax (%)						18
	Labor tax and contributions (%)						11
	Other taxes (%)						5
	Total tax rate (% profit)				36	36	35
Trading across borders	Rank	All				30	13
		OECD				16/23	8/24
	Documents for export (number)				5	5	4
	Time for export (days)				12	12	11
	Cost to export (US$ per container)				780	780	745
	Documents for import (number)				8	8	6
	Time for import (days)				12	12	10
	Cost to import (US$ per container)						745
Enforcing contracts	Rank	All				10	10
		OECD				6/23	7/24
	Procedures (number)		35	35	35	35	35
	Time (days)		230	230	230	230	230
	Cost (% of debt)		10	10	10	10	10
Closing a business	Rank	All				10	11
		OECD				9/23	10/24
	Time (years)		2	2	2	2	2
	Cost (% of estate)		4	4	4	4	4
	Recovery rate (cents on the dollar)		81	81	82	82	81

Source: Data are from World Bank (2008a).

Note: East Asia includes China, Hong Kong, Indonesia, Malaysia, Philippines, Singapore, Taiwan, Vietnam.

	OECD					East Asia			
2004	2005	2006	2007	2008	2004	2005	2006	2007	2008
		6	6	6			8	8	8
		5	5	5			4	4	4
		7	7	6			6	6	6
		6	6	6			6	6	6
		14	14	14			31	31	30
		187	187	179			402	402	365
				20					21
				23					16
				3					4
		47	47	47			41	41	41
		5	5	5			7	7	6
		11	10	10			17	17	16
		715	737	740			580	597	585
		6	5	5			8	7	7
		12	11	10			18	17	16
		718	655	655			633	650	616
32	32	32	31	31	34	34	34	34	34
427	425	423	423	418	470	457	448	448	448
19	19	18	18	18	31	31	31	31	31
1	1	1	1	1	3	3	3	3	3
7	7	8	8	8	18	18	18	18	18
74	67	75	75	74	44	29	45	44	45

Table 6.8. Determinants of Bilateral Foreign Direct Investment Flows

	(1)	(2) Korea dummy (host)	(3) Korea dummy (source)	(4) Korea dummy (both)
GDP in host country	0.611** [0.011]	0.619** [0.011]	0.606** [0.011]	0.613** [0.011]
GDP in source country	0.658** [0.011]	0.662** [0.011]	0.655** [0.011]	0.659** [0.011]
GDP per capita in host country	0.048* [0.021]	0.054** [0.021]	0.054** [0.021]	0.060** [0.021]
GDP per capita in source country	1.208** [0.029]	1.209** [0.029]	1.262** [0.031]	1.258** [0.031]
Distance	−0.426** [0.018]	−0.419** [0.018]	−0.437** [0.019]	−0.429** [0.019]
No. of landlocked	0.010 [0.032]	0.006 [0.032]	0.018 [0.032]	0.013 [0.032]
No. of islands	0.017 [0.033]	0.007 [0.033]	0.030 [0.033]	0.020 [0.033]
Land border dummy	0.557** [0.063]	0.557** [0.063]	0.563** [0.063]	0.562** [0.063]
Dummy for common language	0.631** [0.043]	0.652** [0.044]	0.597** [0.044]	0.620** [0.044]
Dummy for common colonizer post-1945	2.178** [0.466]	2.188** [0.466]	2.220** [0.466]	2.226** [0.466]
Dummy for pairs ever in colonial relationship	1.035** [0.062]	1.017** [0.062]	1.074** [0.063]	1.054** [0.063]
Dummy for pairs currently in colonial relationship	0.900 [0.502]	0.857 [0.502]	0.965 [0.502]	0.918 [0.502]
Strict currency union	1.774** [0.433]	1.781** [0.432]	1.778** [0.432]	1.785** [0.432]
RTA dummy	0.363** [0.046]	0.353** [0.046]	0.373** [0.046]	0.361** [0.046]
Product of land areas	−0.041** [0.007]	−0.047** [0.007]	−0.035** [0.007]	−0.041** [0.007]
Transparency of host country	0.088** [0.010]	0.082** [0.010]	0.088** [0.010]	0.082** [0.010]
Korea dummy (host country)		−0.611** [0.114]		−0.577** [0.114]

Table 6.8. (Continued)

	(1)	(2) Korea dummy (host)	(3) Korea dummy (source)	(4) Korea dummy (both)
Korea dummy (source country)			0.355** [0.079]	0.325** [0.079]
Observations	17,859	17,859	17,859	17,859
R-squared	0.48	0.48	0.48	0.48

Note: Standard errors in brackets. The dependent variable is log of bilateral real foreign direct investment (FDI). FDI data are collected from OECD International Direct Investment Statistics and converted into real values by dividing the current U.S. dollar values by the U.S. consumer price index. The sample includes 30 source countries (OECD) and 149 host countries. GDP data are obtained from Penn World Table 6.2. Other variables are from Rose (2000). All explanatory variables except the dummy variables are expressed in logarithms. RTA dummy takes one if the pair countries have formed a regional trade agreement. Intercept and time dummy variables are included (not reported).

** and * indicate that the estimated coefficients are statistically significant at 1 percent and 5 percent, respectively.

given that the dependent variable is the log of the FDI inflow, that Korea's FDI receipts are 46 percent lower than would be predicted on the basis of international experience.

In Table 6.9 we interact the indicator for Korea with a dummy for successive five-year periods. The coefficient on this interaction is negative throughout. There is some sign that this negative coefficient declined in magnitude (in absolute value) over time as Korea's FDI policies were liberalized, but a sizable and statistically significant negative coefficient reemerges in the most recent five-year period. Indeed, not too much should be made of the relatively small coefficient on the dummy variable for the second half of the 1990s. This was when Korea saw large quantities of "firesale" FDI, as noted earlier—when the collapse of stock prices and the won exchange rate as a result of the financial crisis encouraged foreign investors to swoop in and purchase Korean firms at distress prices. When we break the decade not into two equal halves but into 1991–1997 and 1998–1999 subperiods, in Table 6.10 (column 1) we find that the zero coefficient indicating that Korean FDI is not unusually low is limited to the post-crisis fire-sale years. (When we allow for separate estimated coefficients for the

Table 6.9. Determinants of Bilateral Foreign Direct Investment Flows (Interaction of Korea and Period Dummies)

	(1) Korea dummy (host)	(2) Korea dummy (source)	(3) Korea dummy (both)
GDP in host country	0.619** [0.011]	0.605** [0.011]	0.612** [0.011]
GDP in source country	0.662** [0.011]	0.656** [0.011]	0.660** [0.011]
GDP per capita in host country	0.054** [0.021]	0.055** [0.021]	0.060** [0.021]
GDP per capita in source country	1.209** [0.029]	1.271** [0.031]	1.267** [0.031]
Distance	−0.419** [0.018]	−0.435** [0.018]	−0.428** [0.019]
No. of landlocked	0.006 [0.032]	0.017 [0.032]	0.013 [0.032]
No. of islands	0.007 [0.033]	0.028 [0.033]	0.018 [0.033]
Land border dummy	0.557** [0.063]	0.568** [0.063]	0.568** [0.063]
Dummy for common language	0.652** [0.044]	0.591** [0.044]	0.613** [0.044]
Dummy for common colonizer post-1945	2.188** [0.466]	2.224** [0.466]	2.229** [0.466]
Dummy for pairs ever in colonial relationship	1.017** [0.062]	1.079** [0.063]	1.059** [0.063]
Dummy for pairs currently in colonial relationship	0.856 [0.502]	0.982 [0.502]	0.935 [0.502]
Strict currency union	1.781** [0.432]	1.777** [0.432]	1.784** [0.432]
RTA dummy	0.353** [0.046]	0.373** [0.046]	0.362** [0.046]
Product of land areas	−0.047** [0.007]	−0.034** [0.007]	−0.040** [0.007]
Transparency of host country	0.082** [0.010]	0.088** [0.010]	0.083** [0.010]
Korea 1985–1990 dummy (host country)	−0.738* [0.290]		−0.695* [0.289]

Table 6.9. (Continued)

	(1) Korea dummy (host)	(2) Korea dummy (source)	(3) Korea dummy (both)
Korea 1991–1995 dummy (host country)	−0.625* [0.244]		−0.556* [0.244]
Korea 1996–2000 dummy (host country)	−0.395 [0.227]		−0.360 [0.227]
Korea 2001–2006 dummy (host country)	−0.688** [0.178]		−0.665** [0.178]
Korea 1985–1990 dummy (source country)		0.582** [0.201]	0.546** [0.201]
Korea 1991–1995 dummy (source country)		1.010** [0.150]	0.979** [0.150]
Korea 1996–2000 dummy (source country)		0.229 [0.130]	0.202 [0.130]
Korea 2001–2006 dummy (source country)		−0.066 [0.128]	−0.092 [0.128]
Observations	17,859	17,859	17,859
R-squared	0.48	0.48	0.48

Note: See note for Table 6.8.

Korea dummy variable, the results carry over—see Table 6.11.) With the exception of this one unusual episode, then, it appears that inward FDI remained depressed throughout.

A further factor potentially depressing Korea's FDI receipts is the diversion of investment to China. In an exercise analogous to what we do for trade in Chapter 5, we consider the impact of China's increasing absorption of FDI on Korea's FDI receipts. The ordinary-least-squares results in column 1 of Table 6.12 show a positive correlation between China's FDI receipts and those of other countries. In some cases the positive correlation may have economic meaning—foreign companies may wish to invest in Korea, for example, to produce capital goods for use by foreign investment enterprises in China. In other cases, however, the positive correlation may simply be picking up omitted factors that cause FDI flows to different countries to rise or fall simultaneously. A solution to this last problem, following Eichengreen and Tong (2007), is to use the distance from the

Table 6.10. Foreign Direct Investment Flows with Individual Korea/Year Dummy Variables: Distinguishing the Post-Crisis Fire-Sale Period

	(1) Korea dummy (host)	*(2)* Korea dummy (source)	*(3)* Korea dummy (both)
GDP in host country	0.619**	0.605**	0.612**
	[0.011]	[0.011]	[0.011]
GDP in source country	0.662**	0.656**	0.660**
	[0.011]	[0.011]	[0.011]
GDP per capita in host country	0.054**	0.054**	0.060**
	[0.021]	[0.021]	[0.021]
GDP per capita in source country	1.209**	1.271**	1.267**
	[0.029]	[0.031]	[0.031]
Distance	−0.419**	−0.436**	−0.428**
	[0.018]	[0.018]	[0.019]
No. of landlocked	0.006	0.016	0.012
	[0.032]	[0.032]	[0.032]
No. of islands	0.007	0.029	0.019
	[0.033]	[0.033]	[0.033]
Land border dummy	0.557**	0.567**	0.567**
	[0.063]	[0.063]	[0.063]
Dummy for common language	0.652**	0.593**	0.615**
	[0.044]	[0.044]	[0.044]
Dummy for common colonizer post-1945	2.188**	2.221**	2.227**
	[0.466]	[0.466]	[0.465]
Dummy for pairs ever in colonial relationship	1.017**	1.078**	1.058**
	[0.062]	[0.063]	[0.063]
Dummy for pairs currently in colonial relationship	0.856	0.981	0.934
	[0.502]	[0.502]	[0.502]
Strict currency union	1.781**	1.771**	1.778**
	[0.432]	[0.432]	[0.432]
RTA dummy	0.353**	0.374**	0.363**
	[0.046]	[0.046]	[0.046]
Product of land areas	−0.047**	−0.034**	−0.040**
	[0.007]	[0.007]	[0.007]
Transparency of host country	0.082**	0.088**	0.083**
	[0.010]	[0.010]	[0.010]
Korea 1985–1990 dummy (host country)	−0.738*		−0.696*
	[0.290]		[0.289]

Table 6.10. (Continued)

	(1) Korea dummy (host)	(2) Korea dummy (source)	(3) Korea dummy (both)
Korea 1991–1997 dummy (host country)	−0.627** [0.206]		−0.565** [0.206]
Korea 1998–1999 Dummy (host country)	−0.054 [0.347]		−0.005 [0.347]
Korea 2000–2006 dummy (host country)	−0.687** [0.167]		−0.666** [0.167]
Korea 1985–1990 dummy (source country)		0.581** [0.201]	0.547** [0.201]
Korea 1991–1997 dummy (source country)		0.806** [0.120]	0.777** [0.121]
Korea 1998–1999 dummy (source country)		0.478* [0.207]	0.456* [0.207]
Korea 2000–2006 dummy (source country)		−0.184 [0.119]	−0.212 [0.119]
Observations	17,859	17,859	17,859
R-squared	0.48	0.48	0.48

Note: See note for Table 6.8.

source country to China as an instrument for China's FDI receipts. When this is done, in column 2 of Table 6.12, the coefficient on China's FDI receipts turns negative—as if FDI is being diverted to China from other countries—though the effect is not statistically significant.

We do the same in columns 5 and 6 of Table 6.12 for the observations where Korea is the host country. We find the same positive coefficient in the OLS regressions, though it is larger than before. And we find the same negative coefficient on Chinese FDI receipts when the equation is estimated using instrumental variables. Now, however, the point estimate is larger than before and is just on the margin of statistical significance (the t-statistic is 1.82). This is evidence, then, that China's emergence as a magnet for FDI is having a depressing effect on Korea's own FDI receipts. The point estimate of -1.03 suggests that if China's FDI receipts were only half their actual level, Korea's FDI receipts would be nearly twice as high.

Table 6.11. Foreign Direct Investment Flows with Korea/Year Dummies and Separate Korea Coefficients, Distinguishing the Post-Crisis Fire-Sale Period

	Full Sample				Korea host country	
	(1)	(2)	(3)	(4)	(5)	(6)
	OLS	IV			OLS	IV
China's FDI	0.216**	−0.036	−0.040	−0.041	0.346**	−1.034
	[0.011]	[0.021]	[0.021]	[0.021]	[0.110]	[0.567]
GDP in host country	0.623**	0.654**	0.663**	0.663**	−0.141	0.680
	[0.012]	[0.012]	[0.012]	[0.012]	[0.686]	[0.983]
GDP in source country	0.372**	0.677**	0.687**	0.687**	0.441*	2.138**
	[0.019]	[0.029]	[0.029]	[0.029]	[0.188]	[0.719]
GDP per capita in host country	0.092**	0.044*	0.050*	0.051*	—	—
	[0.021]	[0.022]	[0.022]	[0.022]		
GDP per capita in source country	1.009**	1.300**	1.306**	1.305**	1.074**	3.495**
	[0.039]	[0.045]	[0.045]	[0.045]	[0.404]	[1.104]
Distance	−0.471**	−0.439**	−0.431**	−0.431**	−0.638	−0.925
	[0.020]	[0.020]	[0.020]	[0.020]	[0.385]	[0.532]
# of landlocked	0.023	−0.007	−0.011	−0.011	−0.558	−0.682
	[0.035]	[0.036]	[0.036]	[0.036]	[0.360]	[0.489]
# of island	−0.073*	−0.030	−0.041	−0.042	−1.004	−0.359
	[0.036]	[0.037]	[0.037]	[0.037]	[0.670]	[0.941]
Land border dummy	0.540**	0.545**	0.542**	0.543**	—	—
	[0.071]	[0.073]	[0.073]	[0.073]		
Dummy for common language	0.460**	0.492**	0.516**	0.515**	0.335	0.341
	[0.047]	[0.048]	[0.048]	[0.048]	[0.299]	[0.405]
Dummy for common colonizer post 1945	2.750**	2.614**	2.633**	2.633**	—	—
	[0.984]	[1.000]	[0.999]	[0.999]		
Dummy for pairs ever in colonial relationship	1.190**	1.114**	1.094**	1.095**	—	—
	[0.067]	[0.069]	[0.069]	[0.069]		
Dummy for pairs currently in colonial relationship	0.848	0.610	0.553	0.553	—	—
	[0.646]	[0.657]	[0.657]	[0.657]		
Strict currency union	2.197**	1.990**	1.996**	1.997**	—	—
	[0.427]	[0.434]	[0.434]	[0.434]		
RTA dummy	0.324**	0.297**	0.285**	0.285**	—	—
	[0.051]	[0.052]	[0.052]	[0.052]		

Table 6.11. (Continued)

	Full Sample				Korea host country	
	(1)	*(2)*	*(3)*	*(4)*	*(5)*	*(6)*
	OLS		*IV*		*OLS*	*IV*
Product of land areas	−0.010 [0.008]	−0.052** [0.009]	−0.059** [0.009]	−0.059** [0.009]	−0.059 [0.116]	−0.336 [0.191]
Transparency of host country	0.094** [0.011]	0.093** [0.011]	0.087** [0.011]	0.086** [0.011]	—	—
Korea dummy (host country)				−0.650** [0.121]		
Korea 1985–1990 dummy (host country)				−0.543 [0.349]		
Korea 1991–1997 dummy (host country)				−0.639** [0.213]		
Korea 1998–1999 dummy (host country)				−0.021 [0.371]		
Korea 2000–2006 dummy (host country)				−0.815** [0.171]		
Observations	15,250	15,231	15,231	15,231	221	221
R-squared	0.49	0.48	0.48	0.48	0.55	0.17

Note: OLS=ordinary least squares; IV=instrumental variable. See note for Table 6.8.

Outward FDI

Korean companies have long had a considerable foreign presence. POSCO, the leading steelmaker, acquired a U.S. steel producer in response to restrictions on imports into the U.S. market and established operations in Vietnam to capitalize on low labor costs. In the summer of 2008, Dongwon Industries announced that it would acquire StarKist, the U.S. canned-tuna and packaged-foods producer, and Lotte Confectionary Company announced plans to acquire Guylian, the Belgian chocolate manufacturer. Korean firms have also moved aggressively to establish manufacturing operations in China. This has raised fears that investment

Table 6.12. The Impact of China on Foreign Direct Investment Flows to Other Countries

	Full sample				Korea host country	
	(1)	(2)	(3)	(4)	(5)	(6)
	OLS	IV			OLS	IV
FDI to China	0.216** [0.011]	−0.036 [0.021]	−0.04 [0.021]	−0.04 [0.021]	0.346** [0.110]	−1.034 [0.567]
GDP in host country	0.623** [0.012]	0.654** [0.012]	0.663** [0.012]	0.663** [0.012]	−0.141 [0.686]	0.68 [0.983]
GDP in source country	0.372** [0.019]	0.677** [0.029]	0.687** [0.029]	0.687** [0.029]	0.441* [0.188]	2.138** [0.719]
GDP per capita in host country	0.092** [0.021]	0.044* [0.022]	0.050* [0.022]	0.050* [0.022]	—	—
GDP per capita in source country	1.009** [0.039]	1.300** [0.045]	1.306** [0.045]	1.305** [0.045]	1.074** [0.404]	3.495** [1.104]
Distance	−0.471** [0.020]	−0.439** [0.020]	−0.431** [0.020]	−0.431** [0.020]	−0.638 [0.385]	−0.925 [0.532]
No. of landlocked	0.023 [0.035]	−0.007 [0.036]	−0.011 [0.036]	−0.011 [0.036]	−0.558 [0.360]	−0.682 [0.489]
No. of islands	−0.073* [0.036]	−0.03 [0.037]	−0.041 [0.037]	−0.042 [0.037]	−1.004 [0.670]	−0.359 [0.941]
Land border dummy	0.540** [0.071]	0.545** [0.073]	0.542** [0.073]	0.543** [0.073]	—	—
Dummy for common language	0.460** [0.047]	0.492** [0.048]	0.516** [0.048]	0.514** [0.048]	0.335 [0.299]	0.341 [0.405]
Dummy for common colonizer post-1945	2.750** [0.984]	2.614** [1.000]	2.633** [0.999]	2.633** [0.999]	—	—
Dummy for pairs ever in colonial relationship	1.190** [0.067]	1.114** [0.069]	1.094** [0.069]	1.095** [0.069]	—	—
Dummy for pairs ever in colonial relationship	0.848 [0.646]	0.61 [0.657]	0.553 [0.657]	0.554 [0.657]	—	—
Strict currency union	2.197** [0.427]	1.990** [0.434]	1.996** [0.434]	1.997** [0.434]	—	—
RTA dummy	0.324** [0.051]	0.297** [0.052]	0.285** [0.052]	0.285** [0.052]	—	—
Product of land areas	−0.01 [0.008]	−0.052** [0.009]	−0.059** [0.009]	−0.059** [0.009]	−0.059 [0.116]	−0.336 [0.191]

Table 6.12. (Continued)

	Full Sample				Korea host country	
	(1)	*(2)*	*(3)*	*(4)*	*(5)*	*(6)*
	OLS	IV			OLS	IV
Transparency of host country	0.094** [0.011]	0.093** [0.011]	0.087** [0.011]	0.087** [0.011]	—	—
Korea dummy (host country)			−0.650** [0.121]			
Korea 1985–1990 dummy (host country)				−0.543 [0.349]		
Korea 1991–1995 dummy (host country)				−0.607* [0.255]		
Korea 1996–2000 dummy (host country)				−0.441 [0.234]		
Korea 2001–2002 dummy (host country)				−0.828** [0.183]		
Observations	15,250	15,231	15,231	15,231	221	221
R-squared	0.49	0.48	0.48	0.48	0.55	0.17

Note: OLS=ordinary least squares; IV=instrumental variables. See note for Table 6.8.

in Korean industry is being undermined by Chinese competition—that investment by Korean firms in China comes at the expense of investment at home and depresses Korea's own exports of manufactures.

In this context, it is important to also analyze Korea as a source of FDI. We do this using the same data set as above and the analogous empirical model. The results, in columns 3 and 4 of Table 6.8, suggest that Korea's outward FDI has been significantly greater than its other economic characteristics (and those of the host country) would lead one to expect—in contrast to the results for inward FDI. A point estimate of 0.35 suggests, given that the dependent variable is expressed in logs, that the flow of outward FDI from Korea is 42 percent higher than would be predicted on the basis of international experience.

In Table 6.9, as noted, we distinguish results for different five-year periods. Here, once again the results for outflows contrast with those for inflows. Where for FDI receipts Korea's underperformance is accentuated in the most recent period (it is more noticeable in 2001–2006 than it was in the 1990s), the opposite is true for FDI outflows. Outflows in the 1990s were larger than would have been predicted for a country with Korea's characteristics.[18] More recently, in contrast, this is no longer the case. Since 2001, Korea's FDI outflow has been right on target. If the country has an "FDI problem," it is on the inflow side. And the tendency for FDI flows to be diverted toward China rather than Korea accounts for only a portion of this.

Implications for Growth

There is little consensus in the literature about the effects of continuing low levels of inward FDI on the growth of an economy like Korea's. Skeptics, such as Carkovic and Levine (2002), argue that there is no relationship between FDI and economic growth. Using panel data to control for the simultaneity of growth and FDI as well as country-specific effects, they cannot reject the hypothesis that the impact of FDI on growth is negligible overall. Studies finding otherwise, they conclude, are contaminated by omitted variables and reverse causality (countries, industries, and firms with superior growth prospects for other reasons are more successful at attracting FDI). For the same reasons that economists have grown skeptical that brute-force investment is the key to growth, these authors are skeptical that the volume of FDI, in and of itself, is a key determinant of growth.[19]

A number of studies specific to Korea are similarly skeptical. Dhakal, Rahman, and Upadhyaya (2007); Kim and Seo (2003); and Zhang (2001) use time series to quantify the relation between FDI inflows and growth: they find that causality seems to run mainly from growth to FDI, rather than the other way around. Even those effects, according to Zhang, are evident only in the short run. Kim and Hwang (2000) use (industry) cross-section regressions rather than (aggregate) time series regressions for Korea. Their random-effects regressions yield a positive association between FDI and growth, but one that is statistically insignificant at conventional confidence levels.

Other studies reach more positive conclusions. A number argue that the impact of FDI on growth is contingent on the existence of facilitating conditions. Borensztein, De Gregorio, and Lee (1998); Durham (2004); and Zhang (2001) all find evidence that the pro-growth effects of FDI are likely to be larger in countries with an open trade regime, macroeconomic stability, and, in particular, a highly educated work force, such countries being in a superior position to capture the associated productivity spill-overs. This last finding in particular suggests that Korea would benefit from being able to attract more FDI. Alfaro and Charlton (2007), in an analysis of OECD countries, find larger effects of FDI on growth and the productivity of industries that depend on external finance and rely on highly skilled labor. Again, this suggests that a country in Korea's position would benefit from attracting more FDI.

Chun (2000) suggests that the failure of previous studies of Korea to detect much of an impact of FDI on growth at the industry level reflects the practice of aggregating heterogeneous industries. Thus, given that so much FDI in Korea in recent years has been directed toward the service sector, and toward financial services in particular, it may be useful to look at studies that consider the impact of foreign bank entry and acquisition directly. Harada (2005) compares Korean banks with and without foreign ownership, and concludes that those with high foreign ownership per-formed better in terms of technical efficiency in the first five post-crisis years.

Finally, the impact of Korea's outward FDI on exports has been con-sidered by Kim and Kang (1997) and Lee (2008). Kim and Kang analyze a cross section of industries in the period ending in 1993: they find no evi-dence that outward FDI is associated with a reduction in exports. At the same time, there is little sign in their results that outward FDI actually increases exports of parts, components, and other products. In contrast, Lee finds that the country's outward FDI has actually complemented rather than substituted for merchandise exports. These contrasting results may reflect the different time periods considered and changes in the na-ture of Korean manufacturing production in recent years. Lee finds that FDI has had a particularly strong positive impact on exports since the fi-nancial crisis, in relatively high-tech industries and among relatively large Korean multinationals. This suggests that outward investment in China, among other countries, is stimulating rather than depressing Korean exports by providing a low-cost platform on which to assemble the in-creasingly high-tech parts and components produced by Korea's large corporations.

On balance these results suggest that Korea's economic growth would be better supported by policies that attracted more FDI, especially in manufacturing sectors that use highly skilled labor and in service sectors. Here, in connection with FDI in the service sector in particular, the U.S.-Korea free trade agreement could make a difference insofar as it entailed further opening and liberalization of the business services and financial sectors.

Conclusion

Foreign direct investment has always been controversial in Korea, if for no other reason than its historical association with Japanese colonial occupation. In the course of the 1960s and 1970s the Park government shifted from encouraging inward FDI as a way of relaxing binding external constraints to suppressing FDI in order to advance its industrial policy strategy. After the 1980s Korea shifted back toward encouraging inward FDI, both as a way of acquiring foreign technology with a larger tacit component and as a concomitant of its broader strategy of growth through economic and financial integration. And more recently the country came under pressure to open up further to foreign investment, owing to its accession to the OECD and as a result of the 1997–1998 crisis. Meanwhile there has been a steady increase in outward foreign investment by Korean firms seeking secure access to raw materials and markets abroad and attempting to make use of low-cost foreign labor.

These trends are all evident in the data, but not all are as distinctive as they are sometimes made out to be. In particular, there is nothing unusual about the level or motives for outward foreign investment, given Korea's stage of development, labor costs, and energy and raw-material endowment. Contrary to the view that Korea's outward FDI is excessive—that it is "hollowing out" Korean industry—outward FDI is precisely what one would expect for a country with Korea's characteristics.

Where Korea is unusual is in its level of inward direct investment, which remains significantly below what one would expect of a country with its characteristics. One can point to reasons for this in the legacy of past anti-FDI policies, complaints by potential foreign investors that the playing field is still not level, and the tendency for nearby China, which has become a magnet for foreign investment, to divert FDI away from Korea. The data are consistent with a role for all of these factors.

Comparative experience also suggests that Korea is precisely the kind of country that would benefit from attracting more FDI. As Korea moves closer to the technological frontier, any technologies that it might now wish to acquire from abroad would have a significant tacit component. Licensing or purchasing capital goods would therefore not be enough. The fact that the economy is open along other dimensions, and that Korea possesses abundant supplies of skilled and educated labor, suggests that the country is in a favorable position to capitalize on those technologies.

Growth would almost certainly be further stimulated by policy reforms that attract additional FDI. Some of the challenges to attracting FDI are facts of life, such as the preference of some multinationals for investing in China, which has the same geographical advantages but a larger domestic market. Others, however, such as the perception that Korea's regulatory setting is opaque and unpredictable, can be addressed by policy. These are margins on which the Korean authorities can act.

It is also notable that Korea has one of the lowest service-sector shares of inward FDI in the OECD; of 21 OECD countries, only Norway and Italy had lower service-sector shares in 2006.[20] As we saw in Chapters 4 and 5, low service-sector productivity is one of the principal obstacles to faster growth. Anything that can help to remove this obstacle should be a priority. Eliminating impediments to inward FDI in the service sector would seem like one low-cost way of addressing this key problem.

As for outward FDI, the conventional wisdom is that the Korean economy might grow faster if Korea invested less abroad and devoted more of its scarce domestic savings to domestic investment. We will argue to the contrary in Chapter 8—that growth would likely occur more quickly if Korea undertook more outward FDI of the right sort.

CHAPTER 7

Crises and Growth

Although the performance of the Korean economy over the past half century has been resoundingly positive, it is not without blemishes. Growth has been interrupted by currency and banking crises precipitated by sharp reversals in international capital flows. This was the case in 1970–1971, when growing external debt obligations, superimposed on slowing export growth, forced the government to declare a moratorium on all payments of corporate debt owed to private domestic creditors, negotiate an adjustment program with the International Monetary Fund, and devalue the won by 18 percent. It was the case again in 1980–1982, when the assassination of President Park, the second oil shock, a global slowdown, the international debt crisis, and high levels of short-term foreign indebtedness forced painful adjustments. It was prominently the case in 1997–1998, when the collapse of investor confidence led to massive short-term capital outflows, another appeal to the IMF, and a deep recession, rendering Korea one of the principal casualties of the Asian economic crisis. In 2008 Korea experienced yet another episode of large capital outflows, collapsing currency values, and financial distress. Precisely because Korea had gone further than most of its neighbors in opening its securities markets to foreigners, and because its banks had relatively large short-term dollar liabilities, the country was hit hard when dollars became scarce and U.S. investors liquidated their foreign holdings.

Crises are traumatic by their nature. But they are especially traumatic for a country whose self-image rests on its economic prowess, and for governments whose legitimacy derives from their ability to deliver growth. The question is, does the incidence of economic crisis in Korea reflect fundamental weaknesses in the structure of the economy, or has too much been made of the crisis problem? We attempt to answer this question by, once again, placing Korea's experience in international comparative context.

We start by asking whether Korea is unusually crisis prone. Have crises been more frequent, in other words, than one would expect on the basis of the experience of other countries at comparable stages of economic and financial development? The comparative perspective suggests that while one crisis per decade is not unknown among low- and middle-income countries, which by their nature have fragile financial systems, it is nonetheless a bit unusual. Korea, it would appear, has been more crisis prone than most other comparable countries.

What is it, then, about the country's approach to economic and financial development that heightens crisis risk? Our analysis points to the priority attached to growth and the consequent tendency to run the economy under high pressure of demand. The high levels of investment demand associated with a capital-intensive growth strategy have been financed with debt—short-term foreign debt, in particular—which exposes the country to rollover problems and liquidity risk. We show that the relatively high levels of short-term foreign debt resulting from this strategy are a commonplace of Korean history. Those high levels of short-term foreign debt are, in turn, a key predictor of crisis. They have featured in every Korean financial crisis.

Turning from causes to consequences, a number of observers have concluded that financial crises have had a persistent negative impact on Korean growth. Here analysis is heavily informed by 1997–1998 and its aftermath. Following a sharp recovery in 1999–2000, growth and investment rates ratcheted back down. The suggestion is that the crisis, and by implication those preceding it, did some permanent damage, whether by undermining investor confidence or harming the financial system, or through some other channel.

The counterargument is that the drop in growth and investment rates simply reflected the natural tendency for growth to decelerate with the maturation of the economy. The Korean authorities resisted this tendency in the first half of the 1990s, liberalizing the financial system in ways that encouraged artificially high rates of investment underwritten by high levels of short-term external debt. Once the crisis intervened, those artificially high levels of investment collapsed, and unsustainably rapid growth rates came to an abrupt end. Unlike some other countries that have experienced a gradual deceleration in growth as their economies matured, this particular sequence of events caused Korea's growth rate to come down abruptly. But that deceleration in growth and the transition to lower investment rates were coming, crisis or not. The crisis, in this view, was the occasion for the adjustment, but it was not itself the fundamental cause. In light of the analysis in Chapter 2 of the causes of slower growth in the recent decade, we suggest that the bulk of the evidence is consistent with this second view.

Just as comparisons can help us get a handle on whether Korea is unusually prone to crises, they can also help us understand whether its crises have occasioned unusually serious negative output effects. Here we look not just at the 1997–1998 crisis but also at those that Korea experienced at the beginning of the 1970s and the beginning of the 1980s.[1] And we ask whether the output effects of crises in Korea have been larger or smaller—and more or less persistent—than in other countries.

Four Crises

The four financial crises that punctuated post–World War II Korean economic history display striking similarities, starting with conditions of high leverage and extensive reliance on foreign debt. The crisis of the early 1970s capped a period of rapid growth based on labor-intensive, export-oriented manufacturing. Korea entered this period as a poor economy with limited savings. Domestic finance being limited, interest rates were high; even favored exporters had to pay upward of 20 percent for bank loans, circa 1965. But rates on foreign loans were on the order of only 12 percent, and foreign borrowing was effectively guaranteed by Bank of Korea.[2] Insofar as the government limited the scope for inward FDI and other equity purchases by foreign investors, Korea's foreign borrowing disproportionately took the form of bank loans and suppliers' credits. Foreign aid to Korea was also winding down at this time, and diplomatic relations with Japan were being normalized, two developments that further encouraged foreign borrowing. This was a period when the won's exchange rate against the dollar and the yen was relatively stable, encouraging both lenders and borrowers to neglect the risks of foreign-currency-denominated debt.

Debt service to foreigners as a share of exports rose from 6 percent in 1965 to 18 percent in 1968 and 31 percent in 1970.[3] Clearly this position could be sustained only if export revenues grew robustly. But by the early 1970s, Korean labor costs had begun to rise, and the scope for export growth rates in excess of 40 percent diminished. The global economic slowdown that started in the early 1970s did not help. In 1969 some 30 firms had already found themselves unable to pay back their foreign borrowings, and the government had stepped in to assume control of their operations (and guarantee their debts). Korea negotiated an adjustment program with the IMF that prescribed devaluation, the elimination of most export subsidies, and further decontrolling of the interest rate.

With the negotiation of this 1971 program, the authorities devalued the won by 18 percent. Exports doubled in 1972–1973. But devaluation created balance sheet problems for firms with dollar-denominated debts. In response, the government declared a moratorium on all payments on corporate loans by curb lenders and rescheduled firms' bank loans at reduced interest rates. With these reductions in interest payments to domestic creditors, foreign debt service was successfully maintained. Unlike subsequent crises, the limited development and tight regulation of the banking system meant that banks were not destabilized by domestic default.

The second crisis, which broke out in 1980, was a concomitant of the Heavy and Chemical Industry Drive. Heavy industry is scale and capital intensive, so the drive entailed heavy investment. The chaebol undertaking much of this investment preferred debt over equity finance, on the grounds that debt did not threaten the control of incumbent owner-managers. As a result, the debt/equity ratio in Korean manufacturing rose from an already high 300 percent in 1974 to nearly 400 percent in 1980 and 500 percent in 1982.

Prominent among these debts were those owed to foreign banks, as much of the capital equipment required by the heavy and chemical industries was imported from abroad. The money-center banks, for their part, were flush with recycled petrodollars. Meanwhile Korea's relatively stable exchange rate encouraged those on both sides of these transactions to underestimate the risks. The current-account deficit widened as investment surged ahead, and the oil-import bill rose owing to the OPEC oil-price shocks. By 1979 Korea's external-debt/GDP ratio had risen to 33 percent. As questions began to be asked about the country's financial position, it was forced to shorten the term of its borrowing. Thus, short-term debt as a share of GDP rose from 6 percent in 1978 to 8 percent in 1979 and 15 percent in 1980.

Again, this tenuous situation could have been sustained only if everything had gone according to plan—in particular if the Korean economy and its exports had continued growing robustly. Alas, that was not what happened. In 1978–1979 the economy showed signs of overheating, leading the government first to tighten fiscal policy and then to adopt a comprehensive stabilization plan, scaling back preferences for the heavy and chemical industries. External conditions became less favorable. The United States experienced a brief recession in 1980 and then a more serious one in 1981–1982.

The Korean economy, for its part, contracted in 1980 for the first time in more than two decades. The government again negotiated an agreement with the IMF and devalued the won. Unit labor costs remaining stable in won, they fell sharply in dollars and yen. Further fiscal-austerity measures freed up additional resources for export. With the help of these policies, Korea was able to grow and export its way out of this crisis without having to reschedule its debts.

The success of this adjustment should not cause one to overlook the country's tenuous financial position. Short-term foreign debt in 1980 was 150 percent of foreign reserves. Had foreign bank creditors refused to roll over this debt, Korea would have been in dire straits. Here the country benefited from the fact that global financial markets remained open until the Mexican default in 1982. A strong government could clamp down on labor costs, getting the private sector to agree to guidelines for wage increases, the country's weak trade unions being in no position to resist. Finally, domestic saving was rising strongly, reflecting the rapid growth of recent years. This helped to reconcile smaller current-account deficits and reduced foreign borrowing with continuing high investment.[4]

The third crisis, in 1997, is discussed extensively elsewhere in this series. Here we note only some parallels with Korea's other crises. First, there were high leverage ratios among the country's large commercial and industrial conglomerates in particular, a financing strategy designed to avoid diluting insider control.[5] Second, there was a growing tendency to turn to external financing to maintain high rates of investment as the underlying environment for economic growth slowed. The mid-1990s saw increases in domestic labor costs, naturally slowing growth in the maturing economy, deteriorating conditions in global semiconductor markets, and the rise of Chinese competition. Third, there was the progressive shortening of the debt structure as economic difficulties mounted and access to long-term finance deteriorated. Fourth, there was an unbalanced approach to capital-account liberalization that favored short-term debt. This time the authorities discouraged the chaebol from issuing foreign bonds but left them free to access short-term bank loans abroad. The single most notorious statistic from the crisis is that Korea's short-term external debt was allowed to grow to more than 300 percent of reserves.[6] None of these parallels made a crisis inevitable, but they rendered Korea's finances highly vulnerable if markets grew unsettled, as they did in the second half of the year.

The subsequent adjustment was traumatic. It had been two decades since an OECD country had turned to the IMF for help, and the fact that Korea was forced to approach the IMF was a blow to its pride. The subsequent adjustment was disruptive even by the standards of what had come before. The won fell by nearly three times as much in 1997 as it had in 1980. Combined with the fact that banks and firms were even more highly leveraged than earlier, this made for more extensive balance-sheet distress. Again the government sought to avoid default at any cost, which meant fiscal retrenchment to free up resources for export and to reassure investors, as in 1979–1980, but now that debt ratios were higher, the pressure for fiscal austerity was even greater than before. And given that short-term foreign debt was a multiple of reserves, maintaining debt service required raising interest rates sharply, which only deepened financial distress.

Finally, we have the 2008 crisis. This fourth crisis for the Korean economy was the result of events in the global economy more than in Korea. It reflected deleveraging by U.S. hedge funds and other institutional investors who, experiencing subscriber withdrawals and finding it difficult to tap funding, liquidated their Korean investments. Especially following the failure of Lehman Brothers in October 2008, there was a generalized flight to safety and liquidity. Foreigners desperately seeking to deleverage sold their Korean holdings, sending the market into a tailspin. The result was not only a collapse of equity-market valuations but also a sharp depreciation of the won, which plummeted from less than 1,000 to the dollar in July to more than 1,500 in November. Banks and corporations experienced a severe shortage of dollars. In response, Bank of Korea provided exceptional dollar loans that it financed with the help of a three-month swap facility from the U.S. Federal Reserve.[7]

While this crisis was global, Korea was more severely affected than most Asian countries. The question is, why. One view is that international investors in Korea inaccurately inferred the existence of weaknesses from superficial parallels with Korea's earlier crises. One investment bank's newsletter, for example, headed its analysis of the country's financial prospects "South Korea—The Usual Suspect." Korean banks had again borrowed extensively offshore, in dollars, like they had ten years before.[8] Unlike most other Asian countries, moreover, Korea was running a current-account deficit, like ten years before, which exposed it to the risk of a sudden stop. But that deficit was only 1 percent of GDP, barely a quarter of the levels ten years earlier. The parallels may have been superficial, but their existence is one explanation for why the country's finances again came under pressure.

More fundamentally, Korea proved unusually susceptible to financial pressure precisely because it had so faithfully followed IMF and U.S. Treasury advice to internationalize its financial system. Foreign investors, prominently including U.S. hedge funds, held some 50 percent of Korean stock market capitalization on the eve of the crisis. Foreign holdings of Korean domestic bonds and equities, at more than 250 percent of reserves, were higher than in any other major emerging market. When those investors took losses on other investments, they were forced to liquidate their holdings of Korean securities. Through this mechanism Korea suffered larger capital outflows and a sharper stock market decline than many other emerging markets. Korea was also exposed as a result of having a relatively well-developed financial sector. Banks were highly leveraged and funded themselves on the wholesale money market: the country had a higher loan-to-deposit ratio than any emerging market outside the Baltics, exposing the banks to significant credit risk. Financial development and internationalization may have their advantages, but not in periods when global financial markets go haywire.

There was one final difference from the earlier crises. Korea, having strengthened its financial position, was better able to respond with stabilizing monetary and fiscal interventions. While gross foreign debt was still extensive, at more than 40 percent of GDP, net foreign debt had been reduced to zero. While short-term debt approached 20 percent of GDP, foreign exchange reserves were half again as high. Leverage ratios as measured by net-debt-to-book-equity in the corporate sector had fallen dramatically, from 250 percent to 50 percent, meaning that Korean corporations were less exposed to destabilization from exchange rate depreciation. This allowed Bank of Korea to respond to slowing economic

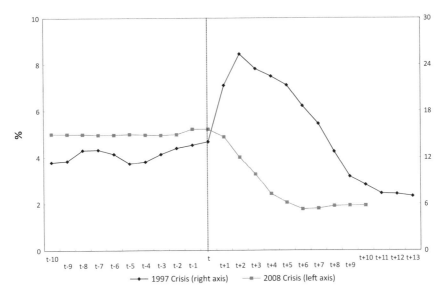

Figure 7.1. Central Bank Policy Rates in Two Recent Crises
Data from Bank of Korea and International Monetary Fund, International Financial Statistics database.

growth by reducing its policy rates, even if this implied a weaker exchange rate. It meant that the authorities could adopt an expansionary fiscal policy rather than cut spending in a desperate effort to attract back capital, as before.

Thus, while there are strong similarities among Korea's four successive economic crises, there are also some reassuring differences, notably in how the authorities were able to respond in the most recent instance.

Comparative Evidence on Crisis Incidence

Four economic crises since 1968 amount to one crisis every ten years. This is not exceptional, but it does make Korea look a bit more crisis prone than is typical. Table 7.1 tabulates crises in both a large sample of 76 countries and a smaller sample of 32 middle-income countries with which Korea has historically been comparable.[9] Data from both samples suggest that roughly 40 percent of the countries experienced at least four crises in the four-plus decades since 1965. Again, this suggests that Korea

Table 7.1. Financial Crises in the Sample Countries (1965–2006)

Number of crises	All countries		Middle-income countries	
	Number of countries	Percent	Number of countries	Percent
0	2	2.6	0	0.0
1	3	3.9	0	0.0
2	24	31.6	10	31.3
3	19	25.0	8	25.0
4	14	18.4	4	12.5
5	5	6.6	4	12.5
6	6	7.9	4	12.5
7	2	2.6	1	3.1
8	1	1.3	1	3.1
Total	76	100.0	32	100.0

Source: Banking crises are those identified in Laeven and Valencia (2008). Additional data from IMF, International Financial Statistics, and World Bank, World Development Indicators.

Note: Financial crises include both currency and banking crises. To identify a currency crisis we adopted two methods and defined a crisis if either method detected one. With the first method, a currency crisis is said to occur when a monthly index of currency pressure changes by a sufficiently large magnitude, namely, that the index is outside of three standard deviations. The monthly index is measured as a weighted average of monthly nominal exchange rate changes and the monthly percentage reserve loss where the weights are assigned to equalize the sample volatility of the two components. Since the nominal exchange rate is supposed to change more rapidly in hyperinflation countries, we considered them in a separate sample. The second method follows Park and Lee (2003): a currency crisis is indicated when there are large nominal depreciations of the currency during any quarter of the year. (A large nominal depreciation of the currency is the case when the depreciation was larger than 25 percent during the given period and exceeded that in the previous period by at least 10 percent.) To avoid measuring the same crisis more than once, we exclude a second observation if it occurred within two years.

is on the crisis-prone end of the distribution, but its experience is not highly exceptional. Twenty to 30 percent of the countries (depending on the sample) experienced more crises than Korea over the period.

We have argued that Korea's susceptibility to crises has been associated with its use of foreign funding—short-term bank funding, in particular—to underwrite extensive investment and aggressively pursue growth. This interpretation is consistent with the findings of Rodrik and Velasco (1999) for a larger sample of countries. Defining crises as sharp reversals in the direction of capital flows, they find that countries where short-term debt owed to foreign banks is greater than foreign reserves have a 10-percentage-point higher probability of experiencing a crisis than countries where this ratio is below unity. (Other variables that significantly heighten crisis risk include the presence of a large current-account deficit and sharp appreciation of the real exchange rate.) Since the average probability of a crisis in a given country in a given year is 6 percent, this is roughly a tripling of crisis risk.

Why short-term debt in excess of reserves heightens an economy's vulnerability to a sharp reversal in the direction of capital flows is clear: if foreign banks are reluctant to roll over short-term loans, for whatever reason, a country whose reserves are less than the value of those loans may find itself unable to pay them back. It will be vulnerable to a capital-flow reversal quite independent of the state of other fundamentals. The authors also consider other forms of short-term debt (not extended by foreign banks): while high levels of other debt also increase crisis risk, the effect is smaller. Medium- and long-term debt, in contrast, has little if any impact on crisis incidence.

We have extended Rodrik and Velasco's analysis beyond the ten-year period that they consider (1988 to 1998). The data for this exercise come from the World Bank's Global Development Finance (GDF) database and cover the period from 1970 to 2005, a considerably longer period than that covered by Rodrik and Velasco. Since the GDF data do not include Korea, data for the country are added from Bank of Korea sources. We exclude Middle Eastern and African countries, where changes in macroeconomic policy often have less of an impact in terms of capital flow reversals than oil prices and political instability. The resulting list of sharp capital-flow reversals is provided in appendix Table 7.A2 at the end of this chapter; reassuringly, Korea in 1998 is among them. (Reversals are measured by the magnitude of the change in total capital flows.) We use a cutoff for reversals of 9 percent of GDP, a sufficiently high threshold to filter out small fluctuations in capital flows but low enough to capture each of the important Korean episodes.

The regression analysis in Table 7.2 confirms that capital flow reversals are more likely in countries with large amounts of short-term debt relative to reserves (and more total debt relative to GNP). The significance of this variable's coefficient varies depending on controls, but the pattern is clear.[10]

We can also look more closely at the composition of Korea's capital inflows during its four crises.[11] In the early 1970s, gross foreign debt as a

Table 7.2. Probit Estimates of Determinants of Capital Flow Reversals, 1970–2005

		Dependent variable takes value of 1 in case of sharp reversal in capital flows				
	(1)	(2)	(3)	(4)	(5)	(6)
Short-term debt/total debt	1.981** [0.379]					
Short-term debt/reserves		0.034* [0.015]	0.031* [0.014]	0.155** [0.040]	0.030* [0.014]	0.029* [0.014]
Medium- and long-term debt/reserves		−0.016 [0.009]	−0.013 [0.009]	−0.028* [0.013]	−0.014 [0.009]	−0.014 [0.009]
Debt/GDP		0.279** [0.075]	0.225** [0.079]	0.687** [0.206]	0.231** [0.080]	0.294* [0.119]
Current account balance/GDP			−0.009 [0.007]	−0.013 [0.009]	−0.008 [0.007]	−0.015 [0.008]
Real exchange rate appreciation (average of previous 3 years)				0.062 [0.108]		
M2/reserves					0.003 [0.008]	
Increase in credit/GDP (average of previous 3 years)						−0.024 [0.068]
Observations	1,840	1,758	1,538	1,334	1,534	1,300
Pseudo R-squared	0.05	0.05	0.05	0.07	0.06	0.05

Note: The dependent variable takes value of one in case of sharp reversals in net capital flows. Coefficients are the changes in probability of sharp reversals associated with changes in the independent variable. Net capital flows are measured based on net flows of total debt, reported in Global Financial Data. Numbers in parentheses are standard errors.

** and * denote statistical significance at 1-percent and 5-percent levels, respectively.

share of GNP rose sharply (from 27 percent in 1969 to 31 percent in 1971 and 34 percent in 1972). Short-term debt as a share of the total also jumped up, from 11 percent in 1969 to 17 percent in 1970.[12] In the late 1970s and the mid-1990s, a sharp increase in foreign indebtedness is again evident. But the debts of the late 1970s were predominantly medium- and long-term, in comparison with the situation fifteen years later. Total short-term debt at the beginning of 1980 was 8.4 percent of GDP and 97 percent of reserves, in comparison with 15 percent of GDP and more than 300 percent of reserves in late 1997. It should not be surprising in this light that the 1997–1998 crisis was more severe. Currency depreciation wreaked more havoc with balance sheets in 1997 than 1980, and financial distress was consequently more widespread. In 2008, both total foreign debt and short-term indebtedness approached 1997 levels, notwithstanding the reforms of the intervening decade. It was this, as noted above, that caused international investors to identify Korea as potentially susceptible to global financial volatility.

Rodrik and Velasco (1999) also use their panel of 32 emerging markets to analyze the determinants of the maturity of external debt. They find that countries whose debts rise over time (that have higher debt ratios in their fixed-effects regressions) rely more on short-term debt. One interpretation of this is that countries anxious to continue borrowing are forced by their creditors to shorten the maturity of their obligations as they become more heavily indebted. There is some evidence of this dynamic in the run-up to the Korean crises of 1972, 1980, and 1997.

Another finding is that middle-income countries with more developed financial markets have a higher share of short-term debt in their total foreign funding. Again this makes sense: countries with underdeveloped financial markets find it difficult to access and intermediate short-term funds. This suggests reasons why Korea would have relied more heavily on short-term foreign borrowing over time and, as a consequence, why the adverse output effects of financial crises should have grown more severe.

We have updated these regressions using data spanning the period from 1970 to 2005. Table 7.3 reports the results using the same data and sample of countries as in our analysis of the determinants of capital flow reversals; Table 7.4 adds back in the Middle Eastern and African countries. The results are basically the same for both samples. Reliance on short-term debt is greater in countries with relatively well-developed banking and financial systems. It is greater in countries carrying and forced to finance relatively

Table 7.3. Determinants of Maturity of External Debt, 1970–2005

	Short-term debt/total debt						
	(1)	*(2)*	*(3)*	*(4)*	*(5)*	*(6)*	*(7)*
Debt/GNP	0.011**	0.006	0.005	0.011*	0.000	0.008*	0.007
	[0.004]	[0.004]	[0.004]	[0.004]	[0.004]	[0.004]	[0.004]
Investment rate		14.237**			24.653**		9.453
		[4.318]			[4.232]		[4.981]
M2/GDP			8.179**		5.574**	−1.902	
			[1.668]		[1.640]	[2.429]	
Per capita GDP				6.334**		8.262**	5.272**
				[1.138]		[1.405]	[1.183]
Observations	2,330	1,716	1,769	1,632	1,636	1,561	1,515
R-squared	0.00	0.01	0.02	0.02	0.03	0.03	0.02

Note: The dependent variable is the ratio of short-term debt to total debt. Numbers in parentheses are standard errors.

** and * denote statistical significance at the 1- and 5-percent levels, respectively.

Table 7.4. Determinants of the Maturity of External Debt, Including Middle East and Africa, 1970–2005

	Short-term debt/total debt						
	(1)	*(2)*	*(3)*	*(4)*	*(5)*	*(6)*	*(7)*
Debt/GNP	0.019**	0.006*	0.015**	0.010**	0.001	0.006*	0.007*
	[0.002]	[0.003]	[0.003]	[0.003]	[0.003]	[0.003]	[0.003]
Investment rate		4.658			9.599**		0.392
		[2.558]			[2.608]		[2.840]
M2/GDP			0.019		0.014	0.012	
			[0.031]		[0.030]	[0.031]	
Per capita GDP				4.860**		6.119**	4.470**
				[0.831]		[0.815]	[0.859]
Observations	4,040	3,184	3,333	3,040	3,034	2,928	2,846
R-squared	0.02	0.00	0.01	0.01	0.00	0.02	0.01

Note: See note for Table 7.3.

heavy debt loads. Finally, it is greater in countries with relatively high investment rates. From this we surmise that our conclusion that Korea relied heavily on short-term debt as a result of its debt- and investment-intensive growth and development strategy—and more recently because of the relatively large size of its financial markets—is consistent with the international evidence.

Comparative Evidence on Effects

What impact do economic crises have on GDP, investment, and export growth? There is less than full agreement among economists about what to expect, although the literature does provide some stylized facts. For example, while crises have a permanent negative impact on the level of output and its trend (the output losses caused by the crisis are not fully made up subsequently, in other words), there appears to be little if any discernible impact of the crisis itself on the post-crisis rate of growth. In addition, recessions following crises tend to be more severe when the pre-crisis credit boom was more pronounced and levels of international reserves are lower. These observations provide some guidance as to what we should expect in Korea.

Hong and Tornell (2005), in a study of 103 developing-country currency crises in the period from 1980 to 1999, find that the GDP growth rate in the immediate post-crisis period falls by 2 percentage points relative to the rate in the immediately preceding tranquil period. But within three years following the crisis, the growth rate has recovered almost exactly to its pre-crisis level. Bordo et al. (2000) find essentially the same thing. Thus, some authors argue that crisis countries enjoy a growth spurt following a crisis, with growth accelerating relative to the pre-crisis norm. Indeed they point to Korea in 1999–2000, when growth accelerated to 9 to 10 percent, as an example of this effect. The Hong and Tornell and Bordo et al. studies suggest that this spurt repairs only part of the damage. The negative impact on the level of GDP owing to the crisis is not, in general, made up.

Hong and Tornell then explore the components of national income. They find that the investment rate drops in the year of the crisis and remains persistently below pre-crisis levels for three subsequent years. The drop in their sample is from 20 percent in the tranquil period to 18 percent in the year of the crisis and 17 percent subsequently.[13] In contrast, there is less evidence of differential export growth over time.

In Table 7.5 we show how Korea's four crises fit into these patterns. The literature on the 1997–1998 crisis suggests that this event was followed by a noticeable decline in the investment rate. The table confirms this and generalizes the point. Declines in investment are evident in all four Korean crises, but the 1997–1998 crisis, when the decline in the investment rate was not only large but also long lasting, stands out. In contrast, the drop in investment was short-lived after the 1971 crisis, as the government's policies promoting investment in the heavy and chemical industries kicked in powerfully. Unlike investment rates, savings rates hardly moved in the 1971, 1980, and 2007–2008 crises, just as they hardly moved in the larger sample of control cases. Here the exception is again the 1997–1998 crisis, when savings rates moved up for a brief period, reflecting the severity of the output decline, the pervasiveness of credit constraints, and the collapse of consumption. It follows that the shift of the current account into surplus was larger after 1997 than in the other three cases or, for that matter, in the control group of countries. This also reminds us that the current-account deficit, which reflects the high pressure of investment demand under which the economy was being run, was a factor in the first two crises but not, in any obvious sense, in 1997–1998 or 2007–2008.

In contrast to the current-account deficit, little was exceptional about the behavior of the budget deficit around the time of Korea's four crises. Reflecting this, bond spreads were low by the standards of other crisis countries. Credit growth was fast, reflecting the fast growth of the economy. But—as we have emphasized—Korea stands out most clearly in its levels of foreign indebtedness, short-term foreign indebtedness in particular. Depending on the crisis in question, short-term indebtedness was two to three times the average in the control group of crisis countries.

What we want to determine is whether the decline in investment and the other changes noted above translated into a drop in output, both in general and specifically in Korea. Table 7.5 offers a clear answer. Economic crises have been a big deal in Korea because they have been associated with unusually large output losses. Whereas growth falls on average by 1 percentage point in a crisis, it fell by fully 7 percentage points in the 1971 Korean crisis, by 10 percentage points in the 1980 crisis (although in this case, for the reasons noted, recovery was unusually swift), by 15 percentage points over two years in the 1997–1998 crisis, and by 2 percentage points in the 2007–2008 crisis, when growth fell sharply but again quickly bounced back. It can be argued that a fast-growing country naturally also slows

Table 7.5. Macroeconomic Adjustment to Currency Crises

	Currency crises defined by depreciation and reserve losses (%)					
	Pre-crisis period	*t*	*t+1*	*t+2*	*t+3*	*Tranquil period*
(1) GDP growth	2.04**	1.16**	1.35**	3.32	3.87	3.33
	1.68**	**1.20****	**2.64****	**3.82**	**4.21**	**3.98**
Korea (1971)	11.37	8.20	4.50	12.00	7.20	
Korea (1980)	8.70	−1.50	6.20	7.30	10.80	7.11
Korea (1997)	8.23	4.70	−6.90	9.50	8.50	
Korea (2008)	4.77	2.3	0.3	6.0		
(2) Current account	−4.20	−3.29**	−2.99**	−2.89**	−2.14**	−4.75
	−3.78	**−2.20****	**−2.40****	**−3.10****	**−1.97****	**−4.61**
Korea (1971)	−6.99	−8.60	−3.46	−2.26	−10.52	
Korea (1980)	−2.81	−8.32	−6.45	−3.35	−1.80	0.16
Korea (1997)	−2.26	−1.62	11.69	5.51	2.39	
Korea (2008)	1.03	0.3	3.9	2.80		
(3) Investment rate	18.20**	18.12**	17.26**	16.94**	17.15**	20.29
	18.03**	**18.23***	**17.13****	**17.06****	**16.99****	**19.44**
Korea (1971)	25.71	25.85	21.89	25.96	32.75	
Korea (1980)	33.35	32.64	30.38	29.36	29.77	32.64
Korea (1997)	37.83	35.97	25.00	29.12	31.00	
Korea (2008)	29.11	31.0	26.2	29.2		
(4) Saving rate	13.48	14.28	13.07*	13.27*	13.95	15.47
	12.63	**15.20**	**11.45**	**12.37**	**14.50**	**14.96**
Korea (1971)	18.44	16.12	17.31	23.25	22.60	
Korea (1980)	30.84	25.25	25.01	26.06	29.61	34.40
Korea (1997)	35.93	35.41	37.23	35.03	33.60	
Korea (2008)	31.51	30.5	30.2	32.0		
(5) Foreign debt	7.12	6.56	6.18	4.48**	3.00**	7.72
	6.77	**5.45**	**5.28**	**3.21****	**2.88****	**7.20**
Korea (1971)	41.57	26.36	20.50	17.12	33.20	
Korea (1980)	21.89	29.21	17.71	13.40	8.51	13.06
Korea (1997)	28.03	10.18	−6.17	−6.87	−3.20	
Korea (2008)	26.56	10.64				

(continued)

Table 7.5. (Continued)

	Currency crises defined by depreciation and reserve losses (%)					
	Pre-crisis period	t	t+1	t+2	t+3	Tranquil period
(6) Short-term debt	14.85	14.40	12.63	12.03*	10.43**	14.06
	12.41	**11.12**	**10.91**	**9.68**	**9.41**	**11.86**
Korea (1971)	11.90	16.40	17.84	16.47	20.88	
Korea (1980)	25.84	34.51	31.53	33.51	30.00	23.81
Korea (1997)	45.61	36.59	24.16	28.15	33.53	
Korea (2008)	40.25	44.56				
(7) CPI inflation	12.45**	24.42**	24.05**	16.56**	23.35**	9.69
	12.64	**23.03**	**20.76**	**13.15**	**16.97**	**8.62**
Korea (1971)	13.16	13.44	11.67	3.22	24.30	
Korea (1980)	14.30	28.70	21.34	7.19	3.42	7.16
Korea (1997)	5.22	4.45	7.51	0.81	2.27	
Korea (2008)	2.50	4.57	2.79	2.88		
(8) Credit growth	16.19	26.45**	19.18**	16.57	20.30**	14.45
	15.80	**22.86**	**16.32**	**18.19**	**17.86**	**14.63**
Korea (1971)	43.56	25.32	25.52	25.93	42.48	
Korea (1980)	29.74	34.05	27.02	22.40	14.82	21.32
Korea (1997)	16.12	20.90	11.01	16.00	15.20	
Korea (2008)	11.41					
(9) Credit/CPI	3.94	0.87	−4.66**	1.79	−2.15**	4.22
	3.19	**−2.45**	**−2.38**	**2.02**	**−2.63**	**5.16**
Korea (1971)	31.20	12.70	14.42	22.77	20.73	
Korea (1980)	16.41	8.83	7.68	15.45	11.47	10.93
Korea (1997)	11.04	16.55	3.76	15.20	12.95	
Korea (2008)	8.94					
(10) Spread	6.83	6.85	7.72	8.06	8.19	7.11
	6.09	**7.38**	**8.00**	**7.20**	**8.39**	**7.25**
Korea (1971)	0.80	1.60	3.50	3.50	0.50	
Korea (1980)	0.80	1.40	0.80	2.00	2.00	0.85
Korea (1997)	0.50	1.07	1.99	1.45	0.61	
Korea (2008)	1.19					

Table 7.5. (Continued)

	Pre-crisis period	*t*	*t+1*	*t+2*	*t+3*	Tranquil period
	Currency crises defined by depreciation and reserve losses (%)					
(11) Deficit/GDP	−4.00	−3.41	−3.01	−3.17	−2.94	−3.22
	−3.29	**−3.07**	**−2.51**	**−2.12**	**−2.64**	**−2.81**
Korea (1971)	−1.00	−2.30	−4.60	−1.60	−4.00	
Korea (1980)	−2.20	−3.11	−4.46	−4.08	−1.49	−0.33
Korea (1997)	0.32	−1.42	−3.87	−2.47	1.13	
Korea (2008)	1.54	1.55				

Source: Hong and Tornell (2005), with additional data from World Bank (2006); IMF, International Financial Statistics database; Bank of Korea; and SaKong (1993). IMF's forecasts are obtained from *World Economic Outlook* (October 2008).

Note: This table is based on Hong and Tornell (2005), table 1; we added data for the four crises in Korea. The table reports the average values first and sample medians below; *t* represents the crisis years: 1971, 1980, 1997, and 2008. Not all of the data are available from 1960; some average values are based on the only available data: the data for investment, saving, current account, and deficit start from 1970, and consumer price index (CPI) data start from 1966; credit growth and credit/CPI for 2005–2007 are the values for 2005–2006.

** and * indicate statistically significant differences from the tranquil period values at the 5- and 10-percent levels, respectively.

down more quickly when it hits a speed bump, and Korea was a fast-growing country throughout the period, by the standards of this sample. We will return to the question of whether its slowdown was in some sense excessive. We will also ask whether the effects were enduring.

To get a handle on why Korea's response differs, studies like Rodrik and Velasco (1999) and Gupta, Mishra, and Sahay (2003) are helpful for their analysis of the severity of crisis-induced recessions and the vigor of post-crisis recoveries in different countries. Rodrik and Velasco find that the severity of the downturn rises with the ratio of short-term foreign debt to reserves (not the ratio of short-term foreign debt to GDP). Countries with higher ratios of short-term foreign debt to reserves are likely to see sharper exchange rate depreciation in a crisis and thus to experience more balance sheet dislocations. Looking at a sample of 195 currency-crisis episodes in 91 developing countries, Gupta, Mishra, and Sahay find that the depth of the post-crisis recession increases with the volume of pre-crisis capital inflows and the magnitude of the subsequent capital-flow reversal. The output loss tends to be larger when growth was unusually rapid in the pre-crisis period and when the authorities were unable to apply expansionary monetary and fiscal policies when the economy turned down. Two other results relevant for thinking about Korea: more-open economies tend to suffer smaller output losses (presumably because they are better able to export their way out of the problem), and output losses are larger when other countries experience crises and are forced to depreciate simultaneously (which presumably makes it harder to export one's way out of the problem). Simultaneous devaluation in other countries has, of course, been a feature of all four Korean crises, suggesting that these events did not simply reflect developments internal to Korea.

To determine whether the impact of crises on growth in Korea was in any way distinctive, we estimated models of the determinants of investment and growth over successive five-year periods. (There are nine five-year periods spanning the years from 1965 to 2006. For reasons of data availability the last period we analyzed was 2005–2006.) The sample is made up of all countries for which information on the vector of control variables is available (76 in all). The specification includes a financial crisis variable set equal to one if either a currency crisis or a banking crisis occurred in the period in question.[14] The list of control variables follows Barro and Lee (2003).

Results for investment are in Table 7.6. Following Barro and Lee (2003), we added the lagged dependent variable as an explanatory variable.[15] The results include a sharp, statistically significant drop in investment in response to a financial crisis. This was found to be true for financial crises as a whole (in columns 1 and 2) and for the Korean crises in particular (columns 3 and 4). Two aspects of these results are particularly noteworthy. First, economic crises have had a larger negative impact on investment in Korea than elsewhere. The coefficient on a crisis in the current period is two to three times greater than that for the full sample of countries. Second, the impact on investment is persistent: the coefficient on the lagged crisis variable (which picks up whether there was a crisis in the preceding five-year period) is also negative and significant. The effect is smaller than that of a concurrent crisis, but again it is significant, and again it is larger in Korea than in the sample of other countries.

The results for growth in Table 7.7 are compatible with these results for investment, although they also differ in important ways. A financial crisis lowers the rate of growth by 1.4 percent a year, on average, over the

Table 7.6. The Impact of the Korean Crisis on Investment: Arellano-Bond Estimates

Investment rate	[1]	[2]	[3]	[4]
Financial crisis	−0.011***	−0.015***	−0.011***	−0.014***
	[0.004]	[0.004]	[0.004]	[0.004]
Financial crisis (−1)		−0.007**		−0.007*
		[0.003]		[0.004]
Korean crisis			−0.025***	−0.048***
			[0.005]	[0.008]
Korean crisis (−1)				−0.028***
				[0.010]
Investment ratio (−1)	0.267***	0.286***	0.262***	0.286***
	[0.070]	[0.068]	[0.069]	[0.068]
Log (per capita GDP)	0.01	0.003	0.011	0.002
	[0.013]	[0.012]	[0.013]	[0.012]
Inflation	−0.009	−0.006	−0.009	−0.007
	[0.008]	[0.008]	[0.008]	[0.008]
Openness	0.067***	0.067***	0.068***	0.068***
	[0.019]	[0.019]	[0.019]	[0.019]
Fertility	0.050**	0.045**	0.053**	0.047**
	[0.021]	[0.022]	[0.021]	[0.022]
Democracy index	−0.015	−0.009	−0.018	−0.011
	[0.067]	[0.066]	[0.067]	[0.066]
Democracy index square	−0.005	−0.011	−0.003	−0.012
	[0.058]	[0.057]	[0.058]	[0.058]
Human capital	−0.016**	−0.014**	−0.016**	−0.013*
	[0.007]	[0.007]	[0.007]	[0.007]
Law and order	0.011***	0.011***	0.012***	0.011***
	[0.003]	[0.003]	[0.003]	[0.003]
Government consumption	−0.122	−0.117	−0.121	−0.117
	[0.075]	[0.078]	[0.076]	[0.078]
Observations	401	401	401	401

Note: Standard errors in brackets. The dependent variable is the investment rate for nine five-year periods, starting with 1965–1970, and then 2005–2006. Log per capita GDP and human capital are for the beginning of each period. The inflation rate is measured by the average annual change in the consumer price index over the period. The investment rate, openness, fertility, democracy index, law and order, and government consumption are similarly measured as averages over each period.

***, **, and * denote statistical significance at 1-, 5-, and 10-percent levels, respectively.

five-year interval in which it occurs; this effect is consistently significant at the 99 percent confidence level (column 1).[16] This effect is robust to the inclusion of a lagged crisis variable indicating whether a crisis occurred in the preceding five-year period (column 2). But, equally important, the coefficient on a financial crisis lagged, while weakly positive, is not statistically significant from zero. It would appear that growth in the period five to ten years following the crisis remains unaffected. This is despite the fact that the decline in investment is persistent (crises in the preceding period as opposed to the current period continue to depress investment, but they do not continue to depress growth). This result points to an increase in efficiency following a crisis. Or, to put the point another way, at least some of the relatively high investment characteristic of the pre-crisis period appears to have been poorly allocated.[17] Once immediate disruptions have passed, there is no sign that the persistent decline in investment rates associated with the crisis produce a persistent decline in growth.

In column 3 of Table 7.7 we add a dummy variable for three Korean crises (1971, 1980, and 1997). We find the same thing for Korea as for other countries. The difference in the output loss relative to the full sample is essentially zero. The point estimate in column 3 suggests that output fell in response to the three Korean crises—0.8 percent per annum *less,* on average, compared with the larger sample—but the standard error is large relative to the point estimate, indicating that the difference is insignificant at conventional confidence levels. Note that this is very different from the unusually large impact we obtained when we estimated the impact of crises on investment.

When we add a dummy variable for lagged Korean crises, we get a large and significant positive coefficient, suggesting that growth bounced back following crises significantly faster than is typical of the countries in our sample. However, this variable appears to be picking up the fact that Korea grew more quickly than most other countries in the sample in both crisis and noncrisis periods (including during the 1975–1980, 1985–1990, and 2000–2005 periods—that is, in the five-year periods that succeeded those containing its crises). When we add a dummy variable for Korea that picks up this faster growth (which ranges from 1.3 to 2.5 percent per annum, depending on whether the specification in column 5 or column 6 is preferred), the coefficients on Korea's current-crisis indicator and its lagged-crisis indicator both go to zero. According to column 5, which we take as definitive, a financial crisis cuts growth by 1.5 percent per annum

Table 7.7. The Impact of Crises on Growth: Random Effects

Growth rate of output	[1]	[2]	[3]	[4]	[5]	[6]
Financial crisis	-0.014*** [0.002]	-0.014*** [0.002]	-0.014*** [0.002]	-0.015*** [0.002]	-0.014*** [0.002]	-0.015*** [0.002]
Financial crisis (-1)		0.001 [0.002]		0.001 [0.002]		0.001 [0.002]
Korean crisis			0.008 [0.013]	0.019 [0.014]	-0.003 [0.014]	0.011 [0.017]
Korean crisis (-1)				0.023* [0.014]		0.015 [0.017]
Korea dummy					0.025** [0.012]	0.013 [0.017]
Log (per capita GDP)	-0.006** [0.003]	-0.006** [0.003]	-0.006** [0.003]	-0.006** [0.003]	-0.006** [0.003]	-0.005** [0.003]
Investment ratio	0.143*** [0.019]	0.151*** [0.021]	0.143*** [0.019]	0.147*** [0.021]	0.137*** [0.019]	0.145*** [0.021]
Inflation	-0.018*** [0.004]	-0.018*** [0.004]	-0.018*** [0.004]	-0.018*** [0.004]	-0.018*** [0.004]	-0.018*** [0.004]
Openness	-0.002 [0.003]	-0.001 [0.003]	-0.002 [0.003]	-0.001 [0.003]	-0.002 [0.003]	-0.001 [0.003]
Fertility	-0.009** [0.005]	-0.008 [0.005]	-0.009** [0.005]	-0.007 [0.005]	-0.008* [0.005]	-0.007 [0.005]

(continued)

Table 7.7. (Continued)

Growth rate of output	[1]	[2]	[3]	[4]	[5]	[6]
Democracy index	0.004	0.005	0.005	0.005	0.005	0.005
	[0.020]	[0.021]	[0.020]	[0.021]	[0.020]	[0.021]
Democracy index square	-0.001	0	-0.001	0	-0.001	0
	[0.017]	[0.017]	[0.017]	[0.017]	[0.016]	[0.017]
Human capital	-0.001	-0.001	-0.001	-0.001	-0.002	-0.001
	[0.001]	[0.001]	[0.001]	[0.001]	[0.001]	[0.001]
Law and order	0.002	0.001	0.002	0.002	0.002*	0.002
	[0.001]	[0.001]	[0.001]	[0.001]	[0.001]	[0.001]
Government consumption	-0.084***	-0.068**	-0.083***	-0.066**	-0.079***	-0.065**
	[0.028]	[0.030]	[0.028]	[0.029]	[0.028]	[0.029]
Observations	537	495	537	495	537	495
R-squared	0.3136	0.3172	0.3168	0.3287	0.3285	0.3299

Note: The estimates are based on panel fixed effect estimation. The dependent variable is the growth rate of real per capita GDP for nine five-year periods, starting with 1965–1970, and then 2005–2006. See also note for Table 7.6.

***, **, and * denote statistical significance at the 1-, 5-, and 10-percent levels, respectively.

over the five-year interval in which it occurs. There is no sign of significantly faster or, for that matter, slower growth in the subsequent five-year period. And there is no sign that either the slowdown immediately following the crisis or the subsequent recovery of growth to the level typical of the pre-crisis period has been different in Korea than elsewhere.

As a robustness check, we estimated the same relationships assuming fixed rather than random effects and by three-stage least squares on the stacked set of cross sections. The results, in Tables 7.8 and 7.9, point to the same conclusions.[18]

Crises are to be avoided, the conclusion follows, because they lead to losses in output that are not recovered subsequently. But there is little evidence at this level of aggregation that they have been responsible for permanently lower growth rates, either in Korea or elsewhere. Multivariate analysis confirms that there is a persistent decline in investment following a crisis and that this has been even larger in Korea than elsewhere. But the decline in growth is only transitory and is no larger in Korea. Evidently other factors, plausibly including an increase in the efficiency of investment, prevent persistently lower investment rates from translating into persistently lower growth rates. This is the positive interpretation in the literature of the impact of lower investment in East Asia following the 1997–1998 crisis. Our analysis establishes that it applies more generally.

Ranciere, Tornell, and Westermann (2008) offer the provocative hypothesis that crises, within limits, are good for growth. Governments and firms that pursue risky strategies that are likely to maximize growth are also exposed to crises. In contrast, cozy environments, where the financial system is tightly cosseted, will be immune from instability but will not be particularly conducive to growth. Korea would seem like an apt example of the point: the chaebol and their regulators consistently pursued policies of high leverage and heavy dependence on foreign debt that accelerated the growth of the economy while at the same time exposing it to crisis risk. The fact that Korea grew faster than most other countries for the past 40 years, despite experiencing periodic financial disturbances, is consistent with their view.

Ranciere, Tornell, and Westermann implement these ideas by regressing the GDP growth rate on the skewness of credit growth and a standard vector of control variables. Intuitively, credit growth will be highly skewed if it is normally relatively rapid (relative to the sample average) but collapses periodically owing to a crisis. Korean credit growth is slightly more

Table 7.8. The Impact of Crises on Growth: Fixed Effects

Growth rate of output	[1]	[2]	[3]	[4]
Financial crisis	−0.015***	−0.016***	−0.015***	−0.016***
	[0.002]	[0.002]	[0.002]	[0.002]
L. financial crisis		0		0
		[0.002]		[0.002]
Korean crisis			−0.009	−0.01
			[0.013]	[0.017]
L. Korean crisis				0.002
				[0.017]
Log (per capita GDP)	−0.028***	−0.029***	−0.028***	−0.030***
	[0.005]	[0.005]	[0.005]	[0.005]
Investment ratio	0.132***	0.131***	0.131***	0.129***
	[0.022]	[0.024]	[0.022]	[0.025]
Inflation	−0.025***	−0.024***	−0.025***	−0.024***
	[0.004]	[0.005]	[0.004]	[0.005]
Openness	0.007	0.01	0.007	0.011*
	[0.006]	[0.006]	[0.006]	[0.007]
Fertility	−0.001	0.004	0	0.004
	[0.006]	[0.007]	[0.006]	[0.007]
Democracy index	−0.028	−0.029	−0.028	−0.03
	[0.024]	[0.025]	[0.024]	[0.025]
Democracy index square	0.023	0.025	0.023	0.026
	[0.019]	[0.020]	[0.019]	[0.020]
Human capital	0.004**	0.005**	0.004**	0.005**
	[0.002]	[0.002]	[0.002]	[0.002]
Law and order	0.001	0.002	0.001	0.002
	[0.001]	[0.001]	[0.001]	[0.001]
Government consumption	−0.114***	−0.082**	−0.114***	−0.082**
	[0.038]	[0.040]	[0.038]	[0.040]
Observations	537	495	537	495
R-squared	0.33	0.34	0.33	0.34

Note: The estimates are based on panel fixed effect estimation. See note for Table 7.7.

Table 7.9. The Impact of Crises on Growth: Three-Stage Least Squares on Cross Sections

Growth rate of output	[1]	[2]	[3]	[4]	[5]	[6]
Financial crisis	-0.013*** [0.002]	-0.013*** [0.002]	-0.014*** [0.002]	-0.013*** [0.002]	-0.013*** [0.002]	-0.013*** [0.002]
Financial crisis (−1)		0.001 [0.002]		0.001 [0.002]		0.001 [0.002]
Korean crisis			0.029** [0.013]	0.032** [0.013]	-0.001 [0.016]	0.007 [0.020]
Korean crisis (−1)				0.037*** [0.013]		0.012 [0.020]
Korea dummy					0.034*** [0.011]	0.027* [0.016]
Log (per capita GDP)	-0.002 [0.002]	-0.002 [0.002]	-0.002 [0.002]	-0.001 [0.002]	0 [0.002]	0 [0.002]
Investment ratio	0.018 [0.034]	0.019 [0.034]	0.011 [0.034]	0.001 [0.035]	-0.005 [0.035]	-0.004 [0.035]
Inflation	-0.020*** [0.005]	-0.021*** [0.005]	-0.020*** [0.005]	-0.020*** [0.005]	-0.020*** [0.005]	-0.021*** [0.005]
Openness	0.004 [0.003]	0.004 [0.003]	0.004 [0.003]	0.004 [0.003]	0.004 [0.003]	0.004 [0.003]
Fertility	-0.010** [0.004]	-0.010** [0.004]	-0.010** [0.004]	-0.007* [0.005]	-0.007* [0.004]	-0.007 [0.005]
Democracy index	0.070*** [0.027]	0.071*** [0.027]	0.071*** [0.027]	0.075*** [0.027]	0.073*** [0.027]	0.074*** [0.027]

(continued)

Table 7.9. (Continued)

Growth rate of output	[1]	[2]	[3]	[4]	[5]	[6]
Democracy index square	-0.060***	-0.060***	-0.060***	-0.060***	-0.059***	-0.060***
	[0.023]	[0.023]	[0.023]	[0.022]	[0.022]	[0.022]
Human capital	-0.002	-0.002	-0.002*	-0.003**	-0.003***	-0.003***
	[0.001]	[0.001]	[0.001]	[0.001]	[0.001]	[0.001]
Law and order	0.003**	0.003**	0.003**	0.003***	0.003***	0.003***
	[0.001]	[0.001]	[0.001]	[0.001]	[0.001]	[0.001]
Government consumption	-0.106***	-0.107***	-0.106***	-0.108***	-0.104***	-0.106***
	[0.038]	[0.038]	[0.038]	[0.038]	[0.038]	[0.038]
Observations	471	471	471	471	471	471
R-squared	0.263	0.264	0.264	0.268	0.267	0.269

Note: The estimates are based on 3SLS (three-stage least squares) estimation. See note for Table 7.7.

negatively skewed than their sample average. (In other words, there are more countries in the sample where negative skewness is less than in Korea than there are countries in which negative skewness is greater than in Korea. This is consistent with our observation that Korea is more crisis prone than the average country, but only slightly more.) They find that negative skewness of credit growth is positively associated with output growth, over the period from 1980 to 2000. Thus, this factor contributes modestly to Korea's relatively fast economic growth over the sample period. According to their estimates, had there been no negative skewness of credit growth in Korea, which would have rendered it typical of the sample, growth would have been half a percentage point per annum slower than was the case. In fact, however, Korean economic growth was fully 2 percentage points per annum faster than predicted by their model for a country with no negative skewness of credit growth. This suggests that the fact that the Korean authorities ran the economy under high pressure of demand and more generally pursued aggressive pro-growth policies that exposed it to crisis risk accounts for perhaps a quarter of the unusually rapid growth of the Korean economy in the last two decades of the twentieth century.[19]

Finally, crises can be catalysts for reform. By bringing financial excesses and economic imbalances to light, they highlight the urgency of adjustment and reform. Crises prompt countries to abandon policies that have outlived their usefulness, and in that way they can lead to long-term rates of growth that are higher than would have been the case otherwise, so long as the crisis incidence is not excessive. It is tempting to interpret Korean experience in this light. The 1971–1972 crisis prompted financial reforms that lowered leverage ratios. It encouraged the authorities to acknowledge the depletion of elastic supplies of underemployed labor from the agricultural sector and to scale back subsidies for labor-intensive manufacturing in favor of more capital-intensive, technologically sophisticated sectors. The 1980–1981 crisis forced the government to acknowledge a real overvaluation that might have been allowed to linger in the absence of that dramatic financial event. The 1997–1998 crisis led to far-reaching reforms in corporate governance and financial regulation that might have been longer in coming in the absence of such severe financial disruptions. It caused the authorities to open up the financial sector more quickly than it otherwise would have.

Conclusion

Growth in Korea, like growth in other emerging markets, has been punctuated by financial crises—in the early 1970s, in the early 1980s, prominently in 1997–1998, and again in 2008. Crises are traumatic because they set back the growth process. The declines in growth have been even larger in Korea than in the typical emerging market, which has made these episodes more than typically traumatic. Beyond that, crises are all the more unsettling for a society and a government that prioritizes economic growth, as Korea does.

Korea's economic crises are best understood as byproducts of a growth model that has involved running the economy under high demand pressure, maintaining high levels of investment, and making heavy use of debt finance. Reliance on debt—short-term debt, in particular—exposes the country to the risk of sharp reversals in the direction of capital flows. This is the downside of the high levels of debt-financed investment that have fueled the engines of Korean growth in normal times. Some would argue that this instability was a price worth paying. The authorities could have clamped down hard on credit growth and debt finance, thereby avoiding financial crises. But the result would have been lower levels of investment, especially by the chaebol, and a slower rate of growth.[20]

After the especially costly crisis of 1997–1998, policymakers determined that it made sense to run the economy more conservatively. They sought to limit the size of the current-account deficit and to keep foreign reserves well in excess of short-term foreign debt. This did not fully insulate Korea from the global credit crisis of 2007–2008, but then few if any countries were fully insulated from that global shock. And some reassurance can be taken from the fact that the damage from the 2007–2008 crisis in Korea was more limited than in the crisis a decade before.

The decade following the 1997–1998 crisis saw lower rates of investment and growth than in earlier years. But although the lower levels of investment appear to be a persistent after-effect of the crisis, the slower growth rates do not. These slower growth rates are mainly attributable, according to our analysis, to other factors, principally the progressive maturation of the economy. The obvious explanation for the existence of a persistent decline in investment with no persistent effect on growth is that the allocation of investable resources has become more efficient. In relying less on brute-force investment and financing it less with short-term debt, the Korean economy should be less exposed to crisis risk going forward.

Appendix

Table 7.A1. Timing of Financial Crises

Country	Currency crisis, 1965–2006	Currency crisis, 1970–2007	Banking crisis, starting year, 1970–2007
Argentina*	1975, 1981, 1987, 2002	1975, 1981, 1987, 2002	1980, 1989, 1995, 2001
Australia*	1974, 1983		
Austria*	1981, 1991		
Afghanistan		N/S	
Antigua and Barbuda		N/S	
Bahamas	1969, 1978	N/S	
Bahrain*		N/S	
Bangladesh*	1975	1976	1987
Barbados	1974, 1999		
Belgium*	1982, 1991		
Belize			
Benin	1980, 1994	1994	1988
Bolivia*	1972, 1982, 1985, 1988, 1991	1973, 1981	1986, 1994
Botswana*	1984, 1996	1984	
Brazil*	1979, 1983, 1987, 1990, 1999	1976, 1982, 1987, 1992, 1999	1990, 1994
Burkina Faso	1994	1994	1990
Burundi	1967, 1976, 1983, 2000		1994
Côte d'Ivoire	1982, 1986, 1994	1994	1988
Cambodia	1969, 1974, 1991, 1997	1971, 1992	
Cameroon*	1984, 1990, 1993, 2000	1994	1987, 1995
Canada*	1981, 1986, 1998		
Cape Verde	1997		1993
Central African Rep.	1968, 1972, 1994	1994	1976, 1995
Chad	1967, 1970, 1979, 1994	1994	1983, 1992
Chile*	1972, 1982	1972, 1982	1976, 1981

(continued)

Table 7.A1. (Continued)

Country	Currency crisis, 1965–2006	Currency crisis, 1970–2007	Banking crisis, starting year, 1970–2007
China, P.R.: Hong Kong		N/S	
China, P.R.: Mainland	1980, 1986, 1989, 1994		1998
China, P.R.: Macao	1984	N/S	
Colombia*	1985	1985	1982, 1998
Comoros	1994	1994	
Congo, Rep. of	1978, 1983, 1993, 1998	1994	1992
Costa Rica*	1981	1981, 1991	1987, 1994
Cyprus	1967, 1991	N/S	
Denmark*	1984, 1992		
Dominica	1979, 1982		
Dominican Rep.*	1985, 1990	1985, 1990, 2003	2003
Egypt*	1979, 1986, 1989	1979, 1990	1980
El Salvador*	1986, 1990	1986	1989
Equatorial Guinea	1988, 1994, 1997	1980, 1994	1983
Ethiopia	1992	1993	
Fiji	1987, 1998	1998	
Finland*	1967, 1977, 1982, 1991	1993	1991
France*	1982, 1992		
Gambia*	1980, 1986	1985, 2003	
Germany*			
Ghana*	1967, 1972, 1978, 1983, 1986, 2000	1978, 1983, 1993, 2000	1982
Greece*	1983, 1992	1983	
Grenada	1978		
Guatemala*	1986, 1989	1986	
Guinea	1986, 1998, 2005	1982, 2005	1985, 1993
Guinea-Bissau	1984, 1991, 2003	1980, 1994	1995
Haiti*	1977, 1991	1992, 2003	1994
Honduras*	1970, 1990	1990	

Table 7.A1. (Continued)

Country	Currency crisis, 1965–2006	Currency crisis, 1970–2007	Banking crisis, starting year, 1970–2007
Hungary*	1989, 1994		1991
Iceland*	1983, 1988, 1992	1975, 1981, 1989	
India*	1976, 1991		1993
Indonesia*	1967, 1978, 1983, 1986, 1997	1979, 1998	1997
Ireland*	1967, 1982, 1992, 2004		
Israel*	1967, 1971, 1975, 1983, 1998	1975, 1980, 1985	1977
Italy*	1976, 1981, 1995	1981	
Jamaica*	1978, 1983, 1991	1978, 1983, 1991	1996
Japan*	1979		1997
Jordan*	1988, 1991	1989	1989
Kenya*	1990, 1997	1993	1985, 1992
Korea*	1971, 1980, 1997	1998	1997
Lesotho	1985, 2001	1985	
Liberia	1993, 1996		1991
Luxembourg	1999		
Madagascar	1979, 1983, 1987, 1994, 2004	1984, 1994, 2004	1988
Malawi*	1981, 1994, 1998	1994	
Malaysia*	1986, 1997	1998	1997
Mali*	1966, 1972, 1994	1994	1987
Malta*	1991, 1997	N/S	
Mauritania	1969, 1985, 1991	1993	1984
Mauritius	1974, 1981		
Mexico*	1976, 1982, 1994	1977, 1982, 1995	1981, 1994
Mongolia	1991	1990, 1997	
Morocco	1981	1981	1980
Mozambique	1971, 1987, 1991, 2005	1987	1987
Nepal	1967, 1975, 1984, 1991	1984, 1992	1988
Netherlands*	1991		

(continued)

Table 7.A1. (Continued)

Country	Currency crisis, 1965–2006	Currency crisis, 1970–2007	Banking crisis, starting year, 1970–2007
New Zealand*	1967, 1975, 1984		
Nicaragua*	1979, 1985, 1988, 1991	1979, 1985, 1990	1990, 2000
Niger*	1966, 1994	1994	1983
Norway*	1978, 1986, 1991, 1997		1991
Oman	1981, 1986	N/S	
Pakistan*	1972, 1990, 1993, 1996	1972	
Panama*	1986		1988
Papua New Guinea*	1995	1995	
Paraguay*	1984, 1988, 1992, 2002	1984, 1989, 2002	1995
Peru*	1967, 1975, 1985, 1988	1976, 1981, 1988	1983
Philippines*	1983, 1986, 1997	1983, 1998	1983, 1997
Poland*	1982, 1986		1992
Portugal*	1976, 1981	1983	
Romania	1973, 1990, 1997	1996	1990
Rwanda	1966, 1969, 1990	1991	
St. Lucia		N/S	
St. Vincent & Grenadines	1982	N/S	
Samoa	1981	N/S	
Senegal*	1976, 1984, 1994	1994	1988
Sierra Leone*	1983, 1986, 1989, 1997	1983, 1989, 1998	1990
Singapore*	1975, 1998		
Solomon Islands	1997, 2002	N/S	
Somalia	1982, 1986	N/S	
South Africa*	1982, 1996	1984	
Spain*	1967, 1977, 1992	1983	1977
Sudan	1981, 1985, 1991	1981, 1988, 1994	
Suriname	1991, 1999	1990, 1995, 2001	

Table 7.A1. (Continued)

Country	Currency crisis, 1965–2006	Currency crisis, 1970–2007	Banking crisis, starting year, 1970–2007
Swaziland	1985, 2001	1985	1995
Sweden*	1977, 1982, 1992	1993	1991
Switzerland*	1969, 1978		
Syrian Arab Rep.	1983, 1986	1988	
Taiwan		N/S	
Tanzania	1984, 1993	1985, 1990	1987
Thailand*	1984, 1997	1998	1983, 1997
Tonga		N/S	
Togo*	1994	1994	1993
Trinidad and Tobago*	1985, 1992	1986	
Tunisia*	1987, 1991		1991
Turkey*	1970, 1980, 1994, 2001	1978, 1984, 1991, 1996, 2001	1982, 2000
Uganda*	1980, 1984, 1987	1980, 1988	1994
United Kingdom*	1967, 1972, 1992		2007
United States*	1967, 1971		1988, 2007
Uruguay*	1965, 1972, 1982, 2002	1972, 1983, 1990, 2002	1981, 2002
Vanuatu	1982	N/S	
Vietnam	1966, 1972, 1981, 1985, 1988, 1997, 2001	1972, 1981, 1987	1997
Zambia*	1981, 1985, 1992, 1995	1983, 1989, 1996	1995
Zimbabwe*	1968, 1982, 1991, 1997, 2003	1983, 1991, 1998, 2003	1995

Source: Data on currency crises, 1970–2007, and banking crises are from Laeven and Valencia (2008).

Note: N/S = not in the sample. Of total of 129 countries considered, 9 never experienced a crisis in the sample period, 1965–2006. The second column reports timing of currency crises identified by our own study. In the regression analysis, only 76 countries (denoted by asterisks) are included, owing to data availability.

Table 7.A2. Episodes of Sharp Reversal in Capital Flows, 1988–2007

Country	Year	Reversal in private capital flows (% of GDP)	Short-term debt/total debt	Short-term debt/reserves
Uruguay	2005	0.17	0.28	1.67
Grenada	2005	0.16	0.18	0.63
Vanuatu	2005	0.14	0.31	0.60
Samoa	2005	0.22	0.67	4.03
Dominica	2004	0.16	0.26	1.53
Belize	2004	0.31	0.08	0.94
St. Kitts and Nevis	2004	0.14	0.01	0.03
Panama	2002	0.10	0.06	0.42
Jamaica	2002	0.09	0.17	0.49
Tajikistan	2002	0.10	0.07	0.84
Ukraine	2002	0.19	0.42	2.77
Turkey	2001	0.16	0.25	1.23
Kyrgyz Rep.	2001	0.14	0.07	0.49
Paraguay	2000	0.11	0.22	0.76
St. Vincent and Grenadines	2000	0.18	0.16	0.75
Uzbekistan	2000	0.13	0.13	0.50
Grenada	1999	0.24	0.37	1.37
Russian Fed.	1999	0.15	0.08	1.22
Bhutan	1999	0.11	0.00	0.00
Nicaragua	1998	0.12	0.14	2.19
Belize	1998	0.42	0.41	3.06
St. Kitts and Nevis	1998	0.12	0.02	0.06
Indonesia	1998	0.15	0.24	1.88
Korea	1998	0.10	0.37	3.12
Malaysia	1998	0.17	0.32	0.70
Philippines	1998	0.18	0.23	1.35
Moldova	1998	0.18	0.00	0.01
Turkmenistan	1998	0.26	0.28	0.42
Latvia	1998	0.11	0.62	2.07
Thailand	1997	0.10	0.42	1.23
Mexico	1996	0.09	0.23	2.19
Georgia	1995	0.15	0.33	—

Table. 7.A2. (Continued)

Country	Year	Reversal in private capital flows (% of GDP)	Short-term debt/total debt	Short-term debt/reserves
Tajikistan	1995	0.12	0.03	—
Turkey	1994	0.14	0.27	2.36
Grenada	1994	0.21	0.29	1.61
Guyana	1994	0.09	0.02	0.18
Papua New Guinea	1993	0.30	0.11	1.59
Mongolia	1993	0.13	0.17	2.59
Solomon Islands	1992	0.15	0.24	3.63
Samoa	1992	0.56	0.19	0.40
Nicaragua	1991	0.49	0.23	14.69
Tonga	1991	0.14	0.17	0.29
Guyana	1989	1.02	0.40	188.45
Dominica	1985	0.12	0.00	0.00
Uruguay	1984	0.12	0.12	0.32
Venezuela	1984	0.12	0.38	1.21
Grenada	1984	0.12	0.04	0.18
Guyana	1984	0.39	0.33	62.42
Jamaica	1984	0.12	0.08	4.54
Argentina	1983	0.15	0.38	3.67
Mexico	1983	0.10	0.30	14.74
Maldives	1983	0.24	0.35	2.74
Philippines	1983	0.10	0.46	6.51
Ecuador	1982	0.13	0.26	2.54
Costa Rica	1981	0.15	0.21	2.92
Belize	1980	0.24	0.53	3.63
Panama	1979	0.11	0.17	2.56
Nicaragua	1978	0.12	0.34	2.81
Peru	1978	0.09	0.23	4.02
Guyana	1977	0.11	0.00	0.04
Jamaica	1976	0.12	0.00	0.00
Papua New Guinea	1972	0.13	0.00	—

Source: World Bank Global Development Finance database and authors' calculations.

Note: Reversals in net capital flows are measured by using net flows on total debt.

CHAPTER 8

Conclusion

Few countries can match Korea's record of rapid growth over the past half century. This period saw the transformation of a desperately poor, primarily agrarian society into an industrial and commercial powerhouse. The quality of life in Korea, whether gauged by Koreans' physical stature and life expectancy or by the quantity and variety of goods and services they consumed, was revolutionized. If this is not testimony to the transformative powers of economic growth, it is hard to imagine what is.

At the same time, there is a sense of impatience and disappointment about the current performance of the economy. Commentators complain that growth has slowed. They worry that the economy should be growing faster. They are pessimistic about the future.

One message of this study is that this sense of pessimism and disappointment is exaggerated. The presumption inherited from the peak growth period, that Korea should grow at rates approaching double digits, is no longer realistic. Growth at near-double-digit rates can be sustained only in relatively backward economies that have recently broken free of their low-level equilibrium trap. Such countries can add several points to their average annual growth rate simply by shifting labor from agriculture to industry, where average productivity is higher, and equipping the new members of the industrial labor force with basic tools and equipment. They can boost the productivity of the work force by raising workers' low level of educational attainment and deepening a shallow capital stock. They can finance this human and physical capital formation with domestic savings, since the younger generations doing the saving will have higher incomes than the older generations, who are dissaving. They can acquire advanced technology embodied in imported capital goods and license techniques from abroad, so long as they develop the capacity to export something else. They can grow on this basis for an extended period if they have started out far behind the technological leader.

Putting Things in Perspective

The foregoing might make what South Korea achieved between the 1960s and 1990s seem almost routine, which it certainly was not. Not all countries have succeeded in initiating catch-up growth, much less in sustaining it for as long as Korea did. But sustaining high growth for an extended period is not the same as sustaining it indefinitely. Indeed, the more successful the catch-up, the more difficult it becomes to maintain rapid growth on this basis. The more rapidly workers are transferred from agriculture to industry, the more completely the pool of underemployed rural labor is drained; by the 1980s Korea had already essentially eliminated its excess labor reserves. The faster the demographic transition is completed, the more rapidly the population will age. Thus Korea, which once enjoyed a disproportionately young working-age population, now has one of the world's fastest rising old-age-dependency ratios. The more rapidly educational attainment is boosted, the more difficult it becomes to raise it further. Korea today has one of the highest university graduation rates of any country, and it is mathematically impossible to boost university graduation rates above 100 percent. The faster capital is accumulated, the higher the capital/labor ratio becomes and the more saving and investment are needed to make up for depreciation of the capital stock. And the closer a country comes to the technological frontier, the less scope it has for technological advancement through the acquisition of machinery and blueprints from abroad. These are all reasons for anticipating that, after half a century of catch-up, the growth of the Korean economy should slow.

The worry is that Korea's growth is slowing excessively. It is that Korea is finding it difficult to navigate the transition to a more innovation-based economy. It is that Korean exporters are being squeezed by Japan from above and by China from below.

With growth having averaged 4.7 percent in Korea between 2001 and 2007, more than double the 2.3 percent average in the advanced countries, it can be argued that even this more nuanced view is exaggerated.[1]

Korea's inventory of economic strengths is formidable. It has a skilled and educated labor force. Korean firms are accustomed to competing on international markets. They include a number of world-class manufacturing firms, Samsung, LG, and Hyundai prominent among them, that enjoy brand recognition internationally for their household appliances, consumer electronics, and motor vehicles. Korea is home to the world's leading shipbuilders; it is the single largest exporter of large container ships, liquefied natural gas tankers, and other heavy oceangoing vessels. The country ranks among the leaders in R&D spending as a share of GDP. It has up-to-date infrastructure, from modern port facilities to an extensive broadband network. Its securities markets are open to foreign as well as domestic investors. Close by is the rapidly growing Chinese market for Korean capital and consumer goods.

Above all, history and tradition cause Korean society to value economic growth. Koreans are willing to sacrifice in order to attain it. The country possesses a government—not just leaders but a permanent civil service—that prioritizes growth and formulates policy accordingly.

None of this is to deny the impatience. Assuming the indefinite continuation of the 4.7 percent and 2.3 percent growth rates that prevailed in Korea and the advanced country group, respectively, between 2001 and 2007, it will take fully another quarter century before Korea's per capita income comes to within 10 percent of that of the United States.[2] And growing faster may be difficult, owing to several factors. Korea's population is aging, which means that a larger share of national income and savings will have to be devoted to services for the elderly as opposed to human and physical capital formation. There is a reluctance in Korea to embrace immigration as a way of refreshing the labor force. The education system is structured to ensure that students score well on internationally standardized tests, not to encourage them to think outside the box. The university system's emphasis on instruction constrains its research capacity and limits the kind of business-university collaboration that has supported the development of high-tech sectors in other countries. Labor relations remain adversarial. Regulation of labor and product markets is restrictive. Outsiders complain of the continuing influence of family and personal connections in business and politics, and this perception that the playing field is not level contributes to Korea's difficulty in attracting FDI. Korea's proximity to China is a two-edged sword: while China offers a rapidly growing market for Korean exports, it is also a magnet for inward foreign investors and an increasingly formidable competitor for Korean exports to third markets.

Most fundamentally, the Korean government remains wedded to an approach to fostering growth that has outlived its usefulness. Once upon a time it was straightforward for government bureaucrats to pick winners. They could observe which industries had been successfully developed by other countries with broadly similar resource endowments and circumstances, and target those industries for development in Korea by offering tax breaks and preferential access to credit. Picking winners is harder now that the economy has approached the technological frontier—now that it possesses in actual or nascent form all the same industries as, say, Japan. There are no more historical examples to emulate, only hypothetical futures. Taking bets on hypothetical futures is something that markets do better than bureaucrats and politicians. To be sure, Korean governments have repeatedly averred their intent to move in the direction of functional interventions—to subsidize R&D on the grounds that it throws off externalities that are difficult for individual firms to capture, for example, rather than subsidizing specific industries. But old habits die hard. The government still has an excessive tendency to micromanage the allocation of resources in the effort to pick winners, when the government announced in September 2008 that it intended to foster the growth of 22 new business sectors, covering a wide spectrum of manufacturing, energy, and service industries, as "future growth engines [of] . . . low-carbon, green growth." There could be no clearer illustration of our point.

Given this litany of complaints, it might seem like a miracle that Korea can grow at all. But once more we say that pessimism and criticism can be overdone. And the upside of this tendency to play up weaknesses is that it sounds a clarion call for pro-growth policy reform.

Priorities for Reform

A first priority for reform should be product and labor market deregulation to stimulate productivity growth in the service sector. Services provide the majority of employment in all advanced economies, even those, like Germany and South Korea, with proud manufacturing traditions. Raising service-sector productivity is therefore essential to raising living standards. Here, competition is key. Boosting service-sector productivity through the application of new information technologies, for example, will entail entry by new providers and exit by incumbents. It will require reorganization of existing service-sector enterprises, be they hospitals, schools, or retail businesses. Korea has already had a taste of how this can work in the case of its banking sector, which was deregulated, thrown open to competition, and fundamentally reorganized, resulting in an increase in productivity.[3] The country needs to pursue such initiatives more broadly.

A second priority should be continued reform of higher education. Total expenditures on education as a share of GDP are 7.2 percent in Korea, the third highest among OECD countries.[4] However, a Korean peculiarity is that 40 percent of that is private education expenditures, whereas the OECD average is only 12 percent. The high level of private expenditure reflects competition among junior and senior high school students to enter universities. Students and their parents spend huge amounts of money on private tutoring institutes to prepare for university entrance exams. However, there is some evidence that these expenditures are not productive; they affect relative but not absolute productivity. After graduation from college, many students have difficulty finding jobs owing to mismatches between the skills provided in tertiary education and those required in the labor market.

To curtail private education expenditures, it would help to establish sound public secondary schooling through which students could signal their eligibility for the best universities. This could be achieved by enhancing competition among public educational institutions through increased transparency about their performance. Universities should be allowed to rank students on the basis of the quality of their high schools, something that is currently prohibited. In addition, it should be made easier to charter private schools, so that students could have a wider variety of pedagogic and curricular choices; currently private schools are almost indistinguishable from public schools. Finally, more autonomy should be granted to private schools so that they might engage in more instructional experimentation and innovation.

It is also important to increase the quality of research at the university level. For example, more public funding could be allocated to national universities through competitive evaluations. The Korean government has moved part way in this direction. In economics, for example, it identified five high-performing institutions and provided half a million dollars annually to each. But too much funding continues to be allocated to universities independent of merit, particularly to subsidize universities in declining regions.

The same can be said of faculty salaries. Traditionally, professors' salaries in Korea are determined on the basis of seniority, so that all professors who have been teaching for the same amount of time are paid equally, irrespective of their research performance. Salaries are also the same for equally experienced professors across different academic departments, whether or not the universities compete with private business for researchers in the discipline in question. A number of Korean universities have sought to improve their ranking on the lists of top institutions compiled by various national and international publications. Seoul National University, Korea University, and Yonsei University, the country's three best universities, announced that they would work to secure a rating as one of the top 100 or top 50 universities worldwide. Achieving this presupposes a system in which they can attract top researchers by offering salaries and stipends significantly greater than those offered to the average instructor.

The government announced in 2010 that the salary system of national universities would move in the direction of a more merit-based system, providing salary incentives for high performance starting from 2011. This is a step in the right direction, but only time will tell whether Korea's traditional ethic of equal pay will permit universities to offer significantly different salaries to professors in different disciplines and according to different levels of research output. There are some promising indications, at least. Even before the government's plan to modify the salary system was announced, several top universities had already begun offering supplementary stipends to outstanding researchers. Some also attempted to attract top professors from other institutions by offering stipends and promising future salary increases.

As one more reform related to education, links between universities and business should be further strengthened. In 2003 Korea adopted legislation equivalent to the Bayh-Dole Act in the United States, designed to promote business-university collaboration. Subsequently a number of universities authorized their faculty to establish joint-venture firms with private business. There are signs that this move toward commercialization is producing results: patent registrations by universities increased from fewer than 1,000 in 2002 to more than 7,000 in 2008.

A third priority for pro-growth reform should be to make Korea more attractive as a destination for FDI. Korea continues to attract less direct investment than would be expected of a country with its characteristics. That it possesses a highly skilled and educated labor force should make it attractive for foreign manufacturing and service-sector firms. Its proximity to China should make it an obvious staging platform for companies seeking to penetrate the Chinese market. Its role as an increasingly important originator of technology should make foreign firms want to participate in that process. But Korea's tradition of resistance to inward foreign investment, the feeling on the part of foreign companies that the rules of the game are not applied equally to domestic and foreign enterprises, restrictive labor market regulations, and, now, growing competition from China for foreign investors all contribute to Korea's underperformance in attracting FDI. Meaningful policy reforms to counter the impression that the playing field is not level, together with labor market reforms, are needed to correct this problem.

To complement these three familiar priorities for reform, we offer two more radical proposals. First, Korea should do more to attract labor from abroad. This could be done by easing the tax on incomes of foreign workers, extending them more generous health-care and pension benefits, and streamlining procedures for acquiring professional credentials. In the face of Korea's exploding old-age-dependency ratio, foreign workers are needed to preserve the viability of Korea's pay-as-you-go social security system. They are a source of entrepreneurship and new ideas. This is obvious in the case of foreign scientists and engineers, whose presence is associated with productivity spillovers and encourages science-related capital accumulation, effects that tend to raise the wages and productivity of unskilled as well as skilled workers.

Moreover, a growing body of evidence suggests that immigration of unskilled workers has limited adverse effects and can even be good for unskilled native workers, insofar as immigrants, with their more limited linguistic skills, tend to specialize in manual tasks, while unskilled natives specialize in more desirable communication-intensive tasks. A greater supply of unskilled workers, in any case, has a strong positive effect on the real earnings of skilled workers.[5] All these are likely to be important effects in Korea.

Embracing foreign workers may be easier in a multiethnic society like the United States than in ethnically homogeneous societies like Korea.

But the experience of one relatively homogeneous nation, the Republic of Ireland, which transformed its labor force in a multiethnic direction in response to the impetus provided by the Single European Act and the country's economic boom, suggests that it can be done. As we saw in Chapters 2 and 3, high growth in Korea was associated with the redeployment of previously underemployed labor to the modern urban sector. If Korea is serious about trying to reattain the high growth rates of earlier years, it will have to find new reservoirs of underemployed labor. Married women are one possibility. North Koreans are potentially another. And immigration is a related option.

The alternative to attracting labor from abroad is to send capital there. Our second radical proposal is that Korea should capitalize on the presence of abundant supplies of low-cost labor elsewhere in Northeast Asia by investing more heavily in regional supply chains and production networks. Rather than resisting the migration of electronic fabrication operations to China, it should actively invest in semiconductor manufacturing facilities there. Rather than attempting to counter the growth of the Chinese shipbuilding industry, it should invest in shipbuilding capacity on the Chinese coastline. Companies headquartered in other countries have been able to cut costs and boost competitiveness by sourcing components made elsewhere and undertaking assembly operations in their own region, be they German motor vehicle manufacturers in Slovakia or U.S. appliance producers in Mexico. Some Korean companies have moved in this direction, and they will have to move faster. Making such a change politically sustainable and socially defensible will then require the government to provide more adjustment assistance and retraining for the domestic workers who are directly affected.

It goes without saying that our final recommendation is that Korean governments should desist from attempting to "pick winners" and focus instead on functional interventions such as encouraging basic research.

Scenarios for the Future

How fast, then, can the Korean economy grow? One approach to answering this question is to use the growth accounting framework of Chapter 2, adding assumptions about the rate of growth of the working-age population, the stock of human capital, the stock of physical capital, and the rate of total factor productivity growth. A second approach is to consider the

GDP growth rates achieved by other high- and middle-income countries, to get a sense of best-case performance.[6]

To be clear, we are concerned here with medium-term scenarios. In the short run, a wide variety of external shocks can affect a country's economic growth. For example, this book is being written in the wake of a global recession that has had a major negative impact on the Korean economy. But this is not our focus: we are analyzing medium-term potential, not the actual outcome this year or next.

Similarly, in the very long run there is an iron law linking the rate of TFP growth to the investment rate, taking the rate of growth of labor input as given. In the standard neoclassical model, the rate of growth of the capital/labor ratio must equal the rate of TFP growth. In this approach, given our assumptions about labor supply and TFP growth, we should derive rather than assume the equilibrium investment rate. But steady-state relationships hold only in the very long run, if at all. While we consider longer-run scenarios below, we are concerned primarily with medium-term adjustments.[7]

In Chapter 2 we estimated that Korea was able to achieve TFP growth of just over 2 percent per year since the early 1980s. At the beginning of the high-growth period it achieved a TFP growth rate of almost 3 percent.[8] One can imagine that comprehensive and effective reforms could lead Korea to reattain that higher rate of TFP growth. For purposes of our projections, we therefore assume TFP growth rates of 2 and 3 percent per annum over the two decades beginning in 2010.

Those who will make up the labor pool over the next decade and a half are already born; the main determinant of how many will enter the work force in a given year will be the share of each age cohort remaining in school.[9] We know that university enrollment is reaching saturation levels. It follows that the share of those old enough to be in the labor force who will still be students will not rise by a large amount. For similar reasons, conventional methods of estimating the contribution of increases in human capital through education are likely to produce only a modest contribution to growth. Put differently, it will be improvements in the quality of education, not the quantity of educated workers, that will have the greatest impact on GDP growth in the future. In our methodology, those quality increases will show up mainly in higher rates of TFP growth.[10]

For the contribution of capital, we assume that Korea will maintain an investment rate of 30 to 35 percent of GDP and that current depreciation rates will continue to apply. An aging population and the resulting rising dependency rates could, of course, reduce savings rates and depress investment below 30 percent of GDP, although the experience of other countries with aging populations, notably Japan, suggests that such societies are generally able to maintain savings and investment rates at this level. We see no reason why investment rates should rise above 35 percent, since they have never exceeded that level for an extended period. Finally, we assume that the share of labor and capital income in total national income remains the same as at present.

The results of these calculations are presented in Table 8.1. They suggest a potential GDP growth rate as high as 6 percent over the next decade, but only if TFP grows at 3 percent per year, faster than it has in fully three decades. Potential growth then falls to 5 percent in the second decade, largely because the labor force begins to decline, reflecting population aging. Even a large increase in the birth rate would not have much of an effect over this horizon, because the newly born would not begin to enter the labor force for 15 to 20 years.

Other scenarios assuming lower rates of investment and TFP growth naturally predict lower potential growth rates. GDP growth falls only slightly with investment at 30 percent instead of 35 percent (dropping from 6.0 to 5.8 percent in the first decade and from 4.7 to 4.6 percent in the second), reflecting the fact that the contribution of physical capital to the growth of productive capacity is relatively small under conventional assumptions. On the other hand, it falls quite sharply with TFP growth at 2 percent per annum rather than 3 (to 4.8 percent in the first decade and 3.4 percent in the second). It is of course even lower when we impose these lower values for both the investment rate and the rate of TFP growth. Still, this analysis places the potential rate of growth of the Korean economy within a well-defined range—4.5 to 6.0 percent per annum in the next decade, and 3.3 to 4.7 percent per annum in the decade following—regardless of assumption.

Our second approach to answering this question involves asking what maximum rate of GDP growth was achieved over a sustained period by countries elsewhere in the world when they were at Korea's current per capita GDP of $20,000.[11] Table 8.2 reports this for the 33 countries and territories that have achieved a purchasing-power-parity GDP per capita of $20,000 in subsequent five- and ten-year periods. The implication for Korean growth is similar to that obtained using the first approach. Only

Table 8.1. Real Potential GDP Growth Rate Forecast

(1) Investment rate=30% and TFP=2%

Period	Real GDP growth rate	Physical capital	Human capital	Labor	TFP
2010–2020	4.55%	1.73%	0.26%	0.56%	2.00%
2020–2030	3.29%	1.46%	0.24%	−0.41%	2.00%

(2) Investment rate=35% and TFP=2%

Period	Real GDP growth rate	Physical capital	Human capital	Labor	TFP
2010–2020	4.81%	1.99%	0.26%	0.56%	2.00%
2020–2030	3.41%	1.59%	0.24%	−0.41%	2.00%

(3) Investment rate=30% and TFP=3%

Period	Real GDP growth rate	Physical capital	Human capital	Labor	TFP
2010–2020	5.76%	1.94%	0.26%	0.56%	3.00%
2020–2030	4.62%	1.79%	0.24%	−0.41%	3.00%

(4) Investment rate=35% and TFP=3%

Period	Real GDP growth rate	Physical capital	Human capital	Labor	TFP
2010–2020	6.04%	2.22%	0.26%	0.56%	3.00%
2020–2030	4.74%	1.92%	0.24%	−0.41%	3.00%

Note: TFP=total factor productivity. For the male labor force we project forward the population of working age (15 to 65). For the female labor force we assume the participation rate gradually rises from its current level to the level of the male population over the next 20 years. We use the population forecast provided by Statistics Korea. We use the conventional method of estimating the contribution of increases in human capital through education based on wage gaps across different levels of educational attainment. The forecast of the education distribution is based on the actual education distribution in the past: we assume that the education distribution of 25-to-29-year-olds will be the same as that of 30-to-34-year-olds in five years, and so on. For physical capital, we use data on capital stock in 2005 from Pyo, Chung, and Cho (2007) and extend it by adding investment with a depreciation rate of 5 percent.

Table 8.2. Five- and Ten-Year Average GDP Growth Rates after Reaching Per Capita GDP of $20,000

Country	Year of $20,000 per capita GDP	Average growth rate for next five years	Average growth rate for next ten years
Switzerland	1970	0.36%	1.52%
Saudi Arabia	1972	12.02%	7.08%
Gabon	1974	−3.63%	−1.06%
United Arab Emirates	1974	15.37%	9.09%
Bahrain	1977	0.93%	0.95%
United States	1977	1.62%	3.12%
Luxembourg	1979	2.12%	4.55%
Norway	1983	3.34%	2.93%
Denmark	1984	1.86%	1.86%
Canada	1985	2.89%	2.38%
Iceland	1986	1.91%	1.60%
Sweden	1987	0.82%	1.27%
Australia	1988	2.23%	3.33%
Austria	1988	2.91%	2.63%
France	1988	1.51%	1.94%
Hong Kong	1988	5.26%	3.97%
Macao	1988	6.43%	4.07%
Bahamas	1989	−3.06%	−0.56%
Belgium	1989	1.73%	2.06%
Finland	1989	−2.73%	0.92%
Germany	1989	2.71%	2.19%
Japan	1989	2.02%	1.56%
Kuwait	1989	0.11%	0.37%
Netherlands	1989	2.15%	2.90%
Singapore	1991	8.70%	6.26%
United Kingdom	1994	3.09%	2.89%
Italy	1995	1.96%	1.48%
Israel	1996	3.03%	2.29%
Ireland	1998	7.47%	6.94%
New Zealand	1999	3.49%	3.49%
Cyprus	2000	2.97%	2.97%
Puerto Rico	2000	2.12%	2.12%
Spain	2001	2.75%	2.75%

Source: Purchasing power parity–adjusted real per capita GDP data are from Penn World Table 6.2.
Note: The sample period ends in 2004.

4 countries achieved an average GDP growth rate above 5 percent per year for a full decade. Only 6 managed this for as long as five years, and 2 of them, Saudi Arabia and the United Arab Emirates, are oil exporters whose experience has little relevance to Korea. Three others, Singapore, Hong Kong, and Macao, are city-states whose experience is similarly of questionable relevance to Korea, and only one of them, Singapore, actually achieved a GDP growth rate above 5 percent for ten years. The remaining country, Ireland, has more in common with Korea in terms of economic structure, but even its experience is of questionable relevance.[12]

The remaining countries grew at between 1.5 and 3 percent a year in their immediate post–$20,000 per capita decade. Thus, if Korea is able to sustain a GDP growth rate of 5 percent for a decade or more, its performance will be virtually unprecedented for a country that is neither oil rich, a city-state, nor a relatively poor region within a richer free-trade bloc. Unprecedented is not impossible. But these comparisons are a clear indication of the challenge the country faces if it is to achieve what growth accounting and the experience of other high-income countries suggests is the country's maximum potential GDP growth rate.

Putting these methodologies together, our judgment is that Korea's maximum potential growth rate over the next one to two decades is more likely to be 5 percent than 6 percent per year.[13]

Of course, the outcome will also hinge on what happens not just in Korea but in the rest of the world. The credit crisis of 2008–2009 is a reminder of how deeply Korea is integrated into global markets. As global growth turned negative in early 2009, Korean growth turned negative as well, reflecting the country's dependence on exports and on foreign finance for its current account deficit. If the United States, Europe, and Japan emerge from their economic problems with heavier burdens of public debt, it is likely that they will grow more slowly in the coming decade. Inevitably, Korean growth will be negatively affected.

The question is, by how much? Regressions of Korean growth on global growth, as in Table 8.3, suggest a Korean "beta" (an elasticity of Korean growth with respect to global growth) between 1 and 2. Ordinary-least-squares regression yields a beta of 1; an error-correction model we regard as more appropriate suggests a beta closer to 2 (Table 8.3).[14] Thus, if the global growth rate is 0.5 percent slower over the coming decade as a result of the financial crisis and its legacy, Korea's rate of growth will be 1 percent slower. The literature on "decoupling" notwithstanding, there is no way around this.

Table 8.3. The Impact of Global Growth on Korea's Growth (1965–2007)

	(1) OLS	(2) VEC
World GDP growth	1.033** [0.358]	2.074** [0.167]
Observations	43	41
R-squared	0.17	—

Source: Data on growth rates obtained from World Bank, World Development Indicators.

Note: OLS=ordinary least squares; VEC=vector error correction. Column 1 reports the OLS coefficient of the world growth rate when Korea's growth rate is regressed on it. Column 2 reports the coefficient of the world growth rate in a cointegration relationship with Korea's growth rate in a VEC model. The values in brackets are standard errors. Growth rates of Korea and the world are in constant 2000 U.S. dollars.

** indicates statistical significance at the 1-percent level.

What happens globally is not under Korea's control, but what happens at home is. Realizing the country's potential in terms of rates of growth will require Korea to implement the reforms suggested in these pages. Only time will tell whether the country is capable of such a sustained reform effort. But Korea has an impressive record, over more than four decades, of moving quickly to reform economic institutions when the need is clear. There is every reason to believe that this reformist spirit will continue into the future.

Reference Matter

Notes

1. At the time of writing, GDP growth in 2011 was back to 4 percent.

2. And given how it had suffered from similar disruptions before.

3. Inevitably, the full story is more complex. In particular, there was some recovery of the relative share of manufacturing following the 1997–1998 financial crisis, which led predictably to a loss of output and employment in financial services. See Chapter 3.

1. In the next chapter, we will explore the sources of growth sector by sector and industry by industry.

2. For example, Young (1995) used the same expression to analyze growth experiences of East Asian countries.

3. Rather than simply presenting the data by decade.

4. The aggregate economy to which we apply these equations includes agriculture, forestry, and fishing; mining and quarrying; manufacturing; electricity, gas, and water; construction; wholesale and retail trade, restaurants, and hotels; transport, storage, and communication; finance, insurance, and real estate business; and community, social, and personal services. In some calculations we exclude agriculture, forestry, and fishing because of the difficulty of collecting meaningful data on labor hours and human capital.

5. We thank Sunbin Kim for providing the hours, wages, and employment data at the industry level for the period 1971–1993.

6. See, for example, Lee and Song (2005) and the literature cited therein.

7. The difference in human capital associated with different years of education is captured by comparing wages of individuals with identical characteristics

but different educational attainment. Lee and Song (2005) used the same methodology to calculate human capital at the industry level in Korea from 1971 to 2003. Our data differ from theirs in minor details, and our data set covers the period until 2005.

8. As we argue later in this chapter, this method probably understates the contribution of human capital to growth in developing economies, but it does capture the contribution of human capital that is rigorously measurable.

9. It is tempting to interpret these patterns as, first, a decade of slow TFP growth (the 1970s) as investments were being made in heavy, chemical, and other modern industries, followed by a decade of faster TFP growth (the 1980s) as those investments began to pay off, a decade when the capital-intensive expansion of those industries began to run into diminishing returns (the 1990s), and finally a post-crisis decade (starting in 1999) when rationalization led to a marked recovery in TFP growth. We develop these ideas later in the chapter.

10. Some authors (e.g., Young 1995) have even suggested that the East Asian experience was just another variant of the capital-intensive growth model of the Soviet Union and its command-economy allies.

11. For given amounts of inputs, including a higher rate of return to capital.

12. If there is anything distinctive about Korea in these estimates, it is that the estimated coefficients of Korea's investment-decade dummy are consistently higher than those of Korea's saving-decade dummy, suggesting that Korea has depended more than many other countries on foreign capital, a fact that is plausibly associated with the persistence of the crisis problem, as we explain and analyze in Chapter 7. Note, however, that the difference in the point estimate on the two dummy variables is not statistically significant at the 95 percent confidence level.

13. As noted above, input data for the 1960s are not as reliable as those for later years. This is particularly true of the capital data. But excluding these data, as most other analysts, starting with Young, have done, does not allow one to really explain what initiated faster growth in Korea. The perpetual inventory method requires the analyst to assume an initial capital stock figure, and the resulting estimates of the growth rate of the capital stock are very sensitive to that assumption in the early years of the constructed time series. After a period of 15 or 20 years of calculations, the initial capital stock figure no longer matters, but for Korea one does not have reliable investment figures for the 1950s, let alone the 1940s, due in part to the Korean War.

14. These reforms are discussed in the first set of volumes produced jointly by Korea Development Institute (KDI) and the Harvard Institute for International Development in the early 1980s. Park Chung Hee was president of South Korea from 1961 to 1979.

15. As analyzed in Chapter 7.

16. The Korean employed labor force grew at a rapid rate during the early years of high growth. The rate was 3.8 percent per year during the first decade of high economic growth (1963–1973), falling to 2.9 percent in the second decade (1973–1983), and to 2.6 percent in the next fourteen years, up to the beginning of the 1997–1998 financial crisis. During the financial crisis, unemployment soared from 425,000 in 1996 to a peak in 1999 of around 1.8 million, with the result that the employed labor force declined during this period by more than 2 million as some dropped out of the labor force altogether. Recovery from the recession was rapid, and by the year 2000 employment in Korea had recovered to levels slightly above those in 1996–1997, although the number of unemployed remained substantially higher than in the 1990s, at more than 800,000 persons. In the next eight years (2000–2008) the employed work force grew at a much slower rate of 1.3 percent a year and then stagnated at a little under 24 million persons as the 2008–2009 crisis hit.

17. See Chapter 3.

18. However, working hours still grew at 1.7 percent a year for an additional 15 to 20 years.

19. To be sure, the growth of the nonagricultural labor force was not exogenous. It responded to investment and productivity growth. In the absence of a high rate of growth of capital, there would not have been rapid growth in nonagricultural employment.

20. Lee (2005), 674. It should be noted that for all the emphasis that Lee puts on education in this article, his growth accounting results for the contribution of education to growth are similar to those used in this chapter.

21. In the 2003 Trends in International Math and Science Study (TIMSS) tests, given internationally, Korean students ranked second in math and third in science among students from 44 participating countries. In the 2003 Programme for International Student Assessment (PISA) tests, fifteen-year-old Koreans ranked first in problem solving, second in reading, third in math, and fourth in science among students from the 40 countries participating. These tests may overstate the achievement of Korean students because so much of Korean teaching involves teaching to the test, but there is little doubt that Korea ranks high even by high-income-country standards. At the university level, the top ranks of Korean universities are now competitive with high-ranking universities elsewhere. The Times Higher Education–QS.com World University Ranking of 2009 placed 11 Korean universities among the top 400 in the world, with 2 in the top 100 and 2 more in the second 100 (http://www.topuniversities.com/university-rankings.com).

22. At least, it will not be possible without importing managers and technicians from abroad. While less-developed economies did import managers and technicians in colonial times, such persons were few in number, and so their growth impact was small.

23. Although it was still at a level comparable to the earlier periods of high growth in Korea.

24. Depending on which measure of profitability is used.

25. The return on equity, for its part, rose slightly from 6.9 percent to 7.2 percent between the two periods. As the data in Table 2.5 indicate, Korea's performance in this regard was substantially better than the other Asian economies hit hardest by the financial crisis.

26. Industry fixed effects are included, though not reported, to control for unobserved industry heterogeneity.

27. Ahn (2005), using manufacturing plant-level data for Korea, also found that greater R&D expenditure was associated with higher productivity at the plant level. Interestingly, however, this positive effect of R&D held only for industry aggregate R&D expenditure, not firm-level R&D expenditure, which may be evidence of the existence of spillover effects of R&D within industries.

28. Since the dependent variable, TFP growth, is serially correlated, the error term in these estimates is also likely to be serially correlated (for example, if there are other important determinants of TFP growth in addition to those we have included). This can bias the coefficient estimates in a panel setting. Further, the standard "fix" of adding a lagged dependent variable to sop up the serial correlation will be inconsistent when the equations are estimated assuming fixed effects. More appropriate is the Arellano-Bond estimator, which uses lagged levels and differences as instruments. The results, shown in Table 2.8, continue to provide strong evidence of the importance of R&D for productivity growth at the industry level. The impact of R&D is on the same order of magnitude as before. Actually the impact is larger in the short run (that is, in the current year). But the longer-run effect, obtained by adjusting for the lagged dependent variable, is very similar to that in the previous table. Again, the message is that R&D is potentially quite important for industry growth in Korea.

29. As India, in particular, began dismantling the "license raj," a term used to describe the excessive amount of government regulation and licensing that slowed growth in India's modern sector.

30. Although they do not tell us the direction of causation.

31. The principal exceptions from most developing countries being certain other countries in East Asia.

32. Doing so requires, at a minimum, a more disaggregated analysis, as we provide in subsequent chapters.

33. This part of the story is of course explained by the sources-of-growth analysis mainly "in the breach," as acknowledged above.

34. Our belief that the causation ran heavily from TFP growth to high rates of investment comes mainly from our analysis of Korea (and Taiwan). It draws in-

ferences from the timing of accelerations in TFP growth and capital formation rates. Of course, causation undoubtedly worked in the opposite direction as well. Only further research across a large number of countries will be able to establish a more precise estimate of the magnitude of causation in both directions.

35. This is documented more systematically in Chapter 7. In the 1980s growth of more than 9 percent resumed, whereas from 2001 through 2005 the growth rate was only 4.7 percent.

36. Council of Economic Planning and Development (2007), 98; figures for 2001–2006. The 6.9 percent figure is for 1992–2007. But then Taiwan had not experienced anything comparable to the chaebol investment frenzy in that earlier period.

37. At least not after the nineteenth century.

38. However, these factors do not provide an adequate explanation for the productivity slowdown of the 1970s, which remains a mystery. In addition, the U.S. slowdown was later reversed in conjunction with the much-vaunted productivity acceleration in the second half of the 1990s.

39. Basically, the country with the highest per capita GDP.

40. The convergence literature is reviewed in the next section. The difference here is that the growth rate does not slow gradually and continuously, as assumed in the typical cross-country growth model specification. In our sample and specification, the drop in growth is abrupt.

41. We study this phenomenon in Chapter 3.

42. Another factor (not in our equation, owing to the difficulty of assembling it for a large cross section of countries) is the end of migration out of low-productivity traditional occupations, notably agriculture, into higher-productivity urban manufacturing and service-sector employment. That migration ends once the reservoir of surplus labor in the countryside has been drained.

43. The 1970s figures for nominal export growth were higher, but because there was rapid worldwide inflation in the 1970s we have not used those data.

44. We analyze the connections between the deceleration in aggregate growth rates and export growth rates in Chapter 5. While real export growth rates were lower, the point remains.

45. Definitive support for this hypothesis would require detailed analysis, industry by industry, of the kinds of technologies used and the origin of those technologies. We will make some progress toward such an effort in the next chapter when we look at the sources of growth of individual industrial sectors. We will also find some support in the next section of this chapter, where we review the cross-country econometric evidence.

46. The starting year is taken as 1982 in order to eliminate any impact of the recession in 1980.

47. Other than perhaps democratization, which may have complicated pursuit of the earlier model of extensive growth based on long hours of work and high investment.

48. Note that we exclude 1998 from the most recent period, during which the economy suffered a severe contraction as a result of the financial crisis. If we include year 1998, the growth of per capita GDP falls further, to 4.9 percent.

49. Extreme bounds analysis is based on the idea that a coefficient on a particular regressor is robust only to the degree that it displays a small variation to the presence or absence of other regressors. The authors define the extreme bounds for a coefficient as ranging between the lowest estimate of its value minus two times its standard error to the highest estimate of its value plus two times its standard error, where the extreme values are drawn from the set of every possible subset of regressors that includes the variable of interest. A variable is then said to be robust if its extreme bounds lie strictly to one side or the other of zero.

50. The specific regression is termed acceptable if it has appropriate statistical properties (white noise error terms), if it is a valid restriction of the general regression, and if it encompasses other parsimonious regressions that are also valid restrictions of the general regression.

51. Being a largely Confucian country, for example, has a positive effect.

52. Specifically, Sala-i-Martin requires that just 95 percent of the distribution of point estimates lie to one side or the other of zero. Like Hoover and Perez, he also finds an impact of religion, and he finds that regional dummy variables are robust (it is good to be in East Asia).

53. Although the official data do not fully capture how far along Korea was in this regard. The econometric approach to measuring the contribution of education in these equations, moreover, likely understates the likely true contribution of education to growth. The specific reasons for this in the two cases (the econometric and growth accounting approaches) are somewhat different, but the main reason is that both treat education as just another variable that independently adds to the growth rate, whereas, as we argued earlier in this chapter, education interacts with the capital stock and with items such as R&D that affect TFP.

54. See Chapter 5.

55. The country did have periods of political instability, which go a long way toward explaining why it did not develop in a sustained way before the 1960s. In contrast, periods of political instability after 1960 have been brief and hence not very disruptive.

56. Nor do the variables associated with slower growth increase in value over time.

57. Only in Taiwan does one see anything like a steady progression to slower and slower growth rates, decade by decade, as we noted earlier.

58. Just as growth accounting understates the contribution of education to the high-growth period, it may also understate the contribution of this slowdown in education growth to the declining growth rate of GDP. The slowdown in the growth of education in recent years in Korea is simply the result of the fact that it is possible to expand the level of education rapidly when large parts of the population have only a few years of education, but it is not possible to do so after all are completing secondary school and a large percentage are already attending a tertiary institution.

59. In the final chapter of this volume we will return to the question of what level of growth further reforms might achieve

CHAPTER THREE

1. Or "deindustrialization of the labor force." Industrial value added continued to grow rapidly from 1988 and maintained its share of GDP at a more or less constant level.

2. See OECD (2008).

3. Because of data limitations our analysis is confined to the period after 1970.

4. We will return to the issue of this decline in manufacturing employment later in the chapter.

5. This has been demonstrated many times throughout history, including in the United States in 2008.

6. Employment in agriculture had already declined to relatively low levels by the 1970s and has continued to fall.

7. As has been well known since Clark (1940).

8. In the case of agriculture, reflecting a large volume of migration off the land.

9. Thus, the static-shift effect accounts for about 40 percent of total labor productivity growth in this period. Combined with the 70 percent attributed to the within effect, this more than fully accounts for the growth of labor productivity economy-wide.

10. For Taiwan, data for the mining industry are not available, and a total of eight one-digit industries are distinguished. Data are from Directorate-General of the Budget, Accounting, and Statistics (various issues).

11. If there is such a correlation, there would be a simple prescription for fixing a sector's productivity problem.

12. This is not to say that education is unimportant for productivity growth, only that many of its effects may be external to the sector in question.

13. In some cases this domestic orientation is inherent in the nature of the sector (in retail and wholesale trade, for example). But in other cases, such as

business, financial, and insurance services, the lack of substantial exports reflects the fact that firms in these sectors are not internationally competitive with the major exporters of these services in the United States and Europe. We discuss the export performance of the service sector in more detail in Chapter 5. The data used in deriving these growth rates are from the same sources as the more aggregated data in the tables but these more disaggregated tables are not included in this book.

14. All for the period as a whole.

15. The period-by-period data are presented in the appendix to this chapter.

16. We can do this by looking at manufacturing.

17. Given that virtually all natural resources had to be imported, this decline was to be expected once Korea abandoned the import-substituting policies of the 1950s.

18. A problem to which we return in Chapter 4.

19. The coefficient in question is often negative.

20. President Syngman Rhee's government also banned virtually all trade with Japan.

21. The same point is asserted for both this and the subsequent period in World Bank (1993). The bank's study argues that price distortions in East Asia were not substantial, providing evidence obtained by averaging the distortions in four economies, Korea, Taiwan, Hong Kong, and Singapore. But two of these four were essentially free ports with few if any product price distortions, and so looking at the average of the four would greatly understate the distortion present in Korea. See World Bank (1993) and Frank, Kim, and Westfall (1975).

22. One major assumption, however, raises a serious question as to whether these border prices really were similar to world prices. The authors assume that all Korean border prices that were in fact well below world prices were in effect similar to or the same as world prices. In our opinion, a more plausible argument would be that the Korean won was probably undervalued and that many prices of exported goods, as a result, were priced very low while goods designed for the domestic market were either just barely competitive internationally or were priced well above world prices (such as, for example, the prices of automobiles).

23. Or this period together with the 1960s.

24. The argument has also been made that the oligopolistic nature of these supported industries (several were given outright but temporary monopolies) may have slowed innovation and R&D. For a recent effort to quantitatively appraise these relationships and review many of the other econometric estimates, see Noland and Pack (2003).

25. Although the magnitude of the estimated impact is small.

26. The signs of the relevant coefficients vary and are, in general, statistically insignificant.

27. This assumes, of course, that in the absence of government intervention, firms would have been unable or unwilling to finance losses in the early years in order to reap benefits subsequently.

28. Although the data needed for a detailed cost-benefit analysis are not available.

29. In 1996 Presidents Chun Doo Hwan and Roh Tae Woo were convicted of accepting illegal payments from businesses (and for their role in suppressing the Kwangju uprising), with Chun being initially sentenced to death and Roh to seventeen years in prison. In late 1997 both were given amnesty and released from jail. President Kim Young Sam, their immediate successor, was not convicted of receiving illegal payments, but his son was.

30. For more on this, see Chapter 6.

31. Such as the Daewoo conglomerate, for example.

32. Beginning even before the 1997–1998 crisis but continuing with more vigor thereafter, Korea has taken steps both to increase the number of lawyers and to raise the capacity of the judiciary to handle complex economic cases. The crisis was one motivation for this change, but it was also fostered by pressure from the business community, which wanted a more accessible legal system for handling commercial disputes of all kinds—disputes that could not easily or efficiently be handled through the informal mechanisms of the past.

33. See Chapter 6.

34. Yoon Won-sup, "S. Korea to Reduce Gas Emissions," *Korea Times*, 17 December 2007, reports on a speech by then Prime Minister Han Duck Soo laying out the various measures Korea was taking to limit the emission of greenhouse gases.

35. See United Nations (2009).

36. Quantitative studies, as we have seen, do not always produce clear results.

37. This is the point made in Frank, Kim, and Westphal (1975).

38. That Korea is, even today, a heavy user of industrial materials and machinery imported from Japan is a legacy of their importance in this earlier period.

39. This is a way of reconciling the results of Lee (1996), discussed above, which suggest that favored sectors displayed relatively low levels and rates of TFP growth in the 1970s, with the fact that many of these sectors became highly competitive internationally in later years.

40. The kind of small and medium-size enterprises from which other economies, like Taiwan's, derive considerable benefit.

41. Or simply "deindustrialization."

42. Indeed, as noted above, Korean industrial value added continued to rise in absolute terms, and at a fairly rapid pace.

43. This table essentially replicates Kim (2006), with minor modifications. He made similar analyses, but his focus was on income inequality. Industry-level

output and employment data are mostly obtained from the OECD STAN database that covers 1971–2005 and then extended back to 1961 by complementing the OECD ISDB database. The OECD STAN database and the OECD ISDB database are not completely consistent with each other. We have granted priority to the STAN database for those years for which both data sets are available. For those years for which only the ISDB database is available, we have made an adjustment to the ISDB figures by comparing the employment shares of the five closest overlapping years of both databases. For example, if the ISDB database covers 1961–1980 and the STAN database covers 1971–2005, by calculating the average difference between the two databases of employment shares for 1971–2005, we adjusted the employment shares for the period 1961–1970 (for which only the ISDB database is available) by subtracting the average difference from the figures constructed from the ISDB database.

44. Another is Canada, an exception for which we do not have an immediate explanation.

45. The pattern in France is slightly different. While the peak was achieved in 1964, deindustrialization of the French labor force effectively began in 1973. We therefore report figures for both years. Though the starting year of deindustrialization is not verified for the United Kingdom, the fact that the manufacturing employment share was 31.9 percent in 1961 indicates that its peak should be higher.

46. This is also the point emphasized by Kim (2006). Again, the exception is Canada.

47. Real per capita GDP is measured at constant 2000 purchasing-power-parity-dollar prices.

48. Notwithstanding the oil shock that hit the economy at the same time, this large decline in the growth rate is likely to be related to deindustrialization of the labor force.

49. Investment rates are calculated using data from the Penn World Tables 6.2.

50. In fact, the average investment rate in the period 1998–2005 (33.4 percent) is comparable to that in 1982–1989 (33.1 percent), before deindustrialization began.

51. To be sure, the slower growth in finance, insurance, and business services may well have been a result of the financial crisis.

CHAPTER FOUR

1. The tendency for the share of services in output and employment to rise with incomes has been well known since the work of Fisher (1939), Clark (1940), and Kuznets (1957).

2. Low-income countries are defined here as those with per capita incomes of less than $935; middle-income countries as those with per capita incomes be-

tween $935 and $11,455. Data on per capita incomes as of 2007 are from the World Bank's *World Development Indicators* using the World Bank Atlas method; see World Bank (2006). That said, the rise in the services share even in the low-income world is suggestive of technological change—of the application of new information and communications technologies, in particular—that may have attenuated the "cost disease" (the tendency for productivity to rise more slowly and costs to rise more quickly in service-producing sectors than in goods-producing ones) while allowing a growing range of services to be traded internationally.

3. That is to say, within two standard errors of the predicted value.

4. The story in Hong Kong is, of course, that it is a service center for all of southern China, and manufacturing that had been confined to the territory by the former embargo on trade with China has gradually shifted to Guangdong Province in China, next door. Japan is a country where policy has traditionally favored manufacturing and where regulation stifling service-sector productivity has held back expansion of the sector—an experience with implications for Korea.

5. Despite the decline in industrial employment in recent years, the service sector's share of GDP did not increase much, peaking at 70 percent in 1999 before falling back to 64 percent in 2005. It should be noted before proceeding that these figures for changes in the structure of GDP are based on GDP in constant prices to measure real changes. If one takes GDP at current prices, the service share rises and manufacturing's share is more or less constant over the most recent two-decade period. The reason for this difference is that the prices of many services rose during this period relative to the prices of manufactured products, because many services are more labor intensive than manufacturing. This results in service-sector prices reflecting more of the impact of rapidly rising real wages in a fast-growing economy, which in turn reflects lower productivity growth in the service sector and nontraded-goods sectors in general, a phenomenon that is known as the Balassa-Samuelson effect. Empirically, there is also the problem that measuring productivity growth in the service sector is more prone to data bias than is the case in manufacturing. These data problems include the fact that labor input into the sector is difficult to measure because so many of those working in the sector are self-employed or part-time workers. Constructing the appropriate price index with which to deflate services is equally difficult, and then there is the fact that many services are intermediate inputs into manufacturing, and their contribution to productivity is often attributed to the manufacturing sector.

6. The data are for labor productivity; there are not enough calculations readily available that look at total factor productivity of disaggregated service sectors across a large sample of countries.

7. Hungary achieved its results largely by inviting in foreign banks. The proximate explanation for the rise in Czech labor productivity in services is less clear to us.

8. Again, rapid productivity growth in a particular sector could simply reflect the fact that that sector lagged further behind the productivity level of other service sectors and hence had more room for improvement from measures designed to raise productivity, such as deregulation. That said, however, there is little question that the service sectors lagging behind in recent years clearly indicate problems with low productivity and barriers to reforms whose removal could raise that productivity.

9. A model developed even earlier by Clark (1937) focused on the demand side, arguing that the income elasticity of demand for services was higher than that for manufactures. (The argument has sometimes been related specifically to such service sectors as social, community, and personal services, which tend to be in higher demand in more wealthy societies.) However, it is not clear how this argument applies to an open economy in which not all countries have wealth. Even if domestic demand for manufactures is growing slowly, so long as it is growing rapidly elsewhere and exporting is possible, Clark's demand-side constraint may not bind. In any case, since manufacturing industry's output share in Korea did not shrink, Clark's argument involving different demand elasticities does not seem to play an important role in explaining the rising employment share of Korean services.

10. See also Fuchs (1969) and Rowthorn and Wells (1987).

11. Jones (2009), 8.

12. Sachs and Schatz (1994) and Wood (1995), among others, have advanced the argument that external factors, such as trade with developing countries, are responsible for the declining share of manufacturing employment.

13. We will have more to say about this when analyzing the impact of trade on employment in Chapter 5.

14. The second highest figure for self-employment in middle-income and higher-income economies is that of Taiwan, at 25 percent of the work force. Self-employment in most such economies represents 10 to 20 percent of the work force.

15. Although it is far above Japan.

16. Revenue from shipping among third countries is half again as important as revenue from shipping Korea's own exports for Korean companies.

17. Somewhat surprisingly, given the prowess of Korean construction companies, the export of construction services in 2006 was a minuscule US$126 million.

18. We analyze Korea's performance as an exporter of services in more detail in Chapter 5.

19. See Kim and Kim (2003).

20. And as we show more systematically in Chapter 5.

21. Jones (2009), 7.

22. This accounts for the vast majority of output in all subsectors but financial services.

23. This cap is higher than in the past, but its effect is still to restrict competition in the legal profession.

24. This brief review of recent efforts at financial deregulation is based on Jones (2009), 27–28.

25. This issue is discussed at length in the overview volume to this series; see Eichengreen, Lim, Park, and Perkins (forthcoming), ch. 8.

26. Jones (2009), 29.

27. Or 80 students per law school; Jones (2009), 29.

28. The situation in Japan was similar, and the position of lawyers and the courts in settling business disputes elsewhere in East and Southeast Asia was worse, with a few exceptions, such as in Singapore.

29. For a discussion of the underdevelopment of the legal profession in East and Southeast Asia, including Korea, see Perkins (2004).

CHAPTER FIVE

1. As opposed to compressing imports, the policy followed less successfully in Latin America. See Corbo and Suh (1993).

2. There are some noticeable differences between Korea and its competitors. Most notably, Korea has moved more quickly into relatively high-tech industries, but it continues to occupy the bottom end of the product space defined by those industries. These two effects thus cancel each other out, from the point of view of the overall technological sophistication of exports.

3. As noted previously, in Chapter 4.

4. Analytical narratives include Findlay 1984; Haggard, Kim, and Moon 1991; Krueger 1982 and 1987; and Yoo 1994.

5. As emphasized in the Korean context by Rodrik (1995).

6. Perhaps predictably, in this light, the empirical literature on whether the export-led growth hypothesis applies to the industrialized countries yields conflicting results (cf. Shan and Sun 1998 and Awokuse 2003).

7. This shift in employment shares from agriculture to manufacturing and services is the so-called Kuznets pattern (after Kuznets 1966).

8. Regional figures are weighted averages of country data, unless otherwise stated. We are grateful for the authors' assistance in helping us to replicate their procedures and extend their figures and tables. The data reported here were constructed independently, in most cases; in a number of cases our figures differ from theirs, for reasons that are not obvious.

9. However, the recent pattern is very similar to that in Taiwan

10. To be sure, countries differ in other ways, besides per capita incomes, that affect their RER and export competitiveness. But it is precisely these other differences that the analysis is designed to expose (by factoring out the effect of per capita incomes). For those concerned about this issue, we can include other determinants of the RER, such as the demographic structure of the population and the nature of the political regime, as additional independent variables.

11. The underlying regression can be found in Table 5.A1 in the appendix to this chapter.

12. According to these results, a country with a relatively low dependency ratio should have a relatively low (depreciated) RER. Intuitively, a low dependency ratio means that a large fraction of the population is in its high-saving years. With saving high relative to investment, the country is a net exporter, which in turn requires a relatively competitive RER. Although Korea is now starting to age rapidly, it is in this low dependency-ratio camp for the bulk of the sample period.

13. The estimated overvaluation is large. At 40 to 50 percent, it is as dramatic as the extent of undervaluation in the 1960s.

14. This assumes, counterfactually, that all infra–free trade agreement trade becomes tariff free at the moment the agreement is reached, and as such may bias downward the estimated effective tariff.

15. Nontariff barriers may be a different matter; we turn to these next.

16. Recalculating these effective tariff rates on a fixed basket of commodities reduces the temporary increase in 1996 by eliminating the compositional effect noted in the text, but there still is a noticeable increase, reflecting policy adjustments in anticipation of WTO accession.

17. As we saw in Table 5.3.

18. If we start in 2001, the growth of Korea's exports is fully 13 percent per annum, putting recent trade performance in an even more favorable light.

19. Note, in particular, the contrast with Taiwan.

20. Since $\exp(1) = 2.71$ approximately 2.7 times.

21. At the 95 percent level of confidence.

22. The indices are constructed using Comtrade data and calculated based on a five-digit breakdown of the Standard International Trade Classification (SITC, Rev2) for 1980 and 1990 and a six-digit breakdown of the International Convention on the Harmonized Commodity and Coding System (HS 92) for 2005.

23. While a number of comparators in both Latin America and East Asia had equally diversified exports in 2006, only Taiwan, Brazil, and (interestingly) China come close to matching Korea's level of export diversification in 1990 (and in 1980 as well). Taiwan is often thought to have a more diversified economy as a result of possessing a large number of relatively small exporting firms, this in turn

being a consequence of its government not having used policies of directed credit to channel resources toward heavy industry to the same extent as in Korea. It is striking, therefore, that these measures show Korean exports as even more diversified than Taiwan's. To check that these results were not being driven by the breakdown of exports into five-digit categories, we redid the calculations for Korea and Taiwan using the two- and three-digit SITC classifications. This too shows Korean exports as more diversified in both 1990 and 2005 (the earlier data not being available for Taiwan). Brazil's case is explained by the fact that the country is generously endowed with raw materials and also exports a range of manufactures. The case of China presumably reflects that economy's size: its abundance of labor meant that moving workers into a narrow range of export industries (e.g., textiles and apparel) threatened to drive down world market prices; hence there was a natural tendency for those resources to flow into a wider range of export industries. From this standpoint Korea's success at diversifying its exports is striking: it is neither an exporter of raw materials, like Brazil, nor does it possess the scale necessary to affect world prices, like China. However, what was truly exceptional once is exceptional no longer: in addition to Brazil and China, Thailand has now overtaken Korea in terms of export diversification.

24. The index is constructed from three-digit SITC data for 182 products and normalized to run from 0 to 1, and a vector of controls is included in the regressions.

25. See Table 5.5.

26. To see the evolution of the coefficients in more detail, we have divided the 1990s dummy into two five-year dummies: 1990–1995 and 1996–2000. When we include year-fixed effects, the coefficients on the dummy variable for Korea in the current decade turn negative, but they are insignificantly different from zero.

27. Interestingly, Chinese competition in those markets is already evident in 1985, even though China sold little if anything in Korea itself.

28. Table 5.A2 in the appendix to this chapter shows which products are taken as constituting the three categories; Tables 5.A3 and 5.A4 show the resulting calculations.

29. Net imports of high-tech products were smaller than net exports of low-tech manufactures, since Korea also had to import energy, raw materials, and natural-resource-based manufactures, which it could not easily export given its modest natural resource endowment.

30. In Latin America, the most prominent trend is toward net exports of resources and resource-based manufactures, reflecting in part strong global growth resulting in high commodity prices around the middle of the present decade. China, these simple aggregates suggest, has developed a revealed comparative advantage in low-tech exports, while the other East Asian countries

have a revealed comparative advantage in either low-tech or resource-based manufactures, depending on which country we are talking about.

31. Reinforcing the point is the fact that the shares of medium- and high-tech exports for China and a number of other countries are certainly overstated by the importance of imported parts and components in measured high-tech exports. The extent of the problem is disputed; see Krugman (2008).

32. The standard errors of the coefficient estimates are adjusted for clustering, to account for the fact that the dependent variables vary by both product and country while the explanatory variables vary only by country.

33. When we add analogous decennial dummy variables for Taiwan, we obtain essentially the same result for that country—namely, negative coefficients on the decennial country dummies. Estimating the relationship with a vector of annual dummy variables for Taiwan (along with the vector of annual dummy variables for Korea) shows, strikingly, that the significant negative coefficient grows more pronounced at the same time in the two countries, toward the end of the 1980s.

34. To be sure, there are some noticeable ups and downs. The chaebol share fell during the financial crisis and again when the high-tech bubble burst, and there was a growth slowdown in 2000–2001. But none of this changes the basic point. It would be nice to have some data on the unit values of exports supplied by large and small/medium-sized firms, but that disaggregation is not available, to our knowledge.

35. Per capita GDP data are from Penn World Table 6.2.

36. See the column headed "China" in Table 5.14.

37. Where all independent variables are industry specific.

38. For more detail on the construction of these measures, see Hahn and Choi (2008).

39. At the time of writing, 2006 was the latest year for which industry-level data were available.

40. The value-added multipliers show a similar picture. Between 1973 and 1990 the value added multipliers associated with consumption, investment, and exports rose by 1.7 percent, 9.4 percent, and 7.4 percent. Between 1990 and 2003, in contrast, the same value-added multipliers rose by 1 percent for consumption, but fell by 1 percent for investment and by 5.9 percent for exports. Again only the value-added multiplier of exports fell significantly in the second period.

41. In addition, there is the shift in the locus of employment from manufacturing to services. As more employment is concentrated in the service sector, exports, which are dominated by manufactures, do not create as much employment as before. When we examine the worker requirement coefficients in the manufacturing and service sectors in the second period, we see that those associated with consumption, investment, and exports declined by 74.4 percent, 68.2 percent,

and 61.8 percent in the manufacturing sector, but declined by 35.8 percent, 31.1 percent, and 49.6 percent in the service sector. Since export goods are produced mainly in the manufacturing sector, their worker requirement coefficient declined least in the manufacturing sector and declined most in the service sector. As the industry structure changes, we believe this trend will continue.

42. Of course, to the extent that the change in IO structure reflects increasing production fragmentation, it will result in not just less employment per unit of exports but also more exports, as more parts and components are shipped across borders. The combination of these two effects on employment is, on net, unclear. But insofar as the value added associated with parts and components is less than that associated with trade in final goods, the interpretation in the text—increases in trade are adding less than before to increases in employment—will continue to hold.

43. Disaggregation allows us to add as an additional explanatory variable the extent of nontariff barriers to trade in specific categories of services, as constructed by the Australian Productivity Commission. These equations are estimated by seemingly unrelated regression. Seemingly unrelated regression increases the efficiency of the estimates but also raises the danger of cross-equation contamination if one of the dependent variables is mismeasured. We show in the chapter appendix that the results carry over when the equations are estimated by OLS.

44. In additional regressions not reported here, we disaggregated miscellaneous commercial services into financial services and insurance services. At this level of disaggregation, data on Korean imports are missing, so we were able to include only one dummy variable for Korea (Korean exports of the services in question). There were large negative coefficients on both financial services and insurance services; these were significantly less than zero at the 99 percent confidence level in OLS regressions and significantly less than zero at the 90 percent level in panel regressions with random effects. This confirms that Korea underperforms as an exporter of these services.

CHAPTER SIX

1. For details see SaKong (1993), 114–115.

2. There were some notable exceptions to these generalizations. The Korean auto parts industry grew out of the partnership between General Motors and the Shin-Jin Corporation established in the 1970s. The transistor industry grew out of a joint venture between Japanese-owned Komi Semiconductor and Motorola Korea. Oil refining began with a joint venture between Gulf Oil and the Korea Development Bank. See Chung (2007), 285.

3. As described in Chapter 7.

4. Chung (2007), 279.

5. Such complaints were not limited, to be sure, to Korea.

6. See Chapter 7.

7. The partially opened sectors included cattle raising, fishing, alcohol distilling, tobacco, power, and gambling, and logistics, communication, and media-related industries. Closed sectors were mainly related to national defense. See Min (2006), 10.

8. Much FDI in Hong Kong is probably an indirect proxy for FDI in China.

9. The other important destinations for Korean FDI include Europe (reflecting market-access considerations) and countries of the Association of Southeast Asian Nations (ASEAN), where Korean multinationals have been able to secure access to natural resources.

10. Here we focus on the same group of countries as in Chapter 5.

11. We follow the industry classification in OECD (2005).

12. Two other countries where the stock of inward FDI was only slightly higher were China and the Philippines. At the same time, the sectoral composition of inward FDI in Korea is not particularly exceptional. The only thing that stands out is the entirely predictable fact that FDI in the primary producing sector is essentially zero.

13. In addition to a summary indicator, this survey provides information for 2006 on the cost of starting a business and the difficulties involved with licenses (the number of procedures, time in days, cost as a share of per capita income), trading across borders (time in days for exports and for imports, cost of containers), registering a property (number of procedures, time in days, cost as a percentage of the property), enforcing a contract (number of procedures, time in days, cost as a percentage of the debt), employing workers (difficulty of hiring, difficulty of firing, rigidity of employment, nonwage labor costs as a percentage of salary), and closing a business (time in years, cost as a percentage of estate, and recovery rate).

14. Cited in Alexander (2008), 8.

15. Wei (1999) in fact includes a much smaller sample of countries than the number considered here.

16. The transparency variable is from Transparency International, the global civil society organization. Three-year averages are used throughout, following Wei, to minimize noise in the data.

17. Such as, but not limited to, the euro area.

18. And, indeed, in the 1980s.

19. Note that this is also an implication of the standard neoclassical growth model, which predicts that higher levels of investment, whether domestic or foreign, will result in faster growth only over the transition to a higher capital-output ratio, not indefinitely.

20. OECD (2008), 107.

CHAPTER SEVEN

1. It is still too early for a definitive analysis of the macroeconomic impact of the 2008 crisis, although we have a few words to say about this in the next section.

2. And subsequently by the Korea Exchange Bank.

3. Krueger (1982), 147.

4. On this see Collins (1994).

5. The debt/equity ratios of the top 30 chaebol reached an astonishing 518 percent in 1997 (Chopra et al. 2001, 21).

6. This was as of 1997.

7. These were subsequently renewed and then supplemented with swaps from the Bank of Japan and the People's Bank of China.

8. This time, however, offshore dollar borrowing was intended to hedge dollar assets (the banks had advanced credits to the shipbuilding industry, which would receive income in dollars once the tankers it had under construction were delivered), not to fund ongoing lending operations. It was argued that Korean banks ended up with more dollar receivables than they otherwise would have insofar as Korean exporters "overhedged." That is, they sold more than 100 percent of their dollar receivables to the banks, betting that the won would appreciate against the dollar—a bet that, in the event, went wrong.

9. Appendix Table 7.A1 provides a complete tabulation of the crisis episodes.

10. Medium-term debt, in contrast, is uniformly insignificant.

11. Rodrik and Velasco do this for the 1980–1981 and 1997–1998 crises; we do so for all four crises.

12. Data from SaKong 1993, table A.35.

13. These are their results when they define the crisis as a weighted average of the rate of currency depreciation and rate of reserve loss.

14. When the crisis variable included either currency crises or banking crises alone, estimates yielded very similar results.

15. The result is a dynamic panel model. So instead of estimating a simple fixed-effects model, which produces inconsistent results when the lagged dependent variable is present, we applied the Arellano-Bond estimator.

16. Otherwise the results conform to the predictions of the recent empirical growth literature. Growth is faster in countries with higher investment rates, greater price stability, and lower levels of government consumption; it is slower in more mature, higher-income countries. A number of other plausible suspects, such as trade openness, human capital (as measured by schooling), democracy, and rule of law do not have statistically significant effects. Again this is consistent with much of the recent empirical literature.

17. Anecdotal accounts for Korea prior to the 1997–1998 crisis are certainly consistent with this view.

18. In Table 7.8, growth declines by 1.6 percent per annum on average over the five-year period in which the crisis occurs. In the subsequent five-year period, growth is neither faster nor slower than it was prior to the crisis. And there is no evidence of a significantly different impact in Korea than in other countries. In Table 7.9 the same is again true so long as we include a dummy variable for Korea, which captures the fact that Korean growth was unusually rapid all through the period.

19. Ranciere, Tornell, and Westermann's sample period extends through 2000, as noted. When we update their calculations through 2006, negative skewness for Korea rises from -0.28 to -0.56. The increase reflects the credit crunch associated with the credit-card crisis of 2003–2004. (Credit growth was 5.2 percent in 2003 but only -1.7 percent in 2004.) This larger absolute value over the longer sample period suggests an even larger impact on growth in Korea.

20. Analyses like that of Ranciere, Tornell, and Westermann suggest that Korea has done well, in terms of overall growth performance, despite—or more to the point, because of—its willingness to shoulder this risk.

CHAPTER EIGHT

1. The 2.3 percent figure is from International Monetary Fund (2008), table A2, line 1.

2. Assuming that the U.S. grows at the advanced country average. As of 2007, per capita incomes in South Korea and the United States were $25,000 and $45,000, respectively. This assumption that global growth will continue at recent rates has, of course, been thrown into question by the global economic and financial crisis of 2008–2009. We will return to this later.

3. Thus, Demirgüç-Kunt and Huizinga (2000) show that interest margins are narrower and other measures of banking-sector efficiency are better in countries with more competitive banking systems. Demirgüç-Kunt, Laeven, and Levine (2004) further show that intermediation costs decline with ease of entry. Nguyen and Williams (2004) find that the intensity of competition ("density of the competitive environment") is a significant predictor of bank efficiency in Korea, as are privatization, foreign ownership, and having listed shares.

4. See OECD (2006a).

5. See, inter alia, Peri 2008 and Peri and Sparber 2008.

6. There are other approaches to forecasting a country's future growth. Some of these approaches use large multi-equation, multivariate models to generate forecasts. Such models are maintained by a variety of government agencies. These elaborate models require many more assumptions; more detail is obtained at the cost of less transparency about what is driving the results. This is not our preferred approach, but the reader seeking to make an informed judgment about the

country's medium-term economic prospects will want to consider the findings that emerge from these alternative frameworks. To then get from Korea's maximum potential to its most likely future growth rate requires a judgment about how far and how fast Korea will be able to carry out the reforms suggested in the first part of this chapter. To be clear, our judgment on these matters is no better than that of hundreds of other analysts of the Korean economy, and our approach to this forecast provides a framework that allows others to reach their own conclusions about whether Korea will or will not reach its full potential growth rate.

7. We do also consider the alternative approach that endogenizes the investment rate, given assumptions about TFP and labor-supply growth, in the steady state.

8. See Chapter 2, Tables 2.1 and 2.2.

9. Absent significant changes in immigration and related policies, as recommended above.

10. Quality increases could also show up in the conventional method for estimating the contribution of human capital if the relative wages of those with increasing educational quality also experienced a rise in relative wages, but we have not assumed any impact of improved educational quality on the structure of wages.

11. As measured at purchasing power parity.

12. Among other things, Ireland's high growth followed a period of dismal economic performance that put it far behind its partners in the European Union. Its membership in the EU and adoption of the euro allowed it to import large amounts of foreign capital and run very large current account deficits without risking a currency crisis. And as part of the Single Market, it was on the receiving end of a very large inflow of foreign workers.

13. Although 6 percent might be sustainable for a shorter period of, say, five years. Of course, over even shorter periods Korea might achieve higher rates of growth, but—to repeat—our interest in this study is Korea's long-term growth potential.

14. To investigate the long-run relationship as well as the short-run relationship, we form a vector error-correction model using two variables, world growth and Korean growth rates. In this error-correction model, the cointegration vector estimate represents the long-run relationship, namely what will eventually happen to the Korean GDP if the world GDP changes. Rolling (ordinary least squares) regressions also suggest that this elasticity may now be higher than it was in the more distant past.

References

Ahn, Sanghoon. 2005. "Global Competition and Productivity Growth: Evidence from Korean Manufacturing Micro-Data." Unpublished manuscript, Korea Development Institute, Seoul (April).

Alesina, Alberto, Sule Ozler, Nouriel Roubini, and Philip Swagel. 1996. "Political Instability and Economic Growth." *Journal of Economic Growth* 1, 189–211.

Alexander, Arthur J. 2008. "Foreign Direct Investment in Korea: Trends, Implications, Obstacles." Korean Economy Series 08-01, U.S.-Korea Institute at School of Advanced International Studies, Johns Hopkins University, Washington, DC (July).

Alfaro, Laura, and Andrew Charlton. 2007. "Growth and the Quality of Foreign Direct Investment: Is All FDI Equal?" Unpublished manuscript, Harvard Business School and London School of Economics (May).

Al-Marhubi, Fahim. 2000. "Export Diversification and Growth: An Empirical Investigation." *Applied Economics Letters* 7, 559–562.

Athukorala, Prema-Chandra. 2005. "Production Fragmentation and Trade Patterns in East Asia." *Asian Economic Papers* 4, 1–27.

Awokuse, Titus. 2003. "Is the Export-Led Growth Hypothesis Valid for Canada?" *Canadian Journal of Economics* 36, 126–136.

———. 2005. "Exports, Economic Growth and Causality in Korea." *Applied Economics Letters* 12, 693–696.

Barro, Robert J., and Jong-Wha Lee. 2000. "International Data on Educational Attainment: Updates and Implications." CID Working Paper 42, Center for International Development, Harvard University (April); http://www.hks.harvard.edu/centers/cid/publications/faculty-working-papers/cid-working-paper-no.-42. Accessed February 2012.

―――. 2003. "Growth and Investment: East Asia before and after the Financial Crisis." *Seoul Journal of Economics* 16, 83–113.

Barro, Robert, and Xavier Sala-i-Martin. 1988. *Economic Growth.* Cambridge, MA: MIT Press.

Baumol, William. 1967. "The Macroeconomics of Unbalanced Growth: The Anatomy of Urban Crisis." *American Economic Review* 57, 415–426.

Bergin, Paul R., and Ching-Yi Lin. 2008. "Exchange Rate Regimes and the Extensive Margin of Trade." NBER Working Paper 14126, National Bureau of Economic Research, Cambridge, MA (June).

Bora, Bijit, Aki Kuwahara, and Samuel Laird. 2002. *Quantification of Nontariff Measures.* New York: United Nations Conference on Trade and Development.

Bordo, Michael, Barry Eichengreen, Daniela Klingebiel, and Maria Soledad Martinez-Peria. 2000. "Is the Crisis Problem Growing More Severe?" *Economic Policy* 21, 51–82.

Borensztein, Eduardo, Jose De Gregorio, and Jong-Wha Lee. 1998. "How Does Foreign Investment Affect Growth?" *Journal of International Economics* 45, 115–172.

Bosworth, Barry, and Gabriel Chodorow-Reich. 2007. "Saving and Demographic Change: The Global Dimension." Working Paper 2007-02, Center for Retirement Research, Boston College.

Bosworth, Barry, and Susan M. Collins. 2003. "The Empirics of Growth: An Update." Unpublished manuscript, Brookings Institution, Washington, DC (September).

Carkovic, Maria, and Ross Levine. 2002. "Does Foreign Investment Accelerate Economic Growth?" Unpublished manuscript, Department of Finance, University of Minnesota (June).

Chopra, Ajai, Kenneth Kang, Meral Karasulu, Hong Liang, Henry Ma, and Anthony Richards. 2001. "From Crisis to Recovery in Korea: Strategy, Achievements and Lessons." In David Coe and Si-Jik Kim, eds., *Korean Crisis and Recovery,* 13–104. Washington, DC: International Monetary Fund.

Chun, Hong-Tack. 2000. "Comment on the Role of Foreign Direct Investment in Korea's Economic Development: Productivity Effects and Implications for the Currency Crisis." In Takatoshi Ito and Anne Krueger, eds., *The Role of Foreign Direct Investment in East Asian Economic Development and Trade,* 290–292. Chicago: University of Chicago Press.

Chung, Young-Iob. 2007. *South Korea in the Fast Lane: Economic Development and Capital Formation.* New York: Oxford University Press.

Clark, Colin. 1937. *National Income and Outlay.* London: Macmillan.

―――. 1940. *The Conditions of Economic Progress.* London: Macmillan.

Collins, Susan. 1994. "Saving, Investment and External Balance in Korea." In Stephan Haggard, Richard Cooper, Susan Collins, Choongsoo Kim, and

Sung-Tae Ro, *Macroeconomic Policy and Adjustment in Korea 1970–1990*, 231–260. Cambridge, MA: Harvard Institute for International Development.

Corbo, Vittorio, and Sang-Mok Suh, eds. 1993. *Structural Adjustment in a Newly Industrialized Country: The Korean Experience*. Washington, DC: World Bank.

Council of Economic Planning and Development. 2007. *Taiwan Economic Forum* 5, no. 12 (December).

Darrat, Ali. 1986. "Trade and Development: The Asian Experience." *Cato Journal* 6, 695–699.

Demirgüç-Kunt, Asli, and Harry Huizinga. 2000. "Determinants of Commercial Bank Interest Margins and Profitability: Some International Evidence." *World Bank Economic Review* 13, 379–408.

Demirgüç-Kunt, Asli, Luc Laeven, and Ross Levine. 2004. "Regulations, Market Structure, Institutions and the Cost of Financial Intermediation." *Journal of Money, Credit and Banking* 36, 593–622.

De Piñeres, Sheila Amin Gutiérrez, and Michael Ferrantino. 1997. "Export Diversification and the Structural Dynamics in the Growth Process: The Case of Chile." *Journal of Development Economics* 52, 35–92.

Dhakal, Dharmendra, Saif Rahman, and Kamal Upadhyaya. 2007. "Foreign Direct Investment and Economic Growth in Asia." Unpublished manuscript, Tennessee State University, Nashville (June).

Directorate-General of the Budget, Accounting and Statistics. Various years. *Statistical Abstract of National Income in Taiwan Area, Republic of China*. Taipei: Government of Republic of China.

Dornbusch, Rudiger, and Yung Chul Park. 1987. "Korean Growth Policy." *Brookings Papers on Economic Activity* 2, 389–444.

Duran, Jose, Nanno Mulder, and Osamu Onodera. 2008. "Trade Liberalisation and Economic Performance: Latin America versus East Asia, 1970–2006." OECD Trade Policy Working Paper 70, OECD Publishing, Paris (February).

Durham, J. Benson. 2004. "Absorptive Capacity and the Effects of Foreign Direct Investment and Equity Portfolio Investment on Economic Growth." *European Economic Review* 48, 285–306.

Eichengreen, Barry. 2008. "The Real Exchange Rate and Economic Growth." Working Paper 5, Commission on Growth and Development, Washington, DC: World Bank.

Eichengreen, Barry, and Poonam Gupta. 2009. "The Two Waves of Service Sector Growth." NBER Working Paper 14968, National Bureau of Economic Research, Cambridge, MA (May).

———. 2011. "The Service Sector as India's Road to Economic Growth." NBER Working Paper 16757, National Bureau of Economic Research, Cambridge, MA (February).

Eichengreen, Barry, Wonhyuk Lim, Yung Chul Park, and Dwight Perkins. Forthcoming. *The Korean Economy: Past, Present and Future.* Cambridge, MA: Harvard University Asia Center.

Eichengreen, Barry, Yeongseop Rhee, and Hui Tong. 2007. "China and the Exports of Other Asian Countries." *Review of World Economics (Weltwirtschaftliches Archiv)* 143, 201–226.

Eichengreen, Barry, and Hui Tong. 2007. "Is China's FDI Coming at the Expense of Other Economies?" *Journal of the Japanese and Asian Economies* 21, 151–172.

Eyanayake, E. M. 1999. "Exports and Economic Growth in Asian Developing Countries: Cointegration and Error Correction Models." *Journal of Economic Development* 24, 43–56.

Feasel, Edward, Yongbeom Kim, and Stephen Smith. 2001. "Investment, Exports and Output in South Korea: A VAR Approach to Growth Empirics." *Review of Development Economics* 5, 421–432.

Feinstein, Charles. 1976. *National Income, Output and Expenditure of the U.K., 1855–1965.* Cambridge, UK: Cambridge University Press.

Findlay, Ronald. 1984. "Trade and Development: Theory and Asian Experience." *Asian Development Review* 2, 23–42.

Fisher, A. G. B. 1939. "Primary, Secondary and Tertiary Production." *Economic Record* 15, 24–38.

Frank, Charles, Kwang Suk Kim, and Larry Westphal. 1975. *Foreign Trade Regimes and Economic Development: South Korea.* New York: Columbia University Press.

Frankel, Jeffrey, and David Romer. 1999. "Does Trade Cause Growth?" *American Economic Review* 89, 379–399.

Fuchs, Victor, ed. 1969. *Production and Productivity in the Service Industries.* New York: Columbia University Press for the National Bureau of Economic Research.

Gouyette, Claudine, and Sergio Perelman. 1997. "Productivity Convergence in OECD Service Industries." *Structural Change and Economic Dynamics* 8, 279–295.

Greenway, David, Robert Hine, and Chris Milner. 1994. "Country-Specific Factors and the Pattern of Horizontal and Vertical Intra-Industry Trade in the U.K." *Weltwirtschaftliches Archiv* 130, 77–100.

Gupta, Poonam, Deepak Mishra, and Ratna Sahay. 2003. "Output Response to Currency Crises." IMF Working Paper 03/230, International Monetary Fund, Washington, DC (November).

Ha, Joonkyung, Yong Jin Kim, and Jong-Wha Lee. 2009. "The Optimal Structure of Technology Adoption and Creation: Basic Research vs. Development in the Presence of Distance to Frontier." *Asian Economic Journal* 23, 373–395.

Haggard, Stephan, Byung-Kook Kim, and Chung-In Moon. 1991. "The Transition to Export-Led Growth in South Korea: 1954–1966." *Journal of Asian Studies* 50, 850–873.

Hahn, Chin Hee, and Yongseok Choi. 2008. "China's Rise and Production and Investment Growth in Korean Manufacturing Industries: Channels and the Effects." Unpublished manuscript, Korea Development Institute and Kyung Hee University, Seoul (July).

Hahn, Chin Hee, and Jong-il Kim. 2003. "Understanding East Asian Growth: Sources and Determinants in a Cross Country Perspective." Paper prepared for Global Research Project of the Global Development Network, New Delhi (December).

Harada, Kimie. 2005. "Measuring the Efficiency of Banks: Successful Mergers in the Korean Banking Sector." CNAEC Research Series 05-03, Korea Institute for International Economic Policy, Seoul (June).

Hausmann, Ricardo, Jason Hwang, and Dani Rodrik. 2007. "What You Export Matters." *Journal of Economic Growth* 12, 1–25.

Hausmann, Ricardo, Lant Pritchett, and Dani Rodrik. 2005. "Growth Accelerations." *Journal of Economic Growth* 10, 303–329.

Hennessy, D. A., and H. Lapan. 2007. "When Different Market Concentration Indices Agree." *Economics Letters* 95, 234–240.

Hong, Kiseok, and Aaron Tornell. 2005. "Recovery from a Currency Crisis: Some Stylized Facts." *Journal of Development Economics* 76, 71–96.

Hoover, Kevin, and Stephen J. Perez. 2004. "Truth and Robustness in Cross-Country Growth Regressions." *Oxford Bulletin of Economics and Statistics* 66, 765–798.

Hsueh, Li-min, Chen-kuo Hsu, and Dwight H. Perkins. 2001. *Industrialization and the State: The Changing Role of the Taiwan Government in the Economy, 1945–1998*. Cambridge, MA: Harvard University Press.

International Monetary Fund. 2008. *World Economic Outlook, October 2008: Financial Stress, Downturns, and Recoveries* (Washington, DC: International Monetary Fund).

Jones, Randall S. 2009. "Boosting Productivity in Korea's Service Sector." OECD Economics Department Working Paper 673, Organization for Economic Cooperation and Development, Paris (February).

Jorgenson, Dale, and Barbara Fraumeni. 1989. "The Accumulation of Human and Nonhuman Capital, 1948–1984." In Robert Lipsey and Helen Tice, eds., *The Measurement of Savings, Investment and Wealth*, 227–282. Chicago: University of Chicago Press.

———. 1992a. "Investment in Education and U.S. Economic Growth." *Scandinavian Journal of Economics* 94 (supplement), 51–70.

———. 1992b. "The Output of the Education Sector." In Zvi Griliches, ed., *Output Measurement in the Service Sector*, 303–342. Chicago: University of Chicago Press.

Kaminsky, Graciela L., and Carmen M. Reinhart. 1999. "The Twin Crises: The Causes of Banking and Balance-of-Payments Problems." *American Economic Review* 89, 473–500.

Kim, David Deok-Ki, and Jong-Soo Seo. 2003. "Does FDI Inflow Crowd Out Domestic Investment in Korea?" *Journal of Economic Studies* 6, 605–622.

Kim, Jong-Il. 2006. "Structural Change and Employment Problem of Korea since the 1990s." *Korean Economy Analyses* 12, 1–57 [in Korean].

Kim, Jong-Il, and June-Dong Kim. 2003. "Liberalization of Trade in Services and Productivity Growth in Korea." In Takatoshi Ito and Anne Krueger, eds., *Trade in Services in the Asia Pacific Region*, 179–208. Chicago: University of Chicago Press.

Kim, June-Dong, and Sang-In Hwang. 2000. "The Role of Foreign Direct Investment in Korea's Economic Development: Productivity Effects and Implications for the Currency Crisis." In Takatoshi Ito and Anne Krueger, eds., *The Role of Foreign Direct Investment in East Asian Economic Development and Trade*, 267–290. Chicago: University of Chicago Press.

Kim, June-Dong, and In-Soo Kang. 1997. "Outward FDI and Exports: The Case of South Korea and Japan." *Journal of Asian Economics* 8, 39–50.

Krueger, Anne O. 1982. *The Developmental Role of the Foreign Sector and Aid.* Cambridge, MA: Harvard University Press for the Council on East Asian Studies of Harvard University.

———. 1987. "The Importance of Policy in Economic Development: Contrasts Between Korea and Turkey." NBER Working Paper 2196, National Bureau of Economic Research, Cambridge, MA (March).

Krugman, Paul. 2008. "Trade and Wages Reconsidered." *Brookings Papers on Economic Activity* 1, 103–154.

Kumar, Subodh, and R. Robert Russell. 2002. "Technological Change, Technological Catch-up, and Capital Deepening: Relative Contributions to Growth and Convergence." *American Economic Review* 92, 527–548.

Kuznets, Simon. 1957. "Quantitative Aspects of the Economic Growth of Nations, II: Industrial Distribution of National Product and Labor Force." *Economic Development and Cultural Change* 5 (supplement), 247–258.

———. 1966. *Modern Economic Growth: Rate, Structure and Spread.* New Haven: Yale University Press.

Laeven, Luc, and Fabian Valencia. 2008. "Systemic Banking Crises: A New Data Base." IMF Working Paper 08/224, International Monetary Fund, Washington, DC (October).

Lall, Sanjaya. 2000. "The Technological Structure and Performance of Developing Country Manufactured Exports, 1995–1998." *Oxford Development Studies* 28, 337–369.

Lee, Geon-woo. 2008. "The Current State of the Service Industry's R&D Investment and Its Future Outlook." *KIET News Brief* 148 (5 November).

Lee, Hongshik, and Joonhyung Lee. 2009. "How, What, and Where to Offshore: A Productivity Comparison at the Firm Level." Unpublished manuscript, Korea Institute for International Economic Policy, Seoul.

Lee, Jong-Wha. 1996. "Government Interventions and Productivity Growth in Korean Manufacturing Industries." *Journal of Economic Growth* 1, 391–414.

———. 2005. "Human Capital and Productivity for Korea's Sustained Economic Growth." *Journal of Asian Economics* 16, 663–687.

Lee, Jong-Wha, and Cheol J. Song. 2005. "Sources of Economic Growth in the Korean Industries, 1970–2001." *Kyong Je Hak Yon Gu* 53, 1–35 [in Korean].

Lee, Siwook. 2007. "Trade Policy and Productivity: Micro-evidence from Korean Manufacturing." Unpublished manuscript, Korea Development Institute, Seoul.

———. 2008. "The Impact of Outward FDI on Export Activities: Evidence from the Korean Case." Unpublished manuscript, Korea Development Institute, Seoul (July).

Levine, Ross, and David Renelt. 1992. "A Sensitivity Analysis of Cross Country Growth Regressions." *American Economic Review* 82, 942–963.

Lim, Wonhyuk, and Randall Morck. Forthcoming. *The Long Shadow of the Big Push Partnership: Groups in Korea's Economic Development.* Cambridge, MA: Harvard University Asia Center.

Min, Byung S. 2006. "Trade and Foreign Direct Investment Patterns in the Republic of Korea in the Aftermath of the 1997 Asian Financial Crisis." *Asia-Pacific Trade and Investment Review* 2, 3–24.

Ministry of Employment and Labor of Korea. Various years. *Survey Report on Wage Structure in Korea.* Downloaded from http://laborstat.moel.go.kr/.

Ministry of Trade and Industry of Singapore. 2008. "Sources of Singapore's Productivity Growth: A Shift-Share Analysis." *Economic Survey of Singapore* (Third Quarter), 12–14.

Nguyen, Nghia, and Jonathan Williams. n.d. "Liberalisation, Ownership and Efficiency Issues: A Comparative Study of Southeast Asian Banking." Unpublished manuscript, University of Wales, Bangor.

Noland, Marcus, and Howard Pack. 2003. *Industrial Policy in an Era of Globalization: Lessons from Asia.* Washington, DC: Peterson Institute for International Economics.

OECD. 2005. *Science, Technology and Industry Scoreboard 2005.* Paris: Organization for Economic Cooperation and Development.

———. 2006a. *Education at a Glance 2006.* Paris: Organization for Economic Cooperation and Development.

———. 2006b. "OECD's FDI Regulatory Restrictiveness Index: Revision and Extension to More Economies." Working Paper on International Investment 2006/4, OECD Publishing, Paris (December).

———. 2007. *Statistics on International Trade in Services.* Paris: Organization for Economic Cooperation and Development.

———. 2008. *Economic Survey of Korea.* Paris: Organization for Economic Cooperation and Development.

Park, Yung Chul, and Jong-Wha Lee. 2003. "Recovery and Sustainability in East Asia." In Michael Dooley and Jeffrey Frankel, eds. *Managing Currency Crises in Emerging Markets*, 275–320. Chicago: University of Chicago Press.

Peri, Giovanni. 2008. "Immigration Accounting: U.S. States, 1960–2006." Unpublished manuscript, University of California, Davis (June).

Peri, Giovanni, and Chad Sparber. 2008. "Task Specialization, Immigration and Wages." Unpublished manuscript, University of California, Davis, and Colgate University, Hamilton, NY (October).

Perkins, Dwight. 2004. "Corporate Governance, Industrial Policy, and the Rule of Law." In Shahid Yusuf, M. Anjum Altaf, and Kaoru Nabeshima, eds., 293–336. *Global Change and East Asian Policy Initiative*, Washington, DC: World Bank.

Perkins, Dwight, and Lora Sabin. 2001. "Productivity and Structural Change." In Li-min Hsueh, Chen-kuo Hsu, and Dwight H. Perkins, eds., *Industrialization and the State: The Changing Role of the Taiwan Government in the Economy, 1945–1998*, 151–174. Cambridge, MA: Harvard Institute for International Development.

Prasad, Eswar, Raghuram Rajan, and Arvind Subramanian. 2006. "Foreign Capital and Economic Growth." Unpublished manuscript, Massachusetts Institute of Technology, Cambridge, MA.

Pyo, Hak K., S. Young Chung, and C. Sam Cho. 2007. "Estimates of Gross Capital Formation, Net Capital Stock and Capital Intensity: 11 Assets and 72 Industries (1970–2005)." *Korean Economy Analyses* 13, 137–191 [in Korean].

Ranciere, Romain, Aaron Tornell, and Frank Westermann. 2008. "Systemic Crises and Growth." *Quarterly Journal of Economics* 123, 359–406.

Riedel, James. 1976. "A Balanced Version of the Linkage Hypothesis." *Quarterly Journal of Economics* 90, 319–322.

Rodriguez, Francisco, and Dani Rodrik. 2000. "Trade Policy and Economic Growth: A Skeptic's Guide to the Cross-National Evidence." *NBER Macroeconomics Annual* 15, 261–325.

Rodrik, Dani. 1995. "Getting Interventions Right: How South Korea and Taiwan Grew Rich." *Economic Policy* 20, 55–107.

———. 2007. "The Real Exchange Rate and Economic Growth: Theory and Evidence." Unpublished manuscript, Kennedy School of Government, Harvard University (August).

Rodrik, Dani, and Andrés Velasco. 1999. "Short-Term Capital Flows." NBER Working Paper 7364, National Bureau of Economic Research, Cambridge MA (September).

Rose, Andrew K. 2000. "One Money, One Market: Estimating the Effect of Common Currencies on Trade." *Economic Policy* 30, 7–46.

———. 2004. "Do We Really Know That the WTO Increases Trade?" *American Economic Review* 94, 98–114.

Rowthorn, Robert, and R. E. Wells. 1987. *Deindustrialization and Foreign Trade*. Cambridge: Cambridge University Press.

Sachs, Jeffrey, and Howard Schatz. 1994. "Trade and Jobs in Manufacturing." *Brookings Papers on Economic Activity* 25, 1–84.

Sachs, Jeffrey, Andrew Warner, and Stephen Radelet. 1997. *Emerging Asia: Changes and Challenge*. Manila: Asian Development Bank.

SaKong, Il. 1993. *Korea in the World Economy*. Washington, DC: Institute for International Economics.

Sala-i-Martin, Xavier. 1997. "I Just Ran Two Million Regressions." *American Economic Review* 87, 187–193.

Schott, Peter K. 2002. "Moving Up and Moving Out: Product Level Exports and Competition from Low Wage Countries." Unpublished manuscript, Yale School of Management, Yale University.

———. 2008. "The Relative Sophistication of Chinese Exports." *Economic Policy* 23, 5–49.

Shan, Jordan, and Fiona Sun. 1998. "Export-Led Growth Hypothesis for Australia: An Empirical Re-Investigation." *Applied Economics Letters* 5, 423–428.

Stern, Joseph J., Ji-hong Kim, Dwight H. Perkins, and Jung-ho Yoo. 1995. *Industrialization and the State: The Korean Heavy and Chemical Industry Drive*. Cambridge, MA: Harvard University Press.

Triplett, Jack, and Barry Bosworth. 2005. "Productivity Measurement Issues in Services Industries: Baumol's Disease Has Been Cured." *Economic Policy Review of the Federal Reserve Bank of New York* 9, 23–33.

UNCTAD. 2009. *World Investment Report 2009*. Geneva: United Nations Conference on Trade and Development.

United Nations. 2008. *World Investment Report*. New York: United Nations.

———. 2009. "Overview of the Republic of Korea's Green Growth National Vision." United Nations Environment Programme, New York (August).

Viovodas, Constantin. 1974. "Exports, Foreign Capital Inflow, and South Korean Growth." *Economic Development and Cultural Change* 22, 480–484.

Wakasugi, Ryuhei. 2007. "Vertical Intra-Industry Trade and Economic Integration in East Asia." *Asian Economic Papers* 6, 27–39.

Walsh, Keith. 2006. "Trade in Services: Does Gravity Hold?" Institute of International Integration Studies Discussion Paper 183, Institute of International Integration Studies, Trinity College Dublin (November).

Wei, Shangjin. 1999. "How Taxing Is Corruption on International Investors?" *Review of Economics and Statistics* 82, 1–11.

Wolfi, Anita. 2005. "The Service Economy in OECD Countries." OECD Working Paper 2005/3, OECD Publishing, Paris (February).

Wood, Adrian. 1995. "How Trade Hurt Unskilled Workers." *Journal of Economic Perspectives* 9, 57–80.

World Bank. 1993. *The East Asian Miracle*. Washington, DC: World Bank.

———. 2008a. "Doing Business: Comparing Regulations." Unpublished manuscript, World Bank, Washington, DC; www.doingbusiness.org.

———. 2008b. *Global Development Finance*. Washington, DC: World Bank.

———. Various years. *World Development Indicators*. Washington, DC: World Bank.

Yoo, Jung-ho. 1994. "South Korea's Manufactured Exports and Industrial Targeting Policy." In Chu-Chin Yang, ed., *Manufactured Exports of East Asian Industrializing Economies*, 149–173. Armonk, NY: M. E. Sharpe.

Yoon, Deok Ryong. 2007. "Korea's Outward FDI in Asia: Characteristics and Prospects." Unpublished manuscript, Korea Institute for International Economic Policy, Seoul (April).

Young, Alwyn. 1995. "The Tyranny of Numbers: Confronting the Realities of East Asian Growth Experience." *Quarterly Journal of Economics* 110, 641–680.

Zhang, K. H. 2001. "Does Foreign Direct Investment Promote Economic Growth? Evidence from East Asia and Latin America." *Contemporary Policy Issues* 19, 175–185.

Index

Harvard East Asian Monographs
(*out-of-print)

Harvard East Asian Monographs

Harvard East Asian Monographs

Harvard East Asian Monographs

Harvard East Asian Monographs

Harvard East Asian Monographs

Harvard East Asian Monographs